THE BRITISH ACADEMY

CLASSICAL AND MEDIEVAL LOGIC TEXTS

General Editors: P. T. Geach and W. Kneale

PAUL OF VENICE

LOGICA MAGNA

PART I

FASCICULE I

PAULI VENETI
LOGICA MAGNA

PRIMA PARS

TRACTATUS DE TERMINIS

———————

Edited with an English Translation
and Notes by

NORMAN KRETZMANN

Published for

THE BRITISH ACADEMY

by the

OXFORD UNIVERSITY PRESS

1979

Oxford University Press, Walton Street, Oxford OX2 6DP

OXFORD LONDON GLASGOW
NEW YORK TORONTO MELBOURNE WELLINGTON
KUALA LUMPUR SINGAPORE HONG KONG TOKYO
DELHI BOMBAY CALCUTTA MADRAS KARACHI
NAIROBI DAR ES SALAAM CAPE TOWN

© *The British Academy 1979*

ISBN 0 19 725980 4

*Printed in Great Britain
at the University Press, Oxford
by Eric Buckley
Printer to the University*

CONTENTS

CHAPTER THREE: COMMON AND DISCRETE TERMS

INTRODUCTION

Life

PAUL OF VENICE was born in Udine, Italy, about 1369. After entering
the Augustinian convent of S. Stefano in Venice, he studied first at Padua.
In 1390 he was assigned to Oxford where he spent at least three years.
By May 1408, he had achieved the status of Doctor of Arts and Theology
and lector in philosophy at the University of Padua.

Although the full details of his biography have yet to be established, it
is clear that Paul had an active career in the political and religious as
well as the academic sphere. More than once he served as ambassador
of Venice to foreign rulers and proved himself an effective diplomat. At
various times he held positions of leadership in his order, including that
of Rector and Vicar General (1409–10), Prior Provincial of Siena (1420),
Prior Provincial of Marche Tarvisine (1420–1), and Regent of the Siena
convent (1421). During his lifetime, he enjoyed international recognition
as a philosopher, and because of this the friars of his convent at S. Stefano
were allowed to wear the black biretta of the patricians (1417). He taught
intermittently at Padua until the end of his life, but also lectured at
Siena (1420), was deputed to lecture at Bologna (1424), and was later
professor at Siena (1427) and rector of the University (1428). He died on
15 June 1429.[1]

Works

Many works in philosophy and theology have been attributed to Paul
of Venice, although a definitive study of their dating, authenticity, and
interrelations has yet to be undertaken. For present purposes, it will be
enough to list the logical writings among them:

(A) Commentaries on Aristotle's *Organon*:

    1. *Expositio super Universalia Porphyrii et in Artem Veterem Aristotelis*
       (*Exposition of Porphyry's 'Universals' and the 'Old Logic' of Aristotle*)
    2. *In Aristotelis Praedicamenta de Ordine Praedicabilium* (*On Aristotle's
       Categories Concerning the Order of the Predicables*)

---

[1] The above biographical data are taken from A. B. Emden, *A Biographical Register of
the University of Oxford to A.D. 1500* (Oxford, Clarendon Press, 1959), vol. 3, 'Paolo
Veneto', pp. 1944–5. Further bibliography on Paul's life is available in this article. The
material in the opening pages of this Introduction, through the list of the treatises com-
prising the *Logica Magna*, is taken from the Introduction to the already published Part II,
Fascicule 6, edited by Francesco del Punta and translated by Marilyn McCord Adams,
who have kindly given their permission to reprint it here.

3. *Commentarius in Libros Posteriorum Aristotelis* (*Commentary on Aristotle's Posterior Analytics*)
4. *Commentarius in Peri Hermeneias Aristotelis* (*Commentary on Aristotle's Peri Hermeneias*)

(B) Other Logical Works:

1. *Logica Parva sive Summulae* (*The Small Logic or Short Summary*)
2. *Logica Magna* (*The Great Logic*)
3. *Sophismata Aurea* (*Golden Sophismata*)
4. *Quadratura sive De Quattuor Dubiis* (*The Square or On Four Doubts*)
5. *De Universalibus* (*On Universals*)[1]

Some of these—e.g. the *Commentarius in Libros Posteriorum Aristotelis* and the *Logica Parva*—circulated widely and survive in numerous manuscripts and editions. In fact, the *Logica Parva* was a popular textbook and was even commented on by several fifteenth-century philosophers.[2] No doubt in part because of its voluminous size—200 folios on both sides with double columns, the rough equivalent of 2,500 modern octavo pages[3]—the *Logica Magna* was not reproduced so often. Wilhelm Risse[4] knows of only two printings—Venice, 1499 (H. 12505), and Venice, 1559—and of these the second does not represent an independent edition but only a reissuing of the first. In addition, there is one surviving complete manuscript: Codex Vaticanus Latinus 2132.[5] A heading on the manuscript added in a later hand attributes the work to Paul of Venice, as does the Venice 1499 edition. We do not know exactly when the *Logica Magna* was written. But assuming that Paul of Venice is the author, there is some reason to fix a date after Paul's sojourn in England.[6]

As impressive in scope as in length, the *Logica Magna* contains chapters on most major topics in medieval logic. The 1499 edition tabulates its contents as follows:

[1] All of these works except for (B5) are listed by Emden, op. cit., p. 1945.

[2] For example, by Menghus Blanchellus Faventinus (Domenico Bianchelli), Jacobus Ritius Aretinus, and Manfredus de Medicis. See *Menghi Faventini Subtilissime Expositiones Questionesque super Summulis Magistri Pauli Veneti, una cum Argutissimis Additionibus Jacobi Ritii Aretini et Manfredi de Medicis* (Venetiis, 1542).

[3] This calculation is made by Allan Perreiah in his introduction to *Logica Magna, Tractatus de Suppositionibus*, edited and translated by Allan Perreiah (The Franciscan Institute, St. Bonaventure, 1971), p. xiii.

[4] Wilhelm Risse, *Bibliographia Logica: Verzeichnis der Druckschriften zur Logik mit Angabe ihrer Fundorte*, Band I (Hildesheim, Georg Olms Verlagbuchhandlung, 1965), pp. 23, 70.

[5] For a description of the manuscript, see A. Maier, *Codices Vaticani Latini, Codices 2118–2192* (Romae, 1961), pp. 27–8. C. H. Lohr, in his 'A Note on the Manuscripts of Paulus Venetus Logica', *Manuscripta*, 1973, pp. 35–6, lists 19 other manuscripts of the *Logica Magna*. Of these, one does contain material from Part I, Treatise 23–viz. Venezia, Biblioteca Marciana, Lat. cl. VI. 30 (2547), ff. 44ra–61rb—but all of the other 18 contain the *Logica Parva* instead.

[6] See *Logica Magna*, Part II, Fascicule 6, pp. x–xii.

Septimus de natura situatorum in figura	*Treatise 7*: On the Nature of Situation in the Figure
Octavus de conversione propositionum	*Treatise 8*: On Converting Propositions
Nonus de hypotheticis propositionibus	*Treatise 9*: On Molecular Propositions
Decimus de veritate et falsitate propositionum	*Treatise 10*: On the Truth and Falsity of Propositions
Undecimus de significato propositionis	*Treatise 11*: On the Significatum of a Proposition
Duodecimus de possibilitate, impossibilitate, et contingentia propositionum	*Treatise 12*: On the Possibility, Impossibility, and Contingency of Propositions
Tertiusdecimus de syllogismis	*Treatise 13*: On Syllogisms
Quartusdecimus de obligationibus	*Treatise 14*: On Obligations
Quintusdecimus de insolubilibus	*Treatise 15*: On Insolubles

Part I, Fascicule 1

The first Treatise of Part I, 'On Terms', is divided into four chapters, each of which is at least initially concerned with a principal division of terms. Paul of Venice, like most other logicians of the later Middle Ages, typically uses the word 'term' very broadly; but he will, when it suits his purposes, employ it in the more precise sense in which only the words essential to an ordinary categorical proposition are the terms of that proposition—its subject and predicate terms. For the sake of clarity in these introductory remarks I will use 'words' instead of 'terms' in the broad sense.

Chapter One takes as its point of departure the distinction between categorematic and syncategorematic words. Traditionally, categorematic words included all and only those that can serve as the subject or predicate terms of categorical propositions, while syncategorematic words were those that can occur in propositions only along with categorematic words. Paul's distinction departs from that tradition, as he explains. But he is far less interested in the distinction itself than in the question whether and in what respects syncategorematic words may be considered to be parts of the terms to which they are attached or in which they occur, a question to which he devotes more than three-quarters of the chapter. As was pointed out above, the treatises of the *Logica Magna* cover most of the topics discussed by medieval logicians; the ordering of those topics is, moreover, roughly the same as would be encountered in a later medieval textbook of logic. Paul has some interest in expounding the elements of logic clearly, but the *Logica Magna* is definitely not a textbook. The author's predilection is for detailed consideration of sophisticated, technical problems related, but sometimes rather remotely, to the elements with which the chapters typically begin.

Chapter Two is initially concerned with natural and arbitrary signification, ordinarily treated by medieval logicians as the most fundamental
semantic distinction: dark clouds and cries of pain have natural signification; the signification of words is arbitrary. Paul, however, makes use of
an extended application of the distinction to words themselves, distin-
guishing between the natural and arbitrary signification of categorematic
words in a way that enables him to explain in terms of signification the
difference between using and merely mentioning a word (formal and
material *suppositio*) and the relationships among the various occurrences,
or tokens, of a single word, or type. His consideration of signification,
particularly of natural signification, leads to the discussion of topics that
would now be thought of as belonging more clearly to epistemology (or,
perhaps, pragmatics) than to logic or semantics. Signification is fundamen-
tally the presentation of something to a mind (nothing more limited will
cover everything that Paul includes under signification), and in understanding the word 'man' a person may have presented to his mind not
only *mortal rational animal* but also, for instance, *substance*, or *Socrates*.
Signification thus shades off into implication, as Paul recognizes in his
distinction between primary and secondary signification, a distinction at
least as important for his further purposes as is the natural/arbitrary
distinction with which this chapter begins.

The distinction between common names and names that are discrete,
singular, or proper is the centre of Paul's attention throughout Chapter
Three, even though the arguments for and against some of the opinions
regarding proper or common names focus on many other logical elements,
such as imposition (of names on things), connotative terms, negation of
various kinds, and distribution (or quantification). Perhaps the most
readily accessible philosophically interesting material in the chapter is
contained in Paul's discussion of proper names, which involves a distinction between grammatically and logically proper names and considerations
of personal identity.

Chapter Four introduces the three sorts of linguistic analysis regularly
employed and discussed in later medieval logic: resolution, exposition, and
functionalization. Although it is primarily propositions that are subjected
to analysis, the sort of analysis appropriate in each case is determined by
the occurrence in the proposition of mediate, or analysable, words of one
sort or another. A proposition containing a mediate word admits of at least
one of the three sorts of analysis; immediate words are the elements of
propositions that are not further analysable. All the remaining treatises of
Part I may be viewed as working out the details of the material presented
in this first treatise, and most of them are concerned with the detailed
consideration of mediate words of one or another sort.

Even the most cursory reading of these chapters will show clearly what this summary description of them suggests: in each of them Paul discusses or employs many concepts and elements of medieval logic that are remote from the explicit subject matter. For that reason the Doctrinal Index at the end of this volume is an indispensable guide to its contents.

The reader will also discover very quickly that the consideration of the opinions of many of Paul's predecessors and contemporaries forms an important part of his encyclopedic aims. I would be delighted to identify all those other medieval logicians for the reader, but I am unable to do so. I undertook the preparation of Part I, Treatise 1, only on the understanding that the publication of this vast work in many separate fascicules represents primarily not the culmination of research but an important stimulus and aid to further research. One reason for the British Academy's decision to publish the *Logica Magna* is that its encyclopedic character and late date will provide the increasing number of scholars working in the history of logic with specific projects and with a context in which to bring together and organize the results of some research that has until now been disparate.

In establishing the text of Paul's treatise on terms I used the Bodleian Library's copy of the Venice 1499 edition together with the only complete manuscript (identified above). My edition and translation were completed in 1970 and delivered to the General Editors. I would do the work differently now, particularly as regards the critical apparatus, but I believe it to be understandable, complete, and accurate as it stands.

I am grateful to Peter Geach for involving me in this project to begin with and for his helpful general counsel and specific suggestions, particularly regarding the notes. And I owe a special debt of gratitude to Anthony Kenny, without whose efforts the publication of this fascicule might well have been delayed even longer.

SIGLA ET ABBREVIATIONES

M = Codex manuscriptus Vaticanus Latinus 2132
(saec. xv, ante an. 1443).

E = Editio typographica Venetiis 1499.

⟨...⟩ Includunt verba ab editore addita.

SIGNS AND ABBREVIATIONS USED IN THE TRANSLATION

⟨...⟩ Enclose words added by the translator.

Superscript lower-case letters indicate English explanatory notes.

LOGICAE MAGNAE

PRIMA PARS

DE TERMINIS

(3ra M, 2ra E) Definiens Aristoteles terminum primo *Priorum* dicit: "Terminus est in quem resolvitur propositio, ut praedicatum et de quo praedicatur, composito vel diviso esse vel non esse" (id est, in propositione affirmativa vel negativa). Et Boethius primo *Topicorum* ait: "Terminos autem voco nomina vel verba quibus nectitur propositio." Quia igitur in terminum resolvitur propositio, ideo primo in terminis est persistendum ut posterius propositionum notitia clarius appareat.

Pro quo primo notatur quod terminorum quidam sunt categorematici, quidam syncategorematici, qui inter se multipliciter distinguuntur.

Terminus categorematicus est signum, tam implicite quam explicite simplex, de communi lege, non extremorum aliqualiter unitivum, sed alterius a se et suo consimili per se in notitiam deductivum.

Particulae huius descriptionis declarantur.

⟨1⟩ Dicitur namque primo 'signum', quod ponitur loco generis, quia omnis terminus categorematicus est signum, et non econverso. Circulus namque ante tabernam est signum, et tamen non est terminus categorematicus. Similiter, quaelibet propositio vocatur signum ratione suae significationis et sui significati, et tamen nulla talis est terminus categorematicus.

⟨2⟩ Secundo dicitur 'tam implicite quam explicite simplex' quia iste terminus 'nihil' est signum explicite simplex, de communi lege, non extremorum aliqualiter unitivum, non tamen est terminus categorematicus sed terminus praegnans, quia non est implicite simplex, cum subordinetur uni tali complexo 'nulla res', composito ex categoremate et syncategoremate.

⟨3⟩ Tertio dicitur 'de communi lege' quia adveniente nova lege, posset per illam quilibet terminus qui modo est categorematicus fore terminus syncategorematicus vel econtra. Excluditur etiam nova impositio.

⟨4⟩ Quarto dicitur 'non extremorum aliqualiter unitivum' ad deno-

⟨Chapter One: The First Division of Terms— Categorematic and Syncategorematic⟩

⟨Aristotle's and Boethius' Definitions of the Term⟩

When Aristotle defines the term in *Prior Analytics* Book I, Chapter 1 ⟨24ᵇ17⟩, he says: "A term is that into which a proposition is analyzed, viz., the predicate and that of which it is predicated, with 'to be' or 'not to be' compounded with it or divided from it" (i.e., in an affirmative or a negative proposition). And in *De differentiis topicis* I ⟨Migne, *PL* 64. 1175B⟩ Boethius says: "I call terms the nouns or verbs out of which a proposition is put together." Thus, since the proposition is analysed into the term, one must concentrate on terms first so that later on one may learn about propositions with greater clarity.

⟨Definition of the Categorematic Term⟩

With that end in view the first thing to notice is that some terms are categorematic and others syncategorematic. These are distinguished from each other in many different ways.

A categorematic term is a sign, inwardly as well as outwardly simple, in accordance with a common law, without any sort of unifying effect on subject and predicate, but leading *per se* to a conception of something other than itself and what is equiform to it.[a]

The details of this description are explained in the following way.

⟨1⟩ 'A sign'. This serves as the genus, for every categorematic term is a sign, but not vice versa. The hoop in front of an inn is a sign, but it is not a categorematic term. Similarly, any proposition is called a sign because of its signification and its significatum, but nothing of the sort is a categorematic term.

⟨2⟩ 'Inwardly as well as outwardly simple'. The reason for saying this is that the term 'nothing' is an outwardly simple sign, in accordance with a common law, and without any sort of unifying effect on subject and predicate; and yet it is not a categorematic term but a pregnant term. For it is not inwardly simple, being subordinated to the complex 'no thing', which is composed of a categorematic and a syncategorematic.

⟨3⟩ 'In accordance with a common law'. The reason for saying this is that if a new law were to arise, any term that is now categorematic could as a result be a syncategorematic term, or vice versa. This rules out a new imposition as well.[b]

⟨4⟩ 'Without any sort of unifying effect on subject and predicate'. This is

tandum quod verba non sunt termini categorematici, cum sint suorum extremorum verba unitiva.

⟨5⟩ Quinto dicitur 'sed alterius a se et suo consimili in notitiam deducti-vum' propter ista signa 'omnis', 'nullus', et huiusmodi, et istos terminos materiales '*A*', '*B*', '*C*', et huiusmodi, qui, licet significent se naturaliter et in suppositione materiali sua consimilia ad placitum, non tamen sunt termini categorematici. Quia oportet quod de communi lege sit signifi-cativus alterius a se et suo consimili, sicut sunt isti termini 'homo', 'animal', et huiusmodi. Significant enim seipsos et in suppositione materiali sua similia, tamen significant homines, qui distinguuntur a talibus terminis et suis consimilibus. Similiter, isti termini 'terminus', 'signum', 'intentio' licet non significent nisi terminos sunt tamen termini categorematici, quia cum aliis conditionibus significant a se et suis consimilibus distincta, nam significant tales terminos 'homo', 'animal', qui non sunt similes alicui tali termino 'signum', 'intentio', vel 'terminus'.

Terminus syncategorematicus est signum officii executivum, nullius a se et suo consimili sine nova impositione per se significativum.

Particulae huius descriptionis declarantur.

⟨1⟩ Dicitur primo 'signum' loco generis, ut prius.

⟨2⟩ Secundo dicitur 'officii executivum' propter terminos categoremati-cos, qui non sunt officiorum executivi. Intelligo enim per esse officii executivum habere vim distribuendi, confundendi, copulandi, disiungendi, conditionandi, atque determinandi. Sicut sunt copulationes, disiunctiones, et notae conditionis: ut 'et', 'vel', 'si', igitur', et huiusmodi; similiter praepositiones et adverbia et interiectiones: ut 'at', 'ab', 'necessario', 'contingenter', 'olim', et huiusmodi.

⟨3⟩ Tertio dicitur 'nullius a se et suo consimili significativum' quia licet ly .nihil., ly .differens., et huiusmodi sunt officii executiva distribuendo, mobilitando, immobilitando, et huiusmodi, tamen quia significant signifi-cata distincta a se at suis similibus, ideo non sunt syncategoremata.

⟨4⟩ Quarto dicitur 'sine nova (2ʳᵇ E) impositione' propter causam dictam, quia non est dubium quod ly .omnis. posset per authenticam impositionem humanam vel divinam significare (3ʳᵇ M) distincta a se et suis similibus. Non tamen sic potest huiusmodi lege absolute dictante ad praesens.

---

2 verbaliter *M*   7–8 quod tales de communi lege sint significativi alterius *M*
13 similibus condistincta *M*   15 vel *om. E*   etc. *add. M*   17 se signum *E*
33 similibus distincta *M*   34 obligatorie et litante ad praesens *M*

said in order to indicate that verbs are not categorematic terms, for verbs do have a unifying effect on subjects and predicates associated with them.[c]

⟨5⟩ 'Leading ⟨per se⟩ to a conception of something other than itself and what is equiform to it'. This is said because of such signs as 'every' and 'no' and such material terms as 'A', 'B', and 'C'. Although they signify themselves naturally and in material *suppositio* signify arbitrarily what is equiform to them, they are are not categorematic terms. A categorematic term must signify in accordance with a common law something other than itself and anything equiform to it, as do the terms 'man', 'animal', and the like. They do signify themselves, and in material supposition they signify things equiform to themselves, but they also signify men, which are distinct from such terms and things equiform to them. Similarly, the terms 'term', 'sign', and 'intention' are categorematic terms even though they signify nothing but terms. This is because in keeping with the other conditions they do signify things distinct from themselves and from the things that are equiform to them. For they signify such terms as 'man' and 'animal', which are not equiform to the terms 'sign', 'intention', or 'term'.

⟨*Definition of the Syncategorematic Term*⟩

A syncategorematic term is a sign that carries out a function and in the absence of a new imposition is significant *per se* of nothing other than itself and what is equiform to it.

The details of this description are clarified in the following way.

⟨1⟩ 'A sign'. As before, this serves as the genus.

⟨2⟩ 'That carries out a function'. This is said because of categorematic terms, which do not carry out functions. By carrying out a function I mean having the force of distributing, confusing,[d] conjoining, disjoining, conditionalizing, and determinating. Conjunctions, disjunctions, and marks of conditionality are of this sort: 'and', 'or', 'if', 'then', and the like. So are prepositions, adverbs, and interjections, such as 'yet', 'by', 'necessarily', 'contingently', 'once', and the like.

⟨3⟩ 'Significant ⟨per se⟩ of nothing other than itself and what is equiform to it'. This is said because although 'nothing', 'different', and words like them do carry out a function in distributing, mobilizing, immobilizing, and the like, they are not syncategorematic words because they signify significata distinct from themselves and equiform to them.

⟨4⟩ 'In the absence of a new imposition'. The reason for saying this is the one already given,[e] for there is no doubt that 'every' could, as a result of an authentic human or divine imposition, signify things distinct from itself and those equiform to it. But it cannot do so at present under an absolutely explicit law of that sort.

Ex praedictis sequitur quod aliquis est terminus simplex qui nec est categorematicus nec est syncategorematicus. Patet de tali termino 'nihil', aut de copula verbi substantivi, aut de talibus materialibus terminis '*A*', '*B*', '*C*', et huiusmodi.

5   Sequitur etiam quod aliquis est terminus syncategorematicus qui per se aliquid significat, nam quilibet talis seipsum materialiter significat, sicut et quaelibet res naturalis obiecta virtuti cogitativae.

Item sequitur quod terminus categorematicus non dicitur esse qui significative acceptus potest esse subiectum vel praedicatum, aut pars 10 subiecti aut pars praedicati distributi, propositionis categoricae, sicut aliqui ponunt definitive. Nam de illis terminis '*A*' et '*B*' et de terminis praegnantibus definitio assignata per eos et non definitum.

Etiam sequitur quod ista definitio communis de termino syncategorematico non est vera, videlicet, terminus syncategorematicus dicitur qui, 15 significative acceptus, non potest esse subiectum aut praedicatum, aut pars subiecti aut pars praedicati distributi, propositionis categoricae. Nam dicendo

Omne videns omnem hominem est animal,

vel

20   Omne quod est homo vel asinus currit,

syncategorema est pars subiecti distributi, ut patet. Et ita dicendo

Tu non es videns omnem hominem,

syncategorema est pars praedicati distributi in propositione categorica.

⟨1⟩ Dubitatur primo utrum adiectiva aliqua possunt esse termini cate- 25 gorem.atici aut de facto sint. Et videtur quod non, quia ly .omnis., .nullus., et huiusmodi non sunt termini categorematici; igitur nec aliquid aliud adiectivum. Consequentia patet, vel detur causa diversitatis.

⟨IR⟩ Respondetur quod adiectiva sunt in multiplici differentia. (1) Quaedam enim non significant a se et suis consimilibus distinctum, ut 30 'omnis' et 'nullus'. (2) Quaedam significant, sed dependenter, propter habitudinem ad alterum extremorum, ut 'albus' ⟨vel⟩ 'niger', 'alba' vel 'nigra' in masculino vel in feminino genere, et in neutro genere, ut 'album' vel 'nigrum' pure adiective sumptum. (3) Tertio sunt aliqua quae significant huiusmodi significata sumpta per se et non per respectum ad aliud, 35 ut sunt huiusmodi adiectiva non tenta pure adiective sed in neutro genere substantivata.

---

2 'vel' *E*   6 aliquid *om. E*   materialiter *om. M*   15 significative
sumptus *E*   30–1 per habitudinem *M*   35 tempta *E*

⟨*Conclusions drawn from the Definitions of Categorematic and Syncategore-matic Terms*⟩

From what has been said so far it follows that there is a simple term that is neither categorematic nor syncategorematic. This is clear as regards such a term as 'nothing', or the copula (i.e., the substantive verb), or the material terms '*A*', '*B*', '*C*', and the like.

It follows also that there is a syncategorematic term that signifies something *per se*, for any such term materially signifies itself, just as any real thing is a natural object for the faculty of thought.

It follows also that a categorematic term is not "that which, taken as significant, can be the subject or the predicate, or a part of the distributed subject or predicate, of a categorical proposition", as some propose to define it. For the definiens chosen by them is verified of the terms '*A*' and '*B*' and of pregnant terms, while the definiendum is not.

It follows also that the common definition of a syncategorematic term is not true—viz., "A syncategorematic term is that which, taken as significant, cannot be the subject or the predicate, or a part of the distributed subject or predicate, of a categorical proposition." For when one says

Everything seeing every man is an animal,

or

Everything that is a man or a donkey is running,

a syncategorematic word is obviously a part of the distributed subject. And when one says

You are not seeing every man,

a syncategorematic word is a part of the distributed predicate in a categorical proposition.

⟨*Doubts and Replies*⟩

⟨I⟩ There is a doubt whether some adjectives can be or in fact are categorematic terms. It seems they cannot, for 'every', 'no', and the like are not categorematic terms; therefore neither is any other adjective. The inference is clear. Or ⟨if it is not⟩, explain the diversity.

⟨IR⟩ Adjectives differ in many ways. (1) Some, such as 'every' and 'no', do not signify anything distinct from themselves and things equiform to them. (2) Others do signify, but dependently, as a consequence of a relation to one or the other of the extremes—e.g., 'white' or 'black' in the masculine or the feminine gender and, when taken purely adjectivally, in the neuter gender. (3) There are some of this sort that do signify significata taken *per se* and not as a consequence of a relation to something else—e.g., adjectives of this sort not taken purely adjectivally but used substantivally in the neuter gender.

Dico ergo quod adiectiva primo modo sumpta non sunt termini categorematici sed syncategorematici, ut dictum est.

Secundo modo sumpta sunt termini categorematici sed dependenter
tales. Sicut enim significant dependenter, ita categorematici sunt depen-
5 denter. Unde dicendo

Albus (vel niger) est (vel erit),

si nihil aliud intelligatur, intelligibiles enuntiationes non sunt. Sed haec
est intelligibilis:

Homo est albus,

10 quia iam ly .albus. significat hominem, distinctum a se et quolibet suo
consimili. Et quod dependenter patet, quia sicut iam significat hominem,
ita potest significare asinum ex sola mutatione in subiecto, dicendo

Asinus est albus.

Notandum tamen quod licet ly .albus. significet hominem album aut
15 asinum album non tamen est praedicatum aliquis talis terminus 'homo
albus' aut 'asinus albus', sed solum ly .albus.

Adiectiva vero sumpta tertio modo significant de per se et non per habitudinem ad aliud. Ideo possunt esse termini categorematici, et independ-
denter tales, sicut ly .homo. vel ly .animal. Unde dicendo

20 Album currit,

vel

Nigrum disputat,

ita intelligibiles propositiones sunt sicut ista:

Homo est animal.

25 Et hoc sumendo ly .album. vel .nigrum. ut dictum est, quia si sumerentur
pure adiective, sicut hic:

Animal est album,

intelligendo implicite quod animal est animal album, tunc inintelligibiles
essent orationes, sicut istae nominatae:

30 Albus currit,

Niger disputat.

⟨II⟩ Secundo dubitatur numquid syncategorema possit esse subiectum
aut praedicatum propositionis. Et videtur quod non, quia ly .omnis.,
.nullus., non possunt esse extrema propositionum, semper significative
35 intelligendo; igitur nec (3ᵛᵃ M) aliqua alia.

⟨IIR⟩ Dicendum quod syncategoremata distributiva aut confusiva aliter
probabilia quam officiabiliter non possunt esse extrema propositionum
significative personaliter sumpta, sicut supra dicta. Et alia similiter, ut

---

11 quod dependeat patet *E*   iam *om. E*   14 tamen *om. E*   18 et *om. E*
23 propositiones *om. E*

I maintain, therefore, that adjectives taken in the first way are not categorematic but syncategorematic terms, as has been said.[f]

Taken in the second way they are categorematic terms, but dependently so. For they are dependently categorematic just as they signify dependently. Thus when one says

White (or black) is (or will be),

if nothing else is understood, these are unintelligible statements. But

The man is white

is intelligible, because now 'white' signifies a man, something distinct from itself and from each thing equiform to it. And it is obvious that it does so dependently, for just as it now signifies a man, so it can signify a donkey, solely in virtue of a change in the subject, when one says

The donkey is white.

Note, however, that although 'white' signifies a white man or a white donkey, the predicate is not any such term as 'white man' or 'white donkey', but 'white' alone.

Adjectives taken in the third way, however, signify *per se* and not as a consequence of a relation to something else. Hence they can be categorematic terms, and independently so, just like 'man' or 'animal'. Thus when one says

A white is running,

or

A black is engaged in disputation,

they are propositions just as intelligible as

A man is an animal,

provided that 'white' or 'black' is taken in the way described. If they were taken purely adjectivally, as in

The animal is white,

where one understands implicitly that the animal is a white animal, then the expressions would be unintelligible, just like the ones already mentioned:[g]

White is running,

Black is engaged in disputation.

⟨II⟩ There is a doubt whether a syncategorematic word can be the subject or the predicate of a proposition. It seems it cannot, for 'every' and 'no' cannot be the extremes of propositions in any case in which they are understood to be signifying; therefore neither can any others.

⟨IIR⟩ It must be said that distributive or confusive syncategorematic words[h] that can be accepted otherwise than functionally cannot be the extremes[i] of propositions taken as signifying personally,[j] as was said above.[k] The same is true of others, such as 'necessarily', 'contingently', and the

'necessario' et 'contingenter' et huiusmodi. Syncategoremata autem offi-
ciabilia possunt subici vel praedicari ad intellectum datum, ut

    (1) Sortem currere est possibile,

    (2) Contingens est Antichristum fore.

5 In prima ly .possibile. est praedicatum, et in secunda ly .contingens. est
subiectum, et tamen sunt syncategoremata, ut patet quia non videtur quod
significent praeter se et sua similia.

    Notandum tamen quod ly .possibile., .contingens., et huiusmodi nomina-
liter sumpta possunt dupliciter sumi, aut (2ᵛᵃ E) officiabiliter aut resolubi-
10 liter in propositione. Primo modo sunt syncategoremata, ut dictum est.
Sed secundo modo sunt categoremata et significant entia possibilia vel
contingentia. Quare, etc.

    ⟨III⟩ Tertio dubitatur utrum haec syncategoremata 'omnis', 'nullus',
'quilibet', 'uterque', et similia possunt esse partes subiecti vel praedicati
15 propositionis significative sumpti.

    ⟨IIIR⟩ Circa istud dubium duae sunt opiniones. ⟨1⟩ Prima dicit quod ly
.omnis. et similia possunt esse partes subiecti vel praedicati significative
sumpti, ut

    Tu es omnis homo,

20   Videns omnem hominem est animal.

    ⟨2⟩ Secunda dicit quod aliqua syncategoremata bene possunt esse partes
subiecti vel praedicati, sed ly .omnis. non. Unde sic dicendo

    Tu es non asinus,

ly .non. est pars praedicati. Sed dicendo

25   Tu es omnis homo,

ly .homo. solum est praedicatum.

    ⟨1.1⟩ Contra primam opinionem arguitur tale signum distributivum
'omnis' positum a parte subiecti, praecedens totam propositionem, non est
pars subiecti, sed aeque syncategorematice sumitur a parte praedicati
30 vel inter partes subiecti sicut quando praecedit totam propositionem;
igitur a pari non potest esse pars subiecti vel praedicati. Consequentia
videtur teneri cum minori. Et maior probatur, nam in illa propositione

    Omnis homo est animal

ly .omnis. non potest esse pars subiecti.

11–12 possibilia et contingentia *E*   14 'uterque' *om. E*   26 est solum *E*
29–30 praedicati et inter *M*

like. But functional syncategorematic words can be subjects or predicates with respect to a given idea, as in

    (1) That Socrates is running is possible,
    (2) Contingent it is that Antichrist will be.

In (1) 'possible' is the predicate, and in (2) 'contingent' is the subject, and yet they are syncategorematic words, as is clear from the fact that they evidently do not signify anything besides themselves and things equiform to them.

Note, however, that when 'possible', 'contingent', and the like are taken as names[l] they can be taken in one of two ways in a proposition, either as functionalizable or as resoluble.[m] Taken in the first way they are syncategorematic words, as has been said.[n] But taken in the second way they are categorematic and signify possible or contingent beings.[o] Therefore, etc.

⟨III⟩ There is a doubt whether the syncategorematic words 'every', 'no', 'each', 'both', and the like can be parts of the subject or the predicate of a proposition when they are taken to be signifying.

⟨IIIR⟩ There are two opinions regarding this doubt. ⟨1⟩ The first maintains that 'every' and the like can be parts of the subject or the predicate when they are taken to be signifying, as in

    You are every man,
    Seeing every man is an animal.

⟨2⟩ The second maintains that some syncategorematic words can rightly be parts of the subject or the predicate, but not 'every'. Thus when one says

    You are a not-donkey,

'not' is a part of the predicate. But when one says

    You are every man,

'man' alone is the predicate.

⟨*Arguments against Opinion 1*⟩

⟨1.1⟩ A distributive sign such as 'every' placed in the subject position preceding the whole proposition is not a part of the subject, but when it is placed in the predicate position or between parts of the subject it is taken just as syncategorematically as when it precedes the whole proposition; therefore by parity of reasoning it cannot be a part of the subject or the predicate. The inference evidently holds good along with the minor premiss. And the major premiss is proved, for in the proposition

    Every man is an animal

'every' cannot be a part of the subject.

⟨1.2⟩ Secundo si ly .omnis. est pars praedicati, sit igitur in illa:

Tu es omnis homo.

Contra: omne praedicatum illius est universale universaliter sumptum, sed hoc totum 'omnis homo' non est universale universaliter sumptum; igitur
5 hoc totum non est praedicatum illius propositionis. Patet discursus in *Baroco*. Et maior patet per Aristotelem primo *Peri Hermeneias*, ubi dicit quod nulla affirmatio est vera in qua universale universaliter sumptum praedicatur, ponentem exemplum de illa:

Omnis homo est omne animal.
10 Minor patet de se.

⟨1.3⟩ Quaero utrum ly .omnis homo. sit terminus transcendens vel non. Si non, ergo cum sit praedicatum videtur quod sit terminus inferior ad transcendens. Et si sic, de ipso potest vere praedicari transcendens, quod non est verum, quia non potest esse subiectum. Nec est transcendens,
15 quare tunc omne ens esset omnis homo.

⟨1.4⟩ Quarto haec propositio

Sortes est omnis homo

est singularis vel indefinita affirmativa. Igitur habet converti simpliciter. Sed non potest aliter converti quam sic:
20   Omnis homo est Sortes,

ubi ly .omnis homo. non est subiectum. Igitur prius non erat praedicatum. Nec potest dici quod sic debet converti:

Aliquid quod est omnis homo est Sortes,

quia tunc non fieret praecise de praedicato subiectum, quod tamen oportet
25 ad hoc quod esset conversio simplex.

⟨1.5⟩ Quinto sic: pono quod continue ante instans quod est praesens componebas sic:

Tu es homo,

et quod nunc primo describas illam intentionem *omnis* a parte praedicati.
30 Tunc arguo sic. Quicquid iam componis cum subiecto huius propositionis prius componebas et econtra, sed prius componebas istam intentionem *homo* de subiecto illius et non aliud; ergo et iam. Ista consequentia patet, et maior similiter, eo quod solum componis istam intentionem *homo* de subiecto. Quia iste actus componendi solum (3vb M) dependet ab istis duabus in-
35 tentionibus et intellectu quo modo continue ab eisdem dependebat prius.

---

6 patet *om.* E   23 quod est *om.* M   29 *homo* M   30 arguitur E
31 prius solum componebas *M*   34 componendi est solum *M*   35 intellectu
eo quod continue *M*

⟨1.2⟩ If 'every' is a part of the predicate, then it is so in

You are every man.

But, on the contrary, every predicate of this proposition is a universal taken universally, but the whole 'every man' is not a universal taken universally; therefore that whole is not the predicate of the proposition. This reasoning in *Baroco* is obvious. And the major premiss is well known from the passage in Aristotle, *De interpretatione* I ⟨Ch. 7, 17^{b}13⟩, where he says that no affirmation is true in which a universal taken universally is predicated, and provides the example

Every man is every animal.

The minor premiss is obvious in itself.

⟨1.3⟩ I ask whether or not 'every man' is a transcendental term.[b] If not, then since it is the predicate it is evidently a term inferior to a transcendental term.[q] And if it is transcendental, then a transcendental term can be predicated of it truly. But that is not true, for it cannot be a subject.[r] Nor is it a transcendental term, because in that case every being would be every man.

⟨1.4⟩ The proposition

Socrates is every man

is a singular or indefinite affirmative proposition. Therefore it has to be converted simply. But it cannot be converted otherwise than this:

Every man is Socrates,

in which 'every man' is not the subject. Therefore it was not the predicate in the former case. Nor can one say that it must be converted in this way:

Something that is every man is Socrates,

since it would not be the case that nothing more nor less than the ⟨former⟩ predicate would become the subject. But that is what is required in order for there to be simple conversion.

⟨1.5⟩ Suppose that just before the present instant you were uninterruptedly compounding[s]

You are a man,

and that just now for the first time you are putting into writing the intention *every* in the predicate position. Then I argue as follows. Whatever you are now compounding with the subject of this proposition you were previously compounding and vice versa, but you were previously compounding the intention *man* and nothing else with the subject of it; therefore now as well. The inference is obvious, and so is the major premiss, because you are compounding only the intention *man* with the subject. For the act of compounding depends solely on those two intentions ⟨*you* and *man*⟩ and on the understanding in the way in which it was uninterruptedly depending on those same things previously.

⟨1.6⟩ Sexto sic: data ista opinione, sequitur quod duo contradictoria inter se contradicentia sunt simul vera, vel quod aliqua sunt contradictoria inter se contradicentia quae non sunt de consimili praedicato. Consequens est manifeste falsum. Et consequentia probatur: et capio istam proposi-
5 tionem

Homo animal non est,

et quaero quid est suum contradictorium. Si dicitur quod haec:

Omnis homo animal est,

habetur prima pars conclusionis, certum est quod quaelibet illarum est
10 vera. Si autem dicitur quod istud est suum contradictorium:

Omnis homo omne animal est,

quaeritur si ly .omne animal. est praedicatum vel non. Si sic, igitur altera pars conclusionis, eo quod ly .animal. praecise praedicatur in una, et ly .omne animal. in alia, modo certum est quod talia praedicata non sunt
15 similia. Si vero dicitur quod ly .omne animal. non est praedicatum sed praecise ly .animal., statim habetur oppositum opinionis.

⟨1.7⟩ Septimo sic: in ista propositione

Tantum omnis homo est homo

ly .homo. praecise est subiectum; igitur oppositum opinionis. Consequen-
20 tia patet. Et antecedens arguitur, quia idem debet esse subiectum ex-clusivae et suae praeiacentis, sed in illa praeiacente

Omnis homo est homo

est praecise ly .homo. subiectum; igitur et in exclusiva. Consequentia patet cum maiori. Et minor probatur, nam praeiacens exclusivae debet
25 esse illud quod remanet dempta dictione exclusiva, sed dempta dictione exclusiva nihil remanet nisi ly

.Omnis homo est homo.;

igitur illud est praeiacens exclusivae.

Multa alia argumenta possunt adduci, quae causa brevitatis omitto.
30 ⟨2.1⟩ Contra secundam opinionem arguitur illud signum distributivum 'non' potest esse pars subiecti vel praedicati, sed aeque syncategorema est illud signum 'omnis' sicut ly .non.; igitur per idem ly .omnis. potest esse pars subiecti vel praedicati. Consequentia videtur (2ᵛᵇ E) bona, et minor similiter. Maior vero patet per opinionem, vel aliter periret illa regula quae

---

2 quod *om. E*   3 inter se contradicentia *om. E*   12 sit praedicatum *M*
21 et subiectum praeiacentis *M*   23 est ly .homo. praecise subiectum *E*   exclu-siva praedicta *M*   25 dempto signo exclusivo *E*   29 brevitatis dimittam *E*

⟨1.6⟩ If Opinion ⟨1⟩ is granted, it follows either that two mutual contradictories are true at one and the same time or that there are some mutual contradictories that are not equiform as regards the predicate. This consequent is plainly false. And the inference is proved in the following way. I take the proposition

A man ⟨a certain⟩ animal is not,[t]

and I ask what its contradictory is. If it is said to be

Every man ⟨a certain⟩ animal is,

then the first part of the conclusion is established, for each of these is certainly true. But if its contradictory is said to be

Every man every animal is,

then the question is whether or not 'every animal' is the predicate. If it is so, then the other part of the conclusion is established, because just 'animal' is predicated in the one, and 'every animal' in the other, and such predicates are certainly not alike. But if it is said that not 'every animal' but just 'animal' is the predicate, then the opposite of the Opinion is established at once.

⟨1.7⟩ In the proposition

Only every man is a man

just 'man' is the subject; therefore the opposite of the Opinion ⟨is established⟩. The inference is obvious. And the following argument supports the antecedent. The subject of an exclusive proposition and of its prejacent must be one and the same, but in the prejacent

Every man is a man

the subject is just 'man'; therefore in the exclusive as well. The inference is obvious, along with the major premiss. And the minor premiss is proved in the following way. The prejacent of an exclusive must be what remains when the exclusive word has been withdrawn, but when the exclusive word has been withdrawn nothing remains but

Every man is a man;

therefore that is the prejacent of the exclusive.

Many other arguments can be adduced, but I omit them for the sake of brevity.

⟨*Arguments against Opinion 2*⟩

⟨2.1⟩ The distributive sign 'non-' can be a part of the subject or the predicate, but the sign 'every' is just as syncategorematic as is 'non-'; therefore by the same token 'every' can be a part of the subject or the predicate. The inference is evidently good, and the minor premiss likewise. But the major premiss is manifest as a consequence of Opinion ⟨2⟩, for otherwise the rule that a negative proposition with a finite predicate follows

dicit quod ab affirmativa de praedicato infinito sequitur negativa de praedicato finito. Periret etiam alia, quae dicit quod in conversione per contra-
positionem oportet quod termini finiti mutentur in terminos infinitos.

⟨2.2⟩ Secundo sic: data opinione, sequitur quod haec propositio est vera:

5   Omnis homo est omnis homo.

Consequens est falsum, et consequentia probatur, nam nulla propositio
est verior illa in qua idem praedicatur de seipso, sed in propositione
praedicta idem praedicatur de seipso; igitur nulla propositio est verior
illa:

10   Omnis homo est omnis homo.

Et si sic, illa est vera, quod erat probandum. Consequentia patet cum
minori, quia ly .homo. praecise subicitur et ly .homo. praecise praedicatur,
per opinionem. Maior est Boethii.

⟨2.3⟩ Tertio sequitur quod istae duae propositiones convertuntur:

15   Sortes est homo

et

       Sortes est omnis homo.

Consequens est falsum, quia una est vera et reliqua falsa. Consequentia
probatur, nam subiecta convertuntur, praedicata convertuntur, copulae
20 sunt eadem, et propositiones sunt eiusdem quantitatis et qualitatis, et
termini praecise pro eisdem supponunt; igitur illae convertuntur. Patet
consequentia, quia per istum modum arguendi investigatur aliquas propositiones similiter converti. Et antecedens clarissime patet intuenti.

⟨2.4⟩ Quarto sequitur quod non omnis propositio universalis negativa de
25 consueto modo loquendi est simpliciter convertibilis, quia convertens est
falsa et conversa vera, quod non est possibile. Consequentia probatur: et
capio istam propositionem

       Nullus homo est omnis homo.

Tunc quaero utrum ipsa sit simpliciter convertibilis vel non. Si non,
30 habetur prima pars conclusionis. Si sic, igitur debet sic converti:

       Nullus homo est homo

vel

       Nihil quod est homo est aliquis homo,

quarum quaelibet est falsa. Igitur habetur secunda pars conclusionis. Et

---

1 quod *om. E*   11 quia in propositione praedicta idem praedicatur de seipso. Et
si sic *E*   19 nam *om. E*   21 illae *om. E*   25-6 conversa est vera et convertens falsa *M*

from an affirmative with an infinite predicate[u] would be lost. Another rule, too, would be lost—viz., that in conversion by contraposition finite terms must be changed into infinite terms.[v]

⟨2.2⟩ If Opinion ⟨2⟩ is granted, it follows that the proposition

Every man is every man

is true. This consequent is false, and the inference is proved in the following way. No proposition is truer than one in which one and the same thing is predicated of itself, but in the proposition given above one and the same thing is predicated of itself; therefore no proposition is truer than

Every man is every man.

And if that is the case, then it is true, which is what was to be proved. This inference is obvious, along with the minor premiss, for according to Opinion ⟨2⟩ just 'man' is the subject and just 'man' is the predicate. The major premiss is from Boethius.[w]

⟨2.3⟩ It follows that the two propositions

Socrates is a man

and

Socrates is every man

are interchangeable. The consequent is false, since one is true and the other is false. The inference is proved in the following way. The subjects are interchangeable, the predicates are interchangeable, the copulas are the same, the propositions are of the same quantity and quality, and the terms supposit for precisely the same things; therefore the two propositions are interchangeable. This inference is obvious, for this is the mode of arguing by means of which one discovers that certain propositions are interchangeable in the same manner. And the antecedent is perfectly plain to anyone who considers it.

⟨2.4⟩ It follows that not every universal negative in the ordinary way of speaking is simply convertible, for the convertend is true and the converse false, which is not possible. The inference is proved in the following way. I take the proposition

No man is every man.

Then I ask whether or not it is simply convertible. If not, the first part of the conclusion is established. If so, then it must be converted as follows:

No man is a man

or

Nothing that is a man is some man,

each of which is false. Therefore the second part of the conclusion is established. And it is obvious that they are correctly converted, since in them the predicate is made of the ⟨former⟩ subject, and the subject is

quod illa recte convertantur patet, quia ibi fit de subiecto praedicatum et econverso, manente eadem quantitate et qualitate. Ergo, etc.

⟨2.5⟩ Quinto sequitur quod duo contradictoria inter se contradicentia sunt simul falsa. Consequens est impossibile, et consequentia probatur,
5 nam ista sunt simul falsa:

Omnis homo est omnis homo

et

Aliquid quod est homo non est homo,

et ista sunt contradictoria inter se contradicentia; ergo . . . Consequentia
10 patet cum maiori. Et minor probatur, nam una est universalis affirmativa (4ra M) et alia particularis negativa de consimilibus subiectis, praedicatis, et copulis, et termini praecise pro eisdem supponunt; ergo . . .

Per istud argumentum posset etiam probari quod duo contradictoria inter se contradicentia sunt simul vera, ut captis talibus propositionibus:

15 Omnis homo est homo,

Aliquid quod est homo non est omnis homo,

arguendo ut prius.

⟨2.6⟩ Sexto sequitur ut prius quod haec est vera:

Homo est omne animal.

20 Probatur: ipsa significat primarie hominem esse animal, sed hominem esse animal est verum; igitur, etc. Consequentia patet cum minori. Et maior arguitur sic: subiectum significat primarie hominem, et praedicatum significat primarie animal, et copula primarie esse, et tota propositio significat iuxta compositionem suorum terminorum; igitur tota propositio
25 significat primarie hominem esse animal. Consequentia patet cum maiori, et minor sequitur ex opinione.

⟨2.7⟩ Ultimo arguitur sic. Et capio istam propositionem:

Tantum omnis homo est homo,

et quaero utrum ly .omnis homo. sit subiectum vel non. Si sic, habetur
30 intentum. Si non, contra: ibi subicitur terminus communis signo universali determinatus; igitur ista est universalis. Consequens falsum, eo quod exclusivae nullius sunt quantitatis.

---

1 ibidem *M*   18 sequitur quod haec est vera ut prius *M*   23 significat *om.*
E   esse primarie *E*   propositio *om. E*   24 suorum *om. E*

made of the ⟨former⟩ predicate, while the quantity and quality remain the same. Therefore, etc.

⟨2.5⟩ It follows that two mutual contradictories are false at one and the same time. This consequent is impossible, and the inference is proved in the following way. The propositions

Every man is every man

and

Something that is a man is not a man

are false at one and the same time, and they are mutual contradictories; therefore . . . This inference is obvious, along with the major premiss. The minor premiss is proved in the following way. One is a universal affirmative proposition and the other a particular negative with their subjects, predicates, and copulas just alike, and the terms supposit for precisely the same things; therefore . . .

By means of this argument one can prove also that two mutual contradictories are true at one and the same time if, for example, one takes such propositions as

Every man is a man

and

Something that is a man is not every man

and then argues as before.

⟨2.6⟩ It follows, as before, that

A man is every animal

is true. Proof: This proposition primarily signifies that a man is an animal, but that a man is an animal is true; therefore, etc. The inference is obvious, along with the minor premiss. The major premiss is supported by the following argument. The subject primarily signifies a man, the predicate primarily signifies an animal, the copula primarily signifies being, and the whole proposition signifies in accordance with the composition of its terms; therefore the whole proposition primarily signifies that a man is an animal. This inference is obvious, along with the major premiss, and the minor premiss follows from Opinion ⟨2⟩.

⟨2.7⟩ Finally, there is this argument. I take the proposition

Only every man is a man

and I ask whether or not 'every man' is the subject. If it is, then what was intended is established. If not, then on the contrary: a common term governed by a universal sign is the subject in the proposition; therefore the proposition is universal. This consequent is false, for exclusives are of no quantity at all.

Quia huiusmodi opiniones probabiles et sustentabiles sunt, nec argumenta contra eas militare videntur, restat solum ut argumenta contra eas facta brevissime dissolvantur.

⟨1.1R⟩ Ad primum igitur contra primam opinionem respondetur breviter negando consequentiam. Sicut non sequitur:

> Ly .omnis. positum a parte praedicati non potest confundere aliquem terminum confuse tantum, sed aeque syncategorematice sumitur a parte praedicati sicut quando praecedit totam propositionem; ergo quando praecedit totam propositionem non potest facere stare aliquem terminum confuse tantum.

Consequens enim est falsum, ut patet, eo quod ly .omnis. distribuens totum subiectum praedicatum facit stare confuse tantum si fuerit terminus communis.

⟨1.2R⟩ Ad secundum respondetur primo negando auctoritatem illam adductam. Ex illa enim sequitur quod haec est falsa:

> Omnes homines sunt omnes homines;
>
> Omnes apostoli Dei sunt omnes apostoli Dei.

Quod tamen est falsum, quaelibet enim istarum est vera tenendo ly .omnes. utrobique collective. Nec valet dicere quod auctoritas intelligitur in singulari numero, quia adhuc quaelibet illarum est vera, scilicet:

> Ista phoenix est omnis phoenix,
>
> Iste deus est omnis deus,
>
> Iste sol est omnis sol,

et tamen in qualibet illarum praedicatur universale universaliter sumptum. Et si quaeritur quare negas auctoritatem Aristotelis, dicitur quod non est auctoritas Aristotelis, sed una propositio male translata.

Vel aliter potest responderi magis sophistice dicendo quod ista auctoritas, quod nulla affirmatio est vera in qua universale universaliter sumptum praedicatur, intelligitur quod nulla affirmatio est vera in qua universale universaliter sumptum, id est, cum signo universali, praedicatur. Et tunc ad argumentum, admitto hunc casum et nego minorem ad eundem (3ra E) intellectum, quia certum est quod in ista propositione

> Tu es omnis homo

praedicatur ly .homo. sumptum cum signo universali. Nec ex hoc sequitur

⟩*Replies to the Arguments*⟩

Since opinions of that sort are acceptable and supportable, and arguments seem not to militate against them, it remains only to refute the arguments raised against them as briefly as possible.

⟨*Replies to the Arguments against Opinion 1*⟩

⟨1.1R⟩ The short reply is to reject the inference. It does not follow any more than does this:

> 'Every' placed in the predicate position cannot give any term merely confused *suppositio*, but in the predicate position it is taken just as syncategorematically as when it precedes the whole proposition; therefore when it precedes the whole proposition it cannot make any term have merely confused *suppositio*.

This consequent is obviously false, for when 'every' distributes the whole subject it makes the predicate have merely confused *suppositio* if it is a common term.

⟨1.2R⟩ One replies first by rejecting the authority appealed to. For it follows from that authority that these propositions are false:

> All men are all men;
> All of God's apostles are all of God's apostles.

But that is false, for each of these is true if 'all' is taken as being used collectively in both of its occurrences.* Nor will it do to say that the authority is understood to apply to the singular number, since each of these is true as well:

> This phoenix is every phoenix,
> This god is every god,
> This sun is every sun,

and yet in each of them a universal taken universally is predicated. And if someone asks, "Why do you reject the authority of Aristotle?", the answer is that it is not the authority of Aristotle, but a badly translated proposition.

Alternatively, one can reply in a more technical way by saying that this authority—that no affirmation is true in which a universal taken universally is predicated—means that no affirmation is true in which a universal taken universally—i.e., together with a universal sign—is predicated. As for the argument, I accept the hypothesis and I deny the minor premise on the basis of this same interpretation, for in the proposition

> You are every man

'man' certainly is predicated taken together with a universal sign. Nor

quod in illa praedicetur ly .homo., sicut non sequitur apud viam communem:

> In ista propositione 'iste homo currit' subicitur terminus communis
> cum pronomine demonstrativo; igitur ibidem subicitur terminus
> 5   communis.

Ita eodem modo potest dici quod ibidem praedicatur universale universaliter sumptum, id est, sumptum cum signo universali, non tamen praedicatur aliquid universale.

⟨1.3R⟩ Ad tertium dico quod ly .omnis homo. non est terminus transcendens, et cum infertur igitur est terminus inferior ad transcendens nego consequentiam. Sicut in ista propositione

> Tu es homo vel non homo

ly .homo vel non homo. est praedicatum et non est terminus transcendens. Nec inferior ad transcendens, quia praedicatur de termino transcendente universaliter, sic dicendo:

> Omne ens est homo vel non homo

iuxta (4ʳᵇ M) illam regulam: de quolibet dicitur alterum contradictorium incomplexorum et de nullo eorum ambo. Unde termini compositi non proprie dicuntur inferiores vel superiores ad aliquid, saltem de per se, nisi forte per reductionem, sicut ly .omnis homo., ly .homo vel non homo., ly .Sortes vel Plato., et sic de aliis, sed bene termini simplices, sicut ly .homo., ly .animal., et sic de aliis.

Aliter potest dici quod terminus transcendens potest praedicari de isto termino 'omnis homo', sic dicendo:

> 25   Aliquid omnis homo est ens,

volendo quod ly .aliquid. teneatur pure syncategorematice. Et sic argumentum nihil concludit.

⟨1.4R⟩ Ad quartum dico quod ista propositio

> (1) Sortes est omnis homo

debet converti sic:

> (2) Aliquid omnis homo est Sortes.

Et tunc ad argumentum id quod fuit praedicatum in prima non est subiectum in secunda igitur conversio nulla, respondetur dupliciter. Primo negando antecedens, dicendo quod sicut ly .omnis homo. prius fuit praedicatum, ita est modo subiectum, tenendo ly .aliquid. pure syncategorematice. Respondetur secundo negando consequentiam. Unde in conversione vocali vel scripta non oportet quod subiectum unius sit praedicatum alterius, vel econverso: praedicatum unius sit subiectum alterius. Quia in ista propositione

> Quilibet homo est unus homo

14 ad ly .transcendens. *E*   19 ad aliud *E*   33 dupliciter *om. E*

does it follow from this that 'man' is predicated in that proposition any more than this follows in a commonly accepted way:

> In the proposition 'this man is running' a common term together with a demonstrative pronoun is subject; therefore a common term is subject in it.

Thus in the same way one can say that in the example a universal taken universally—i.e., together with a universal sign—is predicated, but it is not the case that some universal is predicated.

⟨1.3R⟩ I say that 'every man' is not a transcendental term, and when it is inferred that in that case it is a term inferior to a transcendental I reject the inference. For instance, in the proposition

> You are a man or a non-man

'a man or a non-man' is the predicate, and it is not a transcendental term.[y] Nor is it inferior to a transcendental, for it is predicated universally of a transcendental term, as when one says

> Every being is a man or a non-man

in accordance with the rule that one or the other of a pair of noncomplex contradictories is said of anything whatever and both are said of nothing at all. Thus composite terms—e.g., 'every man', 'a man or a non-man', 'Socrates or Plato', and so on—are not properly said to be inferior or superior to anything, at any rate *per se*, unless perhaps as a result of reduction;[z] but simple terms are—e.g., 'man', 'animal', and so on.

Alternatively, one can say that a transcendental term can be predicated of the term 'every man', as when one says

> Some every man is a being,

intending 'some' to be taken purely syncategorematically.[a] And so the argument concludes nothing.

⟨1.4R⟩ I say that the proposition

> (1) Socrates is every man

must be converted as follows:

> (2) Some every man is Socrates.

As for the argument that that which was the predicate in (1) is not the subject in (2) and that therefore this is no conversion, the reply is twofold. First, to deny the antecedent, saying that just as 'every man' was previously the predicate, so is it now the subject, taking 'some' purely syncategorematically. Second, to reject the inference. Thus in a spoken or written conversion it is not necessary that the subject of the one proposition be the predicate of the other, or vice versa: that the predicate of the one proposition be the subject of the other. For in the proposition

> Any man is an individual man

ly .homo. est praecise subiectum. Et tamen in sua exclusiva non debet esse praedicatum, dicendo sic:

> Tantum unus homo est homo,

quia tunc universalis esset vera et exclusiva falsa, quod non est possibile.
5 Ista igitur:

> Quilibet homo est unus homo

debet sic converti in suam exclusivam:

> Tantum unus homo est aliquis homo

vel

10 > Tantum unus homo est homo masculus.

Similiter,

> Nullus homo currit

non debet sic converti:

> Nullum currens est homo,

15 quia in casu possibili posito antecedens est verum et consequens falsum. Sed sic debet converti:

> Nullum currens est aliquis homo

vel

> homo masculus.

20 Et sic de multis aliis.

⟨1.5R⟩ Ad quintum respondetur admittendo casum. Et ulterius ad argumentum:

> Quicquid iam componis cum subiecto istius propositionis prius componebas et econtra, sed prius componebas istam intentionem
25 > *homo* de subiecto istius; ergo et iam sic facis.

Dicitur concedendo consequentiam et consequens. Et si ex hoc infertur quod praecise ista intentio *homo* est praedicatum, negatur consequentia. Unde dico quod in ista propositione mentali

> *Sortes est omnis homo*

30 praecise componitur ista intentio *homo* cum subiecto eiusdem. Quia componere non est aliud nisi unam intentionem affirmare de alia, et dividere non est nisi unam intentionem ab alia negare. Sed quia talis intentio *homo* distribuitur per actum animae distributivum, ideo simul intentio et actus animae distributivus praedicatur.

35 Vel aliter potest dici concedendo primam consequentiam et negando antecedens pro maiori, dicendo quod continue ante hoc componebam solum istam intentionem *homo* cum subiecto eiusdem, quia non fuit distributa per actum animae distributivum. Sed quia iam primo distribuitur,

4 universalis erit vera E   31 aliud *om.* E   34 distributus E   35 Ulterius
aliter E   36 compono M

just 'man' is the subject. But it must not be the predicate in the corresponding exclusive,[b] when one says

Only an individual man is a human being.[c]

since in that case the universal proposition would be true and the exclusive false, which is not possible. Therefore

Each man is an individual man

must be converted into the corresponding exclusive as follows:

Only an individual man is some man

or

Only an individual man is a male human being.

Similarly,

No man is running

must not be converted as follows:

Nothing running is a human being,

for if one possible state of affairs is assumed,[d] the antecedent is true and the consequent false. Instead it must be converted as follows:

Nothing running is some man

or

⟨Nothing running is⟩ a male human being.

And many others are to be treated in the same way.

⟨1.5R⟩ I accept the hypothesis. And then as for the argument:

Whatever you are now compounding with the subject of this proposition you were previously compounding and vice versa, but you were previously compounding the intention *man* with the subject of it; therefore you are doing so now as well.

I grant the inference and the consequent. But if one infers from this that just the intention *man* is the predicate, I reject that inference. Thus I maintain that in the mental proposition

Socrates is every man

just the intention *man* is compounded with the subject of it. For to compound is nothing other than to affirm one intention of another, and to divide is nothing other than to deny one intention of another. But because an intention such as *man* is distributed by a distributive act of the mind, the intention and the distributive act of the mind are predicated together.

Alternatively, one can grant the first inference and deny the antecedent because of the major premiss, saying that just before now I was uninterruptedly compounding only the intention *man* with the subject of the proposition, because it was not then distributed by a distributive act of the mind.

ideo non solum componebam illam de subiecto eiusdem, sed unum terminum composui ex intentione et actu distribuendi, qui quidem terminus est ly .omnis homo. Quare etc.

⟨1.6R⟩ Ad sextum concedo conclusionem adductam pro secunda parte.
5 Unde non est inconveniens quod in contradictoriis subiecta et praedicata dissimilia sint ratione terminorum syncategorematicorum. Secus est de terminis categorematicis, qui utrobique in contradictoriis debent esse similes. Dicimus enim quod ista sunt contradictoria:

Sortes et Plato currunt;
10   Sortes vel Plato non currit.

Et tamen subiecta ratione coniunctionum sunt dissimilia. Similiter, ista sunt contradictoria:

Sortes est aliquid animal

et

15   Sortes non est quoddam animal.

Et tamen praedicata, ut patet, sunt dissimilia. Similiter, concedimus quod ista sunt contradictoria:

Omnis homo currit

et

20   Aliquid quod est homo non currit.

Et tamen subiecta non sunt eadem nec similia, ut patet. Igitur, etc.

Verumtamen est aliter dicendum, videlicet, quod in ista

Omnis homo omne animal est

non est ly .omne animal. (4ᵛᵃ M) praedicatum, sed praecise ly .animal.
25 Nec ex hoc sequitur oppositum opinionis, quia ipsa praetendit quod quando ly .omnis. vel .omne. non cadit supra copulam principalem, tunc (3ʳᵇ E) est pars subiecti vel praedicati. Sed iam sicut ly .omnis. cadit supra verbum principale, ita et ly .omne., signum sequens. Et si dicitur:

Istae convertuntur: 'omnis homo omne animal est' et 'omnis homo est
30   omne animal', sed in secunda signum est pars praedicati; ergo similiter in prima,

non valet argumentum, sicut non sequitur:

'Iste homo est omnis homo' et 'omnis homo est iste homo' convertuntur, sed in prima ly .omnis. est pars praedicati; ergo et in
35   secunda.

⟨1.7R⟩ Ad septimum dicitur quod in illa propositione

Tantum omnis homo est homo

ly .omnis homo. est subiectum. Ad argumentum:

Idem debet esse subiectum praeiacentis et exclusivae (concedo), sed

10 currunt M et E   22 videlicet om. E   26 .omne. signum universale non E
33-4 convertuntur om. M   34 est pars praedicati ly .omnis.; M   38 Et tunc ad M
39 et subiectum exclusivae M

But since now it is distributed for the first time, I was not only compounding that intention with the subject of the proposition, but I compounded a term out of that intention and the act of distributing, and this term is 'every man'. Therefore, etc.

⟨1.6R⟩ I grant the inferred conclusion because of its second part. Thus it is not absurd that in contradictories subjects and predicates are dissimilar because of syncategorematic terms. It is otherwise as regards categorematic terms, which must be alike in contradictories on both sides. For we say that these are contradictories:

> Socrates and Plato are running;
> Socrates or Plato is not running.

But the subjects are dissimilar because of the conjunctions.
Similarly, these are contradictories:

> Socrates is some animal;
> Socrates is not any animal.

But the predicates are obviously dissimilar. Likewise, we grant that these are contradictories:

> Every man is running;
> Something that is a man is not running.

But the subjects are obviously neither the same nor alike. Therefore, etc.

Another reply must be made, however—viz., that in the proposition

> Every man every animal is

not 'every animal' but just 'animal' is the predicate. Nor does the opposite of Opinion ⟨1⟩ follow from this, for Opinion ⟨1⟩ assumes that the universal sign 'every' is a part of the subject or the predicate when it does not cover the principal copula. But in the present example the first 'every' covers the second 'every', the following sign, just as it covers the principal verb. And if someone says:

> 'Every man every animal is' and 'every man is every animal' are interchangeable, but in the second the sign is a part of the predicate; therefore likewise in the first,

the argument is unacceptable, just as this does not follow:

> 'This man is every man' and 'every man is this man' are interchangeable, but in the first 'every' is a part of the predicate; therefore also in the second.

⟨1.7R⟩ In the proposition

> Only every man is a man

'every man' is the subject. As for the argument:

> The subject of the prejacent and of its exclusive must be one and the

istius praeiacentis 'omnis homo est homo' est praecise ly .homo. subiectum; igitur, etc.,

concedo consequentiam et nego minorem. Pro quo nota quod ista propositio

5   Omnis homo est homo

potest considerari ut est pars illius exclusivae vel ut non est pars eiusdem. Primo modo dico quod ipsa est praeiacens exclusivae et eiusdem subiectum est ly .omnis homo. Secundo modo non est praeiacens exclusivae nec ly .omnis homo. est subiectum, sed solum ly .homo.

10   Sed forte arguitur: ista consequentia est bona:

Tantum omnis homo est homo; igitur omnis homo est homo, quia arguitur ab exclusiva ad suum praeiacens. Igitur illud consequens est praeiacens exclusivae. Sed subiectum illius consequentis est praecise ly .homo. Igitur subiectum praeiacentis est praecise ly .homo., quod erat

15   probandum.

Huic dicitur concedendo consequentiam primam, non tamen quia arguitur ab exclusiva ad suum praeiacens, sed quia praeiacens exclusivae infert tale consequens in bona consequentia. Unde dico quod consequens illud illatum non est praeiacens exclusivae nec secum convertibile, quia ipsum

20   est verum et praeiacens falsum. Significat enim quod aliquid omnis homo est homo, quod est falsum. Et si dicitur quomodo igitur debet inferri praeiacens illius exclusivae, dicitur quod in voce vel in scripto non potest bene, sed solum unum secum convertibile, scilicet,

Aliquid omnis homo est homo.

25   Vel potest dici quod inferendo istam:

Aliquid omnis homo est homo

infertur eius praeiacens tenendo ly .aliquid. pure syncategorematice, quia tunc subiectum est praecise ly .omnis homo. Ex his infero illam conclusionem, quod ab exclusiva affirmativa ad suum praeiacens non valet conse-

30   quentia (intelligendo de 'exclusiva' vocali vel scripta) eo ipso quod talis exclusiva infert aliquam propositionem quam non infert suum praeiacens, cum hoc sit impossibile.

Solutis argumentis factis contra primam opinionem, restat, ut superius est praemissum, solvere obiectiones contra opinionem secundam ad-

35   ductam.

same (I grant that), but the subject of the prejacent 'every man is a man' is just 'man'; therefore, etc.,

I grant the inference and deny the minor premiss. In support of this it should be noted that the proposition

Every man is a man

can be considered either as if it is a part of that exclusive or as if it is not a part of it. If it is considered in the first way, I say that it is the prejacent of the exclusive and that its subject is 'every man'. If it is considered in the second way, it is not the prejacent of the exclusive nor is 'every man' the subject, but 'man' only.

But perhaps some will argue in the following way.

The inference

Only every man is a man; therefore every man is a man

is good, because it argues from an exclusive to its prejacent. Therefore the consequent is the prejacent of the exclusive. But the subject of this consequent is just 'man'. Therefore the subject of the prejacent is just 'man', which is what was to be proved.

The reply to this is to grant the first inference; not, however, because it argues from an exclusive to its prejacent, but because the prejacent of the exclusive entails such a consequent in a good inference. Thus I say that the entailed consequent is neither the prejacent of the exclusive nor interchangeable with it, since it is true and the prejacent is false. For the prejacent signifies that some every man is a man, which is false. And if one asks how then the prejacent of that exclusive is to be inferred, the answer is that whether in speech or in writing ⟨the prejacent itself⟩ cannot be correctly ⟨inferred⟩, but only a proposition interchangeable with it, viz.,

Some every man is a man.

Or it can be said that in inferring

Some every man is a man

one is inferring the prejacent of the exclusive if 'some' is taken purely syncategorematically, for in that case the subject is just 'every man'. From these observations I infer this conclusion, that the inference from an affirmative exclusive to its prejacent is unacceptable (meaning by 'exclusive' a spoken or written exclusive proposition) just because such an exclusive entails a proposition that its prejacent does not entail, for that is impossible.

Now that the arguments raised against Opinion ⟨1⟩ have been resolved, it remains to resolve the objections introduced against Opinion ⟨2⟩, as was announced above.[e]

⟨2.1R⟩ Ad primum, igitur, cum dicebatur:

Illud signum 'non' potest esse pars subiecti vel praedicati, sed aeque syncategorema est ly .omnis. sicut ly .non.; igitur . . . ,

respondeo negando consequentiam, et causa est quia ex ista negatione
5 infinitante 'non' et termino categorematico fit unus terminus significativus cuiuslibet rei non significatae per istum terminum categorematicum. Sed sic non est de illo syncategoremate 'omnis' addito alicui termino categorematico. Unde iste terminus 'non homo' significat quicquid non est homo et per consequens oppositum istius termini 'homo'. Sed iste terminus
10 'omnis homo' non aliud significat quam iste terminus 'homo', quia aeque bene ly .homo. significat omnem hominem sicut ly .omnis homo.

⟨2.2R⟩ Ad secundum, cum inferebatur quod haec esset vera:

Omnis homo est omnis homo,

nego consequentiam. Et concedo quod nulla propositio est verior illa, etc.,
15 nec ex hoc sequitur quod illa sit vera, cum ex negativa non sequitur affirmativa. Et pro hoc glossatur auctoritas Boethii, dicendo quod ipsa est vera de virtute sermonis, eo quod ipsa est una negativa non ponens aliquam propositionem esse veram vel falsam. Ideo conceditur quod nulla propositio est verior illa:

20   Homo est asinus

nec aliqua est falsior (4vb M) illa:

Deus est,

quia dato opposito sequeretur inconveniens. Adhuc si auctoritas illa intelligatur affirmative, id est, omnis propositio affirmativa est vera in qua
25 idem praedicatur de seipso, potest negari auctoritas. Primo quia in ista propositione:

Chimaera est chimaera

idem praedicatur de seipso, et tamen est falsa. Secundo quia sequitur:

Omnis propositio affirmativa est vera in qua idem praedicatur de
30   seipso, sed haec propositio 'Deus est asinus' est propositio affirmativa; ergo ipsa est vera in qua idem praedicatur de seipso.

Consequentia bona, et consequens est falsum. Et non minor; ergo maior.
Vel aliter potest dici quod auctoritas illa intelligitur affirmative sic: omnis propositio affirmativa est vera in qua idem praedicatur de seipso.
35 Et hoc quando praedicatum non sumitur universaliter (qualiter est in

---

2 'non' est pars *M*   3 igitur *om. E*   5 et ex uno alio termino *M*   unus
om. E   6 categorematicum 'homo' *E*   14 etc. *om. M*   15 sequatur *M*
16 Et propter hoc *E*   ipsa *om. E*   17 una *om. E*   21 est *om. E*   illa
om. M   25 idem praedicatum de *M et E*   29–30 de seipso praedicatur *E*   32 Et
om. E

⟨*Replies to the Arguments against Opinion 2*⟩

⟨2.1R⟩ To the first argument, therefore, when it was said:

The sign 'non-' can be a part of the subject or the predicate, but 'every' is just as syncategorematic as is 'non-'; therefore . . . ,

I reply by rejecting the inference. For the infinitating negation 'non-' and a categorematic term make up a single term significant of each thing not signified by that categorematic term; but this does not happen when the syncategorematic 'every' is added to some categorematic term. Thus the term 'non-man' signifies whatever is not a man and is consequently the opposite of the term 'man'. But the term 'every man' does not signify anything other than what the term 'man' signifies, for 'man' signifies every man just as well as does 'every man'.

⟨2.2R⟩ When it is inferred that

Every man is every man

is true, I reject the inference. I grant that no proposition is truer than one, etc., but not that it follows that that proposition is true, for an affirmative does not follow from a negative. In support of this one glosses the cited passage of Boethius, saying that it is true taken literally as it stands, since it is a negative that does not assert that any proposition is true or false. Thus it is granted that no proposition is truer than

A man is a donkey

and that none is falser than

God is,

for given the opposite an absurdity would follow. Moreover, if that cited passage is understood affirmatively—i.e., every affirmative proposition is true in which one and the same thing is predicated of itself—it can be rejected. First, because in the proposition

A chimera is a chimera

one and the same thing is predicated of itself and yet it is false. Second, because this follows:

Every affirmative proposition is a true one in which one and the same thing is predicated of itself, but the proposition 'God is a donkey' is an affirmative proposition; therefore it is a true one in which one and the same thing is predicated of itself.

The inference is good, and the consequent is false. But is is not the minor premiss ⟨that is false⟩; therefore it is the major premiss.

Alternatively, one can say that that cited passage is understood affirmatively in this way: every affirmative proposition in which one and the same thing is predicated of itself is true. And this is the case provided that

proposito); et etiam quando non praedicatur terminus significans aliquam rem de cuius intentione significative sumpta non est aliquis terminus affirmative cum verbo de praesenti praedicabile deducta quacumque ampliatione. Et per hoc respondetur ad argumentum factum de chimaera.

5   ⟨2.3R⟩ Ad tertium nego consequentiam in qua infertur quod illae duae convertuntur:

> Sortes est homo,
>
> Sortes est omnis homo.

Et ad probationem, cum arguitur (3va E) subiecta, praedicata, et copulae 10 convertuntur, etc., nego consequentiam. Per idem enim probaretur quod illae duae propositiones convertuntur:

> Omnis homo animal non est

et

> Omnis homo non est animal,

15 quarum una est vera et alia impossibilis. Si ergo debet concludi aliquas propositiones tales converti, debet sic argui:

> Subiecta et praedicata et copulae convertuntur, et propositiones sunt eiusdem qualitatis et quantitatis, et termini praecise pro eodem vel pro eisdem supponunt, et eodem modo; ergo tales convertuntur.

20 Sed in proposito negarem ultimam particulam, eo quod ly .homo. in una stat determinate, in alia vero stat confuse et distributive.

⟨2.4R⟩ Ad quartam nego conclusionem adductam pro utraque sui parte. Et tunc quando dicitur quod haec:

> Nullus homo est omnis homo

25 est sic convertibilis cum ista:

> Nihil quod est homo est aliquis homo,

dicitur negando. Et ad argumentum cum dicitur:

> Ibidem fit de subiecto praedicatum et de praedicato subiectum, etc.;
>> ergo . . . ,

30 nego consequentiam. Per idem enim probaretur quod haec esset bona conversio:

> Nullus homo currit; ergo nullum currens est homo.

---

5 consequentiam ex qua *M*   duae *om. E*   10 enim *om. E*   11 duae *om. E*
25 cum ista *om. M*   27 cum dicitur *om. M*   32 ergo *om. E*

the predicate is not taken universally (as it is in the example in question: ⟨'every man is every man'⟩, and provided also that the predicate is not a term signifying some thing such that a term is not predicable affirmatively ⟨and truly⟩ of the intention of that thing taken significantly with a present-tense verb when every possible ampliation has been removed.*f* The reply to the argument involving the chimera is a consequence of this latter proviso.*g*

⟨2.3R⟩ I reject the inference in which it is inferred that the two propositions

    Socrates is a man

and

    Socrates is every man

are interchangeable. As for the proof, in which it is argued that the subjects, the predicates, and the copulas are interchangeable, etc., I reject the inference. For in that same way one could prove that these two propositions are interchangeable:

    Every man an animal is not

and

    Every man is not an animal,

one of which is true and the other impossible.*h* Therefore if one must conclude that some such propositions are interchangeable, one must argue in this way:

    The subjects, the predicates, and the copulas are interchangeable, and
        the propositions are of the same quality and quantity, and the terms
        supposit for precisely the same thing or things, and in the same way;
        therefore such propositions are interchangeable.

But as regards the example in question I would deny the last detail ⟨'and in the same way'⟩, since in the one proposition 'man' has determinate *suppositio* but in the other it has distributive confused *suppositio*.

⟨2.4R⟩ I deny both parts of the conclusion. As for the claim that

    No man is every man

is interchangeable with

    Nothing that is a man is some man,

I deny it. And as for the argument:

    In them the predicate is made of the ⟨former⟩ subject, and the subject
        is made of the ⟨former⟩ predicate, etc.; therefore . . . ,

I reject the inference. For in that same way one could prove that this would be a good conversion:

    No man is running; therefore no running thing is a human being.

Et tamen certum est quod casu possibili posito antecedens esset verum et consequens falsum. Similiter sequitur quod haec esset bona conversio:

> Omnis homo animal non est; igitur omne animal non est homo vel non homo.

5 Et tamen antecedens est necessarium et consequens impossibile.

Dico ergo quod in conversione simplici requiritur quod termini in conversa et convertente supponant praecise pro eodem vel pro eisdem, et eodem modo. Sed quia in conversione praedicta non supponunt termini continue eodem modo, ideo non sit determinata conversio. Unde in ista propositione

10   Nullus homo est omnis homo

ly .homo. a parte praedicati stat determinate ratione duorum signorum praecedentium. Et in ista:

> Nihil quod est homo est homo

ly .homo. stat confuse et distributive. Debet igitur ista sic converti:

15   Nihil quod est omnis homo est homo,

et hoc verum est. Similiter, ista:

> Nullus homo currit

debet sic converti:

> Nullum currens est aliquis homo.

20 Similiter, ista:

> Omnis homo animal non est

debet sic converti:

> Animal non est homo,

sive

25   Animal homo non est,

per accidens, et non simpliciter. Nec omnis universalis negativa est convertibilis simpliciter; puta illa quae est de inconsuetuto modo loquendi, sicut in secunda parte patebit capitulo de conversionibus.

⟨2.5R⟩ Ad quintam respondetur eodem modo, nego conclusionem 30 adductam. Et tunc ad argumentum, dico quod ista consequentia non valet:

> A est universalis affirmativa et B particularis negativa de consimilibus subiectis, praedicatis, et copulis, et termini praecise eodem modo pro eisdem supponunt; ergo A et B contradicunt.

35 Sed oportet in antecedente assumere quod talia subiecta et praedicata

---

4 est *add.* M   14 confuse et *om.* E   24–5 *om.* M   33 praedicatis *om.* E   eodem modo *om.* M   33–4 modo vel pro E   35 praedicata et subiecta talia E

And yet it is certain that if one possible state of affairs is assumed[i] the antecedent would be true and the consequent false. It follows likewise that this would be a good conversion:

> Every man an animal is not; therefore every animal is not a man, or is a non-man.

But the antecedent is necessary and the consequent impossible.

I maintain, therefore, that what is required in simple conversion is that the terms in the converse and the convertend supposit for precisely the same thing or things, and in the same way. But because the terms in the original conversion above do not supposit throughout in one and the same way, it is not a determinate conversion. Thus in the proposition

> No man is every man

'man' in the predicate has determinate *suppositio* because of the two preceding signs. And in

> Nothing that is a man is a man

'man' has distributive confused *suppositio*. It must, therefore, be converted in the following way:

> Nothing that is every man is a man,

and that is true. Similarly,

> No man is running

must be converted in this way:

> No running thing is some man.

Again, the proposition

> Every man an animal is not

must be converted in this way:

> An animal is not a man,

or in this way:

> An animal a man is not,

per accidens, and not simply. Nor is every universal negative proposition convertible simply—e.g., one in an extraordinary mode of speech, as will be shown in Part Two in the chapter on conversions ⟨Treatise VIII: The Conversion of Propositions⟩.

⟨2.5R⟩ I reply to the fifth argument in the same way, by denying the conclusion. As for the argument, I say that this inference is unacceptable:

> *A* is a universal affirmative proposition and *B* a particular negative proposition with their subjects, predicates, and copulas just alike, and whose terms supposit in precisely the same way and for precisely the same things; therefore *A* and *B* contradict each other.

Instead one must include in the antecedent the claim that such subjects and

supponant opposito modo si praedicata fuerint termini communes. Quia ista sunt contradictoria:

>   Quilibet homo est iste homo

et

5   Aliquis homo non est iste homo,

et tamen praedicata utrobique supponunt discrete. Quia igitur in his duabus propositionibus

>   Omnis homo est omnis homo

et

10   Aliquid quod est homo non est homo

praedicata utrobique supponunt confuse et distributive, non ergo (9va M) est mirum si non sunt contradictoria. Et sic non procedit argumentum, dato enim illo modo arguendi multa inconvenientia sequerentur. Quare, etc.

15   ⟨2.6R⟩ Ad sextam cum infertur quod haec est vera:

>   Homo est omne animal,

nego consequentiam. Et ulterius nego quod ista significat primarie hominem esse animal. Et tunc ad argumentum:

>   Subiectum significat primarie hominem, praedicatum significat pri-
20   marie animal, et copula significat primarie esse; ergo, etc.,

nego consequentiam. Per idem enim probaretur quod haec est vera:

>   Omne animal est homo,

quia subiectum significat primarie animal, et praedicatum hominem, et copula esse, et tota propositio significat iuxta compositionem suorum 25 extremorum; ergo tota propositio significat primarie animal esse hominem. Et hoc est verum; igitur ipsa est vera. Similiter probaretur quod homo est asinus, sic arguendo:

>   Ista propositio 'hominis est asinus' est vera, et ipsa significat pri-
>   marie hominem esse asinum; igitur hominem esse asinum est
30   verum. Et per consequens homo est asinus.

Et quod ista significat primarie hominem esse asinum arguitur ut prius:

>   Subiectum significat primarie hominem, et praedicatum asinum,
>   et copula esse, et tota propositio significat primarie iuxta composi-
>   tionem terminorum; igitur ista significat primarie hominem esse
35   asinum.

predicates supposit in an opposed way. (⟨That is,⟩ if the predicates are common terms: for these are contradictories:

Any man is this man

and

Some man is not this man,

and yet the predicates in both have discrete *suppositio*.) Therefore since in the two propositions

Every man is every man

and

Something that is a man is not a man

the predicates in both have distributive confused *suppositio*, it is not surprising if they are not contradictories. Thus the argument does not go through, for given that mode of arguing many absurdities would follow. Therefore, etc.

⟨2.6R⟩ When it is inferred that

A man is every animal

is true, I reject the inference. Moreover, I deny that that proposition primarily signifies that a man is an animal. As for the argument:

The subject primarily signifies a man, the predicate primarily signifies an animal, and the copula primarily signifies being; therefore, etc.,

I reject the inference. For in that same way one could prove that

Every animal is a man

is true, since the subject primarily signifies an animal, the predicate a man, and the copula being, and the whole proposition signifies in accordance with the composition of its extremes; therefore the whole proposition primarily signifies that an animal is a man. And that is true; therefore the proposition itself is true. Similarly, one could prove that a man is a donkey, arguing in the following way:

The proposition 'a man's is a donkey' is true, and it signifies primarily that a man is a donkey; therefore that a man is a donkey is true. And as a consequence a man is a donkey.

That the original proposition does primarily signify that a man is a donkey is argued as before:

The subject primarily signifies a man, the predicate a donkey, and the copula being, and the whole proposition primarily signifies in accordance with the composition of its terms; therefore it primarily signifies that a man is a donkey.

Dico, ergo, quod ad concludendum talem propositionem esse veram oportet assumere tale antecedens:

> Subiectum significat primarie hominem in recto, praedicatum signifi-cat primarie animal in recto, et copula significat primarie esse, et
> 5 propositio componitur solum ex subiecto, praedicato, et copula; igitur talis propositio significat primarie hominem esse animal.

Et tunc in proposito concederem consequentiam et negarem antecedens pro ultima parte, quia ista propositio

> Homo est omne animal

10 vel

> Omne animal est homo

non solum componitur ex illis duabus intentionibus cum actu componendi, sed ex his omnibus et actu distribuendi. Ex eadem scientia infertur quod ista propositio

15 > Hominis est asinus

non significat primarie hominem esse asinum, sed significat primarie hominis esse asinum. Quia licet ly .hominis. significet primarie hominem, hoc est in obliquo et non in recto.

⟨2.7R⟩ Ad ultimam rationem dico quod in ista propositione

20 > Tantum omnis homo est homo

praecise ly .homo. est subiectum. Et ulterius cum infertur quod ista est universalis, dupliciter respondetur: primo, concedendo consequentiam et consequens, et ulterius negando quod propositiones exclusivae non (3ᵛᵇ E) sunt alicuius quantitatis. Immo sunt ita bene quantae sicut et aliae, ex quo
25 sunt categoricae. Et si dicitur cuiuslibet exclusivae subiectum debet stare confuse tantum si est terminus communis, huic dicitur quod verum est nisi impedimentum obviet. Sed in proposito signum distributivum im-pedit ne subiectum exclusivae stet confuse tantum. Eodem modo dico de tali:

30 > Omnis homo est omnis homo,

quod praedicatum stat confuse et distributive, non obstante quod ista est universalis affirmativa. Ex quo sequitur quod istud commune dictum fore falsum, quod cuiuslibet universalis affirmativae praedicatum si fuerit ter-minus communis stat confuse tantum. Oportet enim addere 'deducto
35 impedimento', qualiter non est in proposito.

17 ly om. E   22 dupliciter om. E   26 tantum om. E   si fuerit M   28 ne tamen stet E   dico om. E   32 quod om. M   33 quod om. E   35 im-pedimente E

I maintain, therefore, that in order to conclude that such a proposition is true one must include an antecedent of this sort:

> The subject primarily signifies a man in the nominative, the predicate primarily signifies an animal in the nominative, and the copula primarily signifies being, and the proposition is composed solely of the subject, the predicate, and the copula; therefore such a proposition primarily signifies that a man is an animal.

In that case as regards the example in question I would grant the inference and deny the antecedent because of the last part, for the proposition

> A man is every animal

or

> Every animal is a man

is not composed solely of those two intentions ⟨*man* and *animal*⟩ together with the act of compounding, but rather of all those and the act of distributing. From this knowledge one infers that the proposition

> A man's is a donkey

does not primarily signify that a man is a donkey but primarily signifies that a man's is a donkey. For although 'man's' primarily signifies a man, it is in an oblique case and not in the nominative.

⟨2.7R⟩ I maintain that in the proposition

> Only every man is a man

iust 'man' is the subject. Furthermore, when it is inferred that that proposition is universal, the reply is twofold: first, to grant the inference and its consequent, and then to deny that exclusive propositions are not of any quantity. On the contrary, they have quantity just as properly as do other propositions, as a consequence of the fact that they are categoricals. And if someone says that the subject of each exclusive proposition must have merely confused *suppositio* if it is a common term, the reply is that this is true unless an impediment prevents it. But in the example in question the distributive sign acts as an impediment preventing the subject of the exclusive from having merely confused *suppositio*. In the same way I say of a proposition such as

> Every man is every man

that the predicate has distributive confused *suppositio* even though the proposition is a universal affirmative. It follows from this that what is commonly said will be false—viz., that the predicate of any universal affirmative has merely confused *suppositio* if it is a common term. For one must add 'when any impediment has been removed', as has not been done in the example in question.

Vel aliter potest responderi ad argumentum negando quod aliqua exclusiva sit alicuius quantitatis. Et tunc ad argumentum:

> Ibi subicitur terminus communis signo universali determinatus; igitur ista est universalis,

5 nego consequentiam. Per idem enim probaretur quod ista esset universalis:

> Necessario omnis homo est animal,

quia ibi subicitur terminus communis, etc. Sed hoc est falsum, dicitur enim communiter quod ista est una modalis. Ideo si debet inferri aliquam esse propositionem universalem, debet sic argui:

10 > In ista propositione subicitur terminus communis signo universali determinatus distributive eundem mobiliter; igitur talis est universalis.

Consequentia ista est bona, sed in proposito antecedens est falsum, quia in ista exclusiva stat iste terminus 'homo' confuse et distributive et immobili-
15 ter et non mobiliter. Quia ratione eiusdem non contingit istam propositionem probari, sed solum ratione dictionis exclusivae, quae est primus terminus mediatus in exclusiva praedicta. Quare, etc.

⟨ *Secunda Divisio Terminorum*   *Capitulum Secundum*⟩

(9ᵛᵇ M) Terminorum categorematicorum quidam significant naturaliter et
20 quidam ad placitum. Terminum voco significare naturaliter qui aliquid significat quod impossibile est significando non significare.

Et isto modo significant termini mentales se et sua significata distincta naturaliter, quia non possunt significare quin se et talia sua significata primarie intellectui repraesentent, ut est iste terminus mentalis: *homo,*
25 *animal, corpus*, et similia.

Et non solum termini mentales seipsos et alia significata primaria a se distincta naturaliter significant, sed etiam termini vocales vel scripti seipsos naturaliter significant, sicut etiam aliae res sensibiles. Seipsas enim intellectui per intentionem propriam repraesentant, quemadmodum facit
30 homo, lapis, et sic de aliis. Cum ergo significare non sit aliud quam rei similitudinem memoriae vel virtuti cognitivae repraesentare vel conceptum primum in anima causare, igitur tales seipsos significant et hoc naturaliter,

---

5 ista erit universalis *E*   11 eundem *om. E*   15–16 contingit eandem probari *E*   16 solum *om. M*   17 mediatus *om. M*   21 significat et impossibile *E*   23 et tota sua *E*   27 naturaliter *om. E*   29 facit *om. E*
30 ergo *om. E*   31 vel intellectui repraesentare *M*

Alternatively, one can reply to the argument by denying that an exclusive is of any quantity. And then as for the argument:

> A common term governed by a universal sign is the subject in the proposition; therefore the proposition is universal,

I reject the inference. For in that same way one could prove that

> Necessarily every man is an animal

is universal, since in it a common term, etc., is the subject. But that is false, for it is commonly said that this is a modal proposition. Thus if one must infer that some proposition is universal, one must argue in the following way.

> A common term governed by a universal sign so as to have mobile distributive supposition is the subject in this proposition; therefore it is universal.

This inference is good, but its antecedent is false as regards the example in question, because in that exclusive proposition the term 'man' has immobile and not mobile distributive confused supposition. For it is not because of that term that the proposition can be proved, but solely because of the exclusive word, which is the first mediate term[j] in the exclusive. Therefore, etc.

⟨Chapter Two: The Second Division of Terms —Naturally Significant and Arbitrarily Significant⟩

⟨Every Term Naturally Signifies Itself⟩

Some categorematic terms signify naturally and others arbitrarily. I call a term naturally significant which signifies something which it is impossible for it not to signify as long as it is significant.

It is in this way that mental terms naturally signify themselves and their distinct significata, for they cannot signify without primarily representing themselves and their distinct significata to the understanding, as is the case with such mental terms as *man, animal,* and *body.*

And not only mental terms naturally signify themselves (and other primary significata distinct from themselves), but also spoken or written terms naturally signify themselves, just as other sensible things do. For they present themselves to the understanding through a proper intention,[a] as do a man, a stone, and other ⟨sensible things⟩. Therefore, since to signify is nothing other than to represent the likeness of a thing to the memory or the cognitive faculty, or to cause the first concept ⟨of it⟩ in the mind, such terms do signify themselves and do so naturally, for they cannot signify

quia non possunt significare nisi eorum similitudinem memoriae vel potentiae cognitivae adducant.

⟨1⟩ Item capio talem propositionem

Hoc est terminus,

5 demonstrando praedicatum istius propositionis. Tunc: Haec singularis est vera, et per utrumque extremum aliquid significatur; ergo res significata per subiectum est res significata per praedicatum et econtra. Sed nulla est res significata per subiectum nisi praedicatum. Igitur istud praedicatum significatur per praedicatum illius propositionis. Sed praedicatum illius 10 propositionis est terminus scriptus vel vocalis; igitur terminus scriptus vel voacalis significat seipsum.

⟨2⟩ Item aliquis terminus supponit pro se, sed omne supponere est significare; ergo talis significat se. Consequentia patet cum minori, et maior patet de multis terminis supponentibus materialiter, ut

15   Ly .Deus. est nomen,

Ly .homo. est terminus scriptus.

⟨3⟩ Item sic: Omne sensibile naturaliter significat seipsum, sed terminus vocalis vel scriptus est sensibile; igitur talis seipsum naturaliter significat. Consequentia patet. Et maior arguitur, nam omne sensibile, sive sit pro- 20 prium sive commune, sui ipsius agit intentionem in aliquam virtutem interiorem, mediante qua a virtute cognitiva apprehenditur. Et minor osten- ditur isto modo. Quilibet terminus scriptus vel vocalis est scriptum vel vox. Si sit vox, tunc est sensibile proprium, quia tunc ab unico sensu foret perceptibile, scilicet a sensu auditus. Et si sit scriptum, tunc est sensibile 25 commune, quia a pluribus sensibus est perceptibile, puta a sensu visus et a sensu tactus.

Terminus dicitur significare ad placitum tripliciter.

⟨1⟩ Uno modo terminus significat ad placitum prout ly .ad placitum. est accusativi casus et rectus immediate a ly .significat. . Et isto modo non 30 solum terminus vocalis vel scriptus significat ad placitum, sed etiam ter- minus mentalis, scilicet iste terminus *ad placitum* in mente, qui significat hoc significatum primarie: ad placitum, sicut iste terminus 'homo' signifi- cat primarie hominem.

Et quod iste terminus in mente significat primarie ad placitum probatur, 35 nam haec propositio mentalis

Aliquis terminus significat ad placitum

5 et demonstro praedicatum *M*   7 per subiectum et *E*   9–10 proposi- tionis illius *E*   10–11 vel vocalis *om. E*   15 .domus. *E*   23 proprium, et tunc *M*   ab uno sensu *E*   34 significat in mente *E*

without bringing a likeness of themselves to the memory or the cognitive power.

⟨*Arguments in Support of this Claim*⟩

⟨1⟩ I take a proposition such as

This is a term,

indicating by the demonstrative pronoun the predicate of that very proposition. Then: This singular proposition is true, and something is signified by each of the two extremes; therefore the thing signified by the subject is the thing signified by the predicate and vice versa. But no thing is signified by the subject except the predicate. Therefore the predicate is signified by the predicate of that very proposition. But the predicate of that proposition is a written or spoken term; therefore a written or spoken term signifies itself.

⟨2⟩ Some term supposits for itself, but to supposit is in every case to signify; therefore such a term signifies itself. The inference is obvious, along with the minor premiss; and the major premiss is obvious as regards many terms that have material *suppositio*, as in

'God' is a name,
'Man' is a written term.

⟨3⟩ Every sensible thing naturally signifies itself, but a spoken or written term is a sensible thing; therefore it naturally signifies itself. The inference is obvious. The following argument supports the major premiss. Every sensible, proper or common, arouses an intention of itself in some interior faculty by means of which ⟨intention⟩ it is apprehended by the cognitive faculty. And the minor premiss is shown in this way. Each written or spoken term is an inscription or an utterance. If it is an utterance, then it is a proper sensible, because in that case it would be perceptible by a single sense, the sense of hearing. And if it is an inscription, then it is a common sensible, because it is perceptible by more than one sense—viz., the sense of sight and the sense of touch.

⟨*Three Ways in which a Term is Said to Signify Arbitrarily*⟩

A term is said to signify arbitrarily in three different ways.

⟨1⟩ A term signifies arbitrarily in one way in so far as 'arbitrarily' is the object of the verb 'signifies'. Not only a spoken or written term signifies arbitrarily in this way, but a mental term too—viz., the term *arbitrarily* in the mind, which primarily signifies this significatum: arbitrarily—just as the term *man* primarily signifies man.

That this term in the mind primarily signifies arbitrarily is proved as follows. The mental proposition

Some term signifies arbitrarily

significat aliquem terminum significare ad placitum; igitur aliquis pars istius significat ad placitum, sed nulla nisi ista pars: *ad placitum.* Ex his conceditur quod aliquis terminus significans naturaliter significat (4ʳᵃ E) ad placitum.

5 Et aliquis terminus significans ex impositione significat naturaliter, ut capto tali termino *ex impositione* sic significante. Arguitur ut prius argutum est.

⟨2⟩ Secundo modo terminus significat ad placitum quia subiacet imperio ipsius concipientis intellectus vel voluntatis, ut nunc significet vel nunc 10 non significet. Et sic quilibet terminus vocalis, vel scriptus, vel mentalis significat ad placitum, quia voluntas vult istum terminum nunc significare et postea non, sicut patet de isto termino 'homo', qui aliquando significat, aliquando non significat. Et hoc est solum ratione intellectus, qui aliquando divertit se ad unum, aliquando divertit se ad aliud.

15 Unde non (9ʳᵃ M) est imaginandum quod ideo talis terminus mentalis significet ad placitum intellectus quia intellectus possit mutare suum significatum primarium et aliud intelligere. Sed solum dicitur significare ad placitum ut dictum est.

⟨3⟩ Tertio modo aliquis terminus significat ad placitum quia ad volun-20 tatem primarii instituentis ipse vel sibi consimilis aliquid significat vel significavit.

Dicitur enim 'ipse vel sibi consimilis' quia multi sunt termini vocales vel scripti significantes significata a se distincta, et tamen numquam fuerunt impositi ad significandum, ut si primo scriberetur ly .homo. vel ly 25 .animal. Sed sufficit quod sibi consimiles fuerunt impositi ad significandum.

Dicitur etiam 'significat vel significavit' quia licet termini qui primo fuerunt impositi ad significandum iam non significent quia forte sunt corrupti, sufficit quod pro tunc significabant.

30 Dicitur ergo quod talis terminus 'homo' vel 'animal' significat ad placitum, quia movet intellectum ad concipiendum tale vel tale, non propter convenientiam vel similitudinem (quemadmodum facit terminus mentalis sibi subordinatus), sed ex institutione, conventione, vel consensu. Ut dato

---

5–6 et capto *M*   8 placitum qui subiacet *E*   11 quia voluptas vult *M*
12 postea nolit ipsum significare, sicut *M*   15 Ante non *M*   24 primo modo
scriberetur *M*   25 consimilis fuerit *M*   28 primo modo fuerunt *M*   iam *om. E*
31–2 propter aliquam convenientiam *M*

⟨primarily⟩ signifies that some term signifies arbitrarily; therefore some part of this proposition ⟨primarily⟩ signifies arbitrarily, but the only part that does so is this part: *arbitrarily*. On this basis it is granted that some naturally significant term ⟨primarily⟩ signifies arbitrarily.

Moreover, some term signifying as a consequence of imposition signifies naturally—e.g., if we take the ⟨mental⟩ term *as a consequence of imposition* signifying naturally. This is argued as the former case was argued.

⟨2⟩ A term signifies arbitrarily in a second way because it lies under the control of the understanding or will which conceives it, so that at one time it will signify or at another time not signify. Each spoken, written, or mental term signifies arbitrarily in this way, for the will wills the term now to signify and afterwards not, as is clear in the case of the term 'man', which sometimes signifies and sometimes does not signify. And this is solely because of the understanding, which turns now towards one thing, now towards another.

Thus one must not imagine that such a mental term ⟨as was discussed under 1 above⟩ signifies arbitrarily at the pleasure of the understanding because the understanding can change its primary significatum and understand something else ⟨by it⟩. Instead it is said to signify arbitrarily only in the way already described.

⟨3⟩ A term signifies arbitrarily in a third way because the term itself or one equiform to it signifies or did signify something in accordance with the will of the first person to institute it.

⟨The details of this description are explained in the following way.⟩

'The term itself or one equiform to it'. This is said because there are many spoken or written terms signifying significata separate from themselves which were, however, never imposed for the purpose of signifying those significata[b]—as if one were to write 'man' or 'animal' for the first time. But it is enough that things equiform to them have been imposed for the purpose of signifying.

'Signifies or did signify'. The reason for saying this is that although terms that were at first imposed for the purpose of signifying may not signify now, because they happen to have been lost or destroyed, it is enough that they were significant for that time.[c]

⟨*Conclusions Drawn from this Discussion of Natural and Arbitrary Signification*⟩

⟨1⟩ A term such as 'man' or 'animal' is said to signify arbitrarily, therefore, because it moves the understanding to conceive of something or other not as a result of association or resemblance (as does the mental term subordinate to it), but by institution, convention, or agreement. For

quod mundus habuit initium, primus homo rebus ad placitum imposuit
nomina, et posteriores, tales voces audientes appropriatas rebus talibus,
vocaverunt formationes et articulationes, consentientes quod voces in
aeternum sic formatae vel articulatae pro talibus rebus sumerentur, quam,
5 propter talem assensum vel ordinationem factam ab auctoritate, vocamus
impositionem termini primariam. Non quia forte ipsi considerabant de
termino nunc prolato, sed quia statuerunt primo non solum de uno termino sed de quolibet praesenti vel futuro sibi simili quod ipso audito tales
res vel tales conciperemus. Sicut patet de isto termino 'homo', quem
10 primus homo imposuit ut ipse vel sibi consimilis non solum homines
praesentes significet sed etiam quoscumque futuros. Similiter, illum
terminum 'sol' non ad significandum praecise istum solem, sed si fuerint
mille vel quotcumque soles, aequaliter significaret illos absque ulla nova
institutione.

15 Ex his omnibus imaginandum est quod sicut statua vel imago depicta
significat rem ex convenientia et similitudine eiusdem, et circulus ante
tabernam significat vinum solum ex institutione et non ex convenientia vel
similitudine ad vinum, sic terminus mentalis significat rem ex convenientia
et similitudine accidentali ad talem rem, et terminus vocalis vel ⟨scriptus⟩
20 significat solum ex institutione, ut dictum est, et non ex aliqua tali convenientia vel similitudine.

Ex his adhuc infertur universaliter fore verum quod terminus significans
ad placitum dicitur esse ille qui significat aliquod significatum quod quidem
significatum possibile est significando non significare. Hoc patet de isto
25 termino 'homo', qui potest mihi significare asinum, bovem, vel aliquid
aliud non significando mihi hominem, sicut possibile est quod Sortes
existens a remotis appareat Plato vel asinus et non Sortes.

Sed forte contra istam sententiam arguitur, probando quod terminus
mentalis significans naturaliter significat ad placitum, sumendo 'significare
30 ad placitum' tertio modo, sic.

⟨1⟩ Pono quod A sit intentio Sortis, qui sit coram te, et advertas te ad
istam intentionem. Tunc arguitur sic. A significat tibi modo naturaliter
Sortem propter convenientiam et similitudinem inter A et Sortem,
et stat illam intentionem significare non significando Sortem; igitur
35 ista intentio significat ad placitum. Patet consequentia cum maiori. Et

---

1 habuerit M   9 de secundo termino, quem M   13 significet E   15 statura E
17 vinum solum significat E   18 rem om. E   19 vel om. E   20 ut dictum
est om. E   aliqua om. E   22 adhuc om. M   26 nominem sic possibile E
29–30 sumendo 'significare ad placitum' om. E   34 stat talem intentionem E

example, given that the world had a beginning, the first man arbitrarily imposed names on things. And later men, hearing such utterances appropriated to such things, uttered formations and articulations, agreeing together that utterances so formed or articulated would for ever be taken for such things. Because of such an authoritative assent or arrangement we call that the primary imposition of a term. This is not because those men happened to be considering the term that is pronounced in our own day but because they were prescribing for the first time not only as regards the one term but also as regards any present or future term like it such that when we hear it we think of such and such things. This is clear in the case of the term 'man', which the first man imposed so that it or one equiform to it would signify not only present men but also any future men. Similarly, the term 'sun' is not for the purpose of signifying just the sun. If there were a thousand suns or however many suns you please, it would signify them equally without any new institution.

⟨2⟩ As a result of all these considerations one must imagine that just as a statue or a painted picture signifies a thing because of association with or resemblance to it, so a mental term signifies a thing because of association with and accidental resemblance to such a thing. And just as the hoop in front of the inn signifies wine solely because of institution and not because of any association with or resemblance to wine, so a spoken or ⟨written⟩ term signifies solely because of institution, as has been said, and not because of any such association or resemblance.

⟨3⟩ From these considerations, moreover, one infers that it will be universally true that an arbitrarily significant term is said to be one that signifies some significatum which it is possible for it not to signify while remaining significant. This is clear in the case of the term 'man', which can signify a donkey, a cow, or something else to me while not signifying a man to me, just as Socrates when he is far away may appear to be Plato or a donkey and not Socrates.

⟨*Arguments against Conclusion 2*⟩

One may, however, argue against this view as follows, proving that a naturally significant mental term signifies arbitrarily, where 'to signify arbitrarily' is taken in the third way described above.

⟨1⟩ Suppose that A is the intention[d] of Socrates, with whom you are face to face, and that you are concentrating on that intention. Then the argument proceeds in the following way. A now naturally signifies Socrates to you because of the association and resemblance between A and Socrates, and it is consistent that this intention should signify while not signifying Socrates; therefore this intention signifies arbitrarily. The inference is

minor probatur sic. Ponendo quod Sortes recedat a visu tuo, adveniente
Platone, (9ʳᵇ M) consimiliter disposito manente *A* intentione continue
in animo tuo. Tunc arguitur minor sic: *A* iam significat Platonem non
significando Sortem; ergo etc. Consequentia cum minori patet. Maior
5 arguitur sic. *A* prius significavit Sortem solum propter convenientiam inter
A et Sortem, sed tanta est convenientia inter *A* et Platonem sicut prius fuit
inter *A* et Sortem; ergo *A* iam significat Platonem sicut prius significavit
Sortem. Minor patet ex quo Sortes et Plato sunt omnino aequales. Et
consequentia patet, quia posita causa ponitur et effectus.

10 ⟨2⟩ Item arguitur quod *A* significat Platonem, nam hoc *A* prius significavit Sortem, et nulla est differentia per quam habens iudicare quod hoc *A*
non significat tibi illud obiectum (demonstrando Platonem). Immo credis
quod illud obiectum sit id quod fuit prius. Igitur sicut prius (4ʳᵇ E) fuit ita
quod *A* significat obiectum tibi, iam est ita quod *A* significat obiectum tibi.
15 Sed nullum est obiectum nisi Platonem; igitur *A* iam significat Platonem
et, per consequens, ad placitum.

⟨3⟩ Item arguitur quod *A* intentio non significat Sortem, quia solum
illud quod per istam intentionem apprehenditur ista intentio significat, sed
per istam intentionem solum apprehenditur hoc obiectum; ergo illa
20 intentio solum significat illud obiectum et, per consequens, non significat
Sortem.

Ad ista respondetur semper sustinendo quod nulla intentio repraesentans
modo unam rem primarie a qua primarie talis intentio causatur potest
aliam rem distinctam repraesentare non repraesentando priorem, quia
25 nulla intentio prima repraesentans unam rem potest aliam rem distinctam
repraesentare non repraesentando priorem nisi ista intentio aliter et aliter
se haberet. Sed manente una et eadem intentione non potest eadem intentio aliter et aliter se habere; igitur, etc. Consequentia patet, et maior
per hoc quod idem, inquantum idem, semper facit idem. Et minor similiter
30 apparet, quia nullum accidens est subiectum transmutationis.

Item si quaelibet talis intentio possit indifferenter significare quicquid
homo vellet, tunc frustra generarentur tot intentiones in anima, cum una

---

1 minor arguitur sic *M*   viso *M*   2 continuo *E*   3 anima tua *M*
5 convenientiam et similitudinem inter *E*   13 quod id obiectum *E*   14 sit
illud quod *M*   16 et *om. E*   19–20 ergo . . . obiectum *om. E*   20 intentio
non solum *M*   24–6 quia . . . priorem *om. E*   27 intentione *om. E*   27–8 intentio *om. M*   28 igitur *om. E*   29 Et *om. E*   31 potest *M*

obvious, along with the major premiss. The minor premiss is proved in the following way. Suppose that Socrates is receding from your sight as Plato is approaching and that throughout this process the intention A remains just as it was in your mind. Then: A is now signifying Plato while not signifying Socrates; therefore, etc. This inference is obvious along with the minor premiss. The major premiss is supported by the following argument. A used to signify Socrates solely because of the association between A and Socrates, but there is just as much association between A and Plato as there used to be between A and Socrates; therefore A now signifies Plato just as it used to signify Socrates. The minor premiss is clear on the hypothesis that Socrates and Plato are altogether alike. And this last inference is obvious, because when the cause is posited the effect is posited as well.

⟨2⟩ This argument is offered to show that A signifies Plato. This A used to signify Socrates, and there is no difference by which you can judge that this A does not signify this object (indicating Plato) to you. On the contrary, you believe that this object is the object that used to be here. Therefore just as it used to be the case so it is now the case that A signifies an object to you. But there is no object other than Plato; therefore A is now signifying Plato and, as a consequence, doing so arbitrarily.

⟨3⟩ This argument is offered to show that intention A does not signify Socrates. This intention signifies only what is apprehended through this intention, but only this object ⟨(indicating Plato)⟩ is apprehended through this intention; therefore this intention signifies only this object and, as a consequence, does not signify Socrates.

⟨*Replies to these Arguments*⟩

In replying to these arguments I maintain throughout that no intention that now primarily represents one thing by which the intention is primarily caused can represent another, distinct thing while not representing the former thing. This is because no first intention*e* representing one thing can represent another, distinct thing while not representing the former thing unless it is altered in one way or another. But while the intention remains one and the same it cannot be altered in any way; therefore, etc. The inference is obvious, and the major premiss is clear as a consequence of the fact that what is the same, in so far as it is the same, always produces the same. The minor premiss is likewise clear, because no accident is the subject of a change of state.

Again, if any such intention could indifferently signify whatever a man wished it to signify, then there would be no point to the generation of so many intentions in the mind, for one would be enough. Or it would

sufficeret. Vel sequeretur quod quaelibet intentio foret indifferens ad quemlibet actum, quod non est verum.

⟨1R⟩ Ad argumenta respondetur: ad primum potest dupliciter responderi.

5   ⟨1R1⟩ Primo negando quod *A* intentio significet ad placitum, sumendo 'ad placitum' tertio modo. Et tunc ulterius admitto utrumque casum, et concedo quod *A* significat Platonem et quemcumque hominem similem Sorti, sicut ista intentio *homo* significat mihi asinum dato quod asinus existens remote videatur mihi homo. Tamen non est possibile quod ista

10   intentio *homo* significaret sic asinum quod non significaret hominem. Ideo negatur illud assumptum argumenti, cum dicitur quod *A* significat tibi Platonem non significando Sortem.

⟨3R1⟩ Et tunc quando arguitur quod

Solum illud quod per istam intentionem apprehenditur ista intentio
15   significat, sed per illam intentionem solum apprehenditur hoc
obiectum (demonstrando Platonem); ergo . . . ,

respondetur negando minorem, eo quod intentio Sortis non potest aliud significare non significando Sortem, ut saepius dictum est. Sed quia in casu significat Platonem oportet etiam quod significet Sortem, aliter enim

20   *A* intentio significaret ad placitum, quod est contra praedicta.

⟨3R2⟩ Aliter potest dici ad illud argumentum quod *A* intentio significat Sortem et non significat Platonem. Sed bene Platonem significat.

⟨1R2⟩ Et tunc ad argumentum:

A prius significavit Sortem solum propter convenientiam inter *A* et
25   Sortem, sed tanta est convenientia inter *A* et Platonem sicut prius
fuit inter *A* et Sortem; ergo per idem iam *A* significat Platonem,

respondetur negando consequentiam. Sed solum sequitur quod Platonem iam *A* significat recte. Sicut non sequitur:

Tu scis istam propositionem esse veram, et ista est *A*; ergo tu scis *A*
30   esse verum.

Sed bene sequitur quod *A* scis esse verum. Et sic consequenter conceditur quod Platonem *A* significat, et non significat Platonem; Platonem *A* intellectui repraesentat, et non repraesentat Platonem intellectui; Platonis est *A* similitudo, sed *A* non est similitudo Platonis.

35   ⟨2R1⟩ Ad aliud argumentum potest consimiliter dici quod illud obiectum (demonstrando (5ra M) Platonem) *A* significat, sed non significat illud obiectum, sicut stat quod Sortem cognoscam, et non cognoscam Sortem.

---

1 sequitur *M*   3–4 potest dupliciter responderi *om. M*   9 existens a
remotis videatur *M*   10 significat (*prius et alterum*) *E*   11 negatur id assumptum *E*
29 tu *om. E*

follow that any intention would be indifferent as regards each act, which is not true.[f]

⟨1R⟩ The first argument can be replied to in two ways.

⟨1R1⟩ First, by denying that intention *A* signifies arbitrarily when 'arbitrarily' is taken in the third way. I accept both hypotheses, and I grant that *A* signifies Plato and any man like Socrates, just as the intention *man* signifies a donkey to me in case there is a donkey in the distance that seems to me to be a man. Nevertheless it is not possible that the intention *man* would signify a donkey in such a way that it would not signify a man. Therefore one must deny the argument's assumption that A signifies Plato to you while not signifying Socrates.

⟨3R1⟩ Then when it is argued that

> This intention signifies only what is apprehended through this intention; but only this object (indicating Plato) is apprehended through this intention; therefore . . .

the reply is to deny the minor premiss, because the intention of Socrates cannot signify something else while not signifying Socrates, as has often been said. But since in the example it signifies Plato it must signify Socrates as well, for otherwise intention *A* would signify arbitrarily, which is contrary to what has been said above.

⟨3R2⟩ Alternatively, one can say in reply to this argument ⟨3⟩ that intention *A* signifies Socrates and does not signify Plato. But it does rightly signify Plato.

⟨1R2⟩ As for the argument:

> *A* used to signify Socrates solely because of the association between *A* and Socrates, but there is just as much association between *A* and Plato as there used to be between *A* and Socrates; therefore for the same reason *A* now signifies Plato,

the reply is to reject the inference. Rather it follows only that Plato is what *A* now signifies directly. In the same way this does not follow:

> You know that this proposition is true, and this is proposition *A*; therefore you know that proposition *A* is true.

But it does follow rightly that proposition *A* is what you know to be true. And so as a consequence it is granted that Plato is what *A* signifies, and not that *A* signifies Plato; that Plato is what *A* represents to the understanding, and not that *A* represents Plato to the understanding; that Plato is what *A* is a likeness of, and not that *A* is a likeness of Plato.

⟨2R1⟩ In reply to the other argument one can say in just the same way that this object (indicating Plato) is what *A* signifies, but *A* does not signify this object. In the same way it is consistent that Socrates is what I perceive and I do not perceive Socrates.[g]

⟨2R2⟩ Verumtamen mihi apparet melius fore dicendum concedendo quod *A* significat illud obiectum (demonstrando Platonem). Nec ex hoc sequitur quod *A* significet Platonem sicut non sequitur:

> Ly .homo. significat istam rem (dato quod esset unus asinus apparens homo), et ista res est asinus; ergo ly .homo. significat asinum.

Similiter non sequitur:

> Apparet mihi quod hoc est asinus, et hoc est homo; ergo apparet mihi quod homo est asinus.

Similiter non sequitur in dicto casu:

> Plato apparet solum sicut est, sed Plato est Plato; ergo Plato apparet Plato,

oporteret enim pro minori sumere talem de sensu composito:

> Apparet quod Plato sit Plato,

et tunc negatur minor.

Verumtamen magis physice potest responderi ad ista argumenta, negando breviter quod *A* significat Platonem aut quod Platonem significat si prius fuit propria et distincta cognitio Sortis. Sed iam cognoscitur Plato per proprium conceptum vel intentionem, ab ipso obiective causatum, et distinctam a cognitione vel conceptu Sortis. Et licet hoc credam esse idem quod prius, decipior ratione magnae similitudinis inter proprias intentiones Sortis et Platonis. Et ita in aliis dicatur quod non est possibile aliquid cognosci vel intelligi per receptionem et per speciem propriam alterius. Et ita apparet quod intentio hominis non potest repraesentare asinum nec econtra. Unde si homo esset a longe quem putarem esse asinum, non propter hoc causaretur notitia asini, sed solum hominis, ratione cuius posset moveri species asini existens in memoriam proprie asinum repraesentans. In hoc casu ergo est dicendum quod ista species hominis hominem repraesentaret, sed non repraesentaret hominem ratione appellationis. Quare, etc.

Tria superius tacta sunt contra quae contingit arguere ut eorum veritas magis appareat.

> ⟨1⟩ Dicitur enim primo quod termini vocales vel scripti seipsos naturaliter significant.
>
> ⟨2⟩ Dicitur etiam secundo (4ᵗᵃ E) quod tales res a se distinctas significant ad placitum.
>
> ⟨3⟩ Dicitur tertio quod termini mentales significant naturaliter res a se distinctas ex quadam convenientia et similitudine.

18–19 obiective mentaliter causatum distinctam *M*   21–2 possibile aliud cognosci *E*   24 erit *E*   27 hoc *om. E*   est *om. E*   28 hominis *om. M*

⟨2R2⟩ It seems to me, however, that it would be better to reply by granting that *A* does signify that object (indicating Plato). It no more follows
from this that *A* signifies Plato than this follows:

> 'Man' signifies this thing (suppose it is a donkey that appears to be a
> man), and this thing is a donkey; therefore 'man' signifies a donkey.

Similarly, this does not follow:

> It appears to me that this is a donkey, and this is a man; therefore it
> appears to me that a man is a donkey.

Similarly, this does not follow as regards the case described above:[h]

> Plato appears only as he is, but Plato is Plato; therefore
> Plato appears to be Plato,

for the minor premiss would have to be taken in the compounded sense,[i]
as meaning

> It appears that Plato is Plato,

and in that case the minor premiss is denied.

One can, however, reply to these arguments in a way that takes more
cognizance of natural things by summarily denying either that *A* signifies
Plato or that Plato is what it signifies if it used to be a proper and distinct
cognition of Socrates. Instead Plato is now cognized through a proper concept or intention of which he is the objective cause, distinct from a cognition
or concept of Socrates. And although I believe that he is the same thing as
was there previously, I am deceived because of the great resemblance between the proper intentions of Socrates and of Plato. And so as regards
other cases one may say that it is not possible for one thing to be cognized
or understood through the reception of another and through an appearance
proper to another. Thus it appears that the intention of a man cannot
represent a donkey, or vice versa. If a man is far away and I take him to be
a donkey, the notion of a donkey is not caused by him, but only that of a
man, because of which a memory image of a donkey, properly representing
a donkey, could be aroused. In that case, then, it must be said of this
appearance of a man that there would be a man it represented, but it would
not represent a man, by reason of appellation.[j] Therefore, etc.

⟨Three Theses regarding Natural and Arbitrary Signification⟩

Three matters were touched on above against which one can argue in
order to bring out their truth more plainly.

⟨1⟩ Spoken or written terms signify themselves naturally.[k]
⟨2⟩ Spoken or written terms signify things distinct from themselves
arbitrarily.[l]
⟨3⟩ Mental terms signify things distinct from themselves naturally
because of a certain association and resemblance.[m]

⟨1.1⟩ Contra primum dictum arguitur sic. Nam si quilibet terminus vocalis vel scriptus significat se, sequitur quod quilibet foret terminus communis. Consequens est manifeste falsum, et consequentia probatur. Nam terminus dicitur communis eo quod significat plura, sed quilibet
5 terminus significat plura quia significat se naturaliter et suum significatum distinctum; ergo, etc.

⟨1.2⟩ Secundo sequitur quod nullus foret terminus non significativus immo quilibet terminus foret significativus. Consequens falsum et contra Boethium ponentem voces aliquas nihil significare, ut tales terminos 'bu',
10 'ba', et similes. Consequentia probatur quia quilibet terminus significat seipsum naturaliter, et propter naturalem significationem dicitur terminus maxime significativus.

⟨1.3⟩ Tertio sequitur quod quilibet terminus foret terminus analogus. Consequens falsum, et consequentia probatur per descriptionem termini
15 analogi: dicitur enim quod quilibet terminus significans multa quorum unum significat per prius et reliquum per posterius est terminus analogus, sed quilibet terminus significat multa quorum unum significat per prius et reliquum per posterius; ergo, etc. Consequentia patet, et minor probatur. Nam quilibet terminus significat naturaliter seipsum et rem distinctam ad
20 placitum per impositionem, sed prius significat seipsum et posterius rem distinctam; igitur, etc. Consequentia bona, et antecedens patet quia terminus (5rb M) per prius significat suum significatum naturale quam suum significatum ad placitum.

⟨1.4⟩ Quarto sequitur quod ista propositio est vera:

25 Chimaera est.

Probatur: nam ipsa significat primarie sicut est; ergo . . . Consequentia bona, et antecedens probatur, nam ipsa significat primarie illum terminum 'chimaera' esse, et sic est; ergo, etc. Consequentia patet, et antecedens similiter, quia termini primarie significant seipsos cum naturale prius sit
30 quam ad placitum.

⟨1.5⟩ Quinto sequitur quod ista propositio foret falsa:

  Omnis homo est animal.

Probatur: quia si ipsa esset vera, tunc omnis res significata per subiectum esset res significata per praedicatum; cum igitur iste terminus 'homo' sit
35 res significata per subiectum, iste terminus 'homo' est res significata per praedicatum, et per consequens iste terminus 'homo' esset animal, quod est falsum.

⟨1.6⟩ Confirmatur quod ista sit falsa:

  Omnis homo est animal,

---

2 vocalis et scriptus *M*   5–6 distincte *E*   8 foret terminus significativus *M*
Consequens falsum *om. M*   10 'ba', etc. *E*   13 terminus *om. E*   17–
18 prius, etc.; ergo *E*   26 ipsa *om. E*   28 'chimaeram' *M et E*   35 res (2)
om. E

⟨*Arguments against Thesis 1*⟩

⟨1.1⟩ If each spoken or written term signifies itself, it follows that each term will be a common term. This consequent is plainly false, and the inference is proved in the following way. A term is called common because it signifies more than one thing, but each term signifies more than one thing because it signifies itself naturally in addition to its separate significatum; therefore, etc.

⟨1.2⟩ It follows that no term will be nonsignificant but rather that each term will be significant. This consequent is false and contrary to Boethius when he say that some utterances signify nothing—e.g., such terms as 'bu', 'ba', and the like.[n] The inference is proved because each term signifies itself naturally, and it is because of natural signification that a term is said to be significant in the highest degree.

⟨1.3⟩ It follows that each term will be an analogical term. This consequent is false, and the inference is proved on the basis of the description of an analogical term: each term signifying many things one of which it signifies first and the rest subsequently is an analogical term. But each term signifies many things one of which it signifies first and the rest subsequently; therefore, etc. This inference is obvious, and the minor premiss is proved in the following way. Each term signifies itself naturally and a separate thing arbitrarily as a consequence of imposition, but it signifies itself first and the separate thing subsequently; therefore, etc. This inference is good, and the antecedent is obvious because a term signifies its natural significatum before its arbitrary significatum.

⟨1.4⟩ It follows that the proposition

Pegasus is[o]

is true. Proof: The proposition primarily signifies what is the case; therefore, etc. This inference is good, and the antecedent is proved in the following way. The proposition primarily signifies that the term 'Pegasus' is, and this is so; therefore, etc. This inference is obvious, and so is the antecedent. For terms primarily signify themselves since what is natural is prior to what is arbitrary.

⟨1.5⟩ It follows that the proposition

Every man is an animal

would be false. Proof: If this proposition were true, then every thing signified by the subject would be a thing signified by the predicate; therefore since the term 'man' is a thing signified by the subject, the term 'man' is a thing signified by the predicate, and consequently the term 'man' would be an animal, which is false.

⟨1.6⟩ There is confirmation of the falsity of

Every man is an animal,

nam ipsa significat aliter quam est; igitur . . . Antecedens probatur. Nam ista significat omnem talem terminum 'homo' esse talem terminum 'animal', et sic non est; igitur, etc. Antecedens arguitur. Nam iste terminus 'homo' significat seipsum et hominem et distribuitur; igitur si distribuitur 5 pro quolibet supposito vel significato non naturali, a multo fortiori distribuitur pro quolibet supposito vel significato naturali. Quo dato, sequitur intentum.

⟨1.1R⟩ Ad ista respondetur primo ad primum negando quod quilibet terminus sit terminus communis. Et tunc ad argumentum, dico quod non 10 propter hoc dicitur aliquis terminus communis quia significat plura. Sed ideo dicitur aliquis terminus communis quia significat plura de quorum intentionibus est talis terminus vere praedicabilis. Quia ergo iste terminus 'Sortes' vel quiscumque alius non potest vere praedicari de se pro se, sed solum pro significato distincto (intelligendo de praedicatione 15 significative sumpta), igitur non quilibet terminus est terminus communis. Dicimus enim quod Sortes est Sortes, et non quod iste terminus 'Sortes' est Sortes.

Similiter, ad hoc quod esset aliquis terminus communis oportet quod iste esset pro pluribus simul suppositivus, sed non quilibet terminus est 20 simul pro pluribus suppositivus; igitur non quilibet terminus est terminus communis. Consequentia patet, et minor similiter de isto termino 'hoc', qui licet significet plura, puta se et unum significatum distinctum, non tamen potest supponere pro illis simul. Quia ly .hoc. sumitur personaliter, tunc solum supponit pro suo significato distincto. Si autem sumitur 25 materialiter, tunc non supponit pro tali significato distincto sed solum pro se vel pro sibi consimili termino. Quare, etc.

⟨1.2R⟩ Ad secundum dicitur concedendo consequentiam et consequens. Et tunc ad argumentum, dico quod ipse ponit tales 'bu', 'ba', nihil significare ex impositione, et hoc est verum. Nihilominus bene significant 30 naturaliter seipsos, sicut et aliae res faciunt.

⟨1.3R⟩ Ad tertium cum infertur quod quilibet terminus est terminus analogus, nego consequentiam. Et ad probationem, dico quod non propter hoc dicitur aliquis terminus analogus quia significat plura, unum per prius et aliud per posterius. Aliter enim sequeretur quod iste ter- 35 minus 'animal' et consimiles essent termini analogi, eo quod iste terminus 'animal' significat plura, unum per prius et aliud per posterius. Significat enim animal per prius, per posterius vero significat Sortem et Platonem, et sic de aliis. Et ideo dicitur aliquis terminus esse terminus analogus quia praedicabilis est de rebus diversorum praedicamentorum,

---

14 pro se *om. M*   19 simul *om. E*   20 terminus (1) *om. E*   21 termino 'homo' *E*   23 ly *om. E*   24–5 sumitur naturaliter *E*   28 ad minorem, dico *E*   37 per (2) *om. M*   38 terminus esse *om. E*

for this proposition signifies otherwise than is the case; therefore, etc. The antecedent is proved in the following way. This proposition signifies that every term 'man' is a term 'animal',[p] and this is not the case; therefore, etc. This antecedent is argued for in the following way. The term 'man' signifies itself and man and is distributed; therefore if it is distributed for each nonnatural suppositum or significatum, it a *fortiori* distributed for each natural suppositum or significatum. If this is granted, the intended conclusion follows.

⟨Replies to the Arguments against Thesis 1⟩

⟨1.1R⟩ I deny that each term is a common term. As for the argument, I say that it is not because it signifies more than one thing that a term is called common. Rather, a term is called common because it signifies more than one thing and is predicable truly of the intentions of those things. Since, therefore, the term 'Socrates' or any other ⟨person's name⟩ cannot *per se* be predicated truly of itself but only of the separate significatum (understanding the predication to be taken significantly), not each term is a common term. For we say that Socrates is Socrates, and not that the term 'Socrates' is Socrates.

Similarly, in order for a term to be a common term it would have to supposit at one and the same time for more than one thing, but not every term supposits at one and the same time for more than one thing; therefore not every term is a common term. This inference is obvious, and so is the minor premiss as regards the term 'this', which although it signifies more than one thing—itself and one distinct significatum—cannot supposit for them at one and the same time. For if 'this' has personal *suppositio*, it supposits only for its distinct significatum. If, however, it has material *suppositio*, then it does not supposit for such a distinct significatum but only for itself or a term equiform to itself. Therefore, etc.

⟨1.2R⟩ I reject both the inference and its consequent. As for the argument, I say that Boethius claims that 'bu', 'ba', and the like signify nothing as a consequence of imposition, and that is true. They do, however, signify themselves naturally, just as other things do.

⟨1.3R⟩ I reject the inference in which it is inferred that each term is an analogical term. As for the proof, I say that it is not because it signifies more than one thing, one first and another subsequently, that a term is called analogical. For otherwise it would follow that the term 'animal' and those like it would be analogical terms, because the term 'animal' signifies more than one thing, one first and another subsequently. It signifies animal first, but subsequently it signifies Socrates and Plato and so on. Therefore a term is said to be an analogical term because it is predicable of

quorum unum essentialiter dependet ab alio. Sicut est iste terminus 'ens', qui praedicabilis est de substantia et accidente, quorum unum dependet ab alio, ut patet. Modo certum est quod nullus terminus simul est praedicabilis vere de se pro se et de suo significato distincto, sive (5ᵛᵃ M) capiatur
5 praedicatio talis materialiter sive significative. Similiter, nullus terminus quocumque dato dependet a se vel a suo significato distincto, nec econtra; igitur nullus terminus ratione talis significationis debet dici terminus analogus.

⟨1.4R⟩ Ad quartum, cum infertur quod haec est vera:

10   Chimaera est,

nego consequentiam. Et ad probationem, nego quod ipsa significet primarie sicut est. Nego etiam quod ista similiter significet primarie istum terminum 'chimaera' esse. Et tunc ad argumentum: termini prius significant seipsos quam res alias a se distinctas, dicitur negando. Nec sequitur:

15   Termini significant se naturaliter et sua significata distincta ex impositione vel ad placitum; igitur prius significant se quam sua significata distincta.

Et ratio est quia multotiens termini prius inducunt memoriae similitudinem suorum significatorum distinctorum quam seipsos. Hoc enim satis patet de
20 terminis mentalibus, et per idem sic potest esse de terminis vocalibus vel scriptis. Quod autem termini mentales significant prius sua significata distincta quam se hoc patet ex eo quod se significant solum per magnum discursum. Quia si scio, vel postquam scio, hominem currere, statim invenio quod per talem propositionem in mente repraesentatur mihi quod
25 homo currit; quo facto scio me habere talem propositionem, et sic seipsam repraesentat. Quare, etc.

Aliter, dicitur concedendo quod quilibet terminus prius se quam distinctum a se significat. Non tamen sequitur quod se adaequate vel primarie significat, sumendo ly .primarie. officialiter. Sicut ly .homo. prius
30 significat animal quam hominem, non tamen adaequate. Sed de hoc alias, cum de veritate propositionis agetur.

⟨1.5R⟩ Ad quintum, cum infertur quod haec est falsa:

Omnis homo est animal,

nego consequentiam. Et ulterius cum arguitur:

35   Ipsa est vera; igitur omnis res significata per subiectum est res significata per praedicatum,

1 quarum unam M   ab alia M   est om. E   4 pro se om. M   distincto om. M
5 talis om. M   6 suo simili significato E   12 Nego similiter quod ista
significet M   21 significent E   22 ex om. M   solum significant E
27–8 quam demonstratum a M

things belonging to different categories, one of which depends essentially on the other. The term 'being', for example, is predicable of a substance and of an accident, one of which obviously depends on the other. But of course no term is *per se* predicable truly both of itself and of its distinct significatum at one and the same time, whether the predication is taken materially or significantly. Similarly, no term at all depends on itself or on its distinct significatum, or vice versa; therefore no term must be called an analogical term because of such signification.

⟨1.4R⟩ I reject the inference in which it is inferred that

Pegasus is

is true. As for the proof, I deny that that proposition primarily signifies what is the case. I deny also that it likewise primarily signifies that the term 'Pegasus' is. My reply to the argument that terms signify themselves before they signify other things distinct from themselves is to reject it. Nor does this follow:

Terms signify themselves naturally and their distinct significata as a consequence of imposition or arbitrarily; therefore they signify themselves before their distinct significata.

The reason is that terms often call to mind a likeness of their distinct significata before themselves. This is clear enough as regards mental terms, and in the same way it can be so as regards spoken or written terms. But that mental terms signify their distinct significata before themselves is clear from the fact that they signify themselves only as a consequence of a great deal of reasoning. For if I know, or as soon as I know, that a man is running, I immediately find that by such a proposition in the mind it is represented to me that a man is running; and when that has occurred I know that I have such a proposition ⟨in mind⟩, and in that way it represents itself. Therefore, etc.

Alternatively, one may grant that each term does signify itself before it signifies what is distinct from itself. Even so it does not follow that it signifies itself adequately or primarily, taking 'primarily' in its functional sense. Thus 'man' signifies animal before man, but not adequately. I shall deal with this elsewhere, however, when we are concerned with the truth of a proposition.*q*

⟨1.5R⟩ I reject the inference in which it is inferred that

Every man is an animal

is false. I also reject the inference in which it is argued

This proposition is true; therefore every thing signified by the subject is a thing signified by the predicate.

nego consequentiam, eo quod subiectum significat se, et idem non significat praedicatum. Si tamen arguitur:

> Illa propositio est vera; ergo omnis res pro qua supponit subiectum est res pro qua supponit praedicatum,

5 concedo consequentiam et consequens. Et tunc dico quod licet subiectum significet se, non tamen supponit pro se, eo quod significative supponit. Non enim potest supponere pro se nisi materialiter sumeretur, dicendo

> Ly .homo. est nomen.

⟨1.6R⟩ Ad confirmationem nego illam consequentiam:

10 > *A* vel *B* propositio significat aliter quam est; igitur *A* vel *B* propositio est falsa.

Sicut non sequitur:

> *A* propositio significat sicut est; ergo *A* propositio est vera.

Pro quo dico quod quaelibet propositio vera significat infinitas falsitates, 15 et quaelibet propositio falsa significat infinitas veritates. Unde capta ista propositione:

> Homo est asinus.

Ipsa significat hominem esse, hominem esse animal, hominem esse ens, et sic de infinitis, quorum quodlibet est verum. Et quod ipsa propositio 20 significat illas veritates patet, eo quod quaelibet propositio significat quicquid sequitur ad eam, modo alias declarando. Unde bene sequitur formaliter:

> Homo est asinus; igitur homo est, homo est animal, homo est ens, et sic ulterius.

25 Similiter, capta ista propositione:

> Homo est animal.

Ipsa est vera, et tamen significat infinitas falsitates. Significat enim hominem esse asinum, capram, leonem, et sic de aliis, quorum quodlibet est falsum.

30 Ulterius quando dicitur in argumento quod ista propositio:

> Omnis homo est animal

significat istum terminum 'homo' esse istum terminum 'animal', dicitur negando. Unde licet ista propositio significet se, et quaelibet pars significet se, non tamen sequitur quod una pars significet se esse aliam partem. Et 35 sic subiectum non significat se esse praedicatum. Videmus enim quod lapis vel lignum significat se naturaliter, et etiam quaelibet eius pars, et tamen una pars non significat se esse aliam partem, nec una medietas aliam medietatem. Ita est in proposito. (5vb M)

---

18 hominem esse (2) *om.* E   21–2 formaliter *om.* E   23 igitur homo est homo, homo est animal E   24 sic de aliis E   27 et ipsa significat M 28 de multis M   32 terminum 'hominem' esse M

For the subject signifies itself and the predicate does not signify it. But if one argues in this way:

> The proposition is true; therefore every thing for which the subject supposits is a thing for which the predicate supposits,

I grant the inference and its consequent. And in that case I say that although the subject signifies itself, it does not supposit for itself, because it supposits significantly. For it cannot supposit for itself unless it is taken materially, as when one says

> 'Man' is a noun.

⟨1.6R⟩ In reply to the confirmation I reject this inference:

> Proposition *A* or *B* signifies otherwise than is the case; therefore proposition *A* or *B* is false.

In the same way this does not follow:

> Proposition *A* signifies what is the case; therefore proposition *A* is true.

In support of this I say that any true proposition signifies infinitely many falsities and any false proposition signifies infinitely many truths. For instance, take the proposition

> A man is a donkey.

This signifies that a man is, that a man is an animal, that a man is a being, and so on as regards infinitely many, each of which is true. And it is clear that that proposition does signify those truths, because any proposition signifies whatever follows from it, as is explained elsewhere.[r] Thus this follows formally and correctly:

> A man is a donkey; therefore a man is, a man is an animal, a man is a being, and so on.

Similarly, take the proposition

> A man is an animal.

It is true, and yet it signifies infinitely many falsities. For it signifies that a man is a donkey, a goat, a lion, and so on, each of which is false.

Furthermore, when it is said in the argument that the proposition

> Every man is an animal

signifies that the term 'man' is the term 'animal', I deny it. Although the proposition signifies itself and each part of it signifies itself, still it does not follow that one part signifies that it is another part. And so the subject does not signify that it is the predicate. For we see that a stone or a piece of wood signifies itself naturally, and each part of it signifies itself naturally too, and yet one part does not signify that it is another part, or one half that it is another half. And that is the way it is in the example in question.

Ulterius quando dicitur

Iste terminus 'homo' significat se et hominem et distribuitur; ergo
si distribuitur pro supposito vel significato non naturali, a fortiori
debet distribui pro supposito vel significato naturali,

5 respondetur negando consequentiam. Quia iste terminus 'homo' non
distribuitur pro quolibet suo significato, sed solum pro suis suppositis.
Non enim distribuitur pro omni homine praesenti, praeterito, futuro, et
possibili, quod omnes tamen significant, quia pro eisdem non supponit.
Sed solum distribuitur pro omni homine praesentialiter existente, quorum
10 quilibet vel quaelibet est suppositum istius termini 'homo'. Ita est in
proposito, licet ly .homo. significet se naturaliter et hominem non naturaliter, non tamen sequitur quod sicut distribuitur pro homine, ita debet
distribui pro se. Quia supponit pro homine et non supponit pro se, eo quod
ly .homo. sumitur significative. Si autem supponeret materialiter, (5ra E)
15 supponeret pro se et non pro homine.

Dicebatur secundo quod termini vocales vel scripti res a se distinctas non
naturaliter sed ad placitum significant.

⟨2.1⟩ Contra haec arguitur sic. Et signo istum terminum 'Sortes', qui
nunc primo est, significantem tibi Sortem. Tunc si iste terminus 'Sortes'
20 significat ad placitum, aut quia tu vis eum sic significare, aut quia significat ex impositione. Non primo modo, ut suppono; igitur secundo. Tunc
contra: Iste terminus non significat ex impositione quae est, nec ex
impositione quae fuit; igitur non significat ex impositione. Consequentia
bona. Et quod non significet ex impositione quae est patet quia iam non
25 imponitur ad significandum, ut suppono. Nec etiam significat ex impositione quae fuit, quia prius non imponebatur ad significandum cum nunc
primo sit et numquam ante hoc fuit.

⟨2.2⟩ Secundo primus impositor non cognovit istum terminum 'Sortes',
sed quod non cognovit, non imposuit ad significandum; igitur numquam
30 imposuit ad significandum istum terminum 'Sortes'. Et per consequens
non significat ex impositione quae fuit.

⟨2.3⟩ Tertio si iste terminus 'Sortes' significat ex impositione quae fuit,
ergo ista impositio prima fuit causa significationis istius termini 'Sortes',
nunc primo existentis; igitur haec significatio est causatum istius causae.
35 Sed causa et causatum sunt relativa, et relativa debent esse simul; igitur
simul fuerunt impositio prima et significatio huius termini 'Sortes', quod

---

6 significato naturali, *E*   7–8 praeterito, et futuro possibili *E*   8 tamen *om. M*
11–12 non naturaliter *om. M*   12 debuit *M*   15 homine, etc. *E*   18 sic *om. E*
21 Tunc *om. E*   25 ut suppositio *E*   27 hoc *om. E*   29–30 igitur non imposuit
E   33 primus *M*

Furthermore, I reject the inference in which it is said

The term 'man' signifies itself and man and is distributed; therefore if it is distributed for ⟨each⟩ nonnatural suppositum or significatum, it must *a fortiori* be distributed for ⟨each⟩ natural suppositum or significatum.

For the term 'man' is not distributed for each of its significata, but only for its supposita. It is not distributed for every man present, past, future, and possible—all of which it signifies—because it does not supposit for them. Instead it is distributed only for every human being presently existing, of which each, male or female, is a suppositum of this term 'man'.[s] And so it is in the example in question, for although 'man' signifies itself naturally and man nonnaturally, it does not follow that it must be distributed for itself just as it is distributed for man. For it supposits for man and does not supposit for itself, because 'man' is taken significantly. But if it had material *suppositio*, it would supposit for itself and not for man.

⟨Arguments against Thesis 2⟩

It was said in ⟨2⟩ that spoken or written terms signify things distinct from themselves not naturally but arbitrarily.

⟨2.1⟩ I express the term 'Socrates', which now exists for the first time, signifying Socrates to you. Then if that term 'Socrates' signifies arbitrarily, it does so either because you want it to signify in that way or because it signifies as a consequence of imposition. Not in the first way, *ex hypothesi*; therefore in the second. In that case there is this argument to the contrary. This term does not signify by a present imposition, nor by a past imposition; therefore it does not signify by imposition. The inference is good. And it is clear that this term does not signify by a present imposition, because, *ex hypothesi*, it is not now being imposed for the purpose of signifying. Nor does it signify by a past imposition, because it was not previously imposed for the purpose of signifying since it exists now for the first time and never existed before.

⟨2.2⟩ The first imposer did not know the term 'Socrates', but what he did not know he did not impose for the purpose of signifying; therefore he never imposed the term 'Socrates' for the purpose of signifying. Consequently it does not signify by a past imposition.

⟨2.3⟩ If the term 'Socrates' signifies by a past imposition, then that former imposition was the cause of the signification of this term 'Socrates', which exists now for the first time; therefore this signification is an effect of that cause. But cause and effect are correlatives, and correlatives must exist at one and the same time; therefore that first imposition and the signification of this term 'Socrates' existed at one and the same time. But

est contra casum, eo quod iste terminus 'Sortes' non prius fuit nec eius significatio.

⟨2.4⟩ Quarto imponere terminum ad significandum est intentionem termini cum intentione rei totiens ad invicem referre quousque intentio termini intentionem rei ad memoriam reducat. Sed neque primus impositor neque aliquis alius habuit intentionem huius termini 'Sortes' cum intentione rei. Igitur non significat ex impositione, quod erat probandum.

⟨2.1R⟩ Ad ista respondetur, ad primum dicitur concedendo quod iste terminus 'Sortes' significat ex impositione quae fuit. Et tunc ad argumentum:

> Non prius imponebatur ad significandum; igitur non significat ex impositione quae fuit,

nego consequentiam. Quia licet iste terminus 'Sortes' non fuerit impositus ad significandum, sufficit quod sibi consimilis imponebatur ad significandum.

⟨2.2R⟩ Ad secundum respondetur eodem modo, negando consequentiam ultimam. Quia licet primus instituens non cognovit istum terminum 'Sortes', nunc primo existentem, sufficit quod cognovit sibi similem quem imposuit ad significandum, volendo quod quilibet terminus futurus sibi consimilis eodem modo significet.

⟨2.3R⟩ Ad tertium dicitur concedendo totum quousque dicitur quod relativa semper debent esse simul. Unde prius et posterius sunt relativa, et tamen non oportet quod sint simul, non enim bene dicitur quod prius et posterius simul sunt. Similiter nego quod causa et causatum debeant esse simul. Unde pater qui mortuus iam est viginti annis dicitur causa sui filii iam existentis, et tamen ipse pater et filius non simul sunt.

⟨2.4R⟩ Ad quartum respondetur ut prius, quod licet primus instituens non habuit intentionem huius termini 'Sortes' cum intentione rei, sufficit quod habuit intentionem unius consimilis. Quare, etc.

Contra illud quod tertio dicebatur, videlicet quod termini mentales significant res a se distinctas naturaliter ex quadam (6ra M) convenientia vel similitudine, arguitur sic.

⟨3.1⟩ Nam dato isto, sequitur quod ista intentio *homo* potius deberet

---

4 intentione termini totiens *M*   17 cognoverit *E*   30 Contra id quod *E*
31–2 convenientia et similitudine *E*

that is contrary to the hypothesis, because neither this term 'Socrates' nor its signification existed previously.

⟨2.4⟩ To impose a term for the purpose of signifying is to relate the intention of the term and the intention of the thing to one another so often that the intention of the term recalls the intention of the thing to memory. But neither the first imposer nor any other had the intention of this term 'Socrates' together with the intention of the thing. Therefore it does not signify by imposition, which was to be proved.

⟨*Replies to the Arguments against 2*⟩

⟨2.1R⟩ I say that this term 'Socrates' does signify by a past imposition. As for the argument ‑

> It was not previously imposed for the purpose of signifying; therefore it does not signify by a past imposition,

I reject the inference. For although this term 'Socrates' was not imposed for the purpose of signifying, it suffices that one equiform to it was imposed for the purpose of signifying.

⟨2.2R⟩ I reply to the second in the same way, by rejecting the final inference. For although the first institutor did not know this term 'Socrates', which exists now for the first time, it suffices that he knew one equiform to it which he did impose for the purpose of signifying, intending that each future term equiform to it would signify in the same way.

⟨2.3R⟩ I grant everything up to the point at which it is said that correlatives must exist at one and the same time. The earlier and the later, for instance, are correlatives, and yet they must not exist at one and the same time, for it would be incorrect to say that the earlier and the later exist at one and the same time. Likewise I deny that the cause and the effect must exist at the same time. For example, a father who has been dead now for twenty years is said to be the cause of his son, who now exists, although the father and the son do not exist at one and the same time.

⟨2.4R⟩ I reply to the fourth as I have replied before, by saying that although the first institutor did not have the intention of this term 'Socrates' together with the intention of the thing, it suffices that he had the intention of one just like it. Therefore, etc.

⟨*Arguments against Thesis 3*⟩

One argues in the following way against what was said in ⟨3⟩—viz., that mental terms signify things distinct from themselves naturally because of a certain association or resemblance.

⟨3.1⟩ If this is granted, it follows that the intention *man* ought to signify

F

significare intentiones alias a se quam hominem. Probatur: Nam ista intentio *homo* significat hominem ex quadam convenientia et similitudine, sed maior est similitudo inter istam intentionem et quamcumque aliam quam inter istam et hominem; igitur, etc.

5 ⟨3.2⟩ Secundo sic arguitur. Maior est convenientia inter hominem et asinum vel inter Sortem et Platonem quam est inter intentionem hominis et hominem, vel inter intentionem Sortis et Sortem. Sed asinus non significat hominem, nec Sortes significat Platonem; ergo a fortiori nec talis intentio *homo*.

10 ⟨3.3⟩ Tertio iste terminus ⟨mentalis⟩ *chimaera* significat chimaeram, et non propter aliquam similitudinem istius intentionis ad chimaeram; igitur non quaelibet intentio talis significat solum propter similitudinem talem ad suum significatum. Consequentia patet cum maiori. Et maior arguitur, nam inter istam intentionem et chimaeram non est similitudo ex quo 15 chimaera non est, nec potest esse.

⟨3.4⟩ Quarto ista intentio *homo* significat quemlibet hominem, praesentem, praeteritum, et futurum, et hoc naturaliter et non propter aliquam similitudinem inter istam intentionem et omnem hominem, praesentem praeteritum, et futurum, cum nec (5rb E) talis sit. Igitur, etc.

20 ⟨3.5⟩ Quinto probatur quod nulla intentio in anima significat naturaliter, sed solum ad placitum. Nam ista intentio *homo* potest significare rem distinctam ab homine non significando hominem; ergo, etc. Consequentia patet, et antecedens probatur. Et pono quod tu componas illam propositionem in mente tua:

25 A *est intentio*.

Sit *A* intentio hominis. Tunc arguitur sic: *A* prius significavit hominem, et iam significat aliquid non significando hominem; igitur, etc. Consequentia patet cum maiori, et minor arguitur sic. Ista propositio est vera:

A *est intentio*,

30 et est affirmativa de praesenti; igitur res significata per subiectum est res significata per praedicatum. Sed nihil quod est homo est res significata per praedicatum, quia tunc propositio foret impossibilis, non enim est possibile quod aliquis homo sit intentio. Igitur sequitur quod nihil quod est homo significatur per subiectum, quod est intentum.

35 ⟨3.1R⟩ Ad haec respondetur, ad primum negando quod maior est convenientia inter istam intentionem *homo* et unam aliam intentionem quam

---

5 arguitur *om. E*   6 est *om. E*   8 significat *om. M*   9 *homo om. M*   11 propter aliam similitudinem *M*   17 praeteritum *om. E*   19 praeteritum *om. E*   nec illa talis *M*   23-4 illam intentionem in *M et E*   28 sic *om. E*   34 significetur *E*

intentions other than itself rather than man. Proof: The intention *man* signifies man because of a certain association and resemblance, but the resemblance between this intention and any other intention is greater than the resemblance between it and man; therefore, etc.

⟨3.2⟩ The association between a man and a donkey or between Socrates and Plato is greater that the association between the intention of man and man or between the intention of Socrates and Socrates. But a donkey does not signify man, nor does Socrates signify Plato. Therefore *a fortiori* neither does the intention *man*.

⟨3.3⟩ The mental term *chimera* signifies a chimera, and not because of any resemblance of that intention to a chimera; therefore not every such intention signifies only because of such a resemblance to its significatum. The inference is obvious, along with the major premiss. The following argument supports the minor premiss. There is no resemblance between that intention and a chimera because there is no chimera, nor can there be one.

⟨3.4⟩ The intention *man* signifies each man, present, past, and future, and it does so naturally and not because of any resemblance between that intention and every man, present, past, and future, because there is none. Therefore, etc.

⟨3.5⟩ There is a proof that no intention in the mind signifies naturally, but only arbitrarily. For the intention *man* can signify a thing distinct from man while not signifying man; therefore, etc. The inference is obvious, and the antecedent is proved in the following way. Suppose that in your mind you are compounding the proposition

A *is an intention.*

Let *A* be the intention of man. Then: *A* used to signify man, and now it signifies something while not signifying man; therefore, etc. This inference is obvious, along with the major premiss. The following argument supports the minor premiss. The proposition

A *is an intention*

is true, and it is a present-tense affirmative; therefore the thing signified by the subject is the thing signified by the predicate. But nothing that is man is a thing signified by the predicate, since in that case the proposition would be impossible, for it is not possible that *a* man is an intention. It follows, therefore, that nothing that is man is signified by the subject, which is what was intended.

⟨*Replies to the Arguments against Thesis 3*⟩

⟨3.1R⟩ I deny that there is greater association between the intention *man* and another intention than there is between it and man. For there is

inter istam et hominem. Est enim maior convenientia accidentalis inter istam intentionem *homo* et hominem quam inter istam et unam aliam, quia talis intentio *homo* causatur ab homine et non ab aliqua alia intentione.

⟨3.2R⟩ Ad secundum dicitur eodem modo quod duplex est convenientia:
5 una essentialis et alia accidentalis. Modo verum est quod maior est convenientia essentialis inter hominem et asinum, vel inter Sortem et Platonem, quam inter hominem et talem intentionem. Non tamen est maior convenientia accidentalis, ut dictum est. Intentio enim hominis nullo modo posset ab asino causari.

10 ⟨3.3R⟩ Ad tertium dico quod iste terminus ⟨mentalis⟩ *chimaera* significat chimaeram ex quadam convenientia et similitudine. Et tunc ad argumentum:

Inter istam intentionem et chimaeram non est similitudo; igitur, etc.,

nego consequentiam. Quia licet iste terminus ⟨mentalis⟩ *chimaera* non
15 significet chimaeram ex convenientia et similitudine quae est, sufficit quod significet chimaeram ex convenientia et similitudine ⟨quae fuerit⟩ si esset. Et ratio quia iste terminus ⟨mentalis⟩ significat naturaliter quando directe facit rem cuius est similitudo concipi, et haec est ex convenientia accidentali sui ad talem rem si esset. Ideo non sequitur:

20 Antichristus vel chimaera non est; igitur nulla intentio talis est vel non significat ex aliqua convenientia.

⟨3.4R⟩ Ad quartum respondetur eodem modo.

⟨3.5R⟩ Ad quintum nego quod aliqua intentio in anima significet ad placitum, sumendo 'ad placitum' contra naturam. Et tunc ad argumentum,
25 admitto casum, (6ʳᵇ M) et dico quod *A* ita bene significat hominem sicut prius significavit. Et ulterius nego istam propositionem:

A est intentio

sicut istam:

Homo est intentio,

30 eo quod ipsa significat hominem esse intentionem vel terminum, quod est impossibile. Et quod ista sic significet patet ex eo quod subiectum continue stat personaliter. Et si arguitur quod per idem deberet negare istam:

Homo est species,

quae tamen ab omnibus conceditur, respondetur concedendo conclusionem.
35 Unde numquam talis terminus potest supponere materialiter vel simpliciter nisi ipsum praecedit signum materialitatis, puta 'ly', vel aliquod

---

1 et *om.* M 3 et *om.* E 5 una accidentalis et alia essentialis M 5–6 convenientia est E 7 inter talem intentionem et hominem M 15 chimaeram quae ex E 17 iste *om.* M 18 est (2) *om.* M 20 nulla est talis intentio vel M 21 aliqua *om.* E 35 materialitatis E 36 materialiter E; materialitive M

greater accidental association between the intention *man* and man than between it and another intention because the intention *man* is caused by man and not by some other intention.

⟨3.2R⟩ I reply to the second in the same way, by saying that association is of two kinds: one essential and the other accidental. Now it is true that there is a greater essential association between a man and a donkey or between Socrates and Plato than between the intention *man* and man, but, as has been said, the accidental association is not greater. For the intention of man could in no way be caused by a donkey.

⟨3.3R⟩ I say that the mental term *chimera* does signify a chimera because of a certain association and resemblance. As for the argument

> There is no resemblance between that intention and a chimera; there-
> fore, etc.,

I reject the inference. Although the mental term *chimera* does not signify a chimera because of an association and resemblance which is, it is enough that it signifies a chimera because of an association and resemblance which there would be if a chimera existed. The reason is that this mental term signifies naturally whenever it directly causes one to conceive of the thing of which it is the likeness, and this is because of its accidental association with such a thing if it existed. Thus this does not follow:

> Antichrist or a chimera does not exist; therefore either there is no such
> intention or it does not signify because of any association.

⟨3.4R⟩ One replies to the fourth in just the same way.

⟨3.5R⟩ I deny that an intention in the mind signifies arbitraily, taking 'arbitrarily' in the same way as 'contrary to nature'. As for the argument, I accept the hypothesis, and I say that *A* does signify man just as well as it did signify it. Furthermore, I deny the proposition

> *A* is an intention

just as I deny this one:

> Man is an intention,

because it signifies that man is an intention or a term, which is impossible. That it does signify in that way is clear because the subject has personal *suppositio* throughout. And if one argues that by the same token one would have to deny

> Man is a species,

which, however, is granted by everyone, I grant the conclusion. Such a term can never have material or simple *suppositio* unless some sign of materiality precedes it—i.e., 'ly', or something of that sort.[t] But if one

huiusmodi. Si tamen ponitur in casu quod tu componas talem propositionem:

    Ly .*A*. est intentio,

admitto casum et concedo propositionem illam. Et ulterius dico quod *A*
5 significat hominem sicut prius.

    Et tunc ad argumentum:

       Ista propositio est vera; igitur omnis res significata per subiectum est
       res significata per praedicatum,

nego consequentiam. Sed bene sequitur:

10   . . . igitur omnis res pro qua supponit subiectum est res pro qua
       supponit praedicatum,

et hoc est verum in casu isto. Verumtamen negatur si proponitur quod
subiectum supponat pro homine, supponit enim materialiter et per consequens solum pro se vel sibi consimili, etc.

15 Ex praedictis cadunt tria dubia.

    ⟨I⟩ Primum numquid signum non significaret nisi imponeretur ad
significandum.

    ⟨II⟩ Secundum numquid res possunt ita bene significare terminos sicut
econtra.

20   ⟨III⟩ Tertium quare magis imponimus voces et scripta ad significandum
tales res quam alias qualitates ut caliditatem, frigiditatem, albedinem, vel
nigredinem.

    ⟨IR⟩ Pro primo dubio dicitur quod quaedam est impositio facta per signa
quae non sunt dictiones et quaedam per dictiones. Primo modo concedo
25 dubium, quia tunc talis impositio fit per liberam doctrinam vel naturalem
experientiam, ut circulus vel folia ante tabernam, sive latratus canum.
Secundo nego dubium, quia certum est quod iste terminus 'homo' significat
mihi hominem quando non imponitur ad significandum.

    ⟨IR.o⟩ Sed contra istam (5ᵛᵃ E) responsionem arguitur sic, per Aristo-
30 telem quarto *Metaphysicae* et primo *Elenchorum*, quod oportet ante dis-
putationem praesupponere terminorum significationem. Sed hoc non
oporteret si tunc significarent sine impositione.

    4 casum concedendo propositionem *E*   13–14 consequens supponit pro se solum
vel *E*   14 simili *M*   16 non *om. E*   significet *E*   21 qualitates et caliditatem *E*
21-2 frigiditatem et albedinem *M*; albedinem et nigredinem *E*   26 tabernam et
latratus *E*   28 mihi *om. E*   30 decimo *Metaphysicae M*

supposes that it is part of the hypothesis that you are compounding such a proposition as

'*A*' is an intention,

then I accept the hypothesis and grant the proposition as well. In that case, moreover, I say that *A* signifies man as before.

As for the argument

This proposition is true; therefore every thing signified by the subject is a thing signified by the predicate,

I reject the inference. But this follows rightly:

. . . therefore every thing for which the subject supposits is a thing for which the predicate supposits,

and this is true in the case supposed. I deny it, however, if it is claimed that the subject supposits for man, for it has material *suppositio*, and so it supposits only for itself or what is equiform to it.

⟨Three Doubts⟩

These three doubts arise from what has been said so far.

⟨I⟩ Whether a sign would not signify if it had not been imposed for the purpose of signifying.

⟨II⟩ Whether things can signify terms just as well as terms signify things.

⟨III⟩ Why in order to signify things we impose utterances and inscriptions rather than other qualities such as heat, cold, whiteness, or blackness.

⟨Reply to Doubt I⟩

⟨IR⟩ I say that there is one sort of imposition effected in the case of signs that are not words and another in the case of words. As regards the first case, I reply to the doubt affirmatively, for that sort of imposition is effected by means of informal instruction or natural experience—e.g., the hoop or the bush in front of the inn, or the barking of dogs. As regards the second case, I reply negatively, for it is certain that the term 'man' signifies man to me when it is not imposed for the purpose of signifying.[u]

⟨Argument against Reply IR⟩

⟨IR.o⟩ But according to Aristotle in Book IV of the *Metaphysics* [1006[a] 18] and Book I of the *Sophistical Refutations*,[v] it is necessary to presuppose the signification of the terms before a disputation. But that would be unnecessary if they signified then without imposition.

⟨IR.oR⟩ Ad istud dicitur quod Philosophus intendit de terminis ignotis, sicut de '*A*', '*B*', 'ba', 'bau', vel pronominibus ubi nescitur quid demonstratur. Non debent propositiones in quibus ponuntur concedi vel negari aut dubitari quousque respondens certificetur. Ex quo sequitur quod haec
5 propositio non esset concedenda:

Homo est homo

si ly .homo. non esset impositus ad significandum, nec ista:

Hoc est hoc,

eodem demonstrato, nisi certificetur determinate quid demonstratur.
10 ⟨IR.1⟩ Sed contra ista arguitur. Nam dato quod tu scias illum terminum 'homo' non esse impositum ad significandum, tunc tu scis illum nihil significare nisi se. Sed modo verum est quod ipsa vox 'homo' est ipsa vox 'homo'; ergo tu scis istam esse veram in hoc casu.

⟨IR.2⟩ Secundo sic. Si non scis istam propositionem esse veram in isto
15 casu:

Hoc est hoc,

igitur nec eius contradictorium scis esse falsum. Et tunc sequitur istam copulativam esse nescitam a te esse falsam:

Hoc est hoc, et hoc non est hoc,

20 eodem demonstrato. Et similiter sequitur istam disiunctivam:

Hoc est hoc, vel hoc non est hoc

esse nescitam a te esse necessariam, quod non est verum.

⟨IR.3⟩ Tertio arguitur contra illud quod dicebatur, quod illi termini '*A*' vel '*B*', 'ba' vel 'bau', sunt termini ignoti, nam quilibet istorum significat
25 ad placitum sicut iste terminus 'homo'. Igitur qua ratione iste terminus 'homo' non est terminus ignotus, per idem nec illi. Consequentia patet, et antecedens probatur, nam ista est (6va M) propositio:

Ly .ba. est .ba.,

et est vera. Igitur habet subiectum, et non nisi ly .ba. Igitur ly .ba. est
30 subiectum. Et per consequens reddit suppositum verbo personali. Sed omne quod reddit suppositum verbo personali est nomen. Ergo ly .ba.

---

1 Philosophus intelligit de *M*   3 ponitur *E*   5 propositio *om. M*
6 Homo est animal *E*   7 in suppositione personali si *E*   9 certificarem *M*
demonstretur *E*   23 arguitur quod illud *M*   29 et non nisi ly .ba. *om. M*

⟨*Reply to Argument IR.0*⟩

⟨IR.0R⟩ I maintain that the Philosopher is referring to terms that would not be recognized, such as '*A*', '*B*', 'ba','bau', or to pronouns in cases in which one does not know what is being indicated. Propositions in which such terms are used must not be granted or denied or doubted until the respondent has the information. It follows from this that the proposition

Man is man

ought not to be granted if 'man' has not been imposed for the purpose of signifying, nor the proposition

This is this,

where one and the same thing is being indicated, unless one is determinately informed as to what is being indicated.

⟨*Arguments against Replies IR and IR.0R*⟩

⟨IR.1⟩ Suppose that you know that the term 'man' has not been imposed for the purpose of signifying. In that case you know that it signifies nothing besides itself. But even then it is true that the utterance 'man' is the utterance 'man'. Therefore on that hypothesis you do know that

Man is man

is true.

⟨IR.2⟩ If on that hypothesis you do not know that the proposition

This is this

is true, then neither do you know that its contradictory is false. And in that case it follows that the conjunctive proposition

This is this, and this is not this,

where one and the same thing has been indicated, is not known by you to be false. It follows likewise that the disjunctive proposition

This is this, or this is not this

is not known by you to be necessary. But that is not true.

⟨IR.3⟩ There is an argument against the claim that the terms '*A*', '*B*', 'ba', or 'bau' are unrecognized terms, for each of them signifies arbitrarily just as does the term 'man'. Therefore for the same reason as the term 'man' is not an unrecognized term, neither are they. The inference is obvious, and the antecedent is proved in the following way.

'Ba' is 'ba'

is a proposition and is true. Therefore it has a subject, and the only possibility is 'ba'. Therefore 'ba' is the subject. Consequently it appropriates a personal verb to its suppositum.[w] But anything that appropriates a personal verb to its suppositum is a name. Therefore 'ba' is a name, and

est nomen, et per consequens est vox significativa ad placitum. Consequentia patet ex definitione nominis posita ab Aristotele in capitulo de
nomine.

⟨IR.1R⟩ Ad ista respondetur, ad primum quod si scirem ly .est. ver-
5 baliter significare atque extremorum esse unitivum, concederem istam:

Homo est homo

sicut istam:

A est B;

non tamen personaliter sed materialiter solum. Ubi tamen non haberem
10 notitiam nisi ad placitum illius verbi 'est' sicut nec illius termini 'homo' non
concederem illam orationem, nec dicerem ipsam esse veram vel falsam
sicut si tu mihi proponeres 'A', 'B', 'C' sine ulteriori compositione.

⟨IR.2R⟩ Ad secundum dico quod non intelligo illam:

Hoc est hoc

15 nec suum contradictorium. Et ulterius nego consequentiam in qua infertur
quod nec intelligo copulativam nec disiunctivam compositam ex illis·
Sicut non sequitur:

Non intelligo litteras; ergo non intelligo dictiones ex eis compositas.

⟨IR.3R⟩ Ad tertium dico quod ly .ba. et similia sunt termini ignoti, nec
20 significant ad placitum. Et tunc ad argumentum quando infertur quod ly
.ba. est vox significativa quia est nomen, respondetur quod 'nomen' accipitur
tripliciter: communiter, proprie, et magis proprie.

Communiter, nomen potest esse id quod potest reddere suppositum
verbo personali, sive accipiatur materialiter sive significative. Et sic omnis
25 vox potest esse nomen, ut coniunctio, praepositio, interiectio, 'A' vel 'B',
'ba' vel 'bu'.

Alio modo 'nomen' accipitur proprie pro eo quod significative positum
reddit suppositum verbo personali. Et illo modo sycategoremata non sunt
nomina, nec esse possunt sine nova impositione.

30 Tertio modo accipitur 'nomen' magis proprie pro voce significative
sumpta quae potest reddere suppositum verbo et non est nomen obliquum
nec infinitum nec est pars alicuius nominis. Et illa est strictissima acceptio
nominis sicut sumit Philosophus primo *Peri Hermeneias*.

5 estremarem *M*   10 nisi *om. M*   16 copulativam vel disiunctivam *M*
23 esse illud quod *M*   26 'bau' vel 'bu' *E*   28 personali *om. M*   30 magis
om. M

consequently it is an arbitrarily significant utterance. This inference is clear on the basis of the definition of a name given by Aristotle in the chapter on the name ⟨*De interpretatione*, Chapter 2, 16ᵃ19⟩.

⟨*Replies to these Arguments*⟩

⟨IR.1R⟩ If I knew that 'is' was signifying as a verb and was unifying the extremes, I would grant

Man is man

just as I would grant

A is *B*;

not, however, ⟨if the extremes are taken to have⟩ personal *suppositio*, but only ⟨if they are taken to have⟩ material *suppositio*. But in case I had no cognition except arbitrarily of the verb 'is', just as of the term 'man', I would not grant that expression, nor would I say that it was true or false any more than if you were to say to me '*ABC*', without any further composition.

⟨IR.2R⟩ I say that I do not understand either

This is this

or its contradictory. Furthermore, I reject the inference in which it is inferred that I understand neither the conjunctive nor the disjunctive proposition composed of this proposition and its contradictory. In the same way this does not follow:

I do not understand the letters; therefore I do not understand the words composed of them.

⟨IR.3R⟩ I maintain that 'ba' and the like are unrecognized terms and do not signify arbitrarily. As for the argument in which it is inferred that 'ba' is a significant utterance because it is a name, my reply is that 'name' is taken in three ways: broadly, strictly, and more strictly.

Broadly, a name can be that which appropriates a personal verb to its suppositum, whether it is taken materially or significantly. And in this way any utterance can be a name—e.g., a conjunction, a preposition, an interjection, '*A*' or '*B*', 'ba' or 'bu'.

In the second way 'name' is taken strictly for that which when used significantly appropriates a personal verb to a suppositum. In this way syncategorematic words are not names, nor can they be names without a new imposition.

In the third way 'name' is taken more strictly for an utterance taken significantly which can appropriate a verb to a suppositum and is not an oblique or an infinite name or part of any name. And this is the strictest interpretation of 'name' as the Philosopher uses it in *De interpretatione* ⟨Chapter 2, *passim*⟩.

Et per hoc patet intentio ad argumentum quod ista consequentia non valet:

Hoc est nomen; igitur hoc est vox significativa ad placitum

nisi 'nomen' strictissime accipiatur. Qualiter non potest accipi in huiusmodi
5 propositionibus:

Ly .ba. est vox,

Ly .et. est coniunctio,

Ly .ad. est praepositio,

Ly .omnis. est signum universale,

10 et sic de infinitis. Ideo potest concedi quod aliqui termini supponunt materialiter qui numquam fuerunt impositi ad significandum. Patet per praedicta.

⟨IIR⟩ Ad secundum dubium cum quaeritur utrum res possint ita bene significare terminos sicut econtra, respondeo concedendo illud. Quia res
15 apprehensae aliquando ita faciunt venire intellectum ad cognitionem et re-ducunt ita terminos ad memoriam, sicut termini apprehensi reducunt res quas significant ad memoriam. Consequentia tenet, et antecedens pro-batur. Quia cum video Sortem vel Platonem quem scio significari per istum terminum 'Sortes' vel 'Plato', ita bene intellectus meus fertur in ipsum
20 terminum 'Sortes' vel 'Plato', sicut quando audio nominari istum terminum 'Sortes' vel 'Plato' ratione cuius intellectus fertur in (5vb E) cognitionem ipsius Sortis vel Platonis.

Et si quaeritur, ex quo res significant ipsos terminos, vel significant naturaliter vel ad placitum, dico quod res significatae per terminos mentales
25 significant terminos mentales naturaliter, sed res significatae per terminos ad placitum institutos significant ipsos terminos ad placitum. Non tamen quod res sint impositae ad significandum ipsos terminos quemadmodum ipsi impositi sunt ad significandum tales res. Sed ideo quia sicut fuit ad placitum tales terminos significare tales res, ita erit ad placitum tales res
30 (6vb M) significare tales terminos. Ideo differunt termini et res inter modos significandi ipsorum, quia terminus significat rem ut est signum rei, res vero terminum prout terminus est signum eiusdem rei. Et ratio quia res non sunt aptae natae pro terminis in propositione supponere, sed bene econtra, ideo non sunt signa terminorum saltim suppositiva.

10 supponant E   15 in cognitionem M

In the light of this discussion my intention as regards the argument is clear. The inference

This is a name; therefore it is an arbitrarily significant utterance

it not acceptable unless 'name' is taken most strictly. But it cannot be taken in that way in such propositions as

'Ba' is an utterance,
'And' is a conjunction,
'To' is a preposition,
'Every' is a universal sign,

and so on as regards infinitely many. Thus it can be granted that some terms that were never imposed for the purpose of signifying do have material *suppositio*. This is clear from the foregoing remarks.

⟨*Reply to Doubt II*⟩

⟨IIR⟩ I reply to the second doubt, in which it is asked whether things could signify terms just as well as terms signify things, by granting that they could. For things when apprehended sometimes make the understanding come to cognition and recall terms to memory just as terms when apprehended recall to memory the things they signify. The inference holds good, and the antecedent is proved in the following way. When I see Socrates or Plato, whom I know to be signified by the term 'Socrates' or 'Plato', my understanding is brought to the term 'Socrates' or 'Plato', just as when I hear the term 'Socrates' or 'Plato' named my understanding is brought to a cognition of Socrates or of Plato himself.

If one asks, 'Since things do signify terms themselves, do they signify naturally or arbitrarily?', I reply that things signified by mental terms signify mental terms naturally, but things signified by terms arbitrarily instituted signify those terms arbitrarily. But the things are not imposed for the purpose of signifying those terms in the way in which they themselves are imposed for the purpose of signifying such things. Instead, just as it was arbitrary that such terms signify such things, so will it be arbitrary that such things signify such terms. Thus terms and things differ as regards their modes of signifying, for a term signifies a thing inasmuch as it is a sign of the thing, but a thing signifies a term according as the term is a sign of that very thing. But because things are not suited by nature to supposit for terms in a proposition, but rather vice versa, they are not, at any rate, the sort of signs that supposit for terms.

⟨IIIR⟩ Ad tertium dubium, cum quaeritur quare magis imposimus voces et scripta ad significandum res quam alias qualitates, respondeo quod hoc non est magis naturale ipsis vocibus vel scriptis quam alias qualitatibus, quia similes conceptus posset elicere sibi anima per alias qualitates sicut per

5 scripta vel voces. Videmus enim religiosos servantes silentium innuere silentium cum signis, petere panem, vinum, et alia solummodo cum signis. Et si ex hoc concluditur quod possemus cum baculis syllogizare et cum lapidibus concludere et satis manifeste tractare cum propositionibus scitis et necessariis, conceditur conclusio. Sed quia tales res non sunt ita faciliter

10 per nos operabiles non utimur illis in arguendo sicut scriptis vel vocibus, quae voluntatibus nostris facilius subiugantur. Ideo Philosophus primo *Elenchorum* dicebat quod res ad disputationes ferre non possumus, propter hoc utimur terminis pro rebus. Et licet per signa facta cum digitis vel huiusmodi innuere possumus, tamen quia non sunt apud nos tam com-

15 muniter nota et quia multotiens similia apud bene noscentem non significat nisi pro tempore et loco, ideo non sunt tam digna dici propositiones vel harum partes, sicut voces vel scripta. Quare, etc.

⟨IV⟩ Ex his forte posset oriri aliud dubium: numquid terminus de novo impositus ad significandum dum cessat eius significatio significet illud quod

20 prius vel aliud, aut de novo debeat imponi ad significandum, sicut patet in arte obligatoria.

⟨IVR⟩ Ad istud dicitur quod non oportet, eo quod licet non quilibet terminus actu significet, tamen est significativus. Et isto modo conceditur quod in libro clauso sunt multa vera, non quia actu significent, sed quia

25 sunt significativa veri cum fuerint apprehensa, et hoc sine nova impositione. Aliter enim sequitur quod tu verificares Evangelium et totam Sacram Scripturam quandocumque tu velles, et hoc de novo, solummodo aperiendo talem librum clausum et ibidem considerando de scriptis. Et consequenter claudendo illum librum destrueres totam Sacram Scripturam et Evan-

30 gelicam veritatem, quod minus bene sonat. Unde secundum communem

---

6 solummodo *om.* M   7 concludere E   8 tractari M *et* E   9 con-
cederetur E   sunt tam faciliter M   11 faciliter M   12 possunt M
14 apud omnes tam M   23 significet, cum est M   24 multa verba, M

⟨*Reply to Doubt III*⟩

⟨IIIR⟩ I reply to the third doubt, in which one asks why in order to signify things we impose utterances and inscriptions rather than other qualities, by observing that it is not more natural to do so with utterances and inscriptions than with other qualities, for similar concepts could be elicited in the mind by means of other qualities just as by means of inscriptions or utterances. We see that those religious who maintain silence communicate silently with signs, that they ask for bread, wine, and other things with signs only. If one concludes from this that we could syllogize with sticks and draw conclusions with stones and ⟨in such fashion⟩ deal clearly enough with known and necessary propositions, I grant the conclusion. But because we cannot operate so readily with such things as with inscriptions and utterances, which are more easily subjugated to our wills, we do not make use of them in arguing. Thus the Philosopher said in *Sophistical Refutations*, Book I ⟨Chapter 1, 165ᵃ6⟩, that we cannot bring the things themselves to a disputation, and as a result we use terms for the things. And although we can communicate by means of signs made with the fingers or something of that sort, nevertheless because they are not so generally known among us and because things of that sort often signify only at a certain time and place even to one who knows them well, they are not so worthy to be called propositions or parts of propositions as are utterances or inscriptions. Therefore, etc.

⟨*A Fourth Doubt*⟩

⟨IV⟩ Another doubt may perhaps arise from these considerations—viz., whether a term newly imposed for the purpose of signifying signifies what it previously signified or something else while its signification is inactive, or must be newly imposed for the purpose of signifying, as appears in the *ars obligatoria.*ˣ

⟨*Reply to Doubt IV*⟩

⟨IVR⟩ It need not be newly imposed, for a term is significant even while it is not actually signifying. On this basis it is granted that there are many truths in a closed book—not because they are actually signifying, but because they will be significant of what is true when they have been apprehended, and without any new imposition. Otherwise it follows that you make the Gospel and the whole of Sacred Scripture true whenever you wish, and anew, simply by opening such a closed book and considering the things written down in it. By closing that book you would consequently destroy the whole of Sacred Scripture and the Gospel truth, which sounds

usum loquentium quoddam vocatur actualiter verum, quoddam potentialiter verum. Actualiter verum voco propositionem per se actualiter significantem primarie verum, ut

> Homo est animal,

5 posito quod illa alicui sic significet. Sed potentialiter verum non voco simpliciter quod potest esse verum, sed scriptum, vocale, vel mentale non actualiter apprehensum, quod licet sit nunc non significans tamen significabit in posterum absque nova impositione vel est aptum natum significare.

Ostenso quomodo termini significant, et quomodo quidam significant 10 naturaliter, quidam ad placitum, consequenter est videndum quid tales termini significant ad placitum vel naturaliter, in qua materia sunt tres opiniones.

⟨1⟩ Quarum prima ponit quod nihil significat hominem nisi iste terminus 'homo', nec aequivalens. Nec iste terminus 'homo' significat aliquod 15 inferius, ut istum hominem, nec aliquod superius, ut animal vel corpus. Nec sequitur:

> Iste terminus 'homo' significat hominem, et omnis homo est animal;
>   igitur significat animal,

cum ibidem arguatur ab (6ᵃ E) inferiori ad suum superius cum hoc verbo 20 'significat'.

⟨2⟩ Secunda positio in hac materia est quod terminus inferior significat suum per se superius et nullum inferius. Ideo iste terminus 'homo' significat animal, corpus, et similia, non tamen totum, nec aliquod per accidens superius, nec aliquod inferius, quia nec istum hominem, nec istum 25 hominem.

(Et concordant istae duae opiniones in hoc, quia utraque ponit hoc verbum 'significat' facere sophisma, tam cum complexis quam cum incomplexis.)

⟨3⟩ Tertia opinio dicit quod iste terminus 'homo' (7ᵃ M) significat hominem, animal, corpus, substantiam, istum hominem, et istum, et 30 omnem hominem imaginabilem, praeteritum, praesentem, et futurum, non faciendo sophisma cum incomplexis.

⟨1.1⟩ Contra primam opinionem arguitur sic. Nam data ista, sequitur quod aliquis terminus aliquem hominem significat qui non significat aliquem hominem, quod probatur sic. Et capio istum terminum 'iste homo'. 35 Tunc iste terminus 'iste homo' significat istum hominem; igitur istum hominem iste terminus 'homo' significat. Consequentia tenet quia in singularibus non refert praeponere vel postponere terminum demonstrativum. Et tunc ultra, iste terminus istum hominem significat, sed iste

---

1 vocatur actu verum E   8 De significatione terminorum naturaliter et ad placitum. *add. E*   9 Ostenso qualiter termini E   10 videndum quomodo tales E 11 termini *om. M*   15 vel *om. M*   17 'homo' *om. M*   23-4 per actus superius *M*   29 hominem *om. E*   34 hominem, et probatur M   38-p. 82. 1 est ille homo aliquis M

less good. Thus in accordance with ordinary usage one thing is called actually true, another potentially true. A thing actually true is what I call a proposition actually signifying primarily *per se* what is true—e.g.,

A man is an animal,

provided that this is signifying in that way to someone. But a thing potentially true is what I call not simply what can be true, but rather something written, spoken, or mental not actually being apprehended, which although it is not now signifying either will signify hereafter without any new imposition or is naturally suited to signify.

⟨Three Opinions regarding the Significata of Terms⟩

Now that we have seen how terms signify, and how some signify naturally and others arbitrarily, the next thing is to see what such terms signify, whether arbitrarily or naturally. There are three opinions regarding this matter.

⟨1⟩ Nothing signifies man except the term 'man' itself, and not any equivalent. Nor does the term 'man' signify anything inferior ⟨to man⟩, such as this man, or anything superior, such as animal, or body. Nor does this follow:

The term 'man' signifies man, and every man is an animal; therefore it signifies animal,

since the argument proceeds from the inferior to its superior with the term 'signifies'.

⟨2⟩ An inferior term does signify what is *per se* superior to it, but no inferior. Thus the term 'man' signifies animal, body, and the like, but it does not signify whole, or anthing *per accidens* superior to it. Nor does it signify anything inferior, for it signifies neither this man nor that man.

(Opinions ⟨1⟩ and ⟨2⟩ agree in maintaining that 'signifies' gives rise to a sophisma in connection with complex as well as with noncomplex things.ʸ)

⟨3⟩ The term 'man' signifies man, animal, body, substance, this man, that man, and every man imaginable, past, present, and future, without giving rise to a sophisma in connection with noncomplex things.

⟨Arguments against Opinion 1⟩

⟨1.1⟩ If this opinion is granted, it follows that a term that does not signify some man does signify some man. This is proved in the following way. Take the term 'this man'. Now the term 'this man' signifies this man; therefore ⟨it is⟩ this man the term '⟨this⟩ man' signifies. The inference holds good because in singular propositions it makes no difference whether the demonstrative term is placed before or placed after ⟨the main verb⟩.ᶻ

homo est aliquis homo; igitur iste terminus aliquem hominem significat·
Et tamen iste terminus 'iste homo' non significat aliquem hominem, quia
nullus terminus significat aliquem hominem nisi iste terminus 'aliquis
homo', per positionem.

5 ⟨1.2⟩ Secundo sequitur ex ista propositione quod nulla propositio est
vera nec falsa, nec necessaria nec impossibilis, quorum quodlibet est
falsum. Consequentia probatur, nam si aliqua propositio esset vera, ipsa
significat praecise sicut est vel verum. Et si aliqua esset falsa, ipsa significaret aliter quam est vel falsum. Sed secundum opinionem nihil significat
10 praecise sicut est vel verum nisi iste terminus 'praecise sicut est' vel iste
terminus 'verum'; igitur . . . Similiter, nihil significat aliter quam est vel
falsum nisi iste terminus 'aliter quam est', vel iste terminus 'falsum'.

⟨1.3⟩ Tertio arguitur sic. Sequitur formaliter:
Homo currit; ergo animal currit.

15 Sed in omni consequentia bona et formali consequens est de intellectu
antecedentis, et quicquid est de intellectu antecedentis significatur per
illud antecedens, cum ad intelligere sequatur significare. Igitur animal
currere significatur per antecedens. Et per consequens illud antecedens
Homo currit

20 significat animal currere. Et ita inferius significat suum superius, quod
negat positio.

⟨1.4⟩ Item qualitercumque intelligitur per istum terminum 'homo' ita
iste terminus significat. Sed non stat te intelligere per illum terminum
'homo' hominem non intelligendo animal. Ergo si iste terminus 'homo'
25 significat tibi hominem significat etiam animal. Consequentia patet cum
maiori. Et minor arguitur, quia si intelligis hominem per istum terminum
'homo', ergo homo repraesentatur intellectui; igitur si intelligis hominem,
intelligis animal. Item si intelligis hominem non intelligendo animal, igitur
intelligis hominem non intelligendo animal rationale. Consequentia patet,
30 quia negato superiori negatur et inferius. Et tunc ex consequenti sequatur
quod intelligis hominem non intelligendo hominem, consequens impossibile.

⟨1.5⟩ Quinto Aristoteles primo *Peri Hermeneias* dicit quod oratio est vox
cuius partium aliquid est significativum separatim, et ponit exemplum:
35 'Dico autem ut "homo" significat.' Ergo eadem rationie significat aliquem
hominem et eadem ratione corpus et animal, quod negat positio.

---

2 terminus 'homo' non *M*   33 Quinto per Aristotelem primo *E*   dicitur *E*
35 aliquid . . . significat *om. E*   35-6 Ergo . . . hominem *om. M*

Furthermore, ⟨it is⟩ this man this term signifies, but this man is some man; therefore ⟨there is⟩ some man this term signifies. And yet the term 'this man' does not signify some man, because, according to this view, no term signifies some man except the term 'some man'.

⟨1.2⟩ It follows from this view that no proposition is true or false, or necessary or impossible—all of which is false. This inference is proved in the following way. If some proposition were true, it would signify just what is the case, or what is true. And if some proposition were false, it would signify otherwise than is the case, or what is false. But according to Opinion ⟨1⟩ nothing signifies just what is the case, or what is true, except the term 'just what is the case' or the term 'what is true'; therefore . . . Similarly, nothing signifies otherwise than is the case, or what is false, except the term 'otherwise than is the case' or the term 'what is false'.

⟨1.3⟩ This follows formally:

A man is running; therefore an animal is running.

But in every good formal inference the consequent is part of what is understood in the antecedent, and whatever is part of what is understood in the antecedent is signified by the antecedent, since signifying follows understanding. Therefore that an animal is running is signified by that antecedent. Consequently the antecedent

A man is running

signifies that an animal is running. Thus an inferior signifies its superior, which this view denies.

⟨1.4⟩ The term 'man' signifies in whatever way one understands by means of the term. But it is not consistent that you understand man by the term 'man' without understanding animal. Therefore if the term 'man' signifies man to you it signifies animal as well. The inference is obvious, along with the major premiss. The following argument supports the minor premiss. If you understand man by the term 'man', then a man is represented to your understanding for that term, and consequently an animal is represented. Therefore if you understand man you understand animal. Again, if you understand man without understanding animal, then you understand man without understanding rational animal. This inference is obvious, because when the superior is negated, so is the inferior. And in that case it follows from the consequent that you understand man without understanding man, an impossible consequent.

⟨1.5⟩ In *De interpretatione* ⟨Chapter 4, 16ᵇ26⟩ Aristotle says that a sentence is an utterance some parts of which are separately significant, and he gives an example. 'But I say that "man" signifies something.' Therefore by the same reasoning it signifies some man, and by the same reasoning a body and an animal, which this view denies.

⟨1.6⟩ Sexto arguitur reducendo factorem istius opinionis ad contradictionem. Nam ipse ponit quod hoc verbum 'est' significat esse, et esse
hoc verbum 'est' significat; ergo per idem iste terminus 'homo' significat
hominem, et hominem significat iste terminus 'homo'. Consequentia patet,
5 quia sicut iste terminus 'homo' est terminus mediatus, sic iste terminus
'esse'. Probatur: Ly .esse. est communis pluribus per praedicationem;
igitur est terminus mediatus. Consequentia patet. Et antecedens probatur,
eo quod istae sunt verae praedicationes:

Esse Sortis est esse,
10   Esse Platonis est esse.

⟨1.7⟩ Septimo tota causa cogens illum magistrum ad ponendum talem
propositionem est quia aliter sequeretur quod propositio affirmativa et
necessaria significaret hominem esse asinum, quod sibi videtur inconveniens. Sed pro certo illud non est inconveniens, quod probo sic. Nam haec
15 disiunctiva:

Homo est asinus, vel nullus homo est asinus

est vera et necessaria, et tamen significat hominem esse asinum; igitur . . .
Sed hoc forte dicitur quod ista disiunctiva non significat hominem esse
asinum sed pars eiusdem. Contra: et accipio illam propositionem in voce:

20   A est B,

et suppono quod aliquis concipiat per istam disiunctive, sicut istam dis-
iunctam:

Homo est asinus vel nullus homo est asinus

significat. Tunc sic: ista significat hominem esse asinum, et est vera
25 propositio; igitur . . . Conclusio patet, et minor similiter. Et (6ʳᵇ E) maior
probatur sic. Intelligendo istam intellectus intelligit hominem esse asinum,
et non ratione partis; igitur ratione totius.

⟨1.8⟩ Item signo istam disiunctivam:

Hoc est, vel hoc est,

30 Deo et chimaera demonstratis. Haec significat hoc esse (demonstrando
Deum); igitur a pari significat hoc esse (7ʳᵇ M) (demonstrando chimaeram).
Et est vera propositio; igitur . . . Patet consequentia, et antecedens arguitur
sic. Haec disiunctiva significat hoc esse vel hoc esse (Deo et chimaera
demonstratis). Sed quicquid et qualitercumque est hoc esse vel hoc esse
35 (Deo et chimaera demonstratis), est hoc esse (demonstrando Deum). Igitur
. . . Consequentia patet cum maiori. Et minor probatur quia nihil, nec
aliqualiter nec aliquid, est hoc esse, demonstrando chimaeram.

⟨1.9⟩ Item praecise hoc esse (demonstrando Deum) est praecise hoc esse

2–3 esse iste terminus 'est' E   4–7 'homo' . . . mediatus. om. M   12–13 et negativa significaret M   13–14 videtur et necessaria inconveniens M   21 aliquis
homo concipiat E   disiunctive, arguitur sic: sicut E   21–2 illa disiuncta M;
ista disiuncta E   24 significat hominem esse asinum. Tunc E   25 propositio
om. M   26 sic om. E   29 vel hoc est Deus E   31 igitur apparet a E
32 propositio om. E   36–7 nec aliqua M   38 praecise (2) om. M

⟨1.6⟩ One may argue in a way that reduces the proponent of this opinion to contradiction. For he claims that the verb 'is' signifies being, and ⟨it is⟩ being the verb 'is' signifies; therefore by the same token the term 'man' signifies man, and man ⟨is what⟩ the term 'man' signifies. The inference is obvious, because just as the term 'man' is a mediate term,[a] so is the term 'being'. Proof: 'Being' is common to many things through predication; therefore it is a mediate term. This inference is obvious. And the antecedent is proved, for these are true predications:

The being of Socrates is being,
The being of Plato is being.

⟨1.7⟩ The sole reason why this master is compelled to maintain such a view is that otherwise it would follow that an affirmative necessary proposition would signify that a man is a donkey, which seems to him absurd. But it certainly is not absurd, as I shall prove. The disjunctive proposition

A man is a donkey, or no man is a donkey

is true and necessary, but it signifies that a man is a donkey; therefore . . . But perhaps someone will say that it is not this disjunctive proposition but a part of it that signifies that a man is a donkey. On the contrary, I take the spoken proposition

A is B,

and I suppose that by means of this someone thinks disjunctively, as if it signifies the disjunctive proposition

A man is a donkey, or no man is a donkey.

Then: This ⟨'A is B'⟩ signifies that a man is a donkey, and it is a true proposition; therefore . . . The conclusion is obvious, and so is the minor premiss. The major premiss is proved in the following way. In understanding this proposition the understanding understands that a man is a donkey, and not because of some part of it; therefore because of the whole.

⟨1.8⟩ Take the disjunctive proposition

This is, or this is,

indicating God and a chimera. It signifies that this is (indicating God); therefore by parity of reasoning it signifies that this is (indicating a chimera). And it is a true proposition; therefore . . . The inference is obvious, and the following argument supports the antecedent. That disjunctive proposition signifies that this is or this is (indicating God and a chimera). But whatever and however it is that this is or this is (indicating God and a chimera), so is it that this is (indicating God). Therefore . . . This inference is obvious, along with the major premiss. And the minor premiss is proved because it is nothing, neither anyhow nor anything, that this is (indicating a chimera).

⟨1.9⟩ Nothing more nor less than that this is (indicating God) is nothing

vel hoc esse (demonstrando chimaeram et Deum); igitur qualitercumque est hoc esse vel hoc esse est hoc esse (demonstrando Deum). Consequentia patet: ab exclusiva ad suam universalem de terminis transpositis. Et antecedens patet per exponentes.

5 ⟨1.10⟩ Praeterea aliqua propositio est possibilis quae significat hoc album esse nigrum; igitur pari ratione aliqua est propositio vera et necessaria significans sicut non est. Consequentia tenet, et antecedens probatur. Et capio illam propositionem:

Hoc est nigrum,

10 demonstrando album. Ista est possibilis, iuxta illam positionem, et ista significat hoc album esse nigrum; ergo . . . Consequentia patet, et minor probatur. Haec est propositio affirmativa mere singularis de praesenti cuius subiectum significat hoc album, et copula significat esse, et praedicatum significat nigrum, et tota propositio ista significat praecise iuxta composi-
15 tionem suorum terminorum; igitur tota ista propositio significat hoc album esse nigrum.

⟨1.11⟩ Item haec propositio est necessaria:

Esse est esse

secundum opinionem istius magistri. Sed ipsa significat impossibile.
20 Igitur per idem et quaelibet alia. Consequentia bona, et minor probatur, nam ista propositio est indefinita affirmativa cuius subiectum significat esse Sortis, et copula esse, et praedicatum significat esse Platonis, et tota ista propositio significat iuxta compositionem suorum terminorum; ergo tota ista propositio significat esse Sortis esse esse Platonis, quod est impossibile.
25 Consequentia patet, et maior probatur quia si ly .esse. significat esse, igitur esse significat ly .esse. Consequentia patet per opinionem. Et tunc ultra, esse significat ly .esse., igitur hoc esse significat ly .esse., vel hoc esse, vel sic de singulis.

Et ex his patet falsitas opinionis.

30 Sequitur secunda positio, ponens quod terminus communis significat quodlibet superius per se ad istum et nihil ⟨inferius⟩ nec aliud significat. Contra istam opinionem arguitur per plura media.

---

2 est hoc esse (2) *om. M*   15 ista *om. M*   23 suorum *om. M*   24 **esse**
(3) *om. E*   26 Et *om. E*   29 Et *om. M*   opinionis; igitur etc. *E*   31 **nec**
aliquid significat *M*

more nor less than that this is or this is (indicating a chimera and God); therefore however it is that this is or this is, so is it that this is (indicating God). The inference is obvious: from an exclusive to its universal with the terms transposed. And the antecedent is clear as a consequence of the exponents.[b]

⟨1.10⟩ Besides, there is a possible proposition that signifies that this white thing is black; therefore by parity of reasoning there is a true and necessary proposition signifying what is not the case. The inference holds good, and the antecedent is proved in the following way. Take the proposition

This is black,

indicating a white thing. This is possible, in accordance with this view, and it signifies that this white thing is black; therefore . . . The inference is obvious, and the minor premiss is proved in the following way. That is a purely singular affirmative present-tense proposition the subject of which signifies this white thing, and the copula signifies being, and the predicate signifies black, and the whole proposition signifies precisely in accordance with the composition of its terms; therefore this whole proposition signifies that this white thing is black.

⟨1.11⟩ In this master's opinion the proposition

Being is being

is a necessary proposition. But it signifies what is impossible. Therefore, by the same reasoning, so does any other proposition. The inference is good, and the minor premiss is proved in the following way. That proposition is an indefinite affirmative the subject of which signifies Socrates' being, and the copula signifies being, and the predicate signifies Plato's being, and the whole proposition signifies in accordance with the composition of its terms; therefore the whole proposition signifies that Socrates' being is Plato's being, which is impossible. This inference is obvious, and the major premiss is proved because if 'being' signifies being, then ⟨it is⟩ being that 'being' signifies. This inference is obvious as a consequence of Opinion ⟨1⟩. Then, further, if ⟨it is⟩ being that 'being' signifies, then what 'being' signifies is this being, or this being, and so on in each case.

And from these arguments the falsity of Opinion ⟨1⟩ is apparent.

⟨*Arguments against Opinion 2*⟩

Next is the second view, which maintains that a common term signifies anything that is *per se* superior to it but nothing inferior or different. One argues against this opinion by several different means.

⟨2.1⟩ Et primo sic. Ex ista opinione sequitur quod nullus terminus est significativus. Probatur: nam per Boethium in suis *Divisionibus* dicitur si nulla est res quam terminus significat, terminus significativus non dicitur. Sed nulla est res quam iste terminus 'homo' significat aut aliquis alius

5 terminus communis per opinionem. Igitur nullus terminus est significativus, quod est falsum.

⟨2.2⟩ Secundo iste terminus 'homo' est terminus superior ad istum terminum 'iste homo'; igitur quicquid significat iste terminus 'iste homo' significat illud idem iste terminus 'homo'. Sed istum hominem iste ter-

10 minus 'iste homo' significat; ergo istum hominem iste terminus 'homo' significat, quod est contra positionem.

⟨2.3⟩ Tertio sic. Iste terminus 'homo' significat hominem; igitur homo significatur ab isto termino 'homo'. Et per consequens hominem iste terminus 'homo' significat. Si negatur prima consequentia, contra: iste

15 terminus 'homo' significat hominem; igitur ab isto termino 'homo' significatur homo. Et tunc ultra, ab isto termino 'homo' significatur homo; igitur ab isto termino 'homo' significatum est homo. Consequentia patet per resolutionem verbi passivi in suum participium. Et tunc ultra, ab isto termino 'homo' significatum est homo; igitur homo est significatum ab isto

20 termino 'homo'. Consequentia tenet per conversionem simplicem. Et tunc ultra, homo est significatum ab isto termino 'homo', sed nihil est significatum ab isto termino 'homo' nisi quod iste terminus 'homo' significat; igitur iste terminus 'homo' hominem significat, quod est intentum.

⟨2.4⟩ Quarto quodlibet universale de pluribus praedicatur, sed iste

25 terminus 'homo' est universale; igitur de pluribus praedicatur. Consequentia patet cum minori. Et maior probatur per Porphyrium, ubi ponit expresse quod commune est cuilibet universali de pluribus praedicari. Et tunc arguitur sic. Iste terminus 'homo' est de pluribus praedicabilis, sed non est de pluribus praedicabilis nec de aliquibus praedicabilis quae

30 iste terminus 'homo' non significat; ergo plura iste terminus significat. Et non nisi hominem vel homines; igitur hominem vel homines iste terminus 'homo' significat, quod est contra positionem.

⟨2.5⟩ Quinto arguitur sic. Quicquid et qualitercumque est hominem esse est homo, et econtra, ita quod (7ᵛᵃ M) idem est hominem esse et homo.

35 Sed quicquid et qualitercumque est homo est iste homo, vel iste homo, et sic de aliis. Igitur quicquid et qualitercumque est hominem esse est iste homo, vel iste homo, et sic de aliis. Igitur quicquid significat hominem esse significat istum vel illum. Sed haec propositio:

Homo est

40 significat hominem esse; igitur ipsa significat illum hominem vel illum hominem. Ex quo sequitur immediate quod istum hominem vel istum hominem significat.

⟨2.6⟩ Sexto haec vox 'homo' est species; igitur omne eius individuum

---

1 ista positione sequitur *E*   2 dicitur *om. M*   8 igitur quod significat *E*
10 iste (1) *om. M*   14 contra *om. M*   16 ultra *om. E*   17 'homo' *om. E*
29 praedicabilis (2) *om. E*   33 qualitercumque a parte rei est *E*   34 est et
homo (1) *E*   35 est (2) *om. E*   35–6 et sic de aliis *om. M*   37 de
singulis *M*

⟨2.1⟩ It follows from this opinion that no term is significant. Proof: Boethius says in his *De divisionibus* ⟨*PL* 64. 889D⟩ that if there is no thing that the term signifies, the term is not called significant. But as a consequence of Opinion ⟨2⟩ there is no thing that the term 'man' or any other common term signifies. Therefore no term is significant, which is false.

⟨2.2⟩ The term 'man' is a term superior to the term 'this man'; therefore whatever the term 'this man' signifies the term 'man' signifies the same. But the term 'this man' signifies this man; therefore the term 'man' signifies this man, which is contrary to the position.

⟨2.3⟩ The term 'man' signifies man; therefore man is signified by the term 'man'. Consequently ⟨it is⟩ man the term 'man' signifies. If the first inference is rejected, then on the contrary: the term 'man' signifies man; therefore by the term 'man' man is signified. And then, further, by the term 'man' man is signified; therefore what is signified by the term 'man' is man.[c] This inference is obvious by the resolution of a passive verb into its participle.[d] And then, further, what is signified by the term 'man' is man; therefore man is what is signified by the term 'man'. This inference holds good by simple conversion. And then, further, man is what is signified by the term 'man', but nothing is what is signified by the term 'man' except what the term 'man' signifies; therefore man is what the term 'man' signifies, which was the intended conclusion.

⟨2.4⟩ Each universal is predicated of more than one, but the term 'man' is universal; therefore it is predicated of more than one. The inference is obvious, along with the minor premiss. And the major premiss is proved by reference to Porphyry, where he maintains expressly that it is common to each universal to be predicable of more than one.[e] And then the argument proceeds as follows: the term 'man' is predicable of more than one, but it is not predicable of more than one, or of any, that the term 'man' does not signify; therefore that term signifies more than one. And it signifies nothing but man or men; therefore man or men the term 'man' signifies, which is contrary to the position.

⟨2.5⟩ Whatever and however it is to be man, man is, and vice versa, so that man and being man are one and the same. But whatever and however man is is this man, or this, or this, and so on. Therefore whatever and however it is to be man is this man, or this man, and so on in each case. Therefore whatever signifies that man is signifies this one or that one. But the proposition

Man is

signifies that man is; therefore it signifies this man or that man. From this it follows immediately that ⟨the term 'man'⟩ signifies this man or that man.

⟨2.6⟩ The utterance 'man' is a species; therefore it represents equally every

aequaliter repraesentat, et per consequens omne eiusdem individuum aequaliter significat. Consequentia patet quia significare non est aliud quam virtuti congnitivae repraesentare. Tunc ultra, omne individuum illius aequaliter significat, sed iste homo est individuum istius termini 'homo'; igitur istum hominem iste terminus 'homo' significat. Confirmatur: secundum Avicennam similitudo est inter speciem et figuram sigilli, quia si essent sex vel quattuor (6va E) sigilla similia, figura impressa in cera per aliquod illorum sigillorum aequaliter repraesentaret figuram cuiuslibet sicut unius. Cum igitur intentio in anima causata vel effecta ⟨est species eius individuorum⟩, igitur intentio in anima causata vel effecta ⟨per aliquod illorum individuorum⟩ aequaliter cuiuslibet individui est similitudo sicut unius. Et cuius est similitudo repraesentativa et per consequens significativa. Ergo haec species homo omnem hominem significat.

⟨2.7⟩ Septimo haec propositio est singularis affirmativa vera de terminis simplicibus:

Sortes est homo;

igitur omnis res significata per subiectum est res significata per praedicatum. Sed Sortes significatur per subiectum; igitur Sortes significatur per praedicatum. Et per consequens Sortem hic terminus 'homo' significat, quod est contra positionem.

⟨2.8⟩ Octavo sic. Significet 'A' quod iste homo est, et iste homo est, et sic de aliis, et 'B' quod omnis homo est in universali. Et pono quod utraque propositio significet iuxta compositionem suorum terminorum. Tunc 'A' et 'B' convertuntur. Igitur cum 'A' significat istum hominem esse, et illum, et illum, et sic de aliis, significat 'B' conformiter. Assumptum probatur: subiectum 'A' et subiectum 'B' convertuntur, quia utrumque significat omnem hominem et pro eisdem supponit, et copulae et praedicata convertuntur, et cetera sunt paria; igitur . . . Consequentia patet, nam significare iuxta compositionem terminorum est movere virtutem apprehensivam ad comprehendendum pro illis omnibus quae significantur per extrema.

⟨2.9⟩ Item arguitur quod terminus communis significat suum per accidens superius, nam iste terminus 'homo' significat coloratum; igitur . . . Consequentia bona, et antecedens probatur, nam tota ratio cogens sic loquentes in materia quod iste terminus 'homo' significat hominem, animal, corpus, est quia iste terminus 'homo' significat hominem, et cum omnis homo sit animal, igitur iste terminus 'homo' significat animal. Per idem arguitur sic: iste terminus 'homo' significat hominem, et omnis homo est aliquid coloratum; igitur iste terminus 'homo' significat coloratum.

---

6 quia sicut si *M*   7 in cera *om. E*   9 Cum . . . effecta *om. M*   9–10 effecta aequaliter cuiuslibet individui est similitudo sicut unius *E*   10–12 igitur . . . unius *om. M*   12 est similitudo est similitudo *M et E*   14 affirmativa et vera *M* 22 de singulis *M*   25 de singulis *M*   29–30 apprehensivam *om. M* 32–3 superius per accidens *E*

individual belonging to it, and consequently it signifies equally every individual belonging to it. The inference is obvious because to signify is nothing other than to represent to the cognitive faculty. Then, further, it signifies equally every individual belonging to it, but this man is an individual belonging to the term 'man'; therefore the term 'man' represents this man.

Confirmation: According to Avicenna[f] there is a resemblance between the species and the figure of a seal, for if there were six or four seals alike, a figure impressed in wax by any of those seals would represent the figure of each of them as well as of the one. Since, therefore, an intention caused or effected in the mind is a species of its individuals, an intention caused or effected in the mind by any of those individuals is equally a likeness of each of them as of the one. It is a representative and consequently a significant likeness of it. Therefore the species man signifies every man.

⟨2.7⟩ The proposition

Socrates is ⟨a⟩ man[g]

is a true singular affirmative proposition with simple terms; therefore every thing signified by the subject is a thing signified by the predicate. But Socrates is signified by the subject; therefore Socrates is signified by the predicate. Consequently the term 'man' signifies Socrates, which is contrary to the position.

⟨2.8⟩ Let 'A' signify that this man is, and that that man is, and so on as regards the others, and let 'B' signify that every man is, universally. I assume that both propositions signify in accordance with the composition of their terms. In that case 'A' and 'B' are interchangeable. Therefore, since 'A' signifies that this man is, and that one, and so on, 'B' signifies in conformity with it. Proof of the assumption: The subject of 'A' and the subject of 'B' are interchangeable because both signify every man and supposit for the same things, and the copulas and predicates are interchangeable, and the other things are equal; therefore. . . The inference is obvious, for to signify in accordance with the composition of the terms is to move the apprehending faculty for the purpose of comprehending all those things that are signified by the extremes.

⟨2.9⟩ A common term does signify its *per accidens* superior, for the term 'man' signifies something that has a colour; therefore . . . The inference is good, and the antecedent is proved in the following way. The sole reason compelling those who speak this way on the matter to say that the term 'man' signifies man, animal, and body, is this: the term 'man' signifies man, and since every man is an animal, the term 'man' signifies animal. One argues in the same way as follows: the term 'man' signifies man, and every man is something that has a colour; therefore the term 'man' signifies something that has a colour.

⟨2.10⟩ Item haec consequentia est bona:

Homo est; igitur coloratum est,

quia oppositum consequentis repugnat antecedenti; igitur consequens intelligitur in antecedente. Sed nihil intelligitur in antecedente quod illud
5 antecedens non significat; ergo haec propositio

Homo est

significat coloratum esse. Sed illud verbum 'est' significat esse; igitur iste terminus 'homo' significat coloratum.

Tertia opinio, quae inter ceteras probabilis est, ponit quod quilibet ter
10 minus suum superius et quodlibet eo inferius tam de per se quam de per accidens significat.

⟨3.1⟩ Contra istam positionem arguitur: multi sunt termini per se in praedicamento substantiae qui non significant aliquid per se superius; igitur positio falsa. Antecedens probatur sic. Nullum superius ad tale est
15 nisi vox vel qualitas, sed nullus terminus in praedicamento substantiae significat qualitatem; igitur etc.

⟨3.2⟩ Secundo arguitur sic. Et quaero utrum inferius significet (1) quicquid significat suum superius, vel (2) aliquid sic et aliquid non. Non primo modo, quia tunc iste terminus 'animal' non esset superius nec genus
20 ad istum terminum 'homo', et sic modus arguendi ab inferiori ad suum superius non valeret. Nec foret possibile quod homo esset (7ᵛᵇ M) animal rationale, eo quod asinus et quodlibet animal dandum foret homo. Et sic sicut illa est falsa:

Omnis animal est homo

25 propter generalitatem, sic haec:

Omnis homo est animal.

Si autem dicitur quod inferius significat aliquid quod significat suum superius et aliquid non, quaero numquid iste terminus 'homo' significat solum animal quod est homo vel aliquid animal quod non est homo.
30 Secundum non dabitur, ut probatum est; igitur primum. Ex quo patet quod iste terminus 'homo' solum significat hominem.

⟨3.3⟩ Tertio ex positione sequitur quod ista consequentia sit bona:

Iste terminus 'homo' significat hominem; igitur iste terminus 'homo' significat animal.

35 Sed cum antecedente stat quod iste terminus 'homo' solum significat hominem. Igitur cum consequente stat quod solum significat animal. Et sic iste terminus 'homo' solum significat hominem, et tamen significat animal, corpus, substantiam, et infinita alia, quod non videtur verum.

---

4 Sed nihil intelligitur in antecedente *om. M*   6 Homo *om. M*   8 Quare
etc. *add. E*   10 tam *om. M*   19 tunc *om. E*   20 sic periret modus *M*
21 non valeret *om. M*   22 quod quod asinus *M*   30 igitur primum *om. M*

⟨2.10⟩ This is a good inference:

A man is; therefore something that has a colour is,

for the opposite of the consequent is inconsistent with the antecedent. But nothing is understood in the antecedent that the antecedent does not signify. Therefore the proposition

A man is

signifies that something that has a colour is. But the verb 'is' signifies being; therefore the term 'man' signifies something that has a colour.

⟨*Arguments against Opinion 3*⟩

The third opinion, which is acceptable as compared with the others, maintains that each term signifies its superior and anything inferior to it, *per se* as well as *per accidens*.

⟨3.1⟩ There are many terms that are *per se* in the category of substance that do not signify any *per se* superior; therefore this view is false. The antecedent is proved in the following way. There is no superior to such a thing unless it is utterance, or quality, but no term in the category of substance signifies quality; therefore, etc.

⟨3.2⟩ I ask whether an inferior signifies (1) whatever its superior signifies or (2) only some of what its superior signifies. Not (1), because in that case the term 'animal' would not be the superior or the genus in relation to the term 'man', and so the method of arguing from the inferior to its superior would not be acceptable. Nor would it be possible that a man is a rational animal, because a donkey or any given animal would be a man. Thus just as the proposition

Every animal is a man

is false because of its generality so would be the proposition

Every man is an animal.

If, on the other hand, it is said that (2) an inferior signifies only some of what its superior signifies, then I ask whether the term 'man' signifies only an animal that is a man or some animal that is not a man. The second of these will not be granted, as has been proved; therefore the first. It is clear from this that the term 'man' signifies man alone.

⟨3.3⟩ It follows from this view that this is a good inference:

The term 'man' signifies man; therefore the term 'man' signifies animal.

But it is consistent with the antecedent that the term 'man' signifies man alone. Therefore it is consistent with the consequent that it signifies animal alone. And so the term 'man' signifies man alone and nevertheless signifies animal, body, substance, and infinitely many other things, which is evidently not true.

⟨3.4⟩ Quarto ex ista positione sequitur quod ly .chimaera. et .mons aureus. significarent aliquid. Consequens falsum; igitur et positio. Consequentia patet, quia iste terminus 'chimaera' est de praedicamento substantiae et habet per se superius, quia sequitur:

5   Chimaera est igitur substantia est, et aliquid est,

et non econtra.

Quod non significet aliquid arguitur, quia nullum est argumentum ad probandum quod iste terminus 'homo' significat aliquid nisi quia significat hominem, et omnis homo est aliquid. Sed istud medium deficit ibidem.

10   Forte dicitur quod in talibus debet argui per hoc medium sic:

    Si chimaera est, chimaera est aliquid.

Contra, per idem contingit arguere quod (6vb E) 'chimaera' significat non aliquid, quia si chimaera est, chimaera est non aliquid; cum ex impossibili sequitur quodlibet.

15   ⟨3.5⟩ Quinto sequitur quod ista consequentia sit bona:

    Omnis homo currit; igitur omne animal currit,

quae tamen non valet, ut constat. Et quod illud sequatur, probatur. Nam ista propositio

    Homo currit

20 significat animal currere, per opinionem. Sed qualitercumque significet particularis vel indefinita particulariter, eodem modo significat universalis universaliter, ut patet per communem regulam. Cum igitur haec propositio

    Homo currit

25 significat animal currere, igitur haec propositio

    Omnis homo currit

significat omne animal currere. Et per consequens prior consequentia est bona.

⟨3.6⟩ Sexto sequitur quod quaelibet talis est falsa:

30   Omnis homo est,
    Omne animal est.

Probatur: nam qualibet illarum est immo universalis cuius multae singulares sunt falsae, significando primarie. Et antecedens probatur, nam istae sunt falsae:

35   Iste homo est,
    Iste homo est,
    Iste homo est,

---

2 significaret *E*   et *om. M*   5 substantia est, chimaera est igitur, et aliquid *E*   7 aliquid *om. E*   10 sic *om. M*   21–2 universalis universale, ut *M*   32 immo *om. E*   33 antecedens sic, nam *M*   35, 36 Iste homo est homo *E*   37 *om. E*

⟨3.4⟩ It follows from this view that 'chimera' and 'golden mountain' signify something. This consequent is false; therefore so is this view. The inference is obvious, because the term 'chimera' belongs to the category of substance and has a *per se* superior, for this follows:

A chimera exists; therefore a substance exists, and something exists;

and not vice versa.

The following argument shows that 'chimera' does not signify anything. The only argument that proves that the term 'man' signifies something is that it signifies man, and every man is something. But that means is lacking in the case of 'chimera'.

It may be said that in such cases one must argue by this means:

If a chimera exists, a chimera is something.

But on the contrary, one could argue in the same way that 'chimera' signifies nothing, for if a chimera exists, a chimera is nothing. Anything whatever follows from what is impossible.

⟨3.5⟩ It follows that this is a good inference:

Every man is running; therefore every animal is running.

But of course it is unacceptable. That this does follow from Opinion ⟨3⟩ is proved in the following way. According to Opinion ⟨3⟩ the proposition

A man is running

signifies that an animal is running. But, in accordance with a common rule, the universal proposition signifies universally in whatever way the particular or indefinite proposition signifies particularly. Therefore, since the proposition

A man is running

signifies that an animal is running, the proposition

Every man is running

signifies that every animal is running. Consequently the former inference is good.

⟨3.6⟩ It follows that each proposition of this sort is false:

Every man is,
Every animal is.

Proof: Each of them is certainly a universal proposition many of whose singulars are false, signifying primarily. Proof of the antecedent: The propositions

This man is,
This man is,
This man is,

demonstrando homines praeteritos, futuros, vel possibiles. Et istae sunt
singulares istius universalis:

Omnis homo est.

Igitur, etc. Minor probatur, quia non plus requiritur ad hoc quod sint
5 singulares illius universalis nisi quod conveniant in extremis, et quod subiecta illarum singularium significent eadem supposita quae significantur
per subiectum universalis. Sed sic est in proposito, ut patet per opinionem.

⟨3.7⟩ Septimo ex ista opinione sequitur quod iste terminus 'deus' significet omne quod est, et per consequens est transcendens. Et ita de isto
10 termino 'hoc' et de quolibet alio termino immediato. Et quod iste terminus
'deus' significet omne quod est probatur, nam ipse significat asinum,
capram, leonem, chimaeram, malum, infinitum, quantum, et sic de ceteris;
igitur . . . Consequentia patet, et antecedens probatur. Et capio tales
terminos 'deus asinus', 'deus capra', 'deus leo', deus malus', 'deus in-
15 finitus', 'deus quantus', 'deus chimaera'. Tunc: isti termini significant
asinum, capram, etc., sed iste terminus 'deus' est superior ad omnem talem
terminum compositum, et quodlibet superius significat significatum per
suum inferius; igitur . . . Consequentia cum minori patet, et maior
arguitur, nam sequitur formaliter:

20　　Deus chimaera est; igitur deus est,

et non econtra. Patet consequentia per Philosophum ubi dicit quod inferius est a quo non convertitur subsistendi consequentia. Hoc idem patet
per istam regulam: omne se habens per modum appositionis respectu alterius inferius est eo. Sed sic est in proposito. Igitur, etc.

25　　Antequam ad ista argumenta respondeam est primo opinio aliqualiter
declaranda. Cum enim dicitur quod quilibet terminus significat quodlibet
suum superius et quodlibet suum inferius, non debet intelligi quod (8ra M)
quilibet terminus significet quodlibet significatum sui termini superioris
vel sui termini inferioris. Non enim iste terminus 'homo' significat asinum
30 vel bovem, quorum quodlibet est significatum huius termini 'animal', nec
etiam significat lapidem vel lignum, quorum quodlibet est significatum
huius termini 'corpus'. Similiter, ille terminus 'homo albus' est inferior
ad istum terminum 'homo', et tamen ly .homo. non significat albedinem,
quam significat ly .homo albus. Est ergo opinio intelligenda quod quilibet

---

1 praeteritos et futuros E　　　3 Omnis homo est homo E　　　4 etc. om. E
5 quod om. E　　11 'deus' om. E　　　12 de aliis; E　　15 'deus quantus' om.
M　　25 argumenta ista E　　primo om. E　　33 ly om. E

are false, indicating men past, future, or possible. And those propositions are singulars belonging to the universal proposition

Every man is.

Therefore, etc. Proof of the minor premiss: Their being singulars belonging to that universal proposition requires only that they agree as regards the extremes, and that the subjects of those singulars signify the same supposita as are signified by the subject of the universal proposition. But that is the way it is in the example in question, as is clear from Opinion ⟨3⟩.

⟨3.7⟩ It follows from this opinion that the term 'god' signifies everything there is and is consequently a transcendental term.[h] And the same is true of the term 'this' and of every other immediate term.[i] That the term 'god' signifies everything there is is proved in the following way. It signifies donkey, goat, lion, chimera, evil, infinity, finitude, etc.; therefore . . . The inference is obvious. Proof of the antecedent: Take such terms as 'donkey god', 'goat god', 'lion god', 'evil god', 'infinite god', 'finite god', 'chimera god'. Then: These terms signify donkey, goat, etc., but the term 'god' signifies everything that these term signify; therefore, etc. This inference is obvious, along with the major premiss. Proof of the minor premiss: The term 'god' is superior to every composite term of that sort, and each superior signifies what is signified by its inferior: therefore . . . This inference is obvious, along with the minor premiss. The following argument supports the major premiss. The inference

There is a chimera god; therefore there is a god

follows formally, and not vice versa. This inference is obvious by reference to the Philosopher where he says that the inferior is that from which the inference of existence is irreversible ⟨*Categories*, Ch. 12, 14ᵃ29 ff.⟩. The same is clear by reference to the rule that everything related to another by the mode of apposition[j] is inferior to it. But that is the way it is in the example in question. Therefore, etc.

⟨*Explanation of Opinion 3*⟩

Before I reply to these arguments I must first provide some explanation of Opinion ⟨3⟩. When it is said that each term signifies anything superior to it and anything inferior to it, this must not be understood to mean that each term signifies each significatum of its superior or of its inferior term. The term 'man' does not signify donkey or cow, each of which is a significatum of the term 'animal', nor does it signify stone or wood, each of which is a significatum of the term 'body'. Similarly, the term 'white man' is inferior to the term 'man', but 'man' does not signify whiteness, which 'white man' does signify. The opinion is therefore to be understood to

terminus secundarie significat quicquid terminus superior vel inferior primarie significat. Et sic iste terminus 'homo' significat animal secundarie et, ex consequenti, et iste terminus 'animal' significat illud primarie. Similiter iste terminus 'homo albus' significat primarie hominem album, et 5 illud idem ly .homo. significat secundarie.

⟨3.1R⟩ Ad argumenta: ad primum dicitur quod illa ratio concludit verbaliter verum. Ideo glossetur opinio ut prius.

⟨3.2R⟩ Ad secundum dicitur quod iste terminus 'homo' non significat quicquid significat ly .animal., sed aliquid sic et aliquid non, ut superius 10 dictum est. Et ulterius, quando quaeritur si ly .homo. significat animal quod est homo vel animal quod non est homo, dicitur concedendo utrumque. Primum enim de se patet, et secundum similiter, quia ly .homo. significat omnem hominem praeteritum, futurum, et possibilem, quorum plures non sunt.

15 ⟨3.3R⟩ Ad tertium dicitur concedendo conclusionem adductam, videlicet, quod ly .homo. significat solum hominem et tamen significat animal, corpus, et substantiam; ideo infinita. Similiter conceditur quod ly .homo. praecise significat hominem, et praecise significat animal, et praecise significat corpus, et sic de aliis. Non tamen concedo quod ly .homo. 20 praecise significet Sortem vel Platonem, hominem album vel hominem nigrum. Similiter, ly .Sortes. significat praecise hominem, et tamen ly .homo albus. non significat praecise hominem licet sit eo inferius quia est terminus compositus plura significans quam ly .homo.

⟨3.4R⟩ Ad quartum dico quod ly .chimaera. significat aliquid. Et tunc 25 ad argumentum, dico sic prius, quod in talibus debet sumi illud medium:

Si chimaera est, chimaera est aliquid.

Et tunc quando dicitur quod per idem contingit probare quod 'chimaera' significat non aliquid, nego consequentiam. Quia licet ista consequentia sit bona:

30   Chimaera est; igitur chimaera est non aliquid,

hoc solum est gratia materiae, quia antecedens est impossibile, recte sicut:

Haec chimaera est; igitur non aliquid est.

Modo sic non est de alia consequentia, haec enim consequentia est bona et formalis:

35   Chimaera est; igitur chimaera est aliquid,

quia (7ra E) fundatur supra istam consequentiam, quae est bona et formalis:

Chimaera est; igitur aliquid est,

cum ibi arguitur ab inferiori ad suum superius sine aliqua dictione confundendi.

8–9 non significat quicquid *om.* M   10 quando *om.* E   12 et *om.* E   16–17 corpus, animal, substantiam E   17 immo infinita M   19 ly .homo. *om.* E   30 igitur *om.* E   36 illa consequentia M; ista consequentia E

mean that each term secondarily signifies whatever its superior or inferior term primarily signifies. Thus the term 'man' secondarily signifies animal and, consequently, the term 'animal' primarily signifies it as well. Likewise the term 'white man' primarily signifies white man, and 'man' secondarily signifies the same thing.[k]

⟨Replies to the Arguments against Opinion 3⟩

⟨3.1R⟩ I say that that reasoning does come to a conclusion that is literally true. Therefore let the opinion be glossed as above

⟨3.2R⟩ I say that the term 'man' does not signify whatever 'animal' signifies, but only some of what it signifies, as was said above.[l] Furthermore, the answer to the question whether 'man' signifies an animal that is man or an animal that is not man is that it does both. The first is obvious on the face of it, and the second likewise, for 'man' signifies every man past, future, and possible, most of whom do not exist.

⟨3.3R⟩ I grant the conclusion that is drawn, viz., that 'man' signifies man alone and nevertheless signifies animal, body, substance, and infinitely many others. I grant likewise that 'man' precisely signifies man and precisely signifies animal and precisely signifies body, and so on. But I do not grant that 'man' precisely signifies Socrates or Plato, white man or black man. Similarly, 'Socrates' precisely signifies man, but 'white man' does not precisely signify man even though it is inferior to it because it is a composite term signifying more than 'man' does.

⟨3.4R⟩ I say that 'chimera' does signify something. As for the argument, the first thing I say is that in such cases one must adopt the medium

If a chimera exists, a chimera is something.

And then I reject the inference in which it is said that one can argue in the same way to prove that 'chimera' signifies nothing. For although the inference

A chimera exists; therefore a chimera is nothing

is good, it is so only because of the matter ⟨of the antecedent⟩,[m] for the antecedent is impossible, just as in

This chimera exists; therefore nothing exists.

But the other inference is not of that sort, for this inference is both formal and good:

A chimera exists; therefore a chimera is something,

since it is founded on the inference

A chimera exists; therefore something exists,

which is both formal and good, for in it one argues from an inferior to a superior in the absence of any word that gives rise to confused *suppositio*.

⟨3.5R⟩ Ad quintum cum infertur quod haec consequentia est bona:

Omnis homo currit; igitur omne animal currit,

nego consequentiam. Et tunc ad argumentum, concedo quod quicquid significat particularis vel indefinita particulariter significat sua universalis
5 universaliter. Ideo concedo quod ista propositio:

Omnis homo currit

significat omne animal currere. Non tamen ex ipsa sequitur quod omne animal currit, quia ipsa non significat primarie omne animal currere, sed consequenter et secundarie. Et nota quod licet quicquid significat par-
10 ticularis vel indefinita particulariter significat sua universalis universaliter, non tamen qualitercumque nec omni modo sic significat. Quia universaliter et distributive significat propositio universalis, et sic non significat propositio indefinita vel particularis, sed solum indefinite vel particulariter. Verumtamen concedere illud non esset magnam poenam nec contra
15 rationem, quia non sequitur, secundum aliquos:

Qualitercumque significat particularis significat universalis, sed praecise indefinite significat particularis; igitur praecise indefinite significat universalis.

Sicut non sequitur:

20 Qualitercumque aliquid currit, aliquid movetur, sed contingenter aliquid currit; ergo contingenter aliquid movetur.

Antecedens enim est verum, ut patet, et consequens falsum, quia caelum necessario movetur.

⟨3.6R⟩ Ad sextum cum infertur quod quaelibet istarum esset falsa:

25 Omnis homo est,

Omne animal est,

nego consequentiam. Et tunc ad argumentum, nego istam consequentiam:

Non quaelibet singularis istius universalis est vera; igitur ista universalis non est vera,

30 ponendo quod aliquae sunt singulares (8rb M) actuales, aliquae potentiales. Modo ad veritatem universalis bene requiritur quod quaelibet singularis actualis sit vera, non tamen potentialis. Sed quia iste modus loquendi non est in usu, ideo nego quod aliqua universalis vera habeat aliquam

4 indefinita affirmativa particulariter *M*   9 et *om. E*   11 tamen *om. E*
13 particulariter vel indefinite *E*   14 conceditur illa *M*   magnam inconveniens
nec *E*   17 praecise et indefinite *M*; particulariter *E*   22 esset *E*   28 Non
om. M

⟨3.5R⟩ I reject the inference in which it is inferred that the inference

Every man is running; therefore every animal is running

is good. As for the argument, I grant that a universal proposition signifies universally whatever its particular or indefinite proposition signifies particularly. Thus I grant that the proposition

Every man is running

signifies that every animal is running. But it does not follow from this that every animal is running, for it signifies that every animal is running, not primarily, but only consequently and secondarily. Notice also that although a universal proposition signifies universally whatever its particular or indefinite proposition signifies particularly, it does not do so in every way whatsoever. This is because a universal proposition signifies universally and distributively while an indefinite or particular proposition does not signify in that way but only indefinitely or particularly. All the same, to grant that it did so would not be a great absurdity or contrary to reason, for according to some this does not follow:

The universal proposition signifies in whatever way the particular signifies, but the particular signifies just indefinitely; therefore the universal signifies just indefinitely.

In the same way this does not follow:

In whatever way something is running, something is moving, but contingently something is running; therefore contingently something is moving.

The antecedent is oviously true and the consequent false, for the sky necessarily is moving.

⟨3.6R⟩ I reject the inference in which it is inferred that each of these is false:

Every man is,
Every animal is.

As for the argument, I reject this inference:

Not every singular belonging to this universal proposition is true; therefore this universal proposition is not true,

supposing that some are actual singulars and others potential. It surely is required for the truth of a universal proposition that each actual singular be true, but the requirement does not extend to the potential singulars. But in view of the fact that this is not the accepted way of speaking I will deny that a true universal proposition has any false singular, or that there is

singularem falsam, vel quod alicuius singularis falsae sit aliqua universalis
vera. Et tunc quando dicitur quod istae sunt falsae:

> Iste homo est,
>
> Iste homo est,
>
> 5   ⟨Iste homo est,⟩

demonstrato homine praeterito, futuro, vel possibili, concedo quod istae
sunt falsae. Non tamen sunt singulares istius universalis:

> Omnis homo est.

Et tunc ad argumentum:

10   Non plus requiritur quod illae sint singulares illius universalis nisi
        quod conveniant in extremis, et quod subiecta istarum singularium
        significent eadem supposita quae significantur per subiectum uni-
        versalis.

Huic dicitur quod non solum hoc requiritur, sed oportet quod talis univer-
15 salis asserat illa singularia vel quod subiectum illius universalis supponat
pro eisdem. Sed sic non est in proposito, quia in ista propositione

> Omnis homo est

subiectum solum supponit pro hominibus qui sunt. Similiter illa universalis non asserit talis singularia. Unde licet haec propositio

20   Omnis homo est

significet Antichristum esse vel Adam esse, non tamen asserit aliquem illorum esse, nec pro aliquo illorum supponit.

    Hic tamen dicunt aliqui quod ista propositio asserit me esse, et te esse,
sicut etiam significat idem. Et si quaeritur quae est causa quare asserit te
25 esse et non asserit Antichristum esse, cum aeque bene significet Antichristum esse sicut te esse, dicitur quod quia propositio singularis significans
primo te esse sequitur ex ipsa universali cum medio vero, et propositio
singularis significans primo Antichristum esse non sequitur ex ipsa cum
tali medio vero. Cum hoc tamen stat quod haec universalis aliquando non
30 significabit assertive te esse, ipsa existente et te non existente. Et pro tunc
forte significabit assertive Antichristum esse, ipso existente.

    Sed huic responsioni non assentio, quia ly .homo. non significat te;
igitur nec te asserit esse coniunctum verbo substantivo.

    2 quod *om. E*   27 primo me esse *M et E*   28 singularis *om. E*   primo *om. E*
30 assertive me esse *M et E*   et me non *M et E*   33 coniunctum verbaliter
substantive *M*; coniunctum veraciter substantiae *E*

a true universal proposition belonging to any false singular. And then when it is said that the propositions

This man is,
This man is,
This man is,

are false when a past, a future, or a possible man has been indicated, I grant that they are false. But they are not singulars belonging to the proposition

Every man is.

And then as for the argument:

> Their being singulars belonging to that universal proposition requires only that they agree as regards the extremes, and that the subjects of those singulars signify the same supposita as are signified by the subject of the universal proposition.

My reply to this is to say that this is not all that is required. The universal proposition must assert the singulars or the subject of the universal proposition must supposit for the very same things. But that is not the way it is in the example in question, because in the proposition

Every man is

the subject supposits only for men who are. Likewise that universal does not assert singulars of that sort. Thus although the proposition

Every man is

signifies that Antichrist is or that Adam is, it does not assert that either of them is nor does it supposit for either of them.

But at this point some maintain that that proposition does assert that I am and that you are, just as it signifies those things. If someone asks why it asserts that you are and does not assert that Antichrist is, since it signifies that Antichrist is just as well as it signifies that you are, the answer is that the singular proposition primarily signifying that you are follows from the same universal proposition with a true medium, while the singular proposition primarily signifying that Antichrist is does not follow from it with a true medium. But it is consistent with this that at some time that universal proposition will not assertively signify that you are—⟨viz.,⟩ at a time when it is and you are not. And it may be that for that time it will signify assertively that Antichrist is—⟨viz.,⟩ at a time when he does exist.

I do not approve of that reply, however. 'Man' does not signify you; therefore when it is conjoined with the substantive verb[n] it does not assert that you are.

Item sequitur:

Omne currens est asinus, tu es currens (supposito quod sit ita); igitur tu es asinus,

et tamen maior non asserit significatum conclusionis. Dico igitur quod si ex
5 *A* sequitur *B* formaliter et sic sequeretur dato quod *A* esset contingens, *A* asserit significatum *B*. Et notanter addo 'et sic sequeretur dato quod *A*, etc.' quia ex ista

Tu differs a te

10 sequitur formaliter quod baculum stat in angulo. Non tamen asserit baculum stare in angulo, quia sic non sequeretur deducta impossibilitate formalis contradictionis.

⟨3.7R⟩ Ad ultimum cum infertur quod iste terminus 'deus' significat omne quod est, nego consequentiam. Et ad probationem, nego quod ly
15 .deus. significet asinum, capram, et alia. Et ulterius cum dicitur

Iste terminus 'deus asinus' significat asinum, et iste terminus est inferior ad istum terminum 'deus'; igitur ly .deus. significat asinum,

huic potest responderi ⟨dupliciter⟩.

Primo, negando consequentiam, sicut non sequitur:

20 Iste terminus 'homo albus' est inferior ad istum terminum 'homo' sed ly .homo albus. significat albedinem; ergo ly .homo. significat albedinem.

Antecedens enim est verum et consequens (7rb E) falsum. Si tamen iste terminus 'homo albus' vel iste terminus 'deus asinus' esset terminus
25 simplex, satis bene valeret argumentum, quia tunc terminus inferior non plura significaret quam terminus superior immo pauciora, sicut iste terminus 'Sortes' vel 'Plato' respectu illius termini 'homo'.

Aliter respondetur distinguendo illam propositionem

Ly .deus asinus. est inferius ad ly .deus.,

30 eo quod potest ibi intelligi 'inferius' pro inferioritate consequentiae aut pro inferioritate praedicamentali.

Si primo modo, concedo quod iste terminus 'deus asinus' est inferior ad istum terminum 'deus'. Nec ex hoc sequitur quod ly .deus. significet deum asinum sicut nec ly .non homo. significat hominem licet ly .homo. sit
35 terminus inferior ad ly .non homo. In consequentia ista sequitur:

Omnis homo est; igitur non homo est

formaliter, quia sequitur:

Homo est; igitur pars eius est,

11–12 deducta impositione formalis *M*   29 est terminus inferior *M*   32 est
terminus inferior *M*   33 ly .deus asinus. significet *E*   34 hominem sed ly *M*
35 ista *om. M*

Again, although this follows:

Everything running is a donkey, you are running (suppose that is so);
therefore you are a donkey,

the major premiss does not assert what is signified by the conclusion. I say, therefore, that if *B* follows formally from *A* and would follow formally provided that *A* was contingent, then *A* asserts what is signified by *B*. Notice that I add 'and would follow formally provided that *A* was contingent' because from the proposition

You are different from yourself

it follows formally that a stick is standing in the corner. But it does not assert that a stick is standing in the corner, because that would not follow formally if the impossibility of the formal contradiction were removed.

⟨3.7R⟩ I reject the inference in which it is inferred that the term 'god' signifies everything there is. As for the proof, I deny that 'god' signifies donkey, goat, and the others. Furthermore when it is said that

The term 'donkey god' signifies donkey, and this term is inferior to the
term 'god'; therefore 'god' signifies donkey,

one can reply in either of two ways.

First, by rejecting the inference, just as this does not follow:

The term 'white man' is inferior to the term 'man', but 'white man'
signifies whiteness; therefore 'man' signifies whiteness.

The antecedent is true and the consequent false. But if the term 'white man' or the term 'donkey god' were a simple term, the argument would be acceptable enough, for in that case the inferior term would not signify more than the superior term signifies but less, just as the term 'Socrates' or 'Plato' does in respect of the term 'man'.

The other reply consists in drawing a distinction with respect to the proposition

'Donkey god' is inferior to 'god'.

The word 'inferior' in it can be taken to mean either inferential inferiority or predicamental inferiority.

If it is understood in the first way, I grant that the term 'donkey god' is inferior to the term 'god'. It does not follow from this that 'god' signifies donkey god any more than 'non-man' signifies man even though 'man' is a term inferior to 'non-man'. As a result of that inferiority this follows formally:

Every man is; therefore a non-man is,

for this follows:

A man is; therefore a part of him is,

et ultra:

(8va M) . . . igitur non homo est.

Si autem intelligatur ibidem 'inferius' pro inferioritate praedicamentali, nego quod ly .deus asinus. sit inferius ad ly .deus., primo quia ly .deus. non
5 potest esse in praedicamento. Et adhuc dato quod esset in praedicamento, negaretur idem, sicut nec iste terminus 'homo albus' est inferior proprie ad istum terminum 'homo' inferioritate praedicamentali, sed solum inferioritate consequentiae. Quia sequitur:

Homo albus est; igitur homo est,

10 sed non econverso.

Et tunc ad auctoritatem Aristotelis adductam, dico quod ista intelligitur de inferioritate consequentiae et non praedicamentali. Aliter enim sequeretur quod ly .homo vel asinus. esset superius ad ly .homo. in recta linea praedicamentali, quod est falsum. Et quod sequitur patet, quia omnis
15 homo est homo vel asinus, et non econtra.

Ulterius cum allegatur illa communis regula:

Omne se habens per modum appositionis, etc.,

negatur ista de virtute sermonis, quia tunc sequeretur quod ly .homo risibilis., ly .non homo. essent termini inferiores ad istum terminum 'homo',
20 quod est falsum. Et quod hoc sequatur patet, eo quod quilibet illorum se habet per modum appositionis in arguendo respectu istius termini 'homo'. Verumtamen sane potest intelligi regula sic, videlicet, quod

Omne compositum ex substantivo et adiectivo non convertibili cum
　　　substantivo est inferius ad substantivum (intelligendo ut prius ly
25　　　.inferius.).

Et per hoc dicitur quod ly .homo risibilis. non est inferius ad ly .homo., quia illud adiectivum .risibile. convertitur cum ly .homo. Similiter nec ly .non homo. est inferius ad ly .homo., quia non componitur ex adiectivo et substantivo.

30 ⟨3.7R.1⟩ Contra illud quod dicitur, quod in recta linea praedicamentali non debet poni terminus complexus, arguitur, nam

Iste terminus 'corpus animatum' ponitur in figura pro genere et
　　　specie subalterna, qui tamen est terminus complexus; igitur . . .

and further:

. . . therefore a non-man is.

On the other hand, if the word 'inferior' in that proposition is taken to mean predicamental inferiority, I deny that 'donkey god' is inferior to 'god', first because 'god' cannot belong to a category. But even if it were in a category, I would deny this all the same, just as the term 'white man' is not properly inferior to the term 'man' as regards predicamental inferiority but only as regards inferential inferiority. For this follows:

A white man is; therefore a man is,

but not vice versa.

As for the authority of Aristotle that is brought in, I maintain that it is meant to apply to inferential and not to predicamental inferiority. Otherwise it would follow that 'man or donkey' would be superior to 'man' in a direct predicamental line, which is false. And it is obvious that this does follow, for every man is a man or a donkey, and not vice versa.

Furthermore, I reply to the appeal to the common rule

Everything related to another by the mode of apposition is inferior to it

by rejecting it taken literally as it stands. If it obtained, it would follow that 'risible man' and 'non-man' were terms inferior to 'man', which is false. And it is obvious that this would follow, for each of them is related by the mode of apposition when one argues in respect of the term 'man'. One can, however, provide the following sound interpretation of the rule:

Everything composed of a substantive and an adjective that is not interchangeable with the substantive is inferior to the substantive (understanding 'inferior' in the first sense).[o]

As a consequence it is said that 'risible man' is not inferior to 'man', for the adjective 'risible' is interchangeable with 'man'. Likewise 'non-man' is not inferior to 'man', for it is not composed of an adjective and a substantive.

⟨Argument against 3.7R⟩

⟨3.7R.1⟩ There is an argument against the claim that a complex term cannot be located in a direct predicamental line, viz.,

The term 'animate body' is located in the figure ⟨of the Porphyrian Tree⟩ in the position of a genus and a subaltern species, but it is a complex term; therefore . . .

Similarly:

Porphyry locates 'rational animal' as a genus in relation to 'man' and a species in relation to 'animal', but it is a complex term; therefore the reply is inadequate.[b]

Similiter:

> Porphyrius ponit ly .animal rationale. genus ad ly .homo. et speciem ad ly .animal., et tamen est terminus complexus; igitur responsio insufficiens.

5 ⟨3.7R.1R⟩ Ad ista respondetur quod non ponebatur ab antiquis illa figura tamquam vera, sed gratia exempli. Quia forte non habuerunt nomen simplex immediatum illi termino 'corpus' nec illi termino 'animal'. Quare, etc.

Dubitatur iuxta quaedam superius dicta de significatione primaria 10 terminorum. Dicitur enim ibidem quod quilibet terminus secundarie significat quicquid terminus inferior vel superior primarie significat, ita quod iste terminus 'homo' significat primo vel primarie hominem secundarie vero significat animal, corpus, substantiam, istum hominem album, et sic ultra.

15 ⟨1⟩ Contra ista arguitur probando primo quod ista propositio

> Homo est homo

primarie significat hominem esse risibilem, vel hominem esse animal. Et quaero quid dicit iste terminus 'primo' vel 'primarie'. Si dicis quod modus significandi primarius, sit ille modus B.

20 Tunc sic: ista propositio

> Homo est homo

significat B modo hominem esse risibilem, et B modus est modus primarius; igitur haec propositio significat primario modo hominem esse risibilem. Et si sic, ista propositio significat primo hominem esse risibilem. 25 Consequentia patet, et antecedens probatur, sequitur enim:

> Haec propositio significat B modo hominem esse hominem; igitur haec propositio significat B modo hominem esse risibilem.

Patet consequentia: ab inferiori (7va E) ad suum superius sine impedimento.

⟨2⟩ Secundo sic. Et quaero an eodem modo significandi numero 30 significat hominem esse hominem et hominem esse animal vel diversis. Non potest dici quod diversis, quia tunc infinitis modis significandi significaret, quod non videtur verum. Si primo modo, habetur propositum.

⟨3⟩ Tertio signo modum quo haec significat te esse hominem. Tunc sic: isto modo haec significat te esse hominem; igitur isto modo haec significat 35 hominem esse hominem. Et si sic, ista significat hominem esse hominem ex

---

8 De significatione primaria terminorum. *add E*   11 significat primarie, ita *E*
17 significat primarie hominem *E*   23 significat primarie hominem *M*   24 significat hominem primo *E*   27 *B* modo significat *E*

⟨*Reply to this Argument*⟩

⟨3.7R.1R⟩ The figure ⟨of the Porphyrian Tree⟩ was offered by the ancients not as true but for the sake of example. They may have lacked a simple name that stood immediately next to the term 'body' or to the term 'animal' ⟨in the predicamental line⟩. Therefore, etc.

⟨*A reconsideration of the Doctrine of Primary and Secondary Signification*⟩

A doubt arises in connection with some of the things that were said above[q] about the primary signification of terms. It was said there that each term secondarily signifies whatever an inferior or a superior term primarily signifies. Thus the term 'man' first or primarily signifies man but secondarily signifies animal, body, substance, this white man, and so on.

⟨*Arguments against this Doctrine*⟩

⟨1⟩ One argues against these views first by proving that the proposition

A man is a man

primarily signifies that a man is risible, or that a man is an animal.

I ask what the term 'first' or 'primarily' means. If you say that it means the primary mode of signifying, let that be mode B. Then: The proposition

A man is a man

signifies in mode B that a man is risible, and mode B is the primary mode; therefore this proposition signifies in the primary mode that a man is risible. And if that is the case, the proposition first signifies that a man is risible. The inference is obvious, and the antecedent is proved, for this follows:

This proposition signifies in mode B that a man is a man; therefore this proposition signifies in mode B that a man is risible.

This inference is obvious: from an inferior to its superior without impediment.

⟨2⟩ I ask whether that proposition signifies that a man is a man and that a man is an animal in numerically one and the same mode of signifying or in different modes. One cannot say that it does so in different modes, for in that case it would signify in infinitely many modes of signifying, which is evidently not true. But if it does so in the first way, then the thesis put forward ⟨in 1⟩ is established.

⟨3⟩ I pick out the mode in which that proposition signifies that you are a man. Then: In this mode it signifies that you are a man; therefore in this mode it signifies that a man is a man. And if that is the case, then either it signifies consequentially[r] that a man is a man, or one must say that it

consequenti, vel oportet dicere quod ipsa significat primarie te esse hominem. Consequentia prima patet: ab inferiori ad suum superius sine impedimento.

⟨4⟩ Quarto si iste terminus 'homo' primarie significat hominem et secundarie animal, hoc non esset nisi prius significaret (8ᵛᵇ M) hominem et
5 posterius tempore supraduceret ad memoriam suum universalius animal. Sed stat quodlibet prius esse sine suo posteriori; igitur stat quod iste terminus 'homo' significet hominem non significando animal. Igitur non si significat hominem significat animal. Nec ex hoc sequitur quod quid significat primarie significat secundarie. Antecedens patet per hoc, quia si
10 sub uno conceptu significat hominem et animal, non foret ratio quare primarie significat hominem quin per idem primarie significaret animal, corpus, et substantiam, quae est homo. Igitur sicut sequitur:
      Hoc significat hominem; igitur significat animal,
per idem sequitur:
      Primarie significat hominem; igitur primarie significat animal.
15 ⟨5⟩ Quinto arguitur quod iste terminus 'homo' significat primarie suum inferius, nam iste terminus 'homo' aliquem hominem primarie significat; igitur . . . Consequentia bona, et antecedens probatur, nam si ille terminus 'homo' primarie significat hominem, igitur aliqua significatione primaria significat ⟨aliquem⟩ hominem. Sed omnis significatio est relatio et
20 requirit duo extrema in actu existentia; ergo illius significationis aliqua sunt extrema. Sed nulla videtnur esse extrema nisi illud signum et suum significatum primarium. Igitur aliquid est suum significatum primarium, et non nisi ⟨aliquis⟩ homo; ergo ⟨aliquis⟩ homo est significatum primarium illius termini 'homo'. Ergo ⟨aliquem⟩ hominem primarie significat ly
25 .homo., quod est contra istam responsionem.

⟨6⟩ Sexto arguitur sic. Nam ex illa responsione sequuntur duo contradictoria, videlicet, (1) quod iste terminus 'homo' primarie significat hominem, et (2) non primarie significat hominem. Quod illa sequantur arguitur, nam prima illarum est vera iuxta responsionem datam, et secunda arguitur,
30 nam ille terminus 'homo' non significat primarie illum hominem, nec significat primarie illum hominem, et sic de singulis; igitur ille terminus 'homo' non significat primarie hominem. Consequentia patet, quia arguitur ab omnibus singularibus alicuius termini supponentis confuse et distributive. Et totum antecedens sequitur expositione, quae dicit quod
35 terminus communis non significat primarie suum inferius. Quare, etc.

⟨7⟩ Septimo arguitur sic. Ille terminus 'homo' primo significat animal; igitur non secundarie. Consequentia patet, et antecedens probatur, nam ille terminus 'homo' significat animal, et non prius significat aliquid aliud quam animal; ergo significat primo animal. Consequentia patet: ab
40 exponentibus ad expositum respectu illius termini 'primo'. Et antecedens

6 Sed quod licet prius stat esse M; Sed quodlibet stat esse prius sine posteriori E
8 sequitur om. M   quid om. M   11–12 corpus om. M   12 et om. E
14 animal, etc. M   21 illud significet et E   25 quid E   26 sic om. E
13 hominem, nec sic M   36 arguitur sic om. E   primo om. E   significat
primarie animal E   37 igitur etc. non M   38 significat (2) om. E

signifies primarily that you are a man. The first inference is obvious: from an inferior to its superior without impediment.

⟨4⟩ If the term 'man' signifies man primarily and animal secondarily, it is only because it signified man earlier and then later in time additionally brought to memory the corresponding higher universal, animal. But it is consistent that whatever is earlier should occur without what is later than it. Therefore it is consistent that the term 'man' should signify man while not signifying animal. Therefore it is not the case that if it signifies man it signifies animal. Nor does it follow from this that what it signifies primarily it signifies secondarily. The antecedent is obvious, because if it signified man and animal under one concept there would no reason why it primarily signified man that would not also be a reason why it primarily signified animal, body, and substance, which man is. Therefore just as this follows:

This signifies man; therefore it signifies animal,

so, by the same token, does this:

It primarily signifies man; therefore it primarily signifies animal.

⟨5⟩ The term 'man' primarily signifies its inferior, for the term 'man' primarily signifies some man. The inference is good, and the antecedent is proved in the following way. If the term 'man' primarily signifies man, then in some primary signification it signifies man. But every signification is a relation and requires two extremes in actual existence; therefore some things are the extremes of that signification. But evidently the only extremes are that sign and its primary significatum. Therefore something is its primary significatum, and the only thing it can be is some man. Therefore some man is the primary significatum of the term 'man'. Therefore 'man' primarily signifies some man, which is contrary to the reply.[s]

⟨6⟩ Two contradictories follow from the reply, viz., (1) that the term 'man' primarily signifies man and (2) that it does not primarily signify man. The following argument shows that these do follow. (1) is true in accordance with the reply. As for (2), the term 'man' does not primarily signify this man, nor does it primarily signify this man, and so on as regards the individuals; therefore the term 'man' does not primarily signify man. The inference is obvious, since one is arguing from all the individuals belonging to a term with distributive confused *suppositio*. And the whole antecedent follows from the exposition,[t] which says that a common term does not signify its inferior primarily. Therefore, etc.

⟨7⟩ The term 'man' first signifies animal; therefore not secondarily. The inference is obvious, and the antecedent is proved in the following way. The term 'man' signifies animal, and it does not previously signify anything other than animal; therefore it first signifies animal. This inference is obvious: from the exponents to the expounded in respect of the term 'first'.[u]

probatur pro minori, nam si ille terminus 'homo' significat prius aliquid aliud quam animal, igitur significat primo animal, quod est intentum. Consequentia patet, quia iste terminus 'prius' est terminus comparativus praesupponens suum positivum. Similiter, si ille terminus 'homo' prius significat aliquid aliud quam animal, non est nisi homo. Modo hoc est falsum, quia non prius repraesentat intellectui hominem quam animal, immo aeque cito.

Plura alia argumenta possent fieri in hac forti materia, quae gratia brevitatis dimittuntur.

Ad ista argumenta respondetur ut prius, quod iste terminus 'homo' significat primo vel primarie hominem et non animal, sed solum secundarie. Quia aliter sequeretur ista conclusio: quod eadem est significatio primaria et secundaria respectu unius et eiusdem, quod est falsum. Similiter, si iste terminus 'homo' primarie significat animal, tunc per idem quaelibet propositio primarie significaret omne tale quod sequitur ad eam. Consequens videtur esse absurdum, quia tunc frustra (7vb E) foret aliqua significatio secundaria.

⟨1R⟩ Respondeo ergo ad primum argumentum dicendo quod illa propositio

Homo est homo

significat primarie hominem esse hominem et non hominem esse risibilem, sed solum secundarie. Et ulterius cum ponitur quod iste modus primarius sit *B* admitto, et consequenter nego quod illa significet *B* modo hominem esse risibilem. Et tunc ad argumentum cum dicitur ibi arguitur ab inferiori ad suum superius sine impedimento, nego. Immo dico quod quando arguitur ab inferiori ad suum superius cum tali termino ablative sumpto denotante modum significandi, non valet consequentia. Qualiter est in proposito. Unde quacumque copulativa assignata ipsa significat copulative et significat categorice, eo quod ex ipsa sequitur utraque eius pars. Et tamen non sequitur (10va M) quod eodem modo significet copulative et categorice, immo diversis modis. Ex quo sequitur quod assignata ista copulativa:

Deus est, et homo est animal,

ista consequentia est bona, scilicet,

Ista copulativa significat Deum esse et hominem esse animal; igitur significat Deum esse.

---

1 prius *om. M*   3 terminus (2) *om. E*   comparativum *E*   8 hac forma, quae *E*
16 esse *om. M*   18 argumentum *om. E*   24 tunc *om. E*   cum dicitur *om. M*
25 quod *om. E*   34 scilicet *om. M*

The antecedent is proved for the minor premiss in the following way. If the term 'man' previously signifies something other than animal, then it first signifies animal, which is what we wanted. This inference is obvious because the term 'previously' is a comparative, which presupposes its positive ⟨'first'⟩. Similarly, if the term 'man' does previously signify something other than animal, it can only be man. But that is false, for it represents man to the understanding not earlier than animal but just as soon.

Several other arguments could be produced in connection with this formidable topic, but they are omitted for the sake of brevity.

⟨*Replies to these Arguments*⟩

I reply to these arguments as before, by saying that the term 'man' first or primarily signifies man and not animal, which it signifies secondarily only. Otherwise it would follow that primary and secondary signification are the same in respect of one and the same ⟨term⟩, which is false. Similarly, if the term 'man' primarily signifies animal, then by the same reasoning any proposition would primarily signify everything that follows from it. This consequent is evidently absurd, for in that case secondary signification would be pointless.

⟨1R⟩ I reply to the first argument, therefore, by maintaining that the proposition

A man is a man

primarily signifies that a man is a man and not that a man is risible, which it signifies secondarily only. Furthermore, I accept the hypothesis that the primary mode is *B*, and consequently I deny that the proposition signifies in mode *B* that a man is risible. As for the argument, I deny the claim that it is an instance of arguing from an inferior to its superior without impediment. I say instead that when one argues from an inferior to its superior with such a term ⟨as 'in mode *B*'⟩ in the ablative case denoting a mode of signifying,ᵛ the inference is not acceptable. And that is the way it is in the example in question. Thus in the case of any conjunctive proposition you choose, it signifies conjunctively and it signifies categorically, for each of its parts follows from it. But it does not follow that it signifies conjunctively and categorically in one and the same mode, but rather in different modes. It follows from this that if we take the conjunctive proposition

God is, and a man is an animal,

the following inference is good, viz.,

This conjunctive proposition signifies that God is and that a man is an animal; therefore it signifies that God is.

I

Et tamen non sequitur:

> *B* modo significat Deum esse et hominem esse animal; igitur *B* modo significat Deum esse,

supposito quod modus quo significat copulative sit *B*, et modus quo signifi-
5 cat categorice sit *A* vel *C*. Similiter, ista consequentia est bona:

> Tu curris; ergo tu curris vel tu moveris.

Et tamen non sequitur:

> Ista propositio significat isto modo quod tu curris; ergo significat isto modo quod tu curris vel tu moveris,

10 dato quod *A* esset modus categoricus et *B* disiunctivus. Eodem modo debet dici in proposito quod licet haec consequentia sit bona:

> Haec propositio 'homo est homo' significat hominem esse hominem; igitur significat hominem esse risibilem,

non tamen sequitur cum tali ablativo:

15 > Haec propositio significat *B* modo hominem esse hominem; igitur significat *B* modo hominem esse risibilem.

⟨2R⟩ Ad secundum, cum quaeritur numquid eodem modo significandi numero ista propositio

> Homo est homo

20 significet hominem esse hominem et hominem esse animal vel diversis, dico quod diversis. Et ulterius, cum infertur ergo per idem infinitis modis significandi significaret, concedo conclusionem. Non tamen significat infinitis modis significandi ista duo, sed solum duobus modis. Tamen quia significat infinita secundarie dicitur quod infinitis modis significandi
25 significat.

⟨3R⟩ Ad tertium respondetur eodem modo sicut ad primum, negando illam consequentiam:

> Ista propositio isto modo significat te esse hominem; igitur isto modo significat hominem esse hominem,

30 dicendo quod ibi arguitur ab inferiori ad suum superius cum impedimento. Verumtamen potest concedi iuxta viam aliorum quod qualitercumque haec propositio

> Homo est homo

---

1 tamen *om. E*   5 *C* vel *A E*   9 tu (2) *om. M*   16 ipsa *B* modo significat hominem *M*   20 esse risibilem vel *M et E*   22 significat *E*
23 Quia tamen *E*   24 significandi *om. E*   31 concedi quod iuxta *M*

But this does not follow:

It signifies in mode B that God is and that a man is an animal; therefore it signifies in mode B that God is,

supposing that B is the mode in which it signifies conjunctively and that the mode in which it signifies categorically is A or C. Similarly, this is a good inference:

You are running; therefore you are running or you are moving.

But this does not follow:

That proposition signifies in that mode $\langle A \rangle$ that you are running; therefore it signifies in that same mode $\langle A \rangle$ that you are running or you are moving,

given that A is the categorical mode and B the disjunctive. In the same way it must be said as regards the example in question that although this is a good inference:

The proposition 'a man is a man' signifies that a man is a man; therefore it signifies that a man is risible,

nevertheless it does not follow with such an ablative, i.e.,

That proposition signifies in mode B that a man is a man; therefore it signifies in mode B that a man is risible.

⟨2R⟩ In reply to the question whether the proposition

A man is a man

signifies that a man is a man and that a man is an animal in numerically one and the same mode of signifying or in different modes, I say that it does so in different modes. Moreover, when it is inferred that therefore by the same reasoning it would signify in infinitely many modes of signifying, I grant the conclusion. But it signifies these two things not in infinitely many modes of signifying but in two modes only. All the same, it is said to signify in infinitely many modes of signifying because it signifies infinitely many things secondarily.

⟨3R⟩ I reply to ⟨3⟩ in the same way as to ⟨1⟩, by rejecting this inference:

The proposition signifies in that mode that you are a man; therefore it signifies in that mode that a man is a man,

pointing out that in that case one is arguing from an inferior to a superior with an impediment. But following the way some men have adopted, it can be granted that the proposition

A man is a man

significat te esse hominem, significat hominem esse hominem. Et ulterius
nego consequentiam:

> Sed haec propositio secundarie significat te esse hominem; igitur
> secundarie significat hominem esse hominem.

5　Similiter negatur ista consequentia:

> Qualitercumque haec propositio significat hominem esse hominem,
> taliter significat hominem esse animal, sed primarie significat
> hominem esse hominem; igitur primarie significat hominem esse
> animal.

10　Sicut non sequitur:

> Qualitercumque tu es tu, taliter tu es, sed solummodo tu es tu; igitur
> solummodo tu es.

Sicut etiam non sequitur:

> Qualitercumque aliquis homo est, taliter aliquis homo potest esse, sed
> 15　praecise contingenter aliquis homo est; igitur praecise contingenter
> aliquis homo potest esse.

Antecedens est verum et consequens falsum, quia necessario aliquis homo
potest esse, ut clarissime patet per exponentes.

⟨4R⟩ Ad quartum dicitur negando primam consequentiam. Et causa est
20　quia iste terminus 'homo' non propter hoc dicitur significare primarie vel
primo hominem, quia prius significat hominem et posterius supraducit ad
memoriam suum universalius animal, cum hoc sit impossibile. Sed ideo
dicitur significare primarie hominem (et non animal vel Sortem) quia ex
prima institutione significat hominem (et non animal nec Sortem), licet ex
25　tali significatione primaria sequatur immediate ipsum significare animal vel
Sortem, sic arguendo:

> Ille terminus 'homo' significat hominem, omnis homo est animal; ergo
> iste terminus 'homo' significat animal.

Vel dicitur quod iste terminus 'homo' significat primarie hominem et non
30　animal quia tale significatum apprehensum immediate (8ra E) correspondet
tali dictioni 'homo' vocali vel scripto (et non tale significatum animal). Hinc
est quod solet dici quod primarium significatum alicuius termini vel propositionis est id quod toto signo apprehenditur. Quia igitur tale significatum
animal non apprehenditur toto isto signo 'homo', sed solum illud significa-
35　tum homo. Hinc est quod ly .homo. significat secundarie animal et primarie
hominem. Et sicut dico de tali significato homo respectu illius termini
'homo', ita dico de tali significato animal respectu istius termini 'animal'.

⟨5R⟩ Ad quintum dico quod isti termini 'primo', 'primarie', et 'primarium' vel iis aequivalentes in propositionibus (10vb M) in quibus

2 negatur consequentia M　　11 Qualitercumque tu es totaliter es, sed E　　21 et prius
supraducit E　　22 universale M et E　　23 primarie significare E　　23–4 ex
primaria institutione M　　28 'homo' om. M　　34 non apprehenditur om. E
signo 'A' non apprehenditur hic, sed E　　37 Sed hoc in materia de veritate propositionum dicendo concedente add. E　　38 'primarie' om. E

signifies that a man is a man in whatever way it signifies that you are a man. Moreover, I reject this inference:

But the proposition secondarily signifies that you are a man; therefore it secondarily signifies that a man is a man.

This inference is likewise rejected:

The proposition signifies that a man is an animal in whatever way it signifies that a man is a man, but it primarily signifies that a man is a man; therefore it primarily signifies that a man is an animal.

In the same way this does not follow:

You are in whatever way you are you, but only you are you; therefore only you are.

In the same way this, too, does not follow:

A man can be in whatever way a man is, but contingently is the only way in which a man is; therefore contingently is the only way in which a man can be.

The antecedent is true and the consequent false, for necessarily a man can be, as appears most clearly from the exponents.[w]

⟨4R⟩ I reject the first inference. The term 'man' is not said to signify man first or primarily because it signifies man earlier and then later additionally brings the corresponding higher universal, animal, to memory, for that is impossible. Instead it is said to signify primarily man (and not animal or Socrates) because it signifies man (and not animal or Socrates) as a consequence of its first institution. This is so despite the fact that as a consequence of such a primary signification it follows immediately that it signifies animal or Socrates if we argue as follows:

The term 'man' signifies man, every man is animal; therefore the term 'man' signifies animal.

Alternatively, it is said that the term 'man' primarily signifies man and not animal because such a significatum (and not the significatum animal) when apprehended corresponds immediately with the spoken or written word 'man'. It is for that reason that one usually says that the primary significatum of a term or proposition is what is apprehended by means of the whole sign. For as a consequence the significatum animal is not apprehended by means of the whole sign 'man', but only the significatum man. It is for that reason that 'man' signifies animal secondarily and man primarily. What I have to say regarding the significatum man in respect of the term 'man' is just what I have to say regarding the significatum animal in respect of the term 'animal'.

⟨5R⟩ I say that the terms 'first', 'primarily', and 'primary', or their equivalents, can be taken in the compounded and in the divided sense in

ponuntur possunt teneri in sensu composito et in sensu diviso, sicut et illi termini 'verum' et 'falsum'. Ideo concedo istam propositionem:

⟨Aliquem⟩ hominem significat primarie iste terminus 'homo',

tenendo ly .primarie. in sensu composito. Sed in sensu diviso nego illam,
5 quia tunc oportet eam probare ratione istius termini '⟨aliquis⟩ homo'. Modo quocumque homine demonstrato haec propositio est falsa:

Istum hominem significat primarie ly .homo.

Eodem modo dico de illa propositione:

⟨Aliquis⟩ homo est significatum primarium istius termini 'homo'

10 quod ipsa est vera tenendo ly .primarium. modaliter et in sensu composito sed in sensu diviso est falsa.

Sed forte quaeritur quomodo ista propositio debet probari:

⟨Aliquem⟩ hominem significat primarie ly .homo.

respectu de ly .primarie. Dico quod sic debet probari. Iste terminus 'homo'
15 determinate significat hominem, quo nihil posterius sic determinate significat. Igitur, etc. Sed de hoc alias dicetur cum de veritate propositionum agetur.

⟨6R⟩ Ad sextum, cum infertur quod ex responsione sequantur duo contradictoria, nego consequentiam. Et ulterius concedo quod ly .homo.
20 significat primarie hominem et non significat primarie illum nec illum. Nec ex hoc sequitur quod non significet primarie hominem. Et tunc ad argumentum:

Ibi arguitur ab omnibus singularibus alicuius termini supponentis confuse distributive; igitur . . . ,

25 nego consequentiam, oporteret enim quod talis terminus sub quo arguitur staret confuse et distributive mobiliter. Sed hoc est falsum, eo quod est secundus terminus in illa propositione probabili ratione cuius non contingit illam propositionem probari, sed ratione illius termini 'primarie', qui est terminus primus probabiliter, immobilitans istum terminum 'homo'. Est
30 enim hic eadem fallacia sicut alibi, non enim sequitur:

Ego non promitto tibi istum denarium, nec promitto illum, nec illum, nec illum . . . ; igitur non promitto tibi aliquem denarium.

Antecedens enim est verum in casu et consequens falsum.

⟨7R⟩ Ad ultimum, cum infertur quod iste terminus 'homo' primo
35 significat animal, nego. Et tunc ad argumentum:

Iste terminus 'homo' significat animal, et non prius significat aliquid aliud quam animal ; ergo primo significat animal,

propositions in which they occur, just as can the terms 'true' and 'false'. Thus I grant the proposition

The term 'man' signifies primarily some man

taking 'primarily' in the compounded sense. But if it is taken in the divided sense I deny the proposition, for in that case it must be proved with regard to the term 'some man'.

But the proposition

'Man' signifies primarily this man

is false, no matter which man is indicated. In the same way I maintain as regards the proposition

Some man is the primary significatum of the term 'man'

that it is true if 'primary' is taken as a modality and in the compounded sense but false if it is taken in the divided sense.

But perhaps I shall be asked how the proposition

'Man' signifies primarily some man

is to be proved in respect of 'primarily'. I say that it must be proved in this way. The term 'man' signifies man determinately, and nothing subsequent ⟨to the term 'man'⟩ signifies it so determinately. Therefore, etc. But this will be discussed at another time, when the topic is the truth of propositions.ˣ

⟨6R⟩ I reject the inference in which it is inferred that two contradictories follow from the reply.ʸ Furthermore, I grant that 'man' primarily signifies man and does not primarily signify this one or that one. But it does not follow from this that it does not primarily signify man. As for the argument

One is arguing in that case from all the individuals belonging to a term with distributive confused *suppositio*; therefore . . .

I reject the inference, for it would require that the term under which one is arguing had mobile distributive confused *suppositio*. But that is false, for it is not the second term in that provable proposition with regard to which the proposition can be proved, but rather with regard to the term 'primarily', which is the first term provably immobilizing the term 'man'.ᶻ There is the same fallacy here as elsewhere, for this does not follow:

I do not promise you this penny, nor do I promise you this one, nor this one, nor this one . . . ; therefore I do not promise you a penny.

The antecedent is true, we may suppose, and the consequent false.

⟨7R⟩ I reject the inference in which it is inferred that the term 'man' first signifies animal. As for the argument:

The term 'man' signifies animal, and it does not previously signify anything other than animal; therefore it first signifies animal,

nego consequentiam. Et tunc quando dicitur quod ibi arguitur ab exponentibus ad expositum, nego. Et dico quod in illa propositione ly .primo. non
tenetur exponibiliter, sed officiabiliter. Non enim tenetur ibidem comparative nec superlative, sed prout convertitur cum isto termino 'quo nihil
5 posterius', ut dictum est.

Et haec pro materia significationis terminorum dicta sufficiant.

⟨*Tertia Divisio Terminorum*   *Capitulum Tertium*⟩

Expedita sententia de significationibus terminorum, nunc consequenter
restat tam terminum naturaliter significantem quam ad placitum in ter-
10 minum communem et singularem dividere, qui ex modo suarum imposi-
tionum maxime distinguuntur.

Solet enim communiter definiri terminus communis isto modo: terminus
communis est ille qui est pro pluribus supponibilis.

Terminus vero discretus vel singularis est ille qui non est pro pluribus
15 supponibilis, sed tantum pro uno.

⟨D1.1⟩ Contra definitionem termini communis arguitur sic. Iste terminus
'hoc' est terminus discretus et est pro pluribus supponibilis; ergo definitio
insufficiens. Consequentia cum maiori patet. Et minor similiter in hac
propositione:

20   Hoc est,

demonstrando unum populum vel exercitum.

⟨D1.2⟩ Secundo iste terminus 'hoc' est supponibilis pro te et pro me, et
tu et ego sumus plura; ergo . . . Consequentia patet, et antecedens probatur,
nam in ista propositione vera:

25   Ego sum hoc,

me ipso demonstrato, supponit ly .hoc. pro me. Et idem terminus 'hoc'
supponit pro te, memet ipso demonstrato, in hac propositione:

Tu non es hoc;

igitur, etc.

30   ⟨D1.3⟩ Tertio sic. Sit Sortes coram te, de quo formes in mente tua talem
propositionem:

Hoc est hoc,

1 tunc *om.* E   ibi *om.* E   3 ibi E   5 posterius determinate'
E   6 hoc E   7 *om.* M   9 quam etiam ad M   10 ex modo ex suarum
M   25 hoc *om.* E   27 me ipso M   in hac propositione *om.* M   29 igitur
om. E   etc. *om.* M

I reject the inference. And I reject the claim that in that case one is arguing from the exponents to the expounded. I maintain that in that proposition 'first' is taken not as exponible but as functionalizable.[a] For it is not taken comparatively or superlatively there so as to be interchangeable with 'nothing subsequent', as has been said.[b]

Let these remarks on the topic of the signification of terms suffice.

⟨Chapter Three: The Third Division of Terms—Common and Discrete⟩

⟨First Set of Definitions⟩

Now that the doctrine of the significations of terms has been presented, the next task is to divide the term, whether naturally or arbitrarily significant, into the common and the singular term, two types that are most clearly distinguished on the basis of their impositions.

The common term is ordinarily defined in general as follows: A common term is one that is capable of suppositing for more than one thing.

A discrete or singular term, on the other hand, is one that is not capable of suppositing for more than one thing, but for one thing only.

⟨Arguments against the First Definition of a Common Term⟩

⟨D1.1⟩ The term 'this' is a discrete term and is capable of suppositing for more than one thing; therefore the definition is incomplete. The inference is obvious, along with the major premiss. The minor premiss, too, is obvious as regards the proposition

   This is,

indicating a crowd or an army.

⟨D.1.2⟩ The term 'this' is capable of suppositing for you and for me, and you and I are more than one; therefore . . . The inference is obvious, and the antecedent is proved in the following way. In the true proposition

   I am this,

indicating myself, 'this' supposits for me. And the same term 'this' supposits for you in the proposition

   You are not this,

indicating myself. Therefore, etc.

⟨D1.3⟩ Suppose that Socrates is face to face with you and that you form in your mind the following proposition about him:

   This is this,

qua manente divertas te et obiciatur tibi Plato, consimiliter dispositus sicut
Sortes, in loco Sortis, ita quod credas hoc esse quod prius (10ra M) vidisti.
Quo posito, iste terminus *hoc* in mente tua supponit pro illo quem iam
vides et etiam supponit pro illo quem vidisti prius. Igitur ly *.hoc.* supponit
5 pro pluribus et per consequens est (8rb E) terminus communis.

⟨D1.4⟩ Quarto iste terminus 'isti' (in plurali numero) pro pluribus est
supponibilis, et tamen non est terminus communis; ergo . . . Antecedens
patet in ista propositione:

  Isti currunt,

10 demonstrando Sortem et Platonem. Similiter tales termini 'mei', 'tui', 'sui'
sunt de pluribus praedicabiles, ut patet, et tamen non sunt termini communes.

⟨D1.5⟩ Quinto non omnis terminus communis est de pluribus praedicabilis, ut patet de istis: 'deus', 'sol', 'phoenix', 'vacuum', 'chimaera',
15 'mons aureus', et consimilibus.

⟨D1.6⟩ Sexto ille terminus 'istius' est terminus discretus, ut patet, et
tamen est pro pluribus supponibilis; ergo . . . Consequentia patet, et minor
probatur, nam quaelibet istarum est vera:

  Asinus est istius,

20 Capra est istius,

demonstrando per ly *.istius.* Platonem et Ciceronem.

⟨D1.7⟩ Septimo iste terminus 'Sortes' est pro pluribus supponibilis, et
est terminus discretus vel singularis; ergo . . . Consequentia patet cum
minori, quia iste terminus 'Sortes' est nomen proprium. Et maior probatur,
25 dato quod essent quatuor homines vocati hoc nomine 'Sortes'. Tunc aliquis
istorum esset Sortes. Et non esset ratio quare magis unus quam omnes alii.
Ergo quilibet illorum esset Sortes. Et si sic, ly *.Sortes.* pro pluribus
supponeret.

Pro solutione huius ultimi argumenti quidam solent definire terminum
30 communem et terminum singularem aliter quam huc usque definiti
fuerunt, dicentes quod

  Terminus communis est qui, significative acceptus, naturaliter vel
  secundum modum unicae suae impositionis, est aptus natus praedi-

3 *hoc est* in E   10 demonstratis Sorte et Platone *M*   14 ut *om. E*
'phoenix' *om. E*   16–17 et non est *E*   20 *om. M*   21 Platonem vel Ciceronem *M*   26 alii *om. M*   27 illorum *om. E*   29 argumenti moti quidam *M*
31 fuerint *E*

and that while that proposition remains in your mind you are diverted and Plato is put before you in place of Socrates and looking just like Socrates, so that you believe that this is what you saw earlier. On that hypothesis that term *this* in your mind supposits for him whom you see now and supposits also for him whom you saw earlier. Therefore *this* supposits for more than one and is consequently a common term.

⟨D1.4⟩ The term 'they' is capable of suppositing for more than one but is not a common term; therefore . . . The antecedent is obvious as regards the proposition

They are running,

indicating Socrates and Plato. Likewise such terms as 'mine', 'yours', and 'his' are obviously predicable of more than one thing but are not common terms.

⟨D1.5⟩ Not every common term is predicable of more than one thing, as is obvious in the case of 'god', 'sun', 'phoenix', 'vacuum', 'chimera', 'golden mountain', and the like.

⟨D1.6⟩ The term 'this one's' is obviously a discrete term, and yet it is capable of suppositing for more than one thing; therefore . . . The inference is obvious, and the minor premiss is proved because each of these is true:

The donkey is this one's,
The goat is this one's,

indicating Plato and Cicero by 'this one's'.

⟨D1.7⟩ The term 'Socrates' is capable of suppositing for more than one thing, and it is a discrete or singular term; therefore . . . The inference is obvious, along with the minor premiss, because the term 'Socrates' is a proper name. And the major premiss is proved in the following way. Suppose that there are four men called by the name 'Socrates'. In that case some one of them would be Socrates. But there is no more reason why it should be one rather than all the others. Therefore each of them would be Socrates. And if that is the case, 'Socrates' would supposit for more than one.

⟨*Second Set of Definitions*⟩

For the solution of this last argument certain men are given to defining the common term and the singular term otherwise than they have been defined so far, saying that

> A common term is one which, accepted as significant, whether naturally or in accordance with the mode of a single imposition of it, is naturally suited to be predicated of more than one thing, or to

cari de pluribus, vel significare plura, vel pro pluribus supponere indifferenter, quorum unum non est, nec fuit, nec erit pars alterius. Similiter:

Terminus singularis est ille qui, significative acceptus, naturaliter vel
5   secundum modum unicae suae impositionis, est aptus natus pro uno et non pro pluribus supponere, quorum unum non est, nec fuit, nec erit pars alterius.

Ita quod notanter additur ista particula 'unicae suae impositionis' quia quamvis ly .Sortes. bene significet plura, quorum unum non est pars
10 alterius, hoc tamen non est ex unica eius impositione, sed ex pluribus.

⟨D2.1⟩ Sed contra ista dicta arguitur sic. Si iste terminus 'Sortes' esset terminus discretus, sequeretur quod ista contradicerent:

Sortes currit

et

15   Sortes non currit.

Consequens falsum, cum possibile sit istas primarie significando esse simul veras, ut assignato uno Sorte currente et alio sedente.

⟨D2.2⟩ Secundo si iste terminus 'Sortes' non esset terminus communis, sequeretur quod haec non esset universalis:

20   Omnis Sortes currit,

et a fortiori nec indefinita nec particularis. Et si sic, esset singularis, quod est falsum.

⟨D2.3⟩ Tertio si talis aequivocatio istius termini 'Sortes' salvaret illam descriptionem, pari ratione, si iste terminus 'canis' fuisset impositus a
25 casu uni stellae tali, qualitercumque postea fuisset impositus fuisset singularis, quod est falsum. Similiter, concedendum foret talem terminum 'animal' esse terminum singularem, quia posset unus nesciens latinum hoc nomen 'animal' suo proprio filio imponere. Et tunc qua ratione ly .Sortes. esset nomen proprium, eadem ratione ly .animal., quod est absurdum.

30   ⟨D2.4⟩ Quarto qua ratione ista esset aequivoca:

Sortes currit,

pari ratione et ista:

Nullus Sortes currit.

6–7 nec erit, nec fuit M   10 eius unica E   17 signato M   sedente et alio currente E   23–4 illius descriptionem E   25 postea om. E

signify for more than one thing, or to supposit indifferently for more than one thing, none of which things either is or was or will be a part of any other.

Similarly:

A singular term is one which, accepted as significant, whether naturally or in accordance with the mode of a single imposition of it, is naturally suited to supposit for one thing and not for more than one thing, none of which things either is or was or will be a part of any other.

It should be noted that the words 'of a single imposition of it' are added because although 'Socrates' rightly signifies more than one thing, none of which things is a part of any other, it does so not as a result of a single imposition of it, but as a result of more than one imposition.

⟨*Arguments against the Second Definition of a Discrete Term*⟩

⟨D2.1⟩ If the term 'Socrates' were a discrete term, it would follow that these were contradictory:

Socrates is running

and

Socrates is not running.

The consequent is false, since it is possible that they be true at one and the same time when primarily signifying—if, for example, the one is ascribed to a Socrates who is running and the other to another Socrates, who is seated.

⟨D2.2⟩ If the term 'Socrates' were not a common term, it would follow that

Every Socrates is running

would not be universal and, *a fortiori*, neither indefinite nor particular. If so, it would be singular, which is false.

⟨D2.3⟩ If that sort of equivocation of the term 'Socrates' would save that description, then, by parity of reasoning, if the term 'dog' had by chance been imposed on one such star, it would have been a singular term no matter how it was imposed thereafter, which is false. Similarly, one would have to grant that a term such as 'animal' is a singular term, for one who knew no Latin could impose the name 'Animal' on his own son. In that case 'Animal' would be a proper name for the very same reason as 'Socrates' is a proper name, which is absurd.

⟨D2.4⟩ Since the proposition

Socrates is running

would be equivocal, so, by parity of reasoning, would be the proposition

No Socrates is running.

Et cum in aequivocis non sit contradictio, per Aristotelem primo *Peri Hermeneias*, sequitur quod ista non sunt contradictoria:

>   Sortes currit
> et
> 5   Nullus Sortes currit.

⟨D2.5⟩ Quinto si iste terminus 'Sortes' esset terminus aequivocus, sequeretur quod haec (10vb M) esset fallacia aequivocationis, sic arguendo:

>   Omnis Sortes currit, tu es Sortes; ergo tu curris,

sicut ista:

10   Omnis canis currit, caeleste sidus est canis; igitur caeleste sidus currit, quam consequentiam dicit Aristoteles primo *Elenchorum* non valere.

⟨D2.6⟩ Sexto arguitur quod iste terminus 'Sortes' plura significat unica impositione, nam si quis duobus infantibus aeque primo imposuisset ex intentione hoc nomen 'Sortes' in baptismate, nunc esset iste terminus 15 'Sortes' terminus communis et non singularis. Ista consequentia est bona, et antecedens est a te dubitandum: igitur consequens non est a te negandum.

Vel sic: pono quod sit aliquis homo, Sortes, habens tres filios, quibus simul et semel imponat hoc nomen 'Sortes', dicendo "Volo quod quilibet istorum sit Sortes ea ratione qua ego sum Sortes". Tunc certum est quod 20 iste terminus 'Sortes' verificatur de quolibet illorum unica ratione, quia ratione vocationis prius, quae solum fuit una et non plures.

⟨D2.7⟩ Septimo arguitur sic. Iste terminus 'Sortes' ex primaria sua impositione significat Sortem, sed plures sunt Sortes: ergo quemlibet illorum significat. Consequentia patet, quia non est ratio quare magis 25 significet unum (8va E) quam alium, cum omnes aequaliter sunt Sortes. Tunc ultra iste terminus 'Sortes' significat quemlibet istorum, et hoc ex primaria impositione; igitur plura significat unica impositione. Patet consequentia, cum prima impositio sit et fuerit unica impositio.

Sed forte hic dicitur quod ibidem sumitur 'unica impositio' pro unica 30 ratione, quia licet ly .Sortes. significet plura unica impositione, non tamen unica ratione. Alia est enim ratio quare ego sum Sortes et alia est ratio quare tu es Sortes. Ratio enim quare ego sum Sortes est quia ego sum iste

---

2 sequitur *om. M*   4 et *om. M*   11 consequentiam *om. E*   14–15 nomen esset illum terminum 'Sortes' esse terminum communem et non singularem. *M*   17 Ultra sic *E*   22 sic *om. E*   25 alium, et omnes *E*   27 igitur ... impositione *om. M*   29 quod dicitur *E*   31 alia est ratio *om. E.*   32 ego (2) *om. M*

And since, according to Aristotle in *De interpretatione* ⟨Chapter 8, 18ª26⟩, there is no contradiction as regards equivocal propositions, it follows that

Socrates is running

and

No Socrates is running

are not contradictories.

⟨D2.5⟩ If the term 'Socrates' were an equivocal term, it would follow that there would be a fallacy of equivocation in arguing in the following way:

Every Socrates is running, you are Socrates; therefore you are running,

as there is in

Every dog is running, one of the heavenly constellations is a dog; therefore one of the heavenly constellations is running,

an inference which Aristotle calls unacceptable in *Sophistical Refutations* I ⟨165ᵇ30–166ª7⟩.[a]

⟨D2.6⟩ The term 'Socrates' signifies more than one thing by means of a unique imposition, for if anyone had intentionally first imposed the name 'Socrates' equally on two infants in baptism, the term 'Socrates' would now be a common and not a singular term. This is a good inference, and the antecedent is one about which you must be uncertain; therefore the consequent must not be denied by you.

Alternatively, suppose that there is a certain man, Socrates, who has three sons, and that he imposes on them the name 'Socrates' at one and the same time and initially, saying 'I want each of them to be Socrates for the same reason as I am Socrates'. In that case the term 'Socrates' is verified of each of them for a single reason, because of the earlier naming, which was only one and not more than one.

⟨D2.7⟩ As a consequence of its primary imposition the term 'Socrates' signifies Socrates, but there is more than one Socrates; therefore it signifies each of them. The inference is obvious, for there is no reason why it should signify one more than another, since they are all equally Socrates. In that case, moreover, the term 'Socrates' signifies each of them, and it does so as a consequence of its primary imposition; therefore it signifies more than one by means of a single imposition. This inference is obvious, since the first imposition is and will have been a single imposition.

But someone may say that 'single imposition' is taken there for 'single reason', for although 'Socrates' signifies more than one thing by means of a single imposition, it does not do so for a single reason. For there is one reason why I am Socrates and another reason why you are Socrates. The reason why I am Socrates is that I am this man, and the reason why you

homo, et ratio quare tu es Sortes est quia tu es ille homo. Modo alia est
ratio quare ego sum iste homo et alia est ratio quare tu es ille homo.

Sed contra, ex ista responsione sequitur quod quilibet terminus aequivocus est terminus singularis vel discretus. Consequens falsum, et con-
5 sequentia probatur, quia quilibet talis significat plura diversis rationibus, ut
patet de illo termino 'canis'. Quia alia ratione significat canem latrabilem,
et alia ratione significat canem caelestem vel marinum.

⟨D2.8⟩ Octavo arguitur sic. Dato quod essent tres homines quorum
quilibet vocaretur 'Sortes', haec propositio universalis esset vera:

10   Quilibet istorum est Sortes.

Tunc vel ly .Sortes. esset terminus discretus vel communis stans confuse.
Non discretus, quia illa propositio esset falsa. Oportet ergo quod sit terminus communis. Praeterea sicut iste terminus *homo* in mente est terminus
communis quia plura significat et pro eisdem est supponibilis sine nova
15 impositione, sic etiam videtur de isto termino *Sortes*, qui in mente significat
plura et pro pluribus supponibilis sine aliqua impositione, eo quod non
potest imponi ad significandum sicut termini vocales vel scripti.

Propter ista et consimilia argumenta concedunt aliqui quod iste terminus 'Sortes' est terminus communis, et rationaliter certe. Quapropter
20 aliter describunt terminum communem et terminum singularem, dicendo
quod

Terminus communis est qui impositus est ad significandum (vel sibi
correspondens in mente), cuius non repugnat impositioni primariae
pro pluribus absque nova impositione supponere cum verbo de
25   praesenti non ampliativo.

Terminus discretus sic describitur:

Pro tali qui est significativus ad placitum (vel sibi correspondens in
mente), cuius impositione stante primaria pro pluribus repugnat
illum supponere affirmative cum verbo de praesenti non ampliativo.

30 Pro quarum declaratione notandum quod primo dicitur 'impositus ad
significandum' ut excludantur termini non significativi, ut '*A*' vel '*B*', qui

1 iste homo *E*   1–2 Modo . . . ille homo. *om. E*   3 ista ratione sequitur *E*
6 de isto nomine 'canis'. *E*   7 ratione significat *om. E*   8 sic *om. E*   10 esset
M   15 sic est vera de *E*   19 rationabiliter *M*   23 imponi primarie
M et E   29 affirmative *om. M*   30 quorum *E*   notandum quia primo *E*
imponitur *E*

are Socrates is that you are that man. But there is one reason why I am this man, and there is another reason why you are that man.

But on the contrary, it follows from this reply that each equivocal term is a singular or discrete term. This consequent is false, and the inference is proved because each such term signifies more than one thing for various reasons, as is clear in the case of the term 'dog'. It signifies the barking dog for one reason, and it signifies the heavenly or the marine dog for another reason.

⟨D2.8⟩ Suppose there were three men, each of whom was called 'Socrates'. The universal proposition

Each of them is Socrates

would be true. In that case 'Socrates' would be either a discrete term or a common term with confused *suppositio*. It is not a discrete term, because if it were the proposition would be false. Therefore it must be a common term. Besides, just as the term *man* in the mind is a common term because it signifies more than one thing and is capable of suppositing for them without a new imposition, so also as regards this term *Socrates*, which in the mind signifies more than one thing and is capable of suppositing for them without any imposition, since it cannot be imposed for the purpose of signifying as are spoken or written terms.

⟨Third Set of Definitions⟩

Because of these and similar arguments some men grant that 'Socrates' is a common term, and indeed they do so with reason. They therefore give a different description of a common term and a singular term, maintaining that

A common term is one that is imposed for the purpose of signifying (or what corresponds to that in the mind), the primary imposition of which does not conflict with its suppositing for more than one thing without a new imposition together with a non-ampliative present-tense verb.[b]

A discrete term is described as follows:

One that is arbitrarily significant (or what corresponds to that in the mind), which does not admit of suppositing consistently with its primary imposition for more than one thing affirmatively together with a non-ampliative present-tense verb.

⟨An Explanation of these Definitions⟩

In order to explain these it must be recognized, in the first place, that the phrase 'imposed for the purpose of signifying' is used in order to exclude

licet multotiens fuerint impositi ad significandum, hoc (11ra M) solum erat
pro tali tempore disputationis et non generaliter pro omni tempore.

Dicitur etiam 'cuius non repugnat impositioni primariae pro pluribus
supponere' propter istos terminos: 'deus', 'sol', 'phoenix', qui quamvis
5 non supponant nisi pro uno, tamen eisdem ex sui primaria institutione
non repugnat ut pro multis simul supponant. Unde si, per possibile vel
impossibile, causarentur mille vel quotcumque soles, indifferenter per
istum terminum 'sol' significarentur absque hoc quod oporteret istum
terminum 'sol' de novo imponere ad significandum.

10 Similiter, dicitur 'pro pluribus absque nova impositione' propter
praenomina demonstrativa, quae diversis demonstrationibus bene possunt
pro pluribus supponere.

Et dicebatur 'supponere' et non 'esse praedicabile' propter ampliationem
istius termini 'praedicabile', vere vel false, affirmative vel negative, et
15 propter obliquos, qui de pluribus sunt praedicabiles pro quibus non
supponunt.

Et dicebatur 'supponere' et non 'praedicari' quia posito quod Sortes sit
grammaticus, logicus, et rhetoricus, tunc haec est vera:

Grammaticus est iste homo,

20 demonstrando Sortem, et haec similiter:

Logicus est iste homo.

Ecce qualiter hic terminus 'iste homo' praedicatur de pluribus et non
supponit tamen pro pluribus, sed continue pro uno solo, quia idem homo
est grammaticus, logicus, et rhetoricus.

25 Ultimo dicebatur 'cum verbo de praesenti non ampliativo' propter tales
propositiones quae possunt simul esse verae:

Album fuit hoc,
Nigrum fuit hoc.

His visis, faciliter respondetur ad argumenta in principio facta.

30 ⟨D1.1R⟩ Ad primum dicitur quod licet illud pronomen 'hoc' pro pluribus
possit supponere, hoc erit mediante impositione de novo facta, et hoc
excluditur in definitione termini communis. Vel dicitur quod tunc bene

---

1 multotiem *M*   10 dicitur *om.* *E*   de pluribus *M et E*   10–11 propter nomina
demonstrativa *M*   14 vere et affirmative *M*   17 Vel *M*   20 demonstrando istum Sortem *M*   22 et *om.* *M*   23 tamen supponit *M*   homo *om.* *E*
30–1 pro talibus possit *E*   31 facta de novo *M*

non-significant terms such as '*A*' or '*B*', which although they have been imposed often for the purpose of signifying have been imposed only for the duration of a disputation and not generally for all time.

The phrase 'the primary imposition of which does not conflict with its suppositing for more than one thing' is used because of the terms 'god', 'sun', 'phoenix'. Although they do suppost for one thing only, there is nothing about their primary imposition that conflicts with their suppositing for many things at one and the same time. Thus if, whether or not it is possible, a thousand or however many suns were to be brought into existence, they would be signified indifferently by the term 'sun' without there being any need to impose the term 'sun' anew for the purpose of signifying.

Similarly, the phrase 'for more than one thing without a new imposition' is used because of demonstrative pronouns, which can rightly suppost for more than one thing given different indications.

'Suppositing ⟨for⟩' was used rather than 'being predicable ⟨of⟩' because of the ampliation belonging to the term 'predicable'—truly or falsely, affirmatively or negatively—and because of oblique terms,[c] which are predicable of more than one thing for which they do not suppost.

'Suppositing ⟨for⟩' was used rather than 'being predicated ⟨of⟩' for the following reason as well. Suppose that Socrates is a grammarian, a logician, and a rhetorician. In that case this proposition is true:

The grammarian is this man,

indicating Socrates, and so is this:

The logician is this man.

Notice how the term 'this man' is predicated of more than one and yet does not suppost for more than one but supposts throughout for one alone, since one and the same man is the grammarian, the logician, and the rhetorician.

Finally, the phrase 'together with a non-ampliative present-tense verb' was used because of such propositions as

White was this,

Black was this,

which can be true at one and the same time.

Once these things have been seen, it is easy to reply to the arguments produced at the beginning of the chapter.

⟨*Replies to the Arguments against the First Definition of a Common Term*⟩

⟨D1.1R⟩ Although the pronoun 'this' can suppost for more than one thing, it will do so by means of a newly made imposition, which is excluded in the ⟨third⟩ definition of a common term. Alternatively, it may be said

supponit pro pluribus sed non ut plura sunt, quia per modum unius significat illa multa. Ad hoc enim ut esset terminus communis oporteret quod supponeret pro pluribus ut plura sunt.

⟨D1.2R⟩ Ad secundum dicitur quod argumentum non procedit, quia
5 talis non supponit pro pluribus affirmative, sicut adiunctum est in definitione termini discreti.

⟨D1.3R⟩ Ad tertium dicitur sicut ad primum.

⟨D1.4R⟩ Ad quartum dicitur quod licet ly .isti. in actu supponat pro pluribus, non tamen supponit pro illis divisim, sed per modum unius
10 collective. Vel saltim non supponit pro singulis eorum. Posset tamen aliter dici quod licet ly .isti. significet duo vel tria, non tamen pro eisdem (8ᵛᵇ E) supponit.

⟨D1.5R⟩ Ad quintum dicitur quod quamvis ille terminus 'sol' non supponit pro pluribus, tamen non repugnat suae primariae institutioni ut
15 pro pluribus supponat.

⟨D1.6R⟩ Ad sextum dicitur quod iste terminus 'illius' est bene de pluribus praedicabilis, non tamen pro eisdem supponibilis, ut superius dicebatur.

⟨D1.7R⟩ Ad ultimum dicitur concedendo quod ly .Sortes. est terminus
20 communis, ut argumenta probabant.

Contra istam ultimam responsionem arguitur probando quod ly .Sortes. non sit terminus communis.

⟨7R.1⟩ Nam ly .Sortes. est nomen proprium, ut fatetur omnis grammatica. Igitur ly .Sortes. est terminus singularis, et per consequens non est ter-
25 minus communis. Prima consequentia patet quia idem est nomen proprium, terminus discretus, et terminus singularis.

⟨7R.2⟩ Secundo arguitur sic. Si causarentur mille soles, de omnibus illis vere praedicaretur hic terminus 'sol' sine nova impositione. Sed quotcumque homines generarentur, non de omnibus illis vere diceretur hic
30 terminus 'Sortes' sine nova impositione. Igitur non est terminus communis.

Ad ista argumenta respondetur sicut prius, negando quod iste terminus 'Sortes' vel 'Ioannes' sit terminus singularis. Immo est ita bene communis sicut iste terminus 'homo'.

⟨7R.1R⟩ Et tunc ad primum argumentum cum dicitur ly .Sortes. est
35 nomen proprium, nego, sumendo ly .proprium. quoad logicam, concedendo tamen grammatice loquendo. Nec ex hoc sequitur quod non sit

---

1 sunt, sed per E   2 enim om. E   2–3 oporteret ut supponeret E   8 dicitur om. E
10 supponant M   11 ly om. E   11–12 pro illis supponit E   19 concedendo
om. M   24 per omnem non M   25 Prima om. E   27 sic om. E
31 ista om. E   argumenta om. M   35 ly om. M

that in that case it does rightly supposit for more than one thing but not *as* more than one thing, for it signifies those many things by way of one thing. In order for it to be a common term it would have to supposit for more than one thing *as* more than one thing.

⟨D1.2R⟩ The argument does not go through, for such a word does not supposit for more than one affirmatively, as is additionally specified in the ⟨third⟩ definition of a discrete term.

⟨D1.3R⟩ The reply to the third is just like the reply to the first.

⟨D1.4R⟩ Although 'they' actually does supposit for more than one, it does not supposit for them dividedly but collectively after the fashion of one thing. Or at any rate it does not supposit for the individuals belonging to them. But one can say instead that although 'they' does signify two or three, it does not supposit for them.

⟨D1.5R⟩ Although the term 'sun' does not supposit for more than one thing, it does not conflict with its primary institution that it should supposit for more than one thing.

⟨D1.6R⟩ The term 'this one's' is rightly predicable of more than one thing, but it is not capable of suppositing for them, as was said above.[d]

⟨D1.7R⟩ The reply to the last is to grant that 'Socrates' is a common term, as the arguments proved.

⟨*Arguments against D1.7 R*⟩

One argues against this last reply by proving that 'Socrates' is not a common term.

⟨7R.1⟩ As every grammar book acknowledges, 'Socrates' is a proper name. Therefore it is a singular term and consequently not a common term. The first inference is obvious because a proper name, a discrete term, and a singular term are all the same.

⟨7R.2⟩ If a thousand suns were brought into being, the term 'sun' would be predicated truly of all of them without a new imposition. But however many men might be born, the term 'Socrates' would not be said truly of all of them without a new imposition. Therefore it is not a common term.

⟨*Replies to these Arguments*⟩

I reply to these arguments first of all by denying that the term 'Socrates' or 'John' is a singular term. Instead it is common just as the term 'man' is common.

⟨7R.1R⟩ In reply to the first argument I deny the claim that 'Socrates' is a proper name. I deny it, taking 'proper' as it is taken in logic; but

communis logice, sicut non sequitur: ly .hoc. est pronomen grammatice; (11rb M) igitur non est nomen logice.

Et si arguitur quod Aristoteles dicit in multis locis quod 'Sortes' est terminus singularis, dico quod verum est. Sed Aristoteles tunc sumpsit ly
5 .Sortes. pro re significata, sive personaliter, sicut etiam sumebat istos terminos 'aliquis homo', 'aliquis equus', cum dixit illas esse primas substantias.

Sed contra, igitur a pari homo esset individuum.

Capiendo pro re, conceditur. Et quando Aristoteles dixit quod non fuit
10 individuum, vel saltim fuit secunda substantia, tunc sumpsit ly .homo. materialiter.

Et si arguitur quod nullum fuit ibi signum materialitatis, igitur non potuit stare materialiter, respondeo quod antiqui ceperunt dictiones materialiter isto modo non, (quia frustra esset signum materialitatis
15 addere). Sed forte caruerunt tali signo tunc temporis, sicut non invenitur communiter in textis Aristotelis ly .ergo., sed loco illius invenitur ly .nunc. Vel aliter posset responderi quod Aristoteles posuit illa non ut vera, sed solum gratia exempli, ut dicit primo *Priorum*: 'Exempla enim ponimus non ut ita sint, sed ut assentiant addiscentes.'

20 Et si quaeratur quare grammatici vocant talia nomina propria, respondeo quia quilibet sic nominatus cum audit nomen suum appropriat sibi et non alia nomina.

Et si ex hoc concludatur quod a pari ratione ly .homo. posset esse nomen proprium quia homines possunt illud eis appropriare, concedo quod ly·
25 .homo. posset esse nomen proprium. Sed quia non fit communiter talis appropriatio, ideo grammaticus non vocat eum nomen proprium.

⟨7R.2R⟩ Ad secundum argumentum respondeo negando consequentiam, quia non sumitur antecedens pro isto termino 'Sortes' sicut pro illo termino 'sol'. Sed ad concludendum intentum oporteret sic argui.

30 Si causarentur mille soles, de omnibus illis vere diceretur ly .sol. sine nova impositione, sed quotcumque Sortes generentur, non vere de omnibus illis diceretur hic terminus 'Sortes' sine nova impositione; igitur . . .

Conceditur consequentia et negatur minor.

35 Sed contra, videtur quod ista responsio implicet contradictionem, nam sequitur ex hoc quod nulla erit impositio nova, quia iste non vocabitur 'Sortes' nisi imponeretur sibi pro nomine ly .Sortes. Et si sic, igitur nulla

---

1 commune *M*   2 nomen *om. E*   3 in multis locis dicit *M*   4 terminus *om. M*   6 esse *om. E*   9 Concedo pro re. *E*   dicit *M*   sit *E*   12 sit *E* 15 sicut nec invenitur *M*   16 in testibus *M et E*   invenitur licet nunc *M* 18 enim *om. M*   19 sit *M*   sentiant *M*   20 si dicatur quare grammatica vocat *E*   23 concluditur *M*   a *om. M*   24 homines illud sibi possunt appropriare *E*   28 sumitur *om. M*   pro isto termino 'Sortes' sicut *om. M* 31 generetur *E*   36 esset *E*   37 'Sortes' nec imponeretur *M et E*

grammatically speaking, I grant it. It does not follow from this that it is not logically common, just as it does not follow that since 'this' is grammatically a pronoun it is not logically a name.

And if anyone argues that Aristotle says in many places that 'Socrates' is a singular term,*e* I agree that that is true. But on those occasions Aristotle took 'Socrates' for the signified thing, or personally, just as he also took the terms 'some man', 'some horse', when he said that they were first substances.*f*

But on the contrary, then by parity of reasoning man would be an individual.

If ⟨'man'⟩ is taken for the thing ⟨signified⟩, I grant it. When Aristotle said that it was not an individual, or at any rate that it was a second substance,*g* he was taking 'man' materially.

And if it is argued that there was no sign of materiality there and so it could not stand materially, I reply that that was not the way in which the ancients took words materially (for it would be pointless to add a sign of materiality). Perhaps they lacked such a sign at that time, just as the word 'therefore' is not commonly found in Aristotle's texts, but 'now' instead.*h* Alternatively, one could reply that Aristotle put those things forward not as true but only for the sake of example, as he says in *Prior Analytics*, Book I ⟨49*b*32–50*a*4⟩:*i* 'We put forward examples not as if they were so, but in order that the interlocutors might agree.'

And if someone asks why grammarians call such names proper, I reply that it is because each person who is named in a given way when he hears his name appropriates it and not other names to himself.

If someone concludes from this that by parity of reasoning 'man' would be a proper name because men can appropriate it to themselves, I grant that 'man' could be a proper name. But the grammarian does not call it a proper name because such an appropriation is not commonly made.

⟨7R.2R⟩ I reject the inference. The antecedent is not taken in the same way for the term 'Socrates' as for the term 'sun'. In order to arrive at the intended conclusion one would instead have to argue in the following way.

> If a thousand suns were brought into being, 'sun' would be said truly of all of them without a new imposition, but however many Socrateses might be born, the term 'Socrates' would not be said truly of all of them without a new imposition; therefore . . .

This inference is granted and its minor premiss denied.

But on the contrary, it seems that this reply implies a contradiction, for it follows from it that there will be no new imposition, since he will not be called 'Socrates' unless 'Socrates' is imposed on him as a name. And if that is the case, there will be no reason why Socrates rather than Plato

erit causa danda quare generandus citius erit Sortes quam Plato. Et cum
non erit Plato, sequitur quod non erit Sortes.

Respondeo quod supposita veritate quod unus generandus erit Sortes,
dico quod non erit Sortes quia sic vocabitur vel baptizabitur, quia sic esset
5 asinus, sed hoc erit Sortes quia hoc erit hoc (demonstrando Sortem). Unde
quamvis iste numquam vocabitur 'Sortes', non minus erit Sortes. Poterit
etiam vocari 'asinus' vel 'Brunellus', non obstante hoc tamen iste erit
Sortes. Verumtamen ista propositio in voce vel in scripto

> Iste est Sortes

10 tunc non esset vera, et causa est quia tunc iste terminus 'Sortes' non
significaret Sortem illum sed aliquid aliud vel nihil. Ista tamen propositio
in conceptu

> *Iste est Sortes*

continue esset vera. Unde, dato quod iste Sortes generandus vocabitur
15 'Sortes', prius erit ita quod (9ᵃ E) iste est Sortes et prius erit haec vera in
conceptu

> *Iste est Sortes*

quam aliqua talis in voce vel in scripto erit vera, licet tam in voce quam in
scripto erunt istae propositiones continue a primo instanti in quo Sortes
20 erit, dato quod iste non vocabitur 'Sortes' in primo instanti sui esse sed
aliquando postea. Sicut contingit de quolibet homine qualitercumque
nominato vel vocato.

Unde in materia ista est eodem modo agendum sicut in alia consimili.
Dicimus enim quod aeternaliter homo fuit et quod aeternaliter aliqua talis
25 fuit vera in conceptu

> *Homo est homo.*

Tamen certum est quod antequam iste terminus 'homo' fuisset impositus
ad significandum hominem, non erat haec propositio

> Homo est homo

30 in voce vel in scripto magis vera quam ista modo

> Ba est ba.

Et causa est quia tunc iste terminus 'homo' non significabat hominem, sed

---

7 hoc *om. M*   8 voce et in *M*   10 tunc (1) *om. E*   14 erit *E*   20 iste
om. E   20–21 sed aliqualiter postea *M*   22 vel vocato *om. M*   23 modo arguen-
dum sicut *E*   29–30 homo in voce vel in scripto *om. E*   32 Et ratio est *M*

should be born. And since it will not be Plato, it follows that it will not be Socrates.

I reply that if we assume it to be true that one to be born will be Socrates, then, I maintain, he will be Socrates not because he will be called or baptized thus, for a donkey could be so, but rather this will be Socrates because this will be this (indicating Socrates). Thus even though he will never be called 'Socrates', he will be Socrates no less. He could even be called 'Donkey', or 'Brownie', but all the same he will be Socrates. The spoken or written proposition

He is Socrates

would, however, not be true in that case, because the ⟨spoken or written⟩ term 'Socrates' would in that case signify not Socrates himself but either something else or nothing. But the conceived proposition

He is Socrates

would be true throughout. Thus, given that this Socrates to be born will be called 'Socrates', it will be the case that he is Socrates and the conceived proposition

He is Socrates

will be true before any such spoken or written proposition will be true, even though there will be those spoken and written propositions continuously from the first instant in which he will be Socrates, supposing that he is not called 'Socrates' in the first instant of his existence but sometime later. The same sort of thing can occur regarding any man no matter what he is named or called.

Thus one must deal with this topic in the same way as with another very much like it. For we say that man was eternally and that some such conceived proposition as

Man is man

was true eternally. And yet of course before the term 'man' had been imposed for the purpose of signifying man the spoken or written proposition

Man is man

was no more true than is

Ba is ba

now. This is because at that time the term 'man' was signifying not man but either something else or nothing. In the same way one must say as

aliquid aliud vel nohil. Eodem modo est dicendum in illo casu de Sorte quod ipse erit Sortes quando haec propositio in voce vel in scripto

    Iste est Sortes

erit falsa. Haec autem assero iuxta communem viam.

5 (11va M) Circa materiam ultimo tactam, quare aliquis homo est Sortes, vel Ioannes, versantur tres opiniones.

⟨1⟩ Prima dicit quod homo est Sortes quia vocatur 'Sortes', etc.

⟨2⟩ Secunda dicit quod nullus homo potest esse Sortes nec Plato nec sic de aliis propriis nominibus.

10 ⟨3⟩ Tertia ponit quod iste homo est Sortes quia iste homo est hoc (seipso demonstrato).

⟨1.1⟩ Contra primam opinionem arguitur sic. Ex illa sequitur quod tu potuisses fuisse Deus, vel diabolus, et quicquid nominandum, immo similiter homo et asinus, quia potuisti sic vocari. Et ex isto sequitur quod omne quod

15 potest intelligi potest esse, immo quod nulla propositio potest esse impossibilis. Similiter sequitur quod tu potes facere infinitos mundos, quorum quilibet potest esse Deus, eo quod potest sic vocari. Et similiter tu potes facere infinitos deos, quorum quilibet potest esse chimaera. Et quicquid Deus potest facere, etiam chimaera potest facere, ut patet, cum quilibet

20 potest vocari 'chimaera'.

⟨1.2⟩ Item ex ista opinione sequitur quod fautor istius opinionis est asinus, rationale et irrationale. Quia quicquid erit iam est, sed cras erit asinus quia sic vocabitur; ergo et iam est asinus.

⟨1.3⟩ Et sic secundum istam opinionem destruuntur omnes per se

25 praedicationes et omnes propositiones necessariae. Sequitur enim secundum illam opinionem quod contingenter Deus est Deus, quia Deus est id cui hoc nomen 'Deus' fuit impositum; igitur contingenter Deus est Deus.

Haec omnia, ut patet, sunt absurda.

⟨1.4⟩ Item sequerentur ex illa opinione alia innumerabilia auditui

30 absurda et contra totam physicam, scilicet, quod ignis est congelatus, quod terra naturaliter ascendit, quod album est nigrum, quod chimaera volat, quod papa habet alas, et quod aliqua mulier est aliquis homo. Et quod omnia illa sequantur patet, supposito quod quodlibet illorum sic vocaretur.

7 Hoc dicit E   10 Sortes, et est M   quia iste homo est om. M   13 potuisti M
vel om. M   14 Et om. M   16 Sequitur similiter M   posses E
19 etiam om. M   patet, quod quilibet M   22 Et quicquid M   quicquid iam erit
M et E   cras iam erit E   23 etiam est E   26–7 opinionem contingenter
est quod Deus est quod Deus est illud cui M   26 Deus, quia Deus est om. E
28 patent M   29 sequitur M   numeralia M   30 congelatus,
et quod M et E   31 ascendit, et quod E   31–2 quod chimaera . . . homo. om. E
33 sequitur M; sequatur E

regards the Socrates case that he will be Socrates even when the spoken or written proposition

He is Socrates

is false. But I make these claims in accordance with the common way.

⟨Three Opinions regarding Proper Names⟩

There are three opinions regarding the topic last discussed—the reason why a man is Socrates, or John.

⟨1⟩ A man is Socrates because he is called 'Socrates', and so on ⟨as regards other names⟩.

⟨2⟩ No man can be Socrates, or Plato, and so on as regards the other proper names.

⟨3⟩ That man is Socrates because that man is this (indicating that very one himself).

⟨Arguments against Opinion 1⟩

⟨1.1⟩ It follows from this that you could have been God, or the devil, or whatever might be named—indeed, both man and donkey—since you could have been called that. And from this it follows that everything that can be understood can be—indeed, that no proposition can be impossible. It follows likewise that you can make infinitely many worlds, each of which can be God, because it can be called that. Similarly, you can make infinitely many gods, each of which can be a chimera. And whatever God can make, a chimera can also make, obviously, since anything can be called 'chimera'.

⟨1.2⟩ It follows from Opinion ⟨1⟩ that the proponent of the opinion is a donkey, that he is both a rational and a nonrational thing. For whatever he will be he is now, but tomorrow he will be a donkey because that is what he will be called; therefore he is a donkey now, too.

⟨1.3⟩ According to Opinion ⟨1⟩ it follows that all *per se* predications[j] and all necessary propositions are destroyed. For according to this opinion it follows that God is God contingently, because God is that on which the name 'God' has been imposed; therefore God is God contingently.

All these things are obviously absurd.

⟨1.4⟩ Countless other things absurd to the hearer and contrary to all natural science would follow from Opinion ⟨1⟩—e.g., that fire is frozen, that earth has a natural tendency to rise, that white is black, that a chimera flies, that the Pope has wings, and that a certain woman is a certain man. All these absurdities do clearly follow, on the assumption that each of these things is called that.

Ex his igitur patet opinionem illam non valere.

⟨2.1⟩ Contra secundam opinionem est communis modus loquendi. Solet dici

> Ioannes currit,
> Christus passus est,
> Maria est virgo,
> Petrus est apostolus,

quae omnia habet illa opinio negare.

⟨2.2⟩ Item talia nomina 'Christus', 'Maria', absolute significant individua; ergo stat illos terminos de terminis aliis easdem res significantibus praedicari. Consequentia patet per hoc, quod nulla alia ratio danda est quam ista quare ly .homo. est vere et affirmative praedicabilis de ly .tu.

⟨2.3⟩ Item ex ista opinione sequitur quod aliqua universalis est vera cuius quaelibet singularis est falsa. Probatur, nam haec est vera:

> Omnis homo est animal,

et omnes istae singulares sunt falsae:

> Sortes est animal,
> Plato est animal,

et sic de aliis, quia nec Sortes nec Plato est secundum istam opinionem.

⟨2.4⟩ Item sequitur ex opinione quod nullus homo est albus. Probatur, nam aeque accidentale est tale nomen 'Sortes' sicut illud nomen 'albedo'. Si igitur nullus homo est Sortes, per idem nullus homo est albus.

⟨2.5⟩ Item si tale nomen sit accidens, igitur denotat suum subiectum, in quo est, esse tale quale ipsum est. Sed illud nomen est 'Sortes'. Igitur denotat suum subiectum in quo est esse Sortem. Sed nihil est suum subiectum nisi homo; igitur homo est Sortes sicut homo est albus.

Per haec et alia multa argumenta quae possent fieri apparet falsitas opinionis.

Tertia opinio ponit quod aliquis homo est Sortes quia ipse est iste homo.

⟨3.1⟩ Contra illam opinionem arguitur sic. Et assigno aliquem hominem qui sit Sortes quem nescias esse Sortem. Quo posito probatur tunc quod tu scis illum esse Sortem. Et facio istam consequentiam:

> Iste homo est iste homo; ergo iste homo est Sortes.

---

3 Sole dicitur *M*　　　6 *om. M*　　　9 absolute *om. M*　　　11 quia nulla ratio *E*
12 ista quia ly *E*　　　13 opinione *om. E*　　　16 omnes *om. E*　　　19 Sortes est
nec *M*　　　27 Et per *E*　　　30 sic *om. E*　　　31 tunc *om. E*

As a consequence of these arguments, therefore, it is obvious that Opinion ⟨1⟩ is unacceptable.

⟨*Arguments against Opinion 2*⟩

⟨2.1⟩ The ordinary way of speaking is contrary to Opinion ⟨2⟩. One ordinarily says

John is running,
Christ has suffered,
Mary is a virgin,
Peter is an apostle,

all of which this opinion has to deny.

⟨2.2⟩ Such names as 'Christ' and 'Mary' absolutely signify individuals; therefore it is consistent that those terms be predicated of other terms signifying those same things. The inference is clear as a consequence of the fact that that is the only reason that could be given why 'man' is predicable truly and affirmatively of 'you'.

⟨2.3⟩ It follows from Opinion ⟨2⟩ that a universal proposition each of whose singulars is false is true. Proof: The proposition

Every man is an animal

is true, and all these singulars are false:

Socrates is an animal,
Plato is an animal,

and so on as regards the others, since according to this opinion neither Socrates nor Plato is.

⟨2.4⟩ It follows from this opinion that no man is white. Proof: The name 'Socrates' is just as accidental as is the name 'whiteness'; therefore if no man is Socrates, then by the same token no man is white.

⟨2.5⟩ If such a name is an accident, then it denotes that its subject, in which it is, is such as it itself is. But this name is 'Socrates'. Therefore it denotes that its subject in which it is is Socrates. But its only subject is a man; therefore a man is Socrates in the same way as a man is white.

As a consequence of these and many other arguments that could be produced, the falsity of Opinion ⟨2⟩ is apparent.

⟨*Arguments against Opinion 3*⟩

Opinion ⟨3⟩ claims that a man is Socrates because he is this man.

⟨3.1⟩ I pick out a man who is Socrates and whom you do not know to be Socrates. On that hypothesis there is a proof that you do know that he is Socrates. I produce the following inference:

This man is this man; therefore this man is Socrates.

Ista consequentia est bona scita a te esse bona, et totum antecedens est scitum a te; igitur et consequens. Quod ista consequentia sit bona patet per illam regulam: ab uno convertibili ad reliquum simpliciter.

⟨3.2⟩ Secundo arguitur sic. Ex ista opinione sequitur quod aliquid fuit
5 homo et tamen potest esse modo quod id numquam fuit homo. (9rb E) Quod arguitur sic. Pono (11vb M) quod iste homo qui incipit esse sit catecumenus qui de facto erit Sortes et simus in aliquo instanti intrinseco postquam incipit esse et antequam sit baptizatus. Tunc arguitur sic. Iste Sortes fuit homo. Probatur: aliquis homo fuit Sortes iste; igitur iste
10 Sortes fuit aliquis homo. Ista consequentia patet, et antecedens probatur. Iste homo erit Sortes, sed quicquid iste homo erit iste homo fuit; igitur iste homo fuit Sortes. Ista consequentia est bona et totum antecedens est verum; igitur et consequens. Iam probo aliam partem conclusionis. Et fiat ista consequentia:

15   Ille homo numquam erit baptizatus 'Sortes', nec est, nec fuit; igitur ille homo numquam fuit Sortes.

Ista consequentia est bona, et totum antecedens est possibile; igitur et consequens.

⟨3.3⟩ Tertio arguitur sic. Et sit *A* ista propositio scripta:

20   Hoc est Sortes,

non limitata ad aliquem hominem, et imponatur hoc praedicatum 'Sortes' *B* homini noviter generato. Tunc arguitur: iam est *B* homo Sortes, et per totam illam horam fuit non Sortes. Sed illius non est causa nisi impositio vel vocatio *B* hominis per hoc nomen 'Sortes'. Igitur ex hoc, ceteris
25 paribus, incipit iste homo esse Sortes. Et quod iste homo nunc sit Sortes probatur, quia haec est vera:

     Hoc est Sortes,

praecise sic significans, postquam fuit falsa. Igitur incipit esse ita quod hoc est Sortes.

30 ⟨3.4⟩ Quarto arguitur sic. Sit *A* unus infans nondum nominatus. Tunc ille non est Sortes, nec Plato, nec sic de aliis. Et potest esse Sortes, vel Plato, vel sic de aliis. Igitur potest incipere esse Sortes, vel Plato, vel sic de aliis. Si negatur minor, contra: ista propositio

     Hoc est Ioannes

35 posterius erit vera, sic praecise significans. Ergo potest esse ita quod hoc est Sortes. Antecedens patet, posito quod compater illius componat sic:

     Hoc est Ioannes.

---

3 simpliciter *om. E*   4 sic *om. E*   5 tamen *om. E*   modo *om. M*   6 Et pono *M*   incepit *M*   8 incepit *M*   et *om. E*   10 fuit ille homo *M*   Ista *om. M*   15 numquam fuit baptizatus *E*   19 sic *om. E*   21 limitando *E* 22 Nunc arguo sic. *M*   25 nunc *om. E*   30 sic *om. E*   31 de singulis. *E* 32 aliis nominandis. *E*   Sortes et sic *E*   aliis nominandis. *M*   35 Ergo posterius erit *M*

This inference is good ⟨and⟩ known by you to be good, and the whole antecedent is known by you; therefore also the consequent. That the inference is good is clear by reference to the rule ⟨that one may infer⟩ from one interchangeable term to the other simply.

⟨3.2⟩ It follows from Opinion ⟨3⟩ that something was a man and yet it can be now that it never was a man. This is argued in the following way. Suppose that this man who is beginning to be is a catechumen who will in fact be Socrates and that we are at a time that is wholly after he begins to be and before he is baptized. Then: This Socrates was a man. Proof: Some man was this Socrates; therefore this Socrates was some man. This inference is obvious, and the antecedent is proved in the following way. This man will be Socrates, but whatever this man will be this man was; therefore this man was Socrates. This is a good inference, and the whole antecedent is true; therefore also the consequent. I now prove the other part of the conclusion. Let there be the following inference:

This man never will be, nor is, nor was baptized 'Socrates'; therefore this man never was Socrates.

This is a good inference, and the whole antecedent is possible; therefore so is the consequent.

⟨3.3⟩ Suppose that A is the written proposition

This is Socrates,

not limited to some particular man, and that the predicate 'Socrates' is imposed on the newborn man B. Then: The man B is now Socrates, and he was not Socrates for this whole hour. But the only reason for that is the imposition or the calling of the man B by the name 'Socrates'. Therefore, other things being equal, this man begins to be Socrates from this time. That the man B is now Socrates is proved because the proposition

This is Socrates

is true, signifying just that, after it was false. Therefore it begins to be the case that this is Socrates.

⟨3.4⟩ Let A be an infant not yet named. Then: He is not Socrates, or Plato, and so on. And he can be Socrates, or Plato, and so on. Therefore he can begin to be Socrates, or Plato, and so on. If one denies the minor premiss, then on the contrary: The proposition

This is John

will be true afterwards, signifying just that. Therefore it can be the case that this is Socrates. The antecedent is clear on the hypothesis that his godfather decides as follows:

This is John.

Nec est aliqua evidentia ex qua concludi debet quod aliquis homo est Sortes, quin per idem, haec est vera:

Hoc est Sortes.

Et sic, quilibet ex tibi dubio est Sortes, Plato, Cicero, eo quod nominatio
5 est impertinens sicut et credulitas hominis ad hoc quod homo sit Sortes.

⟨3.5⟩ Quinto arguitur quod non propter hoc

Iste homo erit Sortes quia erit hoc

stat enim quod iste homo erit hoc et tamen non erit Sortes. Igitur ista causa non valet, et sic opinio improbatur.

10   Ad argumenta facta contra istam tertiam opinionem, quae inter ceteras probabilis est, respondetur concedendo quod ratio quare tu es Sortes, vel Ioannes, est quia tu es iste homo et econtra, dato quod tu sis Sortes, vel Ioannes.

Si igitur quaeritur quare est iste homo Sortes, dicatur quia ipse est iste
15 homo et non quia sic vocatur. Quia esses asinus, in casu, quod sic esses vocatus. Nec debes dicere quod ideo es Sortes quia hoc nomen sit tibi impositum legitime in baptismate, quia tunc aliquis homo fuit leo, per illud scriptum 'Sancte Leo, ora pro nobis'. Similiter, multi numquam fuerunt baptizati. Debes igitur dicere quod tu es Sortes quia tu es iste
20 homo.

⟨3.1R⟩ Ad primum ergo argumentum respondeo quod admisso illo casu, non sequitur quod scio istum esse Sortem, nec quod scio istum esse istum hominem. Immo nec sequitur me scire aliquem hominem esse, quia non sequitur:

25   Aliquis homo est, et tu scis illum esse Sortem; igitur tu scis aliquem hominem esse.

Si tamen ponatur, cum toto casu, quod sciam illum hominem esse illum hominem, adhuc non admitto casum. Quia hoc nomen 'Sortes' et omnia nomina propria possunt connotare substantiam simpliciter, sine aliqua
30 appellatione, vel possunt connotare substantiam cum tali appellatione.

Primo modo nego casum, sequitur enim:

Scio illum hominem esse illum hominem; igitur scio illum esse Sortem,

dato quod ille homo sit Sortes. Et si ex hoc concluditur quod eo ipso quod
35 ego video aliquem hominem scio utrum est Robertus, vel Ludovicus, concedo (12ra M) consequentiam, supposito quod talis est Robertus, vel Ludovicus.

7 Iste erit Sortes quare erit homo *E*   11 concedendo et sustinendo ratio *M*
11–12 vel Plato *E*; Ioannes, vel Sortes *M*   12 homo *om. M*   tu (2) *om. E*
12–13 scis Sortem, vel Ioannem *M*; sis Sortes, vel Plato *E*   14 dicatur quod ipse *M*
15 Quia tu es asinus *M*   16 ideo est *M*   nomen fuit *M*   21 illo *om. E*
22 quod (2) *om. E*   25 tu nescis illum *M*   27 ponitur *M*   35–6 vel Ioannes,
etc., concedo *M*   36 esset *M*   36–7 vel Ioannes. *M*

And the only evidence from which one must conclude that a man is Socrates is the very same—viz. that this is true:

> This is Socrates.

And so each person is Socrates, or Plato, or Cicero, regardless of any doubt you may have about it, because the naming is irrelevant just as a man's belief is irrelevant to the fact that a man is Socrates.

⟨3.5⟩ The explanation

> The man will be Socrates because he will be this

does not hold good, for it is consistent that that man will be this and yet will not be Socrates. Therefore the explanation is unacceptable, and so the opinion is disproved.

⟨*Replies to the Arguments against Opinion 3*⟩

In reply to the arguments raised against Opinion ⟨3⟩, which is acceptable as compared with the others, I grant that the reason why you are Socrates, or John, is that you are this man, and vice versa—provided that you *are* Socrates, or John.

Therefore if I am asked why this man is Socrates, I say that it is because he is this man and not because he is called that. It is because you are a donkey (in case you are) that you are called that. Nor must you say that you are Socrates because that name was legitimately imposed on you in baptism, for in that case at least one man was a lion (*leo*), judging by the inscription 'Saint Leo, pray for us'. Likewise, many were never baptized. Therefore you must say that you are Socrates because you are this man.

⟨3.1R⟩ I reply to the first argument, therefore, by saying that even when one has accepted that hypothesis it does not follow that I know that he is Socrates or that I know that he is this man. It does not even follow that I know that a man is, for this does not follow:

> A man is, and you know that he is Socrates; therefore you know that a man is.

But if one supposes, along with the whole hypothesis, that I know that this man is this man, then I do not even accept the hypothesis. The name 'Socrates' and all proper names can (1) connote a substance simply, without any appellation, or they can (2) connote a substance together with such an appellation.[k]

As regards (1), I reject the hypothesis, for this follows:

> I know that this man is this man; therefore I know that he is Socrates,

given that this man is Socrates. And if one concludes from this that by the very fact that I see a man I know whether it is Robert, or Louis, I grant the inference—provided that it *is* Robert, or Louis.

Si autem sumantur nomina propria secundo modo, admitto casum. Et
ulterius nego quod sciam illum esse Sortem. Et tunc ad argumentum:

> Tu scis illum esse illum hominem, et ille homo est Sortes; igitur tu
> scis illum esse Sortem,

5 nego consequentiam. Et tunc quando dicitur quod ibidem arguitur ab uno
convertibili ad reliquum, nego. Dico enim quod iste terminus 'Sortes'
sumptus secundo modo non convertitur cum illo termino 'iste homo' sicut
nec iste terminus 'album' cum isto termino 'homo' licet idem sit homo
et album. Verumtamen si ly .Sortes. solum connotat substantiam, bene
10 convertitur cum ly .iste homo. Verumtamen ab uno convertibili ad reliquum cum termino modali praecedente non valet argumentum, ut

> Hoc scio esse hominem; igitur hoc scio esse risibilem.

⟨3.2R⟩ Ad secundum, cum infertur quod aliquid fuit homo, et potest esse
quod illud numquam fuit homo, nego illam conclusionem. Et ulterius
15 admitto (9ᵛᵃ E) casum, et concedo quod iste est Sortes ante baptisma et
fuit Sortes et non potest non fuisse Sortes. Et tunc ad argumentum:

> Iste numquam baptizabitur 'Sortes'; igitur numquam fuit Sortes,

nego illam consequentiam. Et causa quare est saepius dicta. Non enim est
vel fuit Sortes quia sic vocabatur, licet enim adhuc in baptismate vocaretur
20 'Plato' vel 'asinus', non minus esset vel fuisset Sortes.

⟨3.3R⟩ Ad tertium admitto casum. Et ulterius dubito illam:

> B est Sortes.

Et tunc ad argumentum:

> Ista propositio est vera, significando praecise B esse Sortem; igitur..,

25 huic dicitur concedendo illam propositionem esse veram. Dubito tamen an
illa praecise significet B esse Sortem. Cum toto enim casu stat quod ille
terminus 'Sortes' non significet Sortem vel non significet illum Sortem
(demonstrando B) sed aliquid aliud vel nihil. Unde hic est consimiliter
respondendum sicut in alia arte obligatoria. Ut posito quod

30 > Deus est

> et

> Hoc est hoc

---

2 scio M   14–15 admitto ulterius E   18 saepius *om.* E   dicta est. E   18–19 est
vel *om.* E   19 sic vocabitur M   26 significet praecise M

If, on the other hand, proper names are taken in accordance with (2), I accept the hypothesis. Furthermore, I deny that I know that he is Socrates. As for the argument

> You know that he is this man, and this man is Socrates; therefore you know that he is Socrates,

I reject the inference. And I deny the claim that in that case one is arguing from one interchangeable term to the other. I maintain that the term 'Socrates' taken in accordance with (2) is not interchangeable with the term 'this man' any more than the term 'white' is interchangeable with 'man' even though one and the same thing is a man and white. But if ⟨in accordance with (1)⟩ 'Socrates' connotes substance alone, then it is rightly interchangeable with 'this man'. The argument from one interchangeable term to the other with a preceding modal term[l] is not acceptable, however. For example:

> This I know to be a man; therefore this I know to be risible.

⟨3.2R⟩ I reject the inference in which it is inferred that something was a man and it can be that it never was a man. Moreover, I accept the hypothesis, and I grant that he is Socrates before baptism and was Socrates and cannot not have been Socrates. As for the argument

> He never will be baptized 'Socrates'; therefore he never was Socrates,

I reject the inference. The reason why has been pointed out rather often.[m] It is not the case that he is or was Socrates because he was called that, for even if he were called 'Plato' or 'Donkey' in baptism, he would be or have been Socrates no less.

⟨3.3R⟩ I accept the hypothesis. But I doubt this:

> B is Socrates.

As for the argument

> That proposition is true, signifying just that B is Socrates; therefore
>   . . . ,

I grant that that proposition is true. But what I am in doubt about is whether it does signify just that B is Socrates. It is consistent with the whole hypothesis that the term 'Socrates' does not signify Socrates or does not signify this Socrates (indicating B) but either something else or nothing. Thus one must reply here as in another *ars obligatoria*.[n] Suppose, for example, that the propositions

> God is

and

> This is this

convertantur, et scias hoc bene. Tunc: isto casu posito proponitur haec est vera:

> Deus est.

Concedo, quia verum et impertinens. Deinde si proponitur haec est vera:

5   Hoc est hoc,

concedo, quia sequens ex posito cum concesso sequitur. Enim

> Deus est

et

> Hoc est hoc

10 convertuntur. Sed haec est vera:

> Deus est;

igitur haec est vera:

> Hoc est hoc.

> Sed si ulterius proponitur simpliciter

15   Hoc est hoc,

dubitetur sicut et ante casum.

> Et si tunc arguitur sic:

>> Haec est vera: 'hoc est hoc', quae praecise primarie significat hoc esse hoc; ergo hoc est hoc. Ista consequentia est bona scita a te esse
20   bona, et antecedens est scitum a te; igitur et consequens. Et per consequens male respondes dubitando ipsam.

Respondeo negando quod antecedens est scitum a me. Licet enim concedam in casu illo illam esse veram, dubito tamen an ipsa significet praecise hoc esse hoc. Ex quo per ly .hoc. adhuc non sum certificatus.

25 Similiter iuxta sententiam superius positam, si esset aliquis homo noviter generatus qui non esset Sortes, et sibi imponeretur hoc nomen 'Sortes', proposita mihi ista:

> Iste est Sortes,

negarem eam.

30 Et si tunc argueretur sic:

>> Ista propositio est vera: 'iste est Sortes', quae praecise primarie significat istum esse Sortem; igitur iste est Sortes. Ista consequentia est bona. Antecedens est verum; igitur et consequens.

---

4 Conceditur *M*   6 conceditur *M*   concero *M*   22 Respondetur *M*
24 non certificatur. *E*

are interchangeable, and that you know it. Then: Once this hypothesis has been put forward one maintains that the proposition

God is

is true. I grant it, for it is true and independent. If one then maintains that the proposition

This is this

is true, I grant it, for what follows from the hypothesis along with what was granted does follow. For the propositions

God is

and

This is this

are interchangeable. But the proposition

God is

is true. Therefore the proposition

This is this

is true.

But if, further, one proposes simply

This is this,

let it be doubted just as before the hypothesis.

And if one then argues in the following way:

> The proposition 'This is this' is true, and it primarily signifies just that this is this; therefore this is this. This inference is good ⟨and⟩ known by you to be good, and the antecedent is known by you; therefore also the consequent. Consequently you reply incorrectly when you doubt it.

In that case I reply by denying that the antecedent is known by me. For although as regards the hypothesis I grant that that proposition is true, nevertheless I doubt whether it does signify just that this is this. For that reason I am not even convinced by the 'this'.

Likewise in accordance with the view put forward above,[o] if there were a new-born man who was not Socrates and the name 'Socrates' were imposed on him, then if I were to be confronted with the proposition

This is Socrates,

I would deny it.

And if one then argues in the following way:

> The proposition 'This is Socrates' is true, and it primarily signifies just that this is Socrates; therefore this is Socrates. This is a good inference, and its antecedent is true; therefore also the consequent.

Dicitur quod antecedens non est verum. Licet enim illa sit vera in voce et in scripto:

> Iste est Sortes,

ipsa tamen non sic significat primarie, immo nec iste terminus 'Sortes'
5 significat ipsum Sortem sed bene forte illum hominem, quia tale non subordinatur in mente huic:

> *Iste homo est Sortes,*

cum ipsa est falsa, sed bene huic:

> *Iste homo est iste homo,*

10 seipso demonstrato vel uni alteri.

Exemplum enim huius habemus in consimili materia. Ut posito quod haec sit vera:

> Homo est asinus,

admittitur. Et cum proponitur, (12rb M) conceditur. Deinde si proponitur

15 > Homo est asinus,

negatur, quia falsum et impossibile.

Et si tunc arguitur sic:

> Haec est vera: 'homo est asinus', quae praecise primarie sic significat; ergo homo est asinus,

20 concedo consequentiam, et nego minorem tamquam repugnantem casui.

Et si quaeritur quid illa primarie significat, dicatur quod unum verum. Et si quaeritur quid est illud, non determinetur talis quaestio.

Eodem modo est respondendum in materia de illis pronominibus propriis.

⟨3.4R⟩ Ad quartum cum proponitur quod *A* sit unus infans nondum
25 nominatus, admitto. Et ulterius nego illam copulativam:

> Iste non est Sortes, nec Plato, nec sic de ceteris, et iste potest esse Sortes vel Plato et sic de aliis.

Sequitur enim:

> Iste non est Sortes, nec Plato, nec sic de ceteris; ergo non potest esse
30 > aliquis illorum.

Verumtamen proposita mihi prima parte illius copulativae, nego eam, videlicet, quod iste homo non est Sortes, nec Plato, nec sic de ceteris. Et si

---

1 Licet igitur sit *E*   5 talis *M*   17 sic *om. E*   22 determinatur *E*
24 cum imponitur quod *E*   26 et iste *om. M*   26–7 potest . . . aliis. *om. M*
29 Sortes, vel Plato *E*   32 videlicet *om. E*   32 Et cum *E*

In that case I say that the antecedent is not true. For although the proposition

This is Socrates

is true spoken and written, it does not primarily signify that—indeed, the term 'Socrates' does not signify this Socrates but perhaps rightly signifies this man—because it is not subordinated in the mind to

This man is Socrates,

since that is false, but rather to this:

This man is this man,

indicating that very one himself or another.

We have an example of this in material of the same sort. If, for instance, it is supposed that

A man is a donkey

is true, the hypothesis is accepted. And when that is put forward, it is granted. And if one then puts forward the proposition

A man is a donkey,

it is denied, for it is false and impossible.

And if one then argues in the following way:

The proposition 'a man is a donkey' is true, and it primarily signifies just that; therefore a man is a donkey,

I grant the inference, and I deny the minor premiss on the ground that it conflicts with the hypothesis.

And if one then asks what that does primarily signify, let it be said that it is a truth. And if one asks what that is, let that sort of question go unanswered.

One should reply in the same way as regards the topic of proper pronouns.[p]

⟨3.4R⟩ I accept the hypothesis that A is an infant who has not yet been named. But I deny the conjunctive proposition

He is not Socrates, or Plato, or any of the others, and he can be Socrates, or Plato, or any of the others

on the ground that it is impossible. For this follows:

He is not Socrates, or Plato, or any of the others; therefore he cannot be any of them.

But if I am confronted with the first part of the conjunctive—viz. that this man is not Socrates, or Plato, or any of the others—I deny it. And if it is put to me that he is Socrates, I am in doubt about it; if that he is Plato, I am

proponitur mihi iste est Sortes, dubito, iste est Plato, dubito, et sic ulterius
divisim proponendo. Et tunc quando arguitur:

> Suppono quod compater illius componat sic: *hoc est Ioannes*. Posterius
> erit vera, sic significando praecise,

5 dicitur ut prius, dubitando utrum ipsa sic significabit praecise. Non enim
propter hoc est Ioannes, quia compater sic componet. Posset enim componere quod hoc esset asinus, et tamen non ita esset.

⟨3.5R⟩ Ad ultimum, quando arguitur quod stat quod hoc erit hoc et
quod hoc non erit Sortes, respondeo quaerendo an demonstres Sortem
10 futurum vel non. Si non, nihil concludit argumentum. Si sic, nego copulativam illam.

Et tunc si arguitur haec consequentia non valet demonstrando Sortem:

> Hoc erit hoc; ergo hoc erit Sortes,

respondeo negando illud quod non valet.

15 Et si arguitur:

> Iste homo poterit primo vocari 'Plato', et hoc cum ceteris requisitis;
> ergo ly .Plato. poterit ipsum vere significare et pro illo supponere.
> Et per consequens illa propositio poterit esse vera: 'iste est Plato',
> et si sic iste poterit esse Plato.

20 Ad istud dicitur negando istam ultimam consequentiam, sicut non sequitur:

> Haec potest esse vera: 'tu es asinus'; ergo tu potes asinus.

Sed contra, iste modus arguendi generaliter tenet:

> Haec est vera: 'tu es homo', quae praecise significat et primarie te
> esse hominem; ergo tu es homo.

25 Et per consequens tenet talis modus arguendi respectu talis:

> Tu es (9vb E) asinus.

Respondeo quod bene tenet cum tali medio, cum quo tamen non arguc-
batur. Sequitur enim:

> Haec propositio est vera: 'iste homo est asinus', quae praecise primarie
30   significat sic; ergo iste homo est asinus.

Sed negatur minor. Unde dato quod ly .asinus. solum significet quod 'iste
homo', tunc ita bene esset concedenda ista:

> Iste homo est asinus

sicut

35   Iste homo est homo,

licet numquam concederem cum mihi proponeretur.

---

2 divisim *om. E*   4 erat *M*   6–7 enim sic componere *M*   8 quod (2) *om. E*
13 Hoc erit; ergo *M*   14 respondetur *M*   non sequatur. *E*   19 si *om. E*   iste
om. E   23–9 quae . . . asinus', *om. M*   30 sic significat *M*   31 negetur *M*
significaret *M*

in doubt about it; and so one, putting it dividedly.[q] And then when it is argued

> Suppose that his godfather decides as follows: *This is John.* Then the proposition 'This is John', will be true afterwards, signifying just that,

I say as before that I doubt whether it will signify just that. For he is John not because the godfather decides as he does. He could decide that he was a donkey and yet he would not be so.

⟨3.5R⟩ In reply to the last argument, in which it is argued that it is consistent that this will be this and that this will not be Socrates, I ask whether or not you are indicating the future Socrates. If not, the argument concludes nothing. If so, then I deny that conjunctive proposition.

And if one then argues that the inference

> This will be this; therefore this will be Socrates

is unacceptable if Socrates is indicated, I reply by denying that it is unacceptable.

And if one argues in the following way:

> This man will be able to be called 'Plato' at first (along with the other requirements); therefore 'Plato' will be able to signify him truly and to supposit for him. Consequently the proposition 'This is Plato' will be able to be true, and if that is the case he will be able to be Plato.

My reply is to reject this last inference, just as this does not follow:

> 'You are a donkey' can be true; therefore you can be a donkey.

But on the contrary, this way of arguing does hold good in general:

> The proposition 'You are a man' is true, and it primarily signifies just that you are a man; therefore you are a man.

Consequently such a way of arguing holds good in respect of such a proposition as

> You are a donkey.

I reply that it does hold good with such a medium, but it was not argued with such a medium. For this does follow:

> The proposition 'This man is a donkey' is true, and it primarily signifies just that; therefore this man is a donkey.

But I deny the minor premiss. Thus, given that 'donkey' signifies only what 'this man' signifies, it would be just as correct to grant

> This man is a donkey

as it is to grant

> This man is a man,

although I would never grant it when it was put to me.[r]

Et si quaeritur quare non concedis eam, respondeo 'Quia non mihi placet'. Et causa est quia licet possibile sit ipsam significare me hominem esse, tamen in rei veritate non sic significat, qualitercumque casum ponas. Haec autem et similia magis patent in obligationibus.

5 Et licet haec sint probabiliter dicta, tamen gratia alicuius variationis et ut puto veritatem, dico quod

> Aliquis est Sortes ex eo quod vocatur tali nomine proprio authentica sive stabili impositione.

Primo namque summo illud verbum 'vocatur' non ut dicit actum sed 10 habitum, stat enim quod aliquis sit Sortes licet non actualiter ab aliquo nominetur.

Item dico 'nomine proprio' quia si vocaretur nomine appellativo authentica impositione, non propter hoc de ipso verificaretur talis terminus sive significatum illius. Sicut sunt isti termini vel nomina appellativa: 'homo', 15 'animal', 'lupus', 'equus', et huiusmodi. Unde non sequitur:

> Tu vocaris 'equus' authentica impositione; ergo tu es equus.

Dicitur ultimo 'authentica impositione' quia si aliquis fuisset in baptizmate vocatus 'Sortes', et tunc alius vel ipsemet vocaret ipsum 'Plato', qui non se haberet per modum authenticum imponendi, talis non propter hoc 20 esset Plato. Immo si Sortes proprii nominis oblitus esset et a tota communitate vocaretur (12ᵛᵃ M) 'Plato', non propter hoc esset Plato, quia nominatio illa forte non esset authentica impositio.

Voco ergo authenticam impositionem illam quae fit in baptismo aut aequipollentis quoad hoc (quod dico propter denominationes qui haben-25 tur apud infideles). Est etiam authentica impositio illa quae consurgit in creatione papae vel imperatoris, aut novi religiosi ordinem intrantis, cui nomen authentice similiter potest imponi atque mutari.

Ex quibus sequitur quod aliquis est Sortes qui aliquando erit Plato et non Sortes, et aliquis est Plato et non Sortes qui per totam vitam suam fuit

---

2–3 esse hominem *M*   6 veritatis *E*   7 nomine 'Sortes' authentica *E*
10–11 licet ab aliquo actualiter non nominetur. *E*   12 vocaretur termino appellativo
M   15 'animal', 'lapis', et 'equus' *M*   18 et iam alius *M*   'Platonem' *M*
20 esset oblitus *M*   24 dico quod propter *M*   25 Est autem authentica *E*
26–7 cui non authentice *E*   27 similiter *om. M*   28–9 Plato sive non *M*

And if I am asked why I do not grant it, I reply 'Because it does not please me'. And that is because although it is possible that it signify that I am a man, as a matter of fact it does not signify it, however you put the hypothesis.

But these matters and other like them are clearer in connection with the *obligationes.*[s]

⟨A Fourth Opinion regarding Proper Names⟩

Although these things have been said in such a way as to be acceptable, still, for the sake of some variety and so that I may consider ⟨its⟩ truth, I say that

> Someone is Socrates because he is called by that proper name in an authentic or stable imposition.

⟨Explanation of Opinion 4⟩

First, I use the verb 'is called' not in the sense of an action but in the sense of a disposition, for it is consistent that someone be Socrates even though no one actually calls him by name.

Next, I say 'proper name' because if he were called by an appellative name[t] in an authentic imposition it would not be for that reason that such a term or its significatum would be made true of him. I mean such terms or appellative names as 'man', 'animal', 'wolf', 'horse', and the like. Thus this does not follow:

> You are called 'horse' in an authentic imposition; therefore you are a horse.

Finally, I say 'in an authentic imposition' because if someone had been called 'Socrates' in baptism, and then someone else or he himself were to call him 'Plato', which is not the result of an authentic mode of imposition, he would not for that reason be Plato. Indeed if Socrates had forgotten his proper name and was called 'Plato' by the entire community, he would not for that reason be Plato, since that sort of calling him by the name probably would not constitute an authentic imposition.

What I call an authentic imposition, therefore, is that which is accomplished in baptism or in something equivalent to it. (I say this in order to take into account such name-givings as there are among the heathen.) Another authentic imposition arises in the creation of a pope or an emperor, or of a religious novice entering an order, on whom likewise a name can authentically be imposed and changed.

From these considerations it follows that (1) someone is Socrates who at some time will be Plato and not Socrates, and that (2) some one is Plato and not Socrates who his whole life has been Socrates. ⟨(1) follows⟩ given that

Sortes, dato quod aliquis sit iam Sortes ex impositione facta in baptizmate et aliquando erit papa in cuius creatione nominabitur 'Plato'. Et ita pro altera parte similiter dicatur.

⟨4.1⟩ Contra istam positionem est unum forte argumentum, nam data
5 positione, sequitur quod huiusmodi termini 'Sortes' et 'Plato' non sunt termini praedicamenti substantiae. Probo consequentiam, quia de eodem possunt affirmative verificari et non verificari successive praeter corruptionem subiecti; ergo sunt termini accidentales et connotativi. Consequentia patet per descriptionem accidentis ponentem quod accidens est quod
10 adest vel abest, etc.

⟨4.1R⟩ Ad istud argumentum respondetur negando consequentiam. Pro cuius declaratione est notandum quod ille terminus est in praedicamento substantiae (saltim directe, quia per reductionem multi sunt termini accidentales, de quibus alias dicetur) qui est terminus simplex et non
15 significat nisi substantiam distincte, ita quod non significat aliquid quod se habeat per modum accidentis.

Ex quo patet quod isti termini 'Sortes' et 'Plato' sunt in praedicamento substantiae, cum ipsi non significent distincte aliquid quod se habeat per modum accidentis. Sed iste terminus 'album' est bene praedicamenti
20 accidentium, quia significat aliquid per modum accidentis, puta albedinem. Et ita de aliis dicatur.

Et tunc ad definitionem accidentis:

Accidens est quod adest vel abest praeter subiecti corruptionem.

Hic est dicendum quod si definitio illa sic intelligatur quemadmodum
25 aliqui ipsam explanant, videlicet,

Accidens est terminus universalis praedicabilis denominative de subiecto affirmative et negative successive praeter corruptionem illius pro quo supponit,

dico quod ista est falsa. Nec est de intentione Porphyrii sive Aristotelis.
30 Unde patet quod iste terminus 'homo' est praedicamenti substantiae directe, non terminus accidentalis, et tamen potest verificari affirmative et negative successive praeter corruptionem illius pro quo supponit. Nam

4 istam opinionem est E   4-5 data ipsa impositione, M   10 adest
et abest M   etc. om. M   15 significat E   18 significent determinate
aliquid M   19 est bene om. M   19-20 praedicamento accidentis M   22 accidentis om. M   23 adest et abest M; abest etc. E   praeter subiecti corruptionem
om. E   24 sic distincte intelligatur M   25 aliqui om. M   explanant ipsam E
32 negative et successive M

someone is now Socrates as a consequence of an imposition accomplished in baptism and at some time will be a pope who in his creation will be named 'Plato'. And something of a similar sort may be said in support of (2).

⟨Argument against Opinion 4⟩

⟨4.1⟩ There is a powerful argument against this position, for if the position is granted, it follows that such terms as 'Socrates' and 'Plato' are not terms belonging to the category of substance. I prove the inference in the following way. They can be successively verified and not verified affirmatively of one and the same thing apart from the corruption of the subject; therefore they are accidental and connotative terms.[u] This inference is obvious as a consequence of the description of an accident, which says that an accident is that which is present or absent, etc.[v]

⟨Reply to this Argument⟩

⟨4.1R⟩ One replies to this argument by rejecting the inference. For an explanation of this it must be noted that a term in the category of substance (at any rate directly, for many ⟨terms in the category of substance⟩ are accidental terms as a consequence of reduction, which will be discussed elsewhere)[w] is a simple term that does not signify anything but substance distinctly, in such a way that it does not signify anything that is in the mode of accident.

It is clear from this that the terms 'Socrates' and 'Plato' are in the category of substance, for they do not signify anything that is in the mode of accident distinctly. The term 'white', on the other hand, certainly does belong to the category of accidents, for it does signify something that is in the mode of accident—viz., whiteness. And the same sort of thing may be said of others.

Next, as to the definition of accident:

> An accident is that which is present or absent apart from the corruption of the subject.

Here it must be said that if this definition is understood as some explain it[x]— viz.

> An accident is a universal denominatively predicable of a subject affirmatively and negatively in succession apart from the corruption of that for which it supposits—

then I say that it is false. Nor is it in keeping with Aristotle's or Porphyry's intention.[y] Thus it is clear that the term 'man' belongs to the category of substance directly and is not an accidental term even though it can be made true affirmatively and negatively apart from the corruption of that for which it supposits. For there is a part of a man—viz. all of him except a finger—

aliqua est pars in homine, videlicet totum praeter digitum, quae non est
homo, cum sit pars, et ⟨tamen⟩ erit homo per abscissionem digiti.
   Si autem intelligatur praedicta definitio sic, videlicet,

> Accidens est quod adest vel abest ideo potest inhaerere materiae pri-
> mae et non inhaerere praeter subiecti denominationis corruptionem,

5

sic concedo definitionem. Et statim patet quod nec 'Sortes' nec 'Plato' est
accidens.
   Notanter dico 'praeter subiecti denominationis corruptionem' quia
duplex est subiectum, videlicet, inhaesionis (et hoc est materia prima),
10 aliud vero est subiectum denominationis (et hoc est compositum ex materia
et forma). Non debet definitio illa intelligi de primo subiecto, quia sic
anima intellectiva esset accidens, sed de secundo subiecto, ut naturali
philosophia habet videri.
   Ulterius est notandum quod licet negem illos terminos 'Sortes' et 'Plato'
15 esse terminos accidentales vel alicuius praedicamenti accidentium, non
tamen nego ipsos esse terminos connotativos et quoscumque terminos in
concreto significantes. Voco autem terminum connotativum quemcumque
significantem distincte et adaequate suum significatum et aliquid quod se
habeat ad illud per modum (12ᵛᵇ M) formae. Unde ille terminus 'album'
20 est connotativus quia significando album significat albedinem, quae se
habet ad album per modum formae. Similiter ille terminus 'homo' significando hominem significat animam vel humanitatem, quae se habet ad
hominem per modum formae. Si ergo aliquis terminus significando suum
significatum adaequatum significat aliquid per modum formae substan-
25 tialis, talis terminus est terminus substantialis. Si vero significando tale
significatum significat aliquid per modum accidentis, tunc est terminus
accidentalis. Si vero nec per modum ⟨formae⟩ substantialis nec per modum
accidentis, tunc non est terminus accidentalis nec substantialis.
   Ex praedictis non sequitur quod quilibet terminus substantialis est in
30 praedicamento substantiae, sicut iste terminus 'Deus', nec quilibet terminus accidentalis est in praedicamento aliquo novem accidentium, sicut
isti termini 'iustum' et 'sapiens' vel ipsorum abstracta in sua maxima
communitate, qui sunt termini aequivoci vel analogi. Sed de hoc alias in
materia consequentiarum.
35   Iuxta materiam superius tactam dubitatur utrum aliquis terminus communis sit alio communior vel omnes termini communes sint aeque communes. In qua materia sunt duae opiniones.

1 qui *E*   3 intelligitur *M*   videlicet *om. E*   4 abest etc. ideo *E*
4–5 inhaerere mihi primo et *M*   8 dico 'propter subiecti corruptionis denomina-
tionem' *E*   10 aliud non est *M*   12 subiecto *om. E*   12–13 naturalis
probans habet *M*   14 Ulterius nota quod *E*   14–15 'Sortes' . . . terminos *om. E*
15 praedicamenti continet accidentium *M*   16 cognotationis *M*   17 cogno-
tativum *M*   18 significantem determinate et *M*   adaequatum *E*   19 habet
E   ad illud *om. M*   20 cognotativus *M*; connotatus *E*   21 ad album
om. E   21–2 significat hominem significando animam *E*   24 adaequatum
significatum *E*   25 terminus talis *E*   significando talem *M*   26 significat illud
per *M*   26–7 tunc talis terminus est accidentalis. *M*   27 substantiae nec *M*;
subiecti nec *E*   per modum *om. E*   28 tunc vero non *E*   29 praedictis
vero sequitur *E*   31–2 sicut sunt illi termini *M*   33 aequivoci et analogi *E*
Sed et hoc *E*   34 Quare etc. Utrum aliquis terminus communis sit alio communior. *add. E*   35 tactam dupliciter utrum *E*

which is not a man, since it is a part, and yet will be a man after the finger has been amputated.

If, on the other hand, the above-mentioned definition is understood in this way—viz.

> An accident is that which is present or absent in such a way that it can inhere and not inhere in first matter apart from the corruption of the subject of the denomination—

then I grant the definition. And it is immediately apparent that neither 'Socrates' nor 'Plato' is an accident.

I deliberately say 'apart from the corruption of the subject of the denomination' because there are two sorts of subjects—viz. the subject of inherence (i.e. first matter) and the subject of denomination (i.e. what is composed of matter and form). The definition must not be understood as having to do with the first sort of subject, for in that case the intellective soul would be an accident, but rather with the second, as must be shown in natural philosophy.

Further, it must be noted that while I deny that the terms 'Socrates' and 'Plato' are accidental terms or that they belong to any category of accidents, I do not deny that they and all terms signifying in the concrete are connotative terms. I call a connotative term any that signifies distinctly both its adequate significatum and anything that is related to it in the mode of form. Thus the term 'white' is connotative because in signifying what is white it signifies whiteness, which is related to what is white in the mode of form. Similarly the term 'man' in signifying man signifies soul or humanity, which is related to man in the mode of form. If, therefore, a term in signifying its adequate significatum signifies something in the mode of substantial form, such a term is a substantial term. But if in signifying such a significatum it signifies something in the mode of accident, then it is an accidental term. And if ⟨it signifies something⟩ neither in the mode of substantial form nor in the mode of accident, then it is neither an accidental nor a substantial term.

It does not follow from the foregoing remarks that each substantial term is in the category of substance—e.g. 'God'[z]—nor that each accidental term is in some category of the nine accidents—e.g. the terms 'just' and 'wise' or their corresponding abstracts in their greatest degree of commonness, which are equivocal or analogical terms.[a] But this will be discussed later, in connection with inferences.[b]

⟨*Two Opinions regarding Common Terms*⟩

A doubt arises in connection with the material discussed above—viz. whether one common term is more common than another or all common terms are equally common. There are two opinions in this matter.

⟨1⟩ Prima ponit quod nullus terminus communis est reliquo communior, quia quilibet infinita significata significat.

⟨2⟩ Secunda ponit quod bene est aliquis terminus communis reliquo communior.

⟨1.1⟩ Contra primam opinionem arguitur sic. Si nullus terminus communis est reliquo communior, igitur per idem nullus terminus est reliquo superior. Consequens est contra Philosophum, ubi ponit quod in omni praedicamento est dare unum genus supremum, et genera intermedia sunt inferiora. Consequentia patet, quia ad hoc quod aliquis terminus sit superior oportet quod sit communior.

⟨1.2⟩ Secundo quia sicut praecise primae substantiae sunt magis substantiae quam secundae, ita species sunt magis substantiae quam genera. Et hoc non foret verum nisi illa quae Aristoteles vocat magis substantias forent minus communia. Igitur positio falsa. Minor patet per Philosophum, capitulo de substantia, ubi dicit quod plus in genere quam in specie determinatio fit, et iterum secundarum substantiarum magis substantia est species quam genus.

⟨1.3⟩ Tertio sequitur quod nulla esset praedicatio directa nec aliqua esset praedicatio indirecta. Consequentia tenet, quia praedicatio directa est quando superius praedicatur de inferiori suo, et praedicatio indirecta est quando inferius praedicatur de superiori suo, ut

Animal est homo.

Si ergo nullus terminus est reliquo communior, et per consequens nec superior (quia frustra fieret talis superioritas), ergo conclusio falsa.

Multa alia argumenta possent fieri contra istam opinionem, quae gratia brevitatis dimittuntur.

Dicit ergo secunda opinio quod aliquis terminus est bene reliquo communior.

⟨2.1⟩ Sed contra istam opinionem arguitur sic. Cuiuslibet termini communis communitas attenditur penes multitudinem significatorum, sed aeque multa significat unus terminus communis sicut reliquus; igitur . . . Consequentia patet cum maiori, et minor probatur. Nam quilibet terminus communis significat infinita, sed non plura significat aliquis terminus quam infinita; ergo nullus terminus est reliquo communior. Consequentia

---

2 significata *om. M*   5 Si *om. E*   6 terminus *om. E*   11 quia *om. M* praecise *om. E*   18–19 esset praedicatio *om. E*   24 falsa *om. M*   27 secunda opinio *om. E*   29 sic *om. E*   33 plura signat aliquis *E*   terminus *om. E*

⟨1⟩ No common term is more common than another, for each of them signifies infinitely many significata.

⟨2⟩ One common term is indeed more common than another.

⟨Arguments against Opinion 1⟩

⟨1.1⟩ If no common term is more common than another, then by the same token no term is superior to another. The consequent is contrary to the Philosopher, where he maintains that in every category there is a supreme genus and the intermediate genera are inferior.ᶜ The inference is obvious, for a term must be more common in order to be superior.

⟨1.2⟩ Just as first substances are more fully substances than are second substances, so species are more fully substances than are genera. That would not be true if the things that Aristotle calls more fully substances were not less common. Therefore the position is false. The minor premiss is apparent by reference to the Philosopher's chapter on substance, where he says that determination occurs more in the genus than in the species, and, again, regarding second substances, that the species is more fully substance than is the genus.ᵈ

⟨1.3⟩ It follows that there would be neither any direct predication nor any indirect predication. The inference holds good, for direct predication occurs when a superior is predicated of its inferior, and indirect predication occurs when an inferior is predicated of its superior, as in

An animal is man.

If, therefore, no term is more common than another and consequently not superior (since such superiority would be without foundation), the conclusion is false.

Many other arguments could be produced against this opinion, but they are omitted for the sake of brevity.

⟨First Argument against Opinion 2⟩

The second opinion, then, maintains that one term is indeed more common than another.

⟨2.1⟩ The commonness of each common term is taken to be based on the number of its significata, but one common term signifies just as many as does another; therefore ... The inference is obvious, along with the major premiss, and the minor premiss is proved in the following way. Each common term signifies infinitely many things, but no term signifies more than infinitely many things; therefore no term is more common than another. This inference is obvious, and the major premiss is proved as

patet, et maior probatur de illo termino 'homo', qui significat omnes homines, praeteritos, praesentes, et futuros, possibiles et imaginabiles.

⟨2.1R⟩ Ad istud argumentum breviter respondetur quod communitas termini non attenditur penes multitudinem significatorum, quia iste
5 terminus 'homo albus' est inferior ad ly .homo. et tamen plura significat, eo quod significat omne quod significat ille terminus 'homo' et praeter hoc omne albedinem. Sed ideo dicitur aliquis terminus reliquo communior quia de tali potest universaliter praedicari et non econverso vel saltem non sibi repugnat. Ideo ille terminus 'animal' est superior ad illum terminum
10 'homo', quia haec est vera praedicatio:

Omnis homo est animal,

et haec est falsa:

Omne animal est homo.

Et notanter dicitur (13ʳᵃ M) 'vel saltem non sibi repugnat' quia iste terminus
15 'iste sol' est inferius ad illum terminum (10ʳᵇ E) 'sol', et tamen universaliter praedicatur de eodem, dicendo

Omnis sol est iste sol.

De hoc tamen alias in consequentiis clarius dicetur.

⟨2.21⟩ Contra istam opinionem arguitur sic. Haec propositio est vera:

20 Omnis homo est Sortes;

igitur ille terminus 'homo' non est illo termino 'Sortes' communior, et per consequens nec aliquis alius. Consequentia bona, et antecedens probatur. Nam omnis homo est omnis homo, Sortes est homo; igitur Sortes est omnis homo. Consequentia patet, et antecedens probatur. Ille homo est
25 ille homo, et ille homo est ille homo, et sic de aliis; ergo omnis homo est omnis homo. Consequentia probatur, nam sic sequitur: ille homo est ille homo, et ille homo est ille homo, et sic de aliis; ergo ille homo est ille homo et ille homo et ille, et sic de aliis; et ultra igitur omnis homo est omnis homo. Consequentia patet, quia ex opposito consequentis sequitur
30 oppositum antecedentis. Sequitur enim:

Aliquis homo non est omnis homo; igitur iste homo non est ille homo et ille, et sic de aliis.

⟨2.22⟩ Secundo arguitur sic. Aliquis homo est qui est omnis homo; igitur omnis homo est omnis homo. Consequentia bona, et antecedens

---

2 praesentes, praeteritos M   5–6 et non plura significat esse quod E
7 omnem E   album. M   9 est terminus superior M   16 dicendo om.
M   18 De his E   clarius om. E   19 sic om. E   Haec . . . vera om. M
21 est communior illo M   communior om. M   25 de singulis; M   26 nam
om. M   27 de singulis; M   28 et ille est iste, et sic E; et iste homo et iste,
et sic de singulis; M   31–2 est iste, et sic de singulis, etc. M   33 sic om. E
omnis om. E   34 Consequentia patet, et M

regards the term 'man', which signifies all men, past, present, and future, possible and imaginable.

⟨Reply to the First Argument against Opinion 2⟩

⟨2.1R⟩ The short reply to this argument is to observe that the common-ness of a term is not taken to be based on the number of significata. The term 'white man' is inferior to the term 'man' and nevertheless signifies more things, for it signifies everything that the term 'man' signifies and whiteness besides. But one term is said to be more common than another because the one can be universally predicated of the other and not vice versa, or at any rate this is not self-inconsistent. Therefore the term 'animal' is superior to the term 'man', for the predication

Every man is an animal

is true, and

Every animal is a man

is false. I say 'or at any rate this is not self-inconsistent' quite deliberately, because the term 'this sun' is inferior to the term 'sun', and yet it is univer-sally predicated of it, as when one says

Every sun is this sun.

But this will be discussed more clearly on another occasion in what follows.ᵉ

⟨Second Set of Arguments against Opinion 2⟩

⟨2.21⟩ The proposition

Every man is Socrates

is true; therefore the term 'man' is not more common than the term 'Socrates', and consequently neither is any other. The inference is good, and the antecedent is proved in the following way. Every man is every man, Socrates is a man; therefore Socrates is every man. This inference is obvious, and its antecedent is proved in the following way. This man is this man, and this man is this man, and so on as regards the others; therefore every man is every man. Proof of the inference: This man is this man, and this man is this man, and so on; therefore this man is this man and this man and this, and so on; and so, further, every man is every man. This inference is obvious, since the opposite of the antecedent follows from the opposite of the consequent; for this follows:

Some man is not every man; therefore this man is not this man and this, and so on.

⟨2.22⟩ There is some man who is every man; therefore every man is every man. The inference is good, and its antecedent is proved in the

probatur. Nam aliquis homo est, et quilibet homo est ille; igitur aliquis homo est qui est omnis homo. Consequentia bona, et antecedens probatur quia antecedens est una copulativa cuius prima pars est vera et secunda pars est una universalis cuius quaelibet singularis est vera cum prima parte.

5 Ergo ipsa universalis est vera cum prima parte, et per consequens tota copulativa vera. Consequentia patet cum maiori, et minor probatur. Nam quacumque singulari secundae partis data, illa est vera cum prima parte, demonstrando enim Sortem, haec est vera:

Aliquis homo est, et ille homo est ille.

10 Similiter, demonstrando Platonem, haec est vera:

Aliquis homo est, et ille homo est ille.

⟨2.23⟩ Tertio arguitur sic. Aliquis homo erit omnis homo; igitur omnis homo est omnis homo. Ista consequentia est bona, et antecedens est tibi dubium; igitur consequens non est a te negandum. Quod illa consequentia

15 sit bona arguitur. Sequitur enim Sortes erit omnis homo; igitur ipse est omnis homo vel non est omnis homo. Si est omnis homo, habetur intentum. Si non est omnis homo, et omnis homo est, igitur aliquis homo est qui non erit Sortes, et per consequens Sortes non erit omnis homo, quid est oppositum antecedentis.

20 ⟨2.24⟩ Similiter sequitur: si Sortes erit omnis homo et Plato ⟨qui est⟩ est homo vel erit homo, igitur Sortes erit Plato, qui est, et per idem omnis homo. Consequentia patet, quia arguitur a termino stante confuse et distributive ad suum inferius cum debito medio.

⟨2.25⟩ Similiter: si Sortes erit omnis homo, igitur Sortes erit omnis

25 homo qui erit. Consequentia probatur, nam in ista propositione:

Sortes erit omnis homo

distribuitur ly .homo. pro omni homine respectu verbi de futuro; igitur distribuitur pro omni homine qui erit, et si sic consequentia est bona. Quare etc.

30 ⟨2.21R⟩ Ad ista tria argumenta respondetur. Ad primum, nego tam primam quam secundam consequentiam. Nego primam quia non arguitur inductive sicut argumentum ostendit inducendo. Deberet enim sic argui. Ille homo est omnis homo, et ille homo, etc.; igitur omnis homo est omnis

---

9 homo (2) *om. E*   11 homo (2) *om. E*   12 sic *om. E*   est *E*   13 Ista *om.*
E   14 igitur et consequens *M*   15 est bona *E*   enim *om. M*   Sortes est *E*
16 ipse est homo si est *E*   17 aliquis est homo *E*   18 est Sortes *E*   19 oppositum consequentis. *M*   20 sequitur *om. E*   Sortes est *E*   21 erit igitur Sortes
et Plato *E*   24 omnis *om. M*   27 homine et hoc respectu *E*   28 distribuitur ly .homo. pro *M*   32 ostenditur reducere. *E*   33 homo (3) *om. E*
etc. *om. M*

following way. There is some man, and each man is he; therefore there is some man who is every man. This inference is good, and its antecedent is proved because it is a conjunctive proposition of which the first part is true and the second part is a universal proposition each of whose singulars is true together with the first part. Therefore the universal proposition itself is true together with the first part, and consequently the whole conjunctive proposition is true. This inference is obvious, along with the major premiss. The minor premiss is proved in the following way. Any given singular of the second part is true together with the first part, for

> There is some man, and this man is he

is true, indicating Socrates. Likewise

> There is some man, and this man is he

is true, indicating Plato.

⟨2.23⟩ Some man will be every man; therefore every man is every man. This is a good inference, and you are in doubt about its antecedent; therefore you must not deny its consequent. That this inference is good is argued in the following way. Socrates will be every man; therefore he is every man or he is not every man. If he is every man, we have the intended conclusion. If he is not every man, and every man is, then there is some man who will not be Socrates, and consequently Socrates will not be every man, which is the opposite of the antecedent.

⟨2.24⟩ Similarly, this follows. If Socrates will be every man and Plato, who is, is a man or will be a man, then Socrates will be Plato, who is, and by the same token every man. This inference is obvious, since it argues from a term with distributive confused *suppositio* to its inferior with the required medium.*f*

⟨2.25⟩ Similarly, if Socrates will be every man, then Socrates will be every man who will be. Proof of the inference: In the proposition

> Socrates will be every man

'man' is distributed over every man is respect of a future-tense verb; therefore it is distributed over every man who will be, and if that is the case the inference is good. Therefore, etc.

⟨*Replies to the Second Set of Arguments against Opinion 2*⟩

⟨2.21R⟩ I reject both the first and the second inference. I reject the first because one does not argue inductively in the way indicated by the argument in its induction. One would have to argue in the following way. This man is every man, and this man ⟨is every man⟩, etc.; therefore every man is every man. This is a good inference, but its antecedent is false. One can,

homo. Consequentia est bona, et antecedens est falsum. Potest tamen dubitari prima consequentia quia dubitatur an arguatur ex impossibili an ex vero ratione alterius demonstrationis continue a parte utriusque extremi.

Nego secundam consequentiam quia arguitur a copulativa ad proposi-
5 tionem de copulato extremo, quae quidem significat quod aliquis homo est omnis homo.

Unde est notandum quod quandocumque illum terminum 'et sic de aliis' praecedit una propositio copulativa, tunc tota propositio est copulativa, ut

10　　　Ille homo est ille homo, et ille homo est ille, et sic de aliis.

(13rb M) Quando vero talem terminum praecedit una propositio de copulato extremo, tunc tota sine aliqua distinctione est de copulato extremo, ut

　　　Ille homo est ille homo et ille homo, et sic de aliis.

Si autem talem terminum praecederet una propositio categorica de simplici
15 subiecto et praedicato, talis propositio posset esse tam copulativa quam de copulato extremo, ut haec:

　　　Ille homo est ille homo, et sic de aliis.

Ideo propositio talis est distinguenda secundum compositionem et divisionem. Et tunc in sensu diviso potest concedi eisdem demonstratis per
20 ly .iste. a parte ⟨subiecti et per ly .isti. a parte⟩ praedicati. In sensu autem composito est simpliciter neganda.

⟨2.22R⟩ Ad secundum argumentum cum arguitur quod

　　　Aliquis homo est qui est omnis homo; igitur . . . ,

concedo consequentiam et nego antecedens. Ad probationem illius ante-
25 cedentis respondeo primo negando consequentiam, quia antecedens est possibile et consequens impossibile. Unde dato quod non esset nisi unus homo masculus, haec esset vera:

　　　Aliquis homo est, et quilibet homo est ille,

et haec est falsa:

30　　　Aliquis homo est qui est omnis homo

quia ex ipso sequitur statim quod aliquis homo est aliqua mulier, quod est impossibile. Et quod illud sequatur patet, quia necessario aliqua mulier est, licet non sit necessarium aliquem hominem esse.

Verumtamen si ex illo antecedente concluditur quod aliquis homo est
35 qui est quilibet homo, concedo consequentiam et nego antecedens. Et tunc ad argumentum:

　　　Antecedens est una copulativa cuius prima pars est vera, et

1 est (1) om. E　　　5 de toto extremo E　　　7–8 de singulis M　　　10 et ille homo est ille om. E　　de singulis. M　　　12 aliqua distributione est E 13 homo (3) om. E　de singulis. M　　14 categorica om. E　　15 subiecto vel praedicato M　esse om. E　　　17 Iste homo M et E　　de singulis. M　　　19 concedi diversis demonstratis E　　22 quod om. M　　24 concedendo E　negando E　　24–5 antecedentis nego primo E

however, be in doubt about the first inference because there is some doubt whether the argument proceeds from what is impossible or from what is true by reason of one or the other indication under the demonstrative pronouns in both extremes throughout.

I reject the second inference because the argument proceeds from a conjunctive proposition to a proposition with a conjoined extreme, which does indeed signify that some man is every man.

Thus it must be noted that whenever the term 'and so on' is preceded by a conjunctive proposition, the whole proposition is conjunctive—e.g.

This man is this man, and this man is this man, and so on.

But when such a term is preceded by a proposition with a conjoined extreme, then the whole proposition without any distinction is a proposition with a conjoined extreme—e.g.

This man is this man and this man and so on.

If, however, such a term were preceded by a categorical proposition with a simple subject and predicate, such a proposition could just as well be a conjunctive proposition as a proposition with a conjoined extreme—e.g.

This man is this man and so on.

Therefore such a proposition must be distinguished with respect to composition and division. Then in the divided sense it can be granted provided that the same things are indicated by the 'this' in the subject and the 'this' in the predicate. In the compounded sense, however, it must simply be denied.[g]

⟨2.22R⟩ I grant the inference in which it is argued

There is some man who is every man; therefore . . .

and I deny its antecedent. As for the proof of that antecedent, I reply first by rejecting the inference, since its antecedent is possible and its consequent impossible. Thus if we suppose that there is only one male human being, this would be true:

There is some man (male),[h] and each man (male) is he,

and this would be false:

There is some man (male) who is every man (human being),

because it follows immediately from this that some man (male) is some woman, which is impossible. And obviously it does follow, for necessarily some woman is, although it is not necessary that some man (male) is.

But if one concludes from that antecedent that there is some man (male) who is each man (male), I grant the inference and deny the antecedent. As for the argument

The antecedent is a conjunctive proposition of which the first part is

quaelibet singularis secundae partis est vera cum prima parte;
igitur . . . ,

huic dicitur quod quamlibet singularem esse veram (10va E) cum prima
parte potest intelligi dupliciter: collective vel divisive.

5   Collective, nego quod quaelibet singularis secundae partis sit vera cum
prima parte, quia tunc aequivalet huic:

Aliquis homo est, et ille homo est ille, et ille homo est ille, et sic de aliis.

Modo certum est quod hoc est falsum.

Si autem intelligitur divisive, concedo quod quaelibet singularis secun-
10 dae partis est vera cum prima parte, ut probat argumentum. Et si ex hoc
infertur quod illa universalis est vera cum prima parte, nego consequentiam.
Oporteret enim quod quaelibet singularis secundae partis esset vera cum
prima parte collective. Hoc autem est falsum, ut dictum est.

⟨2.23R⟩ Ad tertium respondetur negando illam consequentiam:

15   Aliquis homo erit omnis homo; igitur omnis homo est omnis homo,

nisi forte argueretur ex impossibili. Dictur enim, et bene, quod illa propositio

Aliquis homo erit omnis homo

est impossibilis, sicut est ista:

20   Aliquis homo erit aliqua mulier.

Si arguitur ergo sic:

Aliquis homo erit quilibet homo, etc.,

nego consequentiam iterum. Et tunc ad argumentum, concedo quod Sortes
non est omnis homo et quod aliquis homo est qui non erit Sortes. Et ex hoc
25 non sequitur quod Sortes non erit omnis homo.

⟨2.24R⟩ Et tunc ad argumentum cum arguitur sic:

Sortes erit omnis homo et Plato, qui est, est vel erit homo; igitur, etc.,

nego consequentiam. Et tunc ad argumentum: ibi arguitur a termino
stante confuse et distributive, etc., dico quod non distribuitur ly .homo.
30 nisi pro omni homine qui tunc erit, demonstrando instans pro quo illa
propositio verificatur. Ideo deberet sic argui:

Sortes erit omnis homo, ⟨et⟩ Plato, qui est, tunc erit homo; igitur
Sortes erit Plato.

Consequentia est bona, sed negatur minor.

2–4 igitur . . . parte *om. M*   4 collective et divisive *E*   5 Copulative, *E*   est *E*
7 Aliquis homo est, et ille homo est ille homo, et sic de singulis. *M*   10 probavit *M*
12 Oportet *E*   13 est (1) *om. E*   14 consequentiam illam: *E*   19 sicut et ista:
E   21 ergo sic *om. E*   22 etc. *om. E*   23 negando *E*
24 quod *om. M*; aliquis est homo qui non est *E*   26 Et tunc ad argumentum *om.*
E   cum arguitur sic *om. M*   27 Sortes est *E*   qui est vel erit, erit homo;
E   29 etc. *om. E*   ly *om. E*   30 instans *om. E*   31 debent *E*

true, and each singular belonging to the second part is true together with the first part; therefore . . . ,

I reply to that by saying that the claim that each singular is true together with the first part can be understood in either of two ways: collectively or dividedly.

If it is understood collectively, I deny that each singular belonging to the second part is true together with the first part, for that is equivalent to

There is some man, and that man is he, and that man is he, and so on.

But that is certainly false.

If, however, it is understood dividedly, I grant that each singular belonging to the second part is true together with the first part, as the argument proves. And if one infers from this that that universal proposition is true together with the first part, I reject the inference. For each singular belonging to the second part would have to be true collectively together with the first part. But that is false, as has been said.

⟨2.23R⟩ I reject the inference

Some man will be every man; therefore every man will be every man,

unless one happens to be arguing from what is impossible. For it is said, and rightly, that the proposition

Some man (male) will be every man (human being)

is impossible, in the same way as

Some man (male) will be a woman

is impossible. But if one argues in this way:

Some man (male) will be each man (male), etc.,

I reject the inference again. As for the argument, I grant that Socrates is not every man and that there is some man who will not be Socrates. But it does not follow from that that Socrates will not be every man.

⟨2.24R⟩ I reject the inference in which it is argued

Socrates will be every man, and Plato, who is, is or will be a man; therefore, etc.

As for the argument that in that case one is arguing from a term with distributive confused *suppositio*, etc., I say that 'man' is distributed only over every man who will be at that time, indicating the time for which that proposition comes out true. Therefore one would have to argue in the following way.

Socrates will be every man, and Plato, who is, will be a man at that time; therefore Socrates will be Plato.

The inference is good, but its minor premiss is denied.

Sicut non sequitur:

> Tu diceres ab asino 'iste est asinus', demonstrando asinum futurum
> per mille annos; igitur tu diceres ab illo.

Antecedens enim est verum (ut patet per expositionem vel per resolutionem), et consequens falsum.

⟨2.25R⟩ Ad aliam confirmationem cum arguitur

> Sortes erit omnis homo; igitur Sortes erit omnis homo qui erit,

nego consequentiam. Et tunc ad argumentum:

> In illa propositione 'Sortes erit omnis homo' distribuitur ly .homo.
> respectu verbi de futuro; igitur ly .homo. distribuitur pro omni
> homine qui erit,

nego consequentiam. Sed secundum sequitur quod ly .homo. distribuitur
pro omni homine qui erit in tali vel in tali instanti. Ad hoc enim quod ly
.homo. deberet distribui pro omni homine qui erit oportet quod distribuatur respectu huius verbi 'erit' a parte subiecti et non a parte praedicati,
sicut dicendo

> Omnis homo erit Sortes.

Sed manifestum est quod illa propositio est impossibilis.

Verumtamen leviter potest concedi illa propositio, videlicet:

> Sortes erit omnis homo qui erit,

sic arguendo ut prius:

> Sortes in A instanti erit omnis homo qui erit; igitur Sortes erit omnis
> homo (13va M) qui erit.

Consequentia patet, et antecedens probatur. Nam Sortes in A instanti
erit homo qui est in A instanti, et nihil erit homo qui erit quin illud erit
Sortes; igitur, etc. Consequentia patet: ab exponentibus ad expositam. Et
antecedens probatur, ut praesuppono in casu.

Ex his omnibus patet possibilitas omnium istarum propositionum:

> Sortes erit omnis homo,
> Sortes fuit omnis homo,
> Sortes potest esse omnis homo,

quae communiter negantur tamquam impossibiles.

⟨2.31⟩ Amplius ad principale arguitur quod omnis homo est Sortes. Nam
tantum Sortes est homo; igitur omnis homo est Sortes. Consequentia
patet: ab exclusiva ad suam universalem de terminis transpositis. Et

1–5 sicut . . . falsum *om.* M   6 confirmationem quando arguitur M   12 Sed
oppositum sequitur M   13 in (2) *om.* E   14 debeat M   16 sic dicendo M
17 est E   18 Sed certum est E   19 propositio illa E   videlicet *om.* E
22 instanti *om.* E   24 instanti *om.* E   25 est homo qui erit et in A instanti, est
nihil M   instanti *om.* E   26 expositum M   27 ut *om.* M   suppono E
28 omnium *om.* E   32 quae consequenter negantur tamquam impossibilia. E
33 Amplius *om.* M   principale iterum arguitur M

In the same way, this does not follow:

> You would deny of a donkey 'this is a donkey', indicating a donkey a thousand years in the future; therefore you would deny it of that one there.

The antecedent is true (this is clear as a consequence of exposition or resolution),[i] and the consequent is false.

⟨2.25R⟩ In reply to the other confirmation, in which it is argued

> Socrates will be every man; therefore Socrates will be every man who will be,

I reject the inference. And as for the argument

> In the proposition 'Socrates will be every man' the term 'man' is distributed for every man who will be,

I reject the inference. But it does follow that 'man' is distributed over every man who will be at such and such a time. For in order for 'man' to be distributed over every man who will be it would have to be distributed in respect of the verb 'will' in the subject and not in the predicate, as when one says

> Every man will be Socrates.

But that proposition is manifestly impossible.

The proposition

> Socrates will be every man who will be

can, however, be readily granted if one argues as before:[j]

> Socrates at t_1 will be every man who will be; therefore Socrates will be every man who will be.

This inference is obvious, and its antecedent is proved in the following way. Socrates at t_1 will be a man who is at t_1, and nothing will be a man who will be but that it will be Socrates; therefore, etc. This inference is obvious: from the exponents to the expounded.[k] And the antecedent is proved, as I presuppose in the hypothesis.

As a consequence of all these considerations it is obvious that all these propositions, which are commonly rejected as impossible, are possible:

> Socrates will be every man,
> Socrates was every man,
> Socrates can be every man.

⟨*Third set of Arguments against Opinion 2*⟩

⟨2.31⟩ One argues further against the main thesis in the following way, proving that every man is Socrates. Only Socrates is a man; therefore every man is Socrates. The inference is obvious: from an exclusive proposition

antecedens probatur sic. Propositio vera et affirmativa de praesenti cuius principale verbum non est ampliativum nec cuius praedicatum est terminus distrahens significat quod tantum Sortes est homo, et qualitercumque significat talis propositio, sic est; igitur sic est quod tantum Sortes
5 est homo. Consequentia patet cum minori, et maior arguitur quia illa propositio

    Sortes est homo

significat quod tantum Sortes est homo; ergo . . . Antecedens probatur, nam illa propositio significat Sortem esse hominem, sed quicquid et quali-
10 tercumque est Sortem esse hominem est tantum Sortem esse hominem; igitur eadem significat tantum Sortem esse hominem. Et per consequens illa significat quod tantum Sortes est homo, quod erat probandum. Et quod Sortem esse hominem sit tantum Sortem esse hominem patet per exponentes et etiam per illam consequentiam necessariam.

15   Sortem esse hominem est Sortem esse hominem; igitur Sortem esse
    hominem est tantum Sortem esse hominem.

Quia quaelibet propositio convertitur cum seipsa dictione exclusiva posita a parte praedicati.

⟨2.32⟩ Secundo arguitur sic. Sortes et omnis homo non differunt, et
20 Sortes est, et omnis homo est; igitur Sortes est omnis homo. Consequentia patet, et maior probatur quia suum oppositum est falsum:

    Sortes et omnis homo differunt.

Quia sequitur:

    Sortes et omnis homo differunt, et Sortes est homo: igitur Sortes et
25   Sortes differunt.

Consequens falsum, et consequentia patet: a termino stante confuse et distributive.

⟨2.33⟩ Tertio arguitur sic. Sortes est omnis homo si potest esse quod Sortes est omnis homo, sed potest esse quod Sortes est omnis homo;
30 igitur Sortes est omnis homo. Consequentia patet: a conditionali cum suo antecedenti ad suum consequens; et similiter minor. Et maior probatur, quia si illa (10vb E) conditionalis est impossibilis, igitur sicut illa primarie significat impossibile est esse; igitur non potest esse sicut illa primarie significat. Et illa primarie significat quod Sortes est omnis homo si potest
35 esse quod Sortes sit omnis homo. Igitur non potest esse quod Sortes sit omnis homo si potest esse quod Sortes sit omnis homo. Consequens falsum et implicans contradictorium, quia potest esse quod Sortes sit omnis homo si potest esse quod Sortes sit omnis homo cum idem sit antecedens et consequens.

3 significans *E*　　3–4 qualitercumque sit talis *E*　　5 arguitur sic quia *M*
9 significat tantum Sortem *E*　　quicquid est et *M*　　10–11 hominem; et per consequens illa propositio significat tantum Sortem esse hominem; igitur *E*　　igitur . . .
hominem *om. M*　　13–14 exponentem *E*　　14 et est per *M*　　15 est tantum
Sortem *E*　　19 sic *om. E*　　20 est (2) *om. E*　　24 et (2) *om. M*
28 sic *om. E*　　37 Sortes est omnis *M*

to the corresponding universal proposition with the terms transposed. The antecedent is proved in the following way. A true, affirmative, present-tense proposition whose principal verb is not ampliative[l] and whose predicate is not a distractive term[m] signifies that only Socrates is a man, and whichever way such a proposition signifies, so it is; therefore it is the case that only Socrates is a man. This inference is obvious, along with the minor premiss, and the following argument supports the major premiss. The proposition

Socrates is a man

signifies that only Socrates is a man; therefore . . . This antecedent is proved in the following way. That proposition signifies Socrates being a man, but whatever and whichever way Socrates being a man is is only Socrates being a man; therefore that proposition signifies only Socrates being a man. Consequently it signifies that only Socrates is a man, which is what was to be proved. That Socrates being a man is only Socrates being a man is clear from the exponents[n] and also from the following necessary inference:

Socrates being a man is Socrates being a man; therefore Socrates being a man is only Socrates being a man.

For every proposition is interchageable with that same proposition with an exclusive word attached to the predicate.

⟨2.32⟩ Socrates and every man do not differ, and Socrates is, and every man is; therefore Socrates is every man. The inference is obvious, and the major premiss is proved because its opposite

Socrates and every man differ

is false. For this follows:

Socrates and every man differ, and Socrates is a man; therefore Socrates and Socrates differ.

This consequent is false, and the inference is obvious: from a term with distributive confused *suppositio* ⟨to its inferior⟩.

⟨2.33⟩ Socrates is every man if it can be that Socrates is every man, but it can be that Socrates is every man; therefore Socrates is every man. The inference is obvious: from a conditional together with its antecedent to its consequent; and so is the minor premiss. Proof of the major premiss: If that conditional is impossible, then it is impossible that what it primarily signifies is; therefore what it primarily signifies cannot be the case. And it primarily signifies that Socrates is every man if it can be that Socrates is every man. Therefore it cannot be that Socrates is every man if it can be that Socrates is every man. This consequent is false and implies a contradictory, for it can be that Socrates is every man if it can be that Socrates is every man, since the antecedent and the consequent are just the same.

⟨2.31R⟩ Ad ista tria argumenta respondetur. Ad primum nego quod tantum Sortes est homo. Et ad probationem, nego quod illa propositio

> Sortes est homo

significat quod tantum Sortes est homo. Sed ipsa bene significat tantum
5 quod Sortes est homo, ita quod ly .tantum. determinet ly .significat. Et ulterius ad argumentum

> Illa propositio 'Sortes est homo' significat Sortem esse hominem (concedo), sed quicquid est Sortem esse hominem est tantum Sortem esse hominem (concedo); igitur illa propositio significat
10 tantum Sortem esse hominem,

huic dicitur distinguendo de ly .tantum., eo quod potest determinare ly .Sortem esse hominem. vel ly .significat. Si determinat orationem infinitivam, nego consequentiam et consequens. Si autem determinat praecise ly .significat., concedo consequentiam et consequens. Et ulterius postea
15 cum infertur quod illa significat quod tantum Sortes est homo, nego consequentiam, quia tunc ly .tantum. in antecedente non determinat ly .Sortem esse hominem. sed ly .significat. Ideo deberet sic concludi, quod

> Illa propositio significat tantum quod Sortes est homo,

et hoc est verum, si ly .tantum. determinat ly .significat.
20 Non obstante hoc, potest concedi quod illa propositio

> Sortes est homo

significat quod tantum Sortes est homo. Ex hoc tamen non sequitur quod illa propositio

> Tantum Sortes est homo

25 sit vera, quia non significat illud primarie sed secundarie. Sicut non sequitur:

> Haec propositio 'homo est animal' est vera, et ipsa significat hominem esse asinum; igitur hominem esse asinum est verum, vel haec est vera: 'homo est asinus.'

30 Et causa est quia illa propositio

> Homo est animal

non significat hominem esse asinum primarie sed secundarie. Eodem modo potest dici in proposito.

⟨2.32R⟩ Ad secundum nego quod Sortes et omnis homo non differunt,
35 quia ex illa sequitur quod Sortes et nullus homo conveniunt, quod est falsum. Et ulterius quando dicitur quod suum oppositum est falsum, concedo de opposito contrario, nego tamen de opposito contradictorio. Ideo dico quod haec est falsa:

> Sortes et omnis homo differunt

---

1 respondetur *om. M*   4 significet quod *M*   5 Et *om. E*   9 igitur quod propositio illa *E*   11 de *om. E*   12–14 determinat ly .significat., concedo consequentiam et consequens. Si autem determinat praecise illam orationem infinitivam, nego consequentiam et consequens *E*   14–15 ulterius patet consequentia cum *E* 16 quia in antecedente ly .tantum. *M*   22–3 sequitur quia illa *E*   30 est quare illa *E* 34 non *om. M*   35 homo differunt, quod *M*   36 quando dicitur ulterius *E*

⟨*Replies to the Third Set of Arguments against Opinion 2*⟩

⟨2.31R⟩ I deny that only Socrates is a man. As for the proof, I deny that the proposition

Socrates is a man

signifies that only Socrates is a man. But it does rightly signify only that Socrates is a man, in such a way that the 'only' governs the 'does signify'. And as for the argument

The proposition 'Socrates is a man' signifies Socrates being a man (granted), but whatever is Socrates being a man is only Socrates being a man (granted); therefore that proposition signifies only Socrates being a man,

one replies to this by drawing a distinction regarding the 'only', for it can govern either 'Socrates being a man' or 'signifies'. If it governs 'Socrates being a man', I reject the inference and its consequent. But if it governs just 'signifies', I grant the inference and its consequent. But then I reject the inference in which it is inferred that that proposition signifies that only Socrates is a man, for the 'only' in the antecedent governs not 'Socrates being a man' but 'signifies'. Therefore one would have to conclude thus:

That proposition signifies only that Socrates is a man,

which is true, if 'only' governs 'signifies'.

Despite all this it can be granted that the proposition

Socrates is a man

does signify that only Socrates is a man. But it does not follow from that that the proposition

Only Socrates is a man

is true, for it signifies that not primarily but secondarily.° In the same way this does not follow:

The proposition 'a man is an animal' is true, and it signifies that a man is a donkey; therefore that a man is a donkey is true, or this is true: 'a man is a donkey.'

This is because the proposition

A man is an animal

signifies that a man is a donkey not primarily but secondarily. The same sort of thing can be said regarding the example in question.

⟨2.32R⟩ I deny that Socrates and every man do not differ, for it follows from that that Socrates and no man are alike, which is false. And I grant the claim that its opposite is false as regards the contrary opposite, but I deny it as regards the contradictory opposite. Thus I say that

Socrates and every man differ

sicut illa

    Sortes et omnis homo non differunt.

Nec illa sunt contradictoria, ex quo utrobique ille terminus 'homo' stat confuse et distributive. Et si quaeritur de contradictorio illius:

5   Sortes et omnis homo non differunt,

dico quod illud est

    Omnis Sortes et aliquid quod est homo differunt,

quod est verum.

    Sed forte arguitur probando illam propositionem affirmativam, scilicet,

10   Sortes et omnis homo differunt,

quia

    Sortes est, et omnis homo est, et Sortes non est omnis homo; igitur
    Sortes et omnis homo differunt.

Consequentia patet: ab exponentibus ad expositam.

15   Respondetur negando consequentiam. Sed solum sequitur quod Sortes differt ab omni homine, quod est verum. Nec ibi arguitur ab exponentibus ad expositam, quia illa propositio

    Sortes et omnis homo differunt

non debet exponi ratione de ly .differunt., sed resolvi ratione de ly .Sortes.,

20 tenendo quod sit terminus communis: et si non sit terminus communis, ratione illius signi 'omnis', sic arguendo:

    Sortes et homo differunt, et nihil est homo quin illud et Sortes dif-
    ferunt: igitur, etc.

Et tunc conceditur consequentia et negatur minor.

25   ⟨2.33R⟩ Ad tertium respondeo negando illam

    Sortes est omnis homo si potest esse quod Sortes est omnis homo.

Et concedo quod ipsa est impossibilis, quia illa est una conditionalis falsa.
Et tunc quando concluditur quod

    Non potest esse quod Sortes est omnis homo si potest esse quod Sortes

30   est omnis homo,

dicitur distinguendo illam, eo quod ly .non potest. potest cadere supra totam conditionalem aut supra primam partem solum. Si primo modo, concedo eam, quia tunc significat quod haec propositio est impossibilis:

    Sortes est omnis homo si potest esse quod Sortes est omnis homo,

35 et hoc est verum.

4 contradictoria *E*   5 non *om. M*   8 propositionem negatam, scilicet, *E*
12 est (1) *om. M*   14 ad expositam ab exponentibus. *M*   17 expositum *E*   19 de (1) *om. E*   .differt. *M et E*   de (2) *om. E*   20 non fuerit
terminus *M*   21 signi *om. M*   29 homo, etc. *E*   29-30 si . . . homo *om. E*

and

> Socrates and every man do not differ

are both false. Nor are they contradictories, because the term 'man' has distributive confused *suppositio* in both. And if I am asked about the contradictory of

> Socrates and every man do not differ,

I say that it is

> Every Socrates and something that is a man differ,

which is true.

In an attempt to prove the affirmative proposition

> Socrates and every man differ

one may perhaps argue in the following way:

> Socrates is, and every man is, and Socrates is not every man; therefore Socrates and every man differ.

The inference is obvious: from the exponents to the expounded.[p]

The reply is to reject the inference. All that follows is that Socrates differs from every man, which is true. Nor is it an argument from the exponents to the expounded, for the proposition

> Socrates and every man differ

is not to be expounded in respect of 'differ' but resolved[q] in respect of 'Socrates', considering it as a common term. And if it is not a common term, then it is to be resolved because of the sign 'every', by arguing as follows:

> Socrates and a man differ, and nothing is a man but that it and Socrates differ; therefore, etc.

And in that case the inference is granted and the minor premiss denied.

⟨2.33R⟩ I reply by denying the proposition

> Socrates is every man if it can be that Socrates is every man.

I grant that it is impossible, for it is a false conditional. And in reply to the conclusion

> It cannot be that Socrates is every man if it can be that Socrates is every man,

I reply by drawing a distinction with regard to that conclusion, for the 'cannot' can cover either the whole conditional or the first part alone.

If it operates in the first way, I grant it, for in that case it signifies that the proposition

> Socrates is every man if it can be that Socrates is every man

is impossible, which is true.

Et cum proponitur eius contradictorium, scilicet,

Potest esse quod Sortes est omnis homo, etc.,

dico hic consimiliter quod ly .potest. potest cadere supra primam partem
solum vel supra totum sequens. Si cadit supra primam partem, concedo
5 illam conditionalem; et tunc non est contradictorium illius negativae
concessae. Si autem cadit supra totum sequens, nego eam, quia tunc illa
significat quod haec propositio est possibilis:

Sortes est omnis homo si potest esse quod Sortes est omnis homo,

quod est falsum. Et tunc verum est quod illa affirmativa contradicit
10 negativae concessae.

Si vero in illa propositione

Non potest esse quod Sortes sit omnis homo, etc.

et negatio cadit supra primam partem, nego eam tamquam impossibilem,
eo quod tunc significat quod si potest esse quod Sortes est omnis homo non
15 potest esse quod Sortes est omnis homo, quod est falsum et impossibile.

Aliter potest responderi et melius. Cum proponitur

Non potest esse quod Sortes est omnis homo, etc.,

concedo eam, eo quod illa negatio 'non' necessario cadit supra totum
sequens, et non terminatur in aliqua parte illius conditionalis. Si tamen
20 proponitur

Potest esse quod Sortes est omnis homo, etc.,

distinguatur sicut prius, eo quod non ita necessitatur ly .potest. transire
supra totum sequens, sicut ista (14ra M) negatio 'non'.

Et si ex hoc concluditur quod impossibile est Sortem currere si possibile
25 est Sortem currere, et impossibile est te stare si tu potes stare, et impossibile
est te esse sophistam si tu potes esse sophista, conceduntur omnia illa.

⟨2.41⟩ Amplius arguitur ad principale sic. Omnis homo est Sortes; igitur
Sortes est omnis homo. Consequentia patet, et antecedens probatur sic.
Omnis homo vel non omnis homo est Sortes; igitur omnis homo est
30 Sortes. Consequentia probatur sic. Omnis homo vel non omnis homo est
Sortes; igitur homo vel non omnis homo est Sortes. Et nihil est homo vel
non omnis homo quin illud est Sortes. Et si sic, Sortes est omnis homo.
Consequentia prima patet: ab exposita ad suas exponentes.

---

6 concessae *om. M*   12 Sortes est omnis *M*   homo *om. E*   etc. *om. M*   13 cadat
M   17 etc. *om. E*   20 proponitur illa *M*   22 distinguitur *E*   25 currere,
et *om. M*   26 tu *om. M*   27 ad principale arguitur *M*   28 sic
om. E

And when its contradictory is propounded—viz.

It can be that Socrates is every man, etc.—

I say here as well that the 'can' can cover either the first part alone or the whole of what follows it. If it covers the first part, I grant that conditional; and in that case it is not the contradictory of the negative proposition already granted. But if 'can' covers the whole of what follows it, I deny it, for in that case it signifies that the proposition

Socrates is every man if it can be that Socrates is every man

is possible, which is false. And in that case it is true that the affirmative contradicts the negative proposition already granted.

On the other hand, if the negation in the proposition

It cannot be that Socrates is every man, etc.

covers the first part, I deny it as impossible, for in that case it signifies that if it can be that Socrates is every man it cannot be that Socrates is every man, which is false and impossible.

There is another and better reply. When

It cannot be that Socrates is every man, etc.

is propounded, I grant it, because the negation '⟨can⟩not' necessarily covers the whole of what follows it, and it is not terminated in some part of the conditional. But if

It can be that Socrates is every man, etc.

is propounded, let the distinction be drawn as before, for the 'can' is not bound to extend over the whole of what follows it as is the negation '⟨can⟩-not'.

And if one concludes from this that it is impossible that Socrates is running if it is possible that Socrates is running, and it is impossible that you are standing if you can stand, and it is impossible that you are a logician if you can be a logician, all these things are granted.

⟨*Fourth Set of Arguments against Opinion 2*⟩

⟨2.41⟩ Every man is Socrates; therefore Socrates is every man. The inference is obvious, and the antecedent is proved in the following way. Every man or not every man is Socrates; therefore every man is Socrates. Proof of the inference: Every man or not every man is Socrates; therefore a man or not every man is Socrates. And nothing is a man or not every man but that it is Socrates. And if that is the case, Socrates is every man. The first inference is obvious: from what is expounded to its exponents.[r]

Similiter, si omnis homo vel non omnis homo est Sortes, et omnis homo vel non omnis homo est omnis homo, igitur omnis homo est Sortes.

Similiter, si omnis homo vel non omnis homo est Sortes, igitur tantum Sortes est homo vel non omnis homo, et per consequens Sortes est omnis homo. Consequentia prima patet: ab universali ad suam exclusivam de terminis transpositis.

Similiter, si omnis homo vel non omnis homo est Sortes, ⟨et⟩ Plato est homo vel non omnis homo, igitur Plato est Sortes. Et per idem Cicero est Sortes. Et si sic, Sortes est omnis homo.

Propter ista argumenta forte negatur principale antecedens, videlicet,

Omnis homo vel non omnis homo est Sortes.

Contra: non omnis homo est Sortes; igitur omnis homo vel non omnis homo est Sortes. Consequentia patet: a parte disiuncti ad totum disiunctum.

Similiter, iste homo vel non omnis homo est Sortes, et iste homo vel non omnis homo est Sortes, et sic de aliis; igitur omnis homo vel non omnis homo est Sortes. Consequentia patet: a singularibus ad universalem. Et quod sint eius singulares patet quia alicuius universalis sunt singulares, et non videtur quod alicuius nisi illius datae; igitur, etc.

⟨2.42⟩ Secundo arguitur sic. Aliquo modo Sortes est omnis homo; igitur Sortes est omnis homo. Consequentia patet: ab inferiori ad suum superius sine impedimento. Antecedens arguitur sic. Isto modo Sortes est omnis homo (demonstrando modum quo Sortes est homo), et iste est aliquis modus; igitur . . . Consequentia patet, et antecedens probatur. Quia isto modo Sortes est homo, et isto modo nihil aliud a Sorte est homo; igitur, etc. Consequentia patet: ab exponentibus ad expositam.

Confirmatur. Omnis homo est Sortes isto modo; igitur isto modo Sortes est omnis homo. Consequentia patet: ab uno convertibili ad reliquum. Et antecedens sic arguitur. Tantum isto modo Sortes est homo; igitur omnis homo est Sortes isto modo. Patet consequentia per illam regulam; ab exclusiva ad suam universalem. Et ultra: ergo omnis homo est Sortes. Consequentia patet: ab inferiori ad suum superius a parte praedicati cum distributione addita subiectis. Antecedens autem principale est verum, scilicet,

Tantum isto modo Sortes est homo,

ut patet per exponentes.

3 si *om.* E   5 prima *om.* E   15 de singulis; M   17 quod sunt eius M   18 etc. *om.* M   21 impedimento praecedente. M   Et antecedens E   sic *om.* E   26 Consimiliter. M   31-2 cum dictione exclusiva addita E

Similarly, if every man or not every man is Socrates, and every man or not every man is every man, then every man is Socrates.

Similarly, if every man or not every man is Socrates, then only Socrates is a man or not every man, and consequently Socrates is every man. The first inference is obvious: from a universal proposition to its exclusive proposition with terms transposed.

Similarly, if every man or not every man is Socrates, and Plato is a man or not every man, then Plato is Socrates. And by the same token Cicero is Socrates. And if that is the case, Socrates is every man.

On account of these arguments one may perhaps deny the main antecedent—viz.,

Every man or not every man is Socrates.

But on the contrary, not every man is Socrates; therefore every man or not every man is Socrates. This inference is obvious: from one part of a disjoined term to the whole disjoined term.

Similarly, this man or not every man is Socrates, and this man or not every man is Socrates, and so on; therefore every man or not every man is Socrates. This inference is obvious: from the singular propositions to the universal proposition. And it is clear that they are its singulars, for they are the singulars of some universal proposition, and it seems that they are not the singulars of any other than the one given; therefore, etc.

⟨2.42⟩ In some respect Socrates is every man; therefore Socrates is every man. This inference is obvious: from an inferior to its superior in the absence of an impediment. The antecedent is argued for in the following way. In this respect Socrates is every man (indicating a respect in which Socrates is a man), and this is some respect; therefore . . . This inference is obvious, and the antecedent is proved in the following way. In this respect Socrates is a man, and in this respect nothing other than Socrates is a man; therefore, etc. This inference is obvious: from the exponents to what is expounded.[s]

This is confirmed in the following way. Every man is Socrates in this respect; therefore in this respect Socrates is every man. The inference is obvious: from one interchangeable proposition to another. And the antecedent is argued for in the following way. Only in this respect is Socrates a man; therefore every man is Socrates in this respect. This inference is obvious under the rule governing inferences from an exclusive to the corresponding universal proposition. Further, therefore every man is Socrates. This inference is obvious: from an inferior to a superior predicate-term with distribution added to the subject. The principal antecedent, however, is true—viz.

Only in this respect is Socrates a man—

as its exponents clearly show.

⟨2.43⟩ Tertio, haec propositio est possibilis:

Sortes est omnis homo, et plures homines sunt;

igitur . . . Antecedens probatur, quia potest esse sicut ipsum primarie significat; ergo illud est possibile. Consequentia patet per definitionem
5 propositionis possibilis. Antecedens sic potest probari. Potest ita esse quod Sortes est omnis homo (et capio), et plures homines sunt, et sic antecedens primarie significat; igitur, etc. Consequentia patet, et antecedens probatur. Et capio illam copulativam:

Potest esse quod Sortes est omnis homo et plures homines sunt.

10 Ista copulativa est vera quia utraque eius pars est vera, sicut patet. Tunc sic: illa copulativa est vera, ut patet; ergo ita est̊sicut illa primarie significat, et ipsa primarie significat quod potest esse quod Sortes est (14rb M) omnis homo et plures homines sunt. Igitur ita est quod potest esse quod Sortes est omnis homo et plures homines sunt. Patet consequentia: ab uno
15 convertibili ad reliquum.

⟨2.41R⟩ Ad ista tria argumenta respondetur. Ad primum dicitur cum arguitur:

Omnis homo vel non omnis homo est Sortes; igitur omnis homo est Sortes,

20 dubito illam consequentiam eo quod signum universale in antecedente potest distribuere totum disiunctum vel solum primam partem disiuncti.

Si autem distribuit totum disiunctum, concedo consequentiam, ut argumenta probant, et nego antecedens, quia tunc antecedens significat quod omne quod est homo vel non omnis homo est Sortes, quod est falsum
25 et impossibile.

Et tunc ad primum argumentum, quando arguitur

Non omnis homo est Sortes; igitur omnis homo vel non omnis homo est Sortes,

nego consequentiam. Et tunc ad regulam, dico quod intelligitur quando
30 notam disiunctionis vel disiunctum non praecedit terminus habens vim confundendi confuse et distributive vel confuse tantum. Quia non sequitur:

Tu differs ab asino; ergo tu differs ab homine vel ab asino,

quia antecedens est verum et consequens falsum. Similiter non sequitur:

Iste terminus 'homo' significat primarie hominem; ergo iste terminus
35   'homo' significat primarie hominem vel asinum,

et sic de infinitis.

2 homines sunt homines; *M et E*   5 Antecedens arguitur sic. *E*   Ita est quod *M*   6 (et capio) *om. M*   10 pars *om. M*   13 et quod plures *E*   16 Et primo ad primum *M*   17 dicitur: *E*   32 differes *E*   35 asinum, etc. *E*

⟨2.43⟩ The proposition

Socrates is every man and there are several men

is possible; therefore . . . Proof of the antecedent: It can be just as the proposition primarily signifies; therefore the proposition is possible. This inference is obvious from the definition of a possible proposition. The antecedent can be proved in the following way. It can be that Socrates is every man (and I am supposing that it is) and there are several men, and that is what the antecedent primarily signifies; therefore, etc. This inference is obvious, and its antecedent is proved in the following way. I take the conjunctive proposition

It can be that Socrates is every man and there are several men.

This conjunctive is true because, as is obvious, each part of it is true. Then: This conjunctive is obviously true; therefore what it primarily signifies is the case, and it primarily signifies that it can be that Socrates is every man and there are several men. This inference is obvious: from one interchangeable proposition to another.

⟨*Replies to the Fourth Set of Arguments against Opinion 2*⟩

⟨2.41R⟩ I am in doubt about the inference in which it is argued

Every man or not every man is Socrates; therefore every man is Socrates,

for the ⟨first⟩ universal sign in the antecedent can either distribute the whole disjoined term or distribute only the first part of it.

If, on the one hand, it distributes the whole disjoined term, I grant the inference, as the arguments prove, and I deny the antecedent, for in that case the antecedent signifies that everything that is either a man or not every man is Socrates, which is false and impossible.

And as for the first argument ⟨to the contrary⟩, in which it is argued

Not every man is Socrates; therefore every man or not every man is Socrates,

I reject the inference. With regard to the rule I maintain that it is meant to apply when a term with the power of producing distributive confused or merely confused *suppositio* does not precede the note of disjunction*t* or the disjoined term. For this does not follow:

You differ from a donkey; therefore you differ from a man or a donkey,

since the antecedent is true and the consequent false. Similarly, this does not follow:

The term 'man' primarily signifies man; therefore the term 'man' primarily signifies man or donkey,

and so on in infinitely many cases.

Ad aliud argumentum quando dicebatur

> Iste homo vel non omnis homo est Sortes, et iste, etc.; igitur omnis
> homo vel non omnis homo est Sortes,

dico ad hoc dubitando hanc consequentiam eo quod ly .vel. in omnibus
5 singularibus antecedentis potest teneri in sensu diviso vel composito.

Si in sensu (11rb E) diviso, nego consequentiam eo quod quaelibet
singularis antecedentis est vera, quaelibet enim tunc significat quod iste
homo est Sortes vel non omnis homo est Sortes, et hoc est verum. Et
ulterius dico quod istae non sunt singulares illius universalis demonstratae,
10 sed illius:

> Omnis homo est Sortes vel non omnis homo.

Si autem ly .vel. teneatur in sensu composito, concedo consequentiam
et nego antecedens, eo quod multae singulares antecedentis sunt falsae.
Haec enim, demonstrando Platonem, est falsa:

15 > Iste homo vel non omnis homo est Sortes

eo quod ipsa tunc significat quod hoc quod est iste homo vel non omnis
homo est Sortes, quod est falsum. Debet enim sic resolvi:

> Hoc est Sortes (demonstrando Platonem), et hoc est iste homo vel
> non omnis homo; igitur iste homo vel non omnis homo est Sortes.

20 Et si arguitur sic:

> Non omnis homo est Sortes; ergo iste homo (demonstrato Platone)
> vel non omnis homo est Sortes,

nego consequentiam. Et si allegatur regula quod a parte disiuncti, etc.,
dico quod regula tenet quando ly .vel. tenetur divisive et non collective.
25 (Qualiter hoc sit intelligendum dicetur inferius.) Et sic patet quomodo ista
propositio

> Omnis homo vel non omnis homo est Sortes

est falsa si ly .omnis. distribuit totum subiectum.

Si autem signum universale solum distribuat partem primam disiuncti,
30 nego consequentiam principalem. Et concedo antecedens eo quod ipsum
tunc significat quod omnis homo est Sortes vel non omnis homo est Sortes,
vel saltem quod Sortes est omnis homo vel non omnis homo, tenendo ly
.omnis. sicut prius.

Et tunc ad primum argumentum, nego consequentiam, quia non arguitur
35 ab exposita ad suas exponentes. Sed sic debet exponi:

> Homo vel non omnis homo est Sortes, et nihil est homo quin illud vel
> non omnis homo est Sortes; igitur, etc.

---

1 Et ad *M*   4 hanc *om. E*   5 composito vel diviso *E*   6 consequentiam
in eo *E*   7 singularis in antecedente *E*   9 demonstratae *om. M*   14 demonstrato Platone *E*   16 tunc *om. E*   20 sic *om. E*   23 etc. *om. E*   regula
intelligitur quando *M*   25 hoc sic intelligendum *M*   26 propositio est falsa *M*
28 est falsa *om. M*   29 solum *om. E*

In reply to the other argument ⟨to the contrary⟩, in which it is said

> This man or not every man is Socrates, and this, etc.; therefore every
> man or not every man is Socrates,

I reply that I am in doubt about the inference because the 'or' in all the
singular propositions of the antecedent can be taken either in a divided
sense or in a compounded sense.

If it is taken in a divided sense, I reject the inference. Each singular
in the antecedent is true, for in that case each one of them signifies that
this man is Socrates or not every man is Socrates, which is true. But those
are not the singulars of the indicated universal proposition but of this one:

> Every man is Socrates or not every man.

But if the 'or' is taken in a compounded sense, I grant the inference and
deny the antecedent, for many of the singulars are false. For the proposition

> This man (indicating Plato) or not every man is Socrates

is false because in that case it signifies that that which is this man or not
every man is Socrates, which is false. It must be resolved in the following
way.

> This is Socrates (indicating Plato), and this is this man or not every
> man; therefore this man or not every man is Socrates.

And if one argues

> Not every man is Socrates; therefore this man (indicating Plato) or not
> every man is Socrates,

I reject the inference. If one appeals to the rule that from a part of a
disjoined term, etc., I say that the rule applies when the 'or' is taken
divisively and not collectively. (How that is to be understood will be discussed below.)[u] Thus it is clear how the proposition

> Every man or not every man is Socrates

is false if the 'every' distributes the whole subject.

If, on the other hand, the universal sign distributes only the first part of
a disjoined term, then I reject the principal inference. But I grant the
antecedent because in that case it signifies that every man is Socrates or not
every man is Socrates, or, at any rate, that Socrates is every man or not
every man, taking the 'every' as before.

As for the first argument ⟨in 2.41⟩, I reject the inference. It is not an
argument from what is expounded to its exponents. Instead, it must be
expounded in the following way:

> A man or not every man is Socrates, and nothing is a man but that it
> or not every man is Socrates; therefore, etc.

Et sic patet veritas exponentium.

    Ad aliud cum arguitur

        Omnis homo vel non omnis homo est Sortes, omnis homo vel non
        omnis homo est omnis homo; igitur omnis homo est Sortes,

5   nego consequentiam. (14va M) Nec est syllogismus in tertia figura, eo quod
maior extremitas non praedicatur de minori extremitate in conclusione,
sed solum pars de parte. Deberet igitur inferri talis conclusio:

        Omnis homo vel non omnis homo est Sortes vel non omnis homo,

    vel sic:

10   Aliquid quod est omnis homo vel non omnis homo est aliquid quod
        est Sortes vel non omnis homo.

    Si enim modus ille arguendi valeret probaretur quod homo est asinus,
sic arguendo:

        Omnis homo vel asinus est asinus, omnis homo vel asinus est homo;
15   igitur homo est asinus.

    Non debet talis conclusio inferri, sed haec:

        Aliquid quod vel asinus est homo est aliquod quod vel asinus est
        asinus.

    Ad aliud cum infertur quod tantum Sortes est homo vel non omnis
20 homo, nego consequentiam. Nec ibi arguitur ab universali ad suam exclusivam, de terminis transpositis, quia non fit de subiecto praedicatum nec
econtra. Et si quaeritur de exclusiva illius universalis, dico quod est ista:

        Tantum Sortes vel non omnis homo est homo,

    ita quod ly .non omnis homo. teneat se a parte subiecti. Eodem modo est
25 dicendum de ista:

        Omnis homo vel asinus est homo

    quod eius exclusiva non est haec:

        Tantum homo est homo vel asinus,

    sed haec:

30   Tantum homo vel asinus est homo,

    quae vera est, ut patet per exponentes.

    Ad ultimum cum arguitur

        Si omnis homo vel non omnis homo est Sortes, ⟨et⟩ Plato est homo vel
        non omnis homo, igitur Plato est Sortes,

   5 in secunda figura *E*   6 extremitate *om. E*   7 inferre *M*   9 vel sit: *M*
12 modus enim *E*   valeret arguendi *M*   esset *M*   16 Non enim debet *M*
sed sic: *E*   24 .non omnis. non teneat *E*   26 est asinus homo *M*   32 ultimum
quando arguitur *M*

And in that case the truth of the exponents is obvious.

As for the ⟨second⟩ argument ⟨in 2.41⟩, in which it is argued

> Every man or not every man is Socrates, every man or not every man is every man; therefore every man is Socrates,

I reject the inference. Nor is it a syllogism in the third figure, for the major extremity is not predicated of the minor extremity in the conclusion, but only a part is predicated of a part. The conclusion that ought to be drawn, therefore, is

> Every man or not every man is Socrates or not every man,

or

> Something that is every man or not every man is Socrates or not every man.

For if that mode of arguing were acceptable one would prove that a man is a donkey by arguing in the following way.

> Every man or a donkey is a donkey, every man or a donkey is a man; therefore a man is a donkey.

It is not that conclusion which is to be inferred, but this:

> Something which itself or a donkey is a man is something which itself or a donkey is a donkey.

As for the ⟨third⟩ argument ⟨in 2.41⟩, in which it is inferred that only Socrates is a man or not every man, I reject the inference. Nor is it an argument from a universal proposition to its exclusive proposition with terms transposed, for the subject is not turned into a predicate or vice versa. And if I am asked about the exclusive of that universal proposition I say that it is this:

> Only Socrates or not every man is a man,

so that 'not every man' is taken as part of the subject. In the same way it must be said that the exclusive of

> Every man or a donkey is a man

is not

> Only a man is a man or a donkey

but

> Only a man or a donkey is a man,

which is true, as is clear from its exponents.

As for the ⟨fourth and⟩ last argument ⟨in 2.41⟩, in which it is argued

> If every man or not every man is Socrates, and Plato is a man or not every man, then Plato is Socrates,

nego consequentiam, quia plus praedicatur in minori quam distribuitur in maiori. Sed deberet sic argui:

> Omnis homo, etc., Plato est homo; igitur Plato est Sortes vel non omnis homo,

5 quod est verum.

⟨2.42R⟩ Ad secundum argumentum principale, cum arguebatur

> Aliquo modo Sortes est omnis homo; igitur Sortes est omnis homo,

nego consequentiam, quia arguitur ab inferiori ad suum superius cum distributione. Et causa est quia ly .homo. in antecedente stat confuse et 10 distributive et restringitur per istum terminum 'aliquo modo', qui cadit tam supra praedicatum quam supra subiectum. Sed in consequente ly .homo. stat confuse et distributive sine aliqua restrictione. Arguitur enim ibi ac si argueretur

> Omnis homo albus currit; igitur omnis homo currit.

15 Ad confirmationem cum proponitur

> Omnis homo est Sortes isto modo,

nego. Et tunc ad argumentum

> Tantum isto modo Sortes est homo; igitur, etc.,

nego consequentiam quia in antecedente ly .isto modo. cadit supra sub-
20 iectum et praedicatum et ipsum restringit. In consequente autem cadit solum supra praedicatum. Ideo si sic argueretur:

> Tantum isto modo Sortes est homo; igitur isto modo omnis homo est Sortes,

concederem consequentiam et consequens, quia suae exponentes sunt 25 verae, scilicet,

> Isto modo homo est Sortes, et isto modo nihil est homo quin illud est Sortes; igitur, etc.

Si enim iste modus arguendi valeret, per idem et iste:

> Aliquando tantum Sortes currebat; igitur omne quod currebat est 30 vel fuit Sortes aliquando.

Similiter:

> Aliquando nullum animal fuit in archa Noe; igitur nullum praeteri-tum in archa Noe est vel fuit animal aliquando.

Et tamen, ut patet, neutra istarum consequentiarum valet. Ex primo enim 35 antecedente solum sequitur quod aliquando omne quod currebat est vel

---

3 Omnis homo et Plato est homo; *M*   7–8 homo, pro nunc nego *M*   11 sub-iectum quam supra praedicatum. *E*   17 Et *om. E*   21 supra solum *E*   arguitur: *M*   25 verae, si *M*

I reject the inference, for more is predicated in the minor premiss than is distributed in the major premiss. Instead one must argue in this way:

> Every man, etc., Plato is a man; therefore Plato is either Socrates or not every man,

which is true.

⟨2.42R⟩ In reply to the second principal argument, in which it was argued

> In some respect Socrates is every man; therefore Socrates is every man,

I reject the inference, for it is an argument from an inferior to its superior with distribution. This is because 'man' in the antecedent has distributive confused *suppositio* and is restricted[v] by the term 'in some respect', which covers the predicate as well as the subject. But in the consequent 'man' has distributive confused *suppositio* without any restriction. For in that case one is arguing as if one were to argue

> Every white man is running; therefore every man is running.

As for the confirmation, I reject the premiss

> Every man is Socrates in this respect.

And as for the argument

> Only in this respect is Socrates a man; therefore, etc.,

I reject the inference because the 'in this respect' in the antecedent covers the subject and the predicate and restricts it. In the consequent, however, it covers the predicate alone. Thus if one were to argue

> Only in this respect is Socrates a man; therefore in this respect every man is Socrates,

I would grant the inference and its consequent, since its exponents are true—viz.

> In this respect a man is Socrates, and in this respect nothing is a man but that it is Socrates; therefore, etc.

For if that mode of arguing were acceptable, then by the same token so would this be:

> At one time only Socrates was running; therefore everything that was running is or was Socrates at one time.

Likewise

> At one time no animal was in Noah's ark; therefore no past thing in Noah's ark is or was an animal at one time.

But of course neither of these inferences is acceptable. From the first antecedent it follows only that at one time everything that was running is or

fuit Sortes. Ex secundo similiter sequitur quod aliquando nullum animal praeteritum in archa Noe est vel fuit animal.

⟨2.43R⟩ Ad tertium principale nego quod haec sit possibilis:

Sortes est omnis homo et plures homines sunt.

5 Et tunc ad argumentum:

Potest ita esse quod Sortes est omnis homo et plures homines (11va E) sunt; igitur . . . ,

respondeo dubitando antecedens, quia ly .potest. vel cadit supra primam partem solum vel supra totum sequens. Si solum supra primam partem, 10 nego consequentiam et concedo antecedens quia tunc est vera copulativa cuius utraque pars est vera. Si autem cadit supra (14vb M) totum sequens, concedo consequentiam et nego antecedens. Et tunc ad argumentum:

Illa est una copulativa cuius utraque pars est vera,

nego quod sit copulativa. Immo est una categorica de copulato extremo, 15 cuius verbum principale est illud verbum 'potest'.

Aliter dicitur concedendo illam sine distinctione, quia ly .potest. non cadit supra secundam partem nisi ponatur ly .quod., quare non potest esse nisi copulativa. Sed nego illam:

Potest esse quod Sortes est omnis homo et quod plures homines sunt,

20 quia categorica est ex quo ly .potest. cadit supra totum sequens. Quare, etc.

⟨2.51⟩ Amplius arguitur ad principale sic. Homo est Sortes; igitur omnis homo est Sortes. Consequentia probatur, sequitur enim:

Homo est Sortes; igitur hominem esse Sortem est verum,

et per consequens nullum hominem esse Sortem non est verum. Conse-
25 quentia patet quia 'non verum' et 'falsum' convertuntur. Tunc ultra:

Nullum hominem esse Sortem non est verum; igitur omnem hominem esse Sortem est verum.

Consequentia patet per illam regulam: negatio postposita, etc. Et si sic, omnis homo est Sortes.

30 ⟨2.52⟩ Secundo: Sortes non differt ab omni homine, et Sortes est, et omnis homo est; igitur Sortes est omnis homo. Consequentia patet cum minori. Et maior probatur sic. Verum est non Sortem differre ab omni

---

11 super *M et E*   14 Ideo est *M*   18 nisi *om. E*   19 omnis *om. E*
22 enim *om. M*   25 Et tunc *E*   28 si *om. M*   31-2 patet,
et antecedens pro minori probatur. *M*

was Socrates. Similarly, from the second antecedent it follows that at one time no past animal in Noah's ark is or was an animal.

⟨2.43R⟩ In reply to the third principal argument I deny that the proposition

Socrates is every man and there are several men

is possible. And then as for the argument

It can be that Socrates is every man and there are several men; therefore . . . ,

I reply by expressing doubt about the antecedent, for the 'can' covers either the first part alone or the whole of what follows it. If it covers only the first part, I reject the inference and grant the antecedent because in that case it is a true conjunctive each part of which is true. But if the 'can' covers the whole of what follows it, I grant the inference and deny the antecedent. And in that case I reply to the argument

This is a conjunctive each part of which is true

by denying that it is a conjunctive. It is instead a categorical proposition with a conjoined extreme, the main verb of which is the verb 'can'.

One may reply alternatively by granting it without distinction, since 'can' does not cover the second part unless a 'that' is inserted, and as a result of this the proposition can only be a conjunctive. But I deny the resultant proposition:

It can be that Socrates is every man and that there are several men,

for it is a categorical in virtue of the fact that the 'can' covers the whole of what follows it. Therefore, etc.

⟨Fifth Set of Arguments against Opinion 2⟩

⟨2.51⟩ A man is Socrates; therefore every man is Socrates. Proof of the inference: This follows:

A man is Socrates; therefore that a man is Socrates is true, and consequently ⟨that no man is Socrates is false, and further⟩ that no man is Socrates is not true. This inference is obvious because 'not true' and 'false' are interchangeable. Then, further:

That no man is Socrates is not true; therefore that every man is Socrates is true.

This inference is obvious under the rule that a negation placed after,[w] etc. And if that is the case, every man is Socrates.

⟨2.52⟩ Socrates does not differ from every man, and Socrates is, and every man is; therefore Socrates is every man. The inference is obvious, along with the minor premiss. The major premiss is proved in the following

homine; igitur non Sortes differt ab omni homine. Consequentia patet, et antecedens probatur. Nam haec propositio

> Deus est

non est Sortem differre ab omni homine, et ipsa est aliquid verum; igitur
5 verum est non Sortem differre ab omni homine. Consequentia patet, et antecedens probatur. Quia ista propositio

> Deus est

non est Sortem differre ab omni homine, et ista propositio est; igitur ipsa est non Sortem differre, etc. Consequentia patet: a negativa de praedicato
10 finito ad affirmativam de praedicato infinito cum debito medio.

⟨2.53⟩ Tertio arguitur sic. Sortes omni homini est idem; igitur Sortes est omnis homo. Consequentia patet, et antecedens probatur. Et pono quod Sortes concludat sibi et omni homini. Tunc arguitur sic. Sorti concludenti et omni homini Sortes est idem; igitur omni homini Sortes est
15 idem. Consequentia patet: a toto copulato ad alteram partem.

Similiter, si Sorti concludenti et omni homini Sortes est idem, igitur alicui homini et omni homini Sortes est idem. Consequentia patet: ab inferiori ad suum superius affirmative. Probatur antecedens principale sic. Huic Sortes est idem (demonstrando Sortem), et hoc est Sorti concludens
20 et omni homini; igitur Sorti concludenti et omni homini Sortes est idem.

⟨2.51R⟩ Ad ista tria argumenta respondetur. Ad primum cum proponitur

> Nullum hominem esse Sortem est falsum,

respondeo dubitando illam, eo quod ly .falsum. potest teneri in sensu
25 composito vel in sensu diviso. Si in sensu composito, concedo eam, eo quod significat quod haec propositio est falsa:

> Nullus homo est Sortes.

Si autem teneatur ly .falsum. in sensu diviso, nego illam, quia suum contradictorium est verum, videlicet,

30   Aliquem hominem esse Sortem est falsum,

---

11 Tertio sic arguitur vel sequitur. *M*   12 homine. *M*   13 sic *om. E*
18 Modo probatur *M*   19 concludenti *E*

way. What is true is not Socrates differing from every man; therefore not Socrates differs from every man. This inference is obvious, and its antecedent is proved in the following way. The proposition

God is

is not Socrates differing from every man, and it is something true; therefore what is true is not Socrates differing from every man. This inference is obvious, and its antecedent is proved in the following way. It is not the case that the proposition

God is

is Socrates differing from every man, and that proposition is; therefore it is not Socrates, etc. This inference is obvious: from a negative proposition with an infinite predicate[x] to an affirmative proposition with the required medium.[y]

⟨2.53⟩ Socrates is the same as every man; therefore Socrates is every man. The inference is obvious. Proof of the antecedent: Suppose that Socrates is drawing a conclusion with reference to himself and every man. Then: Socrates is the same as somebody drawing a conclusion with reference to Socrates and every man; therefore Socrates is the same as every man. This inference is obvious: from a whole conjoined term to one or the other part.[z]

Similarly, if Socrates is the same as somebody drawing a conclusion with reference to Socrates and every man, then Socrates is the same as some man and every man. This inference is obvious: from an inferior to its superior affirmatively. The principal antecedent is proved in the following way. Socrates is the same as this (indicating Socrates), and this is somebody drawing a conclusion with reference to Socrates and every man; therefore Socrates is the same as somebody drawing a conclusion with reference to Socrates and every man.[a]

⟨*Replies to the Fifth Set of Arguments against Opinion 2*⟩

⟨2.51R⟩ I reply to the proposition

That no man is Socrates is false

by expressing doubt about it, for 'false' can be taken either in a compounded or in a divided sense. If it is taken in a compounded sense, I grant the proposition, for in that case it signifies that

No man is Socrates

is false. But if 'false' is taken in a divided sense, I deny the proposition, for its contradictory is true—viz.

That some man is Socrates is false—

quia Platonem esse Sortem est falsum, et Plato est homo. Eodem modo respondendum est ad illam:

Nullum hominem esse Sortem non est verum.

Concedo ipsam in sensu composito et nego ipsam in sensu diviso.

5 Et ulterius, cum concluditur

. . . igitur omnem hominem esse Sortem est verum,

concedo consequentiam si ly .verum. in antecedente teneatur in sensu diviso. Si autem in sensu composito, nego consequentiam.

Et ulterius ad regulam, dico quod non habet veritatem in modalibus. 10 Et causa est quia solum ista negatio praeposita cadit supra copulam principalem, quod tamen non deberet esse iuxta intellectum regulae.

Vel dicitur quod arguitur negatione praeposita, quia in modalibus negatio iuncta modo dicitur praeposita, ut capitulo modalium ostendetur.

⟨2.52R⟩ Ad secundum argumentum nego quod Sortes non differt ab 15 omni homine. (15ra M) Et ad probationem

Verum est non Sortem, etc.; igitur . . . ,

respondeo distinguendo antecedens, quia ly .verum. potest teneri nominaliter (resolutorie) vel modaliter. Si primo modo, concedo antecedens et nego consequentiam. Si modaliter, concedo consequentiam et nego ante-20 cedens, quia tunc significat quod haec propositio est vera:

Non Sortes differt ab omni homine,

quod est falsum. Et tunc ad argumentum

Haec propositio 'Deus est' est non Sortem, etc., et ipsa est aliquid verum; igitur . . . ,

25 nego consequentiam. Nec est syllogismus expositorius, quia ly .verum. in antecedente tenetur nominaliter et in consequente modaliter.

Aliter potest dici iterum dubitando istam:

Verum est non Sortem differre ab omni homine,

eo quod ly .non. potest teneri infinite vel pure negative. Si infinite, nego 30 consequentiam ex qua infertur quod non Sortes differt ab omni homine, quia in illo consequente ly .non. necessario tenetur negative, cum ipsum nihil praecedat. Si autem tenetur pure negative, concedo consequentiam et nego antecedens.

Ad probationem, nego consequentiam. Nec ibi arguitur per regulam 35 dictam, ex quo in consequente ly .non. tenetur pure negative.

1 homo; igitur . . . Eodem M   2 est respondendum M   7 tenebatur E
16 igitur . . . om. M   18 (resolutorie) et modaliter M   26 et om. M
consequente vero modaliter M   27–35 Aliter . . . negative. om. M

because that Plato is Socrates is false, and Plato is a man. One must reply
to the proposition

That no man is Socrates is not true

in the same way. I grant it in the compounded sense and deny it in the
divided sense.

I grant the inference which concludes

. . . therefore that every man is Socrates is true

if the 'true' in the antecedent is taken in a divided sense. If it is taken in
a compounded sense, however, I reject the inference.

As for the rule, I maintain that it has no truth in application to modal
propositions.[b] The reason for this is that only the negation placed *before*
covers the principal copula, which is not as it must be to accord with the
sense of the rule.

Alternatively I say that it is an argument from a negation placed before,
for as regards modal propositions a negation joined to the mode is said to be
placed before, as will be shown in the chapter on modal propositions.[c]

⟨2.52R⟩ I deny that Socrates does not differ from every man. As for the
proof

What is true is not Socrates, etc.; therefore . . . ,

I reply by drawing a distinction regarding the antecedent. 'True' can be
taken either as a name (as regards resolution)[d] or as a modality.[e] If it is
taken in the first way, I grant the antecedent but reject the inference. If it
is taken as a modality, I grant the inference but deny the antecedent, for in
that case it signifies that the proposition

Not Socrates differs from every man

is true, which is false. As for the argument

The proposition 'God is' is not Socrates, etc., and it is something true;
therefore . . . ,

I reject the inference. Nor is it an expository syllogism,[f] for 'true' is
taken as a name in the antecedent but as a modality in the consequent.

Alternatively, one can reply again by expressing doubt about the proposition

What is true is not Socrates differing from every man,

for the 'not' can be taken either as infinitating or as purely negative.[g] If it is
taken as infinitating, I reject the inference by which it is inferred that not
Socrates differs from every man, for the 'not' in that consequent is necessarily taken as negative since nothing precedes it. If, however, it is taken as
purely negative, I grant the inference and reject the antecedent.

As for the proof, I reject the inference. Nor is it an argument in accordance with the cited rule, for the 'not' in the consequent is taken purely
negatively.

⟨2.53R⟩ Ad tertium nego quod Sortes omni homini est idem. Et tunc ad probationem admitto casum. Et ulterius nego istam consequentiam:

Sorti concludenti et omni homini Sortes est idem; igitur omni homini Sortes est idem,

5 si ly .omni homini. regitur ab isto participio 'concludenti'. Et tunc ad argumentum ibi arguitur a copulato ad alteram partem, dico quod non semper tenet nisi copulatum regatur a copula principali et etiam quod ipsum non praecedat signum vel terminus habens vim confundendi. Ideo istae consequentiae non valent:

10   Tu non es homo et asinus; igitur tu non es homo.

Similiter non sequitur:

Istud totum est idem isti medietati ⟨et isti medietati; igitur istud totum est idem isti medietati⟩.

Eodem modo est dicendum in proposito quod consequentia praedicta non 15 valet quia illud totum 'Sorti et omni homini' regitur ab isto termino 'concludenti' et non ab isto termino 'est'. Quare . . .

Ad confirmationem quando dicebatur

Si Sorti concludenti, etc., igitur alicui homini et omni homini Sortes est idem,

20 dicitur negando consequentiam. Primo quia non arguitur ab inferiori ad suum superius, quia ly .Sorti concludenti. non est terminus inferior ad istum terminum 'homini'. Vel dato adhuc quod esset terminus inferior, consequentia non valeret, quia non arguitur ratione totius subiecti, sed solum partis. Modo talis forma non valet, sicut non sequitur:

25   Tu es apparens asinus; igitur tu es aliqualis asinus,

et tamen ly .aliqualis. est terminus superior ad ly .apparens. Similiter non sequitur:

Tu es dominus Platonis; igitur tu es aliquid Platonis,

et tamen ly .dominus. est terminus inferior ad ly .aliquid.

30 Si tamen concludatur in argumento priori quod alicui homini Sortes est idem, concedo consequentiam, et consequens verum. Tamen si in

1 omni homine homini *M*   3 igitur, etc. *E*   3–4 omni . . . idem, *om. E.*   7–
16 semper tenet quia non significatur idem regimen in antecedente et in consequente, modo ly .omni homini. in antecedente regitur a participio et in consequente ab illo termino 'idem'. *M*   29 tamen *om. E*

⟨2.53R⟩ I deny that Socrates is the same as every man. As for the proof I accept the hypothesis but I reject the inference

> Socrates is the same as somebody drawing a conclusion with reference to Socrates and every man; therefore Socrates is the same as every man,

if 'every man' is governed by the participial phrase 'drawing a conclusion'. As for the claim that that argument is from a conjoined term to one or the other part, I maintain that it does not always hold good unless the conjoined term is governed by the principal copula and no sign or term with the power of producing confused *suppositio* precedes it. Thus these inferences are unacceptable:

> You are not a man and a donkey; therefore you are not a man.

Similarly, this does not follow:

> This whole is the same as this half and this half; therefore this whole is the same as this half.[h]

The same sort of thing must be said about the example in question. The above-mentioned inference is unacceptable because the whole 'Socrates and every man' is governed by the term 'drawing the conclusion with reference to' and not by the term 'is'. Therefore . . .

As for the confirmation, in which one says

> If Socrates is the same as somebody drawing a conclusion with reference to Socrates etc., then Socrates is the same as some man and every man,

I reject the inference. First, because this is not an argument from an inferior to its superior; 'somebody drawing a conclusion with reference to Socrates' is not a term inferior to the term 'man'. Alternatively, even if one were to grant that it is an inferior term, the inference would not be acceptable, for the argument proceeds not in regard to the whole subject but a part only. Such a form is unacceptable, however, just as this does not follow:

> You are a donkey in appearance; therefore you are a donkey in some respect,

even though 'in some respect' is a term superior to 'in appearance'. Similarly, this does not follow:

> You are Plato's lord; therefore you are something that is Plato's,

even though 'lord' is a term inferior to 'something'.

If, however, one concludes in the prior argument that Socrates is the same as some man, I grant the inference, and its consequent is true. But if

antecedente principali regitur ly .omni homini. ab isto termino 'idem', concedo consequentiam et nego antecedens. Et tunc ad eius probationem:

> Huic Sortes est idem, et hoc est Sorti concludens et omni homini; igitur, etc.,

5 nego consequentiam. Primo quia in antecedente ly .omni homini. regitur a ly .concludenti. et in consequente regitur a ly .idem. Vel aliter potest dici quod non est syllogismus expositorius. Primo quia in resolvenda solum subicitur ly .Sorti concludenti. et ly .omni homini. tenet se a parte praedicati. Sed debet sic argui:

10   Huic et omni homini Sortes est idem, et hoc est Sortes concludens; igitur Sorti concludenti et omni homini Sortes est idem.

Et tunc conceditur consequentia et negatur maior.

⟨2.61⟩ Amplius ad principale arguitur sic. Omnis homo est Sortes vel hominem esse asinum hoc A significat, sed nullum hominem esse asinum

15 hoc A significat (semper uniformiter demonstrando); igitur omnis homo est Sortes. Consequentia patet disiunctiva cum opposito unius partis ad alteram eius partem. Et antecedens est verum in casu; igitur et consequens. Et quod antecedens sit verum arguitur. Et pono quod A sit haec copulativa:

> Homo est asinus et nullus homo est asinus.

20 Tunc isto posito patet quod hominem esse asinum hoc A significat, quia pars illius copulativae, scilicet, hominem esse asinum, hoc A significat, et quicquid significat pars copulativae significat tota copulativa, ut suppono; igitur, etc. Et per idem argumentum probatur quod nullum hominem esse asinum hoc A significat, quia pars illius copulativae sic significat; igitur,

25 etc.

Confirmatur hoc sic. Nullum hominem differre a Sorte propositio vera primarie significat, et qualitercumque propositio (15rb M) vera primarie significat est; igitur sic est quod nullus homo differt a Sorte. Consequentia patet, et antecedens probatur. Et sit B haec propositio

30   Deus est.

Tunc sic: nullum hominem differre a Sorte B (propositio vera) primarie

---

3 hoc est Sor. *M et E*   concludens sibi et *E*; et *om. M*   4 igitur *om. M*
7 Primo *om. M*   13 principale argumentum. *E*   21 copulativae illius *E*
scilicet *om. M*   hoc *A om. M*   22 quidquid *M*   24 igitur *om. E*
26 Consimiliter hoc *M*   28 quod nihil quod est homo *M*

'every man' in the principal antecedent is governed by the term 'the same', I grant the inference and deny the antecedent. And as for the proof of it,

> Socrates is the same as this, and this is somebody drawing a conclusion with reference to Socrates and every man; therefore, etc.,

I reject the inference. First, because 'every man' is governed by 'drawing the conclusion with reference to' in the antecedent and by 'the same as' in the consequent. Alternatively, one can say that that is not an expository syllogism.[i] First, because for purposes of resolution[j] only 'Socrates drawing the conclusion' is the subject and 'every man' remains in the predicate. Instead the argument must proceed in the following way:

> Socrates is the same as this and ever man, and this is Socrates drawing a conclusion; therefore Socrates is the same as somebody drawing a conclusion with reference to Socrates and every man.

And in that case the inference is granted and the major premiss is denied.[k]

⟨Sixth Set of Arguments against Opinion 2⟩

⟨2.61⟩ Every man is Socrates or that a man is a donkey this A signifies, but that no man is a donkey this A signifies (indicating the same ⟨proposition A⟩ throughout); therefore every man is Socrates. The inference is obvious: from a disjunctive proposition together with the opposite of one part to its other part. And the antecedent is true *ex hypothesi*; therefore so is the consequent. The following argument is offered to show that the antecedent is true. Suppose that A is the conjunctive proposition

> A man is a donkey and no man is a donkey.

Then on that hypothesis it is obvious that that a man is a donkey this A signifies. For a part of that conjunctive—viz. that a man is a donkey—this A signifies, and whatever a part of a conjunctive signifies, the whole conjunctive signifies, as I am supposing; therefore, etc. And by the same argument it is proved that that no man is a donkey this A signifies, because a part of the conjunctive signifies that; therefore, etc.

This is confirmed in the following way. That no man differs from Socrates a true proposition primarily signifies, and whatever way a true proposition primarily signifies is the case; therefore it is the case that no man differs from Socrates. The inference is obvious, and the antecedent is proved in the following way. Let B be the proposition

> God is.

Then: That no man differs from Socrates B (a true proposition) primarily signifies, and B is a true proposition; therefore, etc. The major premiss is

significat, et *B* est aliqua propositio vera; igitur, etc. Maior probanda, et antecedens arguitur, quia si non, proponatur eius oppositum, videlicet,

> Aliquem hominem differre a Sorte *B* (propositio vera) primarie significat.

5 Hoc est falsum, quia primarie Deum esse *B* propositio significat. Et quod ista sint contradictoria patet, quia una est universalis negativa et alia particularis affirmativa.

⟨2.62⟩ Secundo arguitur ad idem sic. Et pono quod Sortes et omnes alii homines disputent. Tunc isto casu posito Sortes est omnis homo disputans;

10 igitur, etc. Consequentia bona, et antecedens probatur sic. Iste Sortes et nihil aliud ab isto Sorte est homo disputans; igitur iste Sortes est omnis homo disputans. Consequentia patet, quia sequitur:

> Iste Sortes et nihil aliud ab isto Sorte est homo disputans; igitur tantum Sortes est homo disputans.

15 Et per consequens sequitur conversim quod omne disputans est Sortes.

Similiter, si iste Sortes et nihil aliud ab isto Sorte est homo disputans, igitur nihil aliud ab isto Sorte est homo disputans. Consequentia tenet; a toto copulato ad alteram eius partem sine aliquo termino habente vim confundendi praeposito. Tunc sic: nihil aliud ab isto Sorte est homo disputans,

20 et iste Sortes est homo; igitur iste Sortes est omnis homo disputans, quod erat probandum.

Sed iam probatur antecedens principale, videlicet,

> Iste Sortes et nihil aliud ab isto Sorte est homo disputans,

quia hoc est homo disputans (demonstrando istum Sortem), et hoc est iste

25 Sortes et nihil aliud ab isto Sorte; igitur . . . Consequentia patet, quia syllogismus expositorius, et antecedens est manifestum.

Similiter, homo disputans est iste Sortes et nihil aliud (12ra *E*) ab isto Sorte; igitur iste Sortes et nihil aliud ab isto Sorte est homo disputans. Consequentia patet: per conversionem simplicem. Et antecedens etiam

30 de se patet resolutorie arguendo.

⟨2.63⟩ Tertio arguitur sic. Tantum Sortes est homo; ergo omnis homo est Sortes. Consequentia patet, et antecedens probatur sic. Tantum homo

---

1 etc. *om. M*   2 proponitur *M*   videlicet, *om. M*   5 primarie debet esse *E*
6 alias *E*   8 ad idem arguitur *E*   9 homines *om. M*   13 nihil aliquid
ab *M*   15 conversim sequitur *M*   18 termino *om. M*   19 sic sit: *M*
22 Sed tamen probatur *M*   29 etiam *om. M*   31 sic *om. E*   32 Tenet
consequentia, et *E*   sic *om. E*

proved and the antecedent is supported by the following argument. Suppose that it is not the case; then let its opposite be put forward—viz.

That some man differs from Socrates *B* (a true proposition) primarily signifies.

That is false, for proposition *B* primarily signifies that God is. That the two propositions are contradictories is obvious; the one is a universal negative and the other a particular affirmative.

⟨2.62⟩ The same conclusion is argued for in the following way. Suppose that Socrates and all the other men are engaged in disputation. Then on that hypothesis Socrates is every man engaging in disputation; therefore, etc. This is a good inference, and the antecedent is proved in the following way. This Socrates and nothing other than this Socrates is a man engaging in disputation; therefore this Socrates is every man engaging in disputation. The inference is obvious, for this follows:

This Socrates and nothing other than this Socrates is a man engaging in disputation; therefore only Socrates is a man engaging in disputation.

Consequently it follows conversely that everything engaging in disputation is Socrates.

Similarly, if this Socrates and nothing other than this Socrates is a man engaging in disputation, then nothing other than this Socrates is a man engaging in disputation. The inference holds good: from a whole conjoined term to one or the other of its parts, when no term with the power of producing confused *suppositio* has been placed before. Then: Nothing other than this Socrates is a man engaging in disputation, and this Socrates is a man; therefore this Socrates is every man engaging in disputation, which is what was to be proved.

The principal antecedent—viz.

This Socrates and nothing other than this Socrates is a man engaging in disputation—

is proved in the following way. This is a man engaging in disputation (indicating this Socrates), and this is this Socrates and nothing other than this Socrates; therefore ... This inference is obvious, since it is an expository syllogism,[*l*] and the antecedent is apparent.

Similarly, a man engaging in disputation is this Socrates and nothing other than this Socrates; therefore this Socrates and nothing other than this Socrates is a man engaging in disputation. The inference is obvious: by simple conversion. The antecedent, too, is obvious in itself when one argues in accordance with resolution.[*m*]

⟨2.63⟩ Only Socrates is a man; therefore every man is Socrates. The inference is obvious, and the antecedent is proved in the following way.

est Sortes; ergo tantum Sortes est homo. Ista consequentia arguitur sic. Sequitur enim: tantum homo est Sortes; igitur nihil aliud ab homine est Sortes. Consequentia patet: ab exposita ad unam suarum exponentium. Et ultra: . . . ergo nihil non idem homini est Sortes. Consequentia patet
5 quia 'aliud' et 'non idem' convertuntur. Tunc ultra: nihil non idem homini est Sortes; igitur omne idem homini est Sortes. Consequentia patet, quia negatio postposita, etc. Et ultra sequitur quod tantum Sortes est homo, quod erat probandum.

⟨2.61R⟩ Ad ista tria argumenta respondetur. Ad primum negando
10 breviter consequentiam primam. Et quando dicitur quod ibidem arguitur a disiunctiva ad alteram partem, nego, eo quod ista non sunt contradictoria:

Hominem esse asinum *A* significat

et

Nullum hominem esse asinum *A* significat.

15 Sunt enim simul vera, ut probavit argumentum. Sed deberet argui cum tali medio:

Non est ita quod hominem esse asinum *A* significat.

Et tunc conceditur consequentia et negatur minor.

Ad confirmationem cum proponitur

20 Nullum hominem differre a Sorte *B* (propositio vera) primarie significat,

huic dicitur distinguendo istam secundum compositionem et divisionem. In sensu diviso concedo eam, ut argumentum probavit. Tamen ex hoc non sequitur quod nullus homo differat a Sorte. Si autem teneatur in sensu
25 composito, concedo consequentiam et nego antecedens, eo quod tunc significat quod aliqua propositio vera, vel *B*, propositio vera, significat primarie nullum hominem differre a Sorte, quod est falsum.

⟨2.62R⟩ Ad secundum, admisso isto casu, (15va M) nego quod Sortes est omnis homo disputans. Et tunc ad argumentum

30 Iste Sortes et nihil aliud ab isto Sorte est homo disputans; ergo, etc., concedo consequentiam et nego antecedens. Et ulterius ad eius probationem nego utramque consequentiam factam. Et causa est quia ly .nihil. continue

Only a man is Socrates; therefore only Socrates is a man. This inference is supported by the following argument, for this follows: Only a man is Socrates; therefore nothing other than a man is Socrates. This inference is obvious: from what is expounded to one of its exponents.[n] Further: ... therefore nothing not the same as a man is Socrates. This inference is obvious because 'other' and 'not the same' are interchangeable. Then further: Nothing not the same as a man is Socrates; therefore everything the same as a man is Socrates. This inference is obvious because a negation placed after, etc.[o] And it follows, further, that only Socrates is a man, which is what was to be proved.

⟨*Replies to the Sixth Set of Arguments against Opinion 2*⟩

⟨2.61R⟩ The short reply is to reject the first inference. And I deny the claim that it is an argument from a disjunctive proposition ⟨together with the opposite of one part⟩ to its other part, for the propositions

That a man is a donkey A signifies

and

That no man is a donkey A signifies

are not contradictories. As the argument has proved, they are true together. Instead one would have to argue with such a medium as this:

It is not the case that that a man is a donkey A signifies.

And then the inference is granted but the minor premiss is denied.

As for the confirmation, in which it is proposed

That no man differs from Socrates B (a true proposition) primarily signifies,

my reply is to draw a distinction with regard to composition and division. In the divided sense I grant it, as the argument has proved. But it does not follow from this that no man differs from Socrates. On the other hand, if it is taken in the compounded sense, I grant the inference and deny the antecedent. For in that case it signifies that some true proposition—or B, a true proposition—primarily signifies that no man differs from Socrates, which is false.

⟨2.62R⟩ Having accepted the hypothesis, I deny that Socrates is every man engaging in disputation. As for the argument

This Socrates and nothing other than this Socrates is a man engaged in disputation; therefore, etc.,

I grant the inference but deny the antecedent. And as for the proof of the antecedent, I reject both the inferences that are produced. This is because 'nothing' in the antecedent is taken as infinitating throughout and in the

in antecedente tenetur infinite et in consequente pure negative. Deberet igitur sic argui.

> Hoc est homo disputans, et hoc est iste Sortes et nihil aliud ab isto Sorte; igitur iste Sortes et ens nihil aliud ab isto Sorte est homo
> 5   disputans.

Et sic concedo consequentiam et consequens. Similiter, ex ista propositione

> Homo disputans est iste Sortes et nihil aliud ab isto Sorte

solum sequitur quod iste Sortes et ens nihil aliud a Sorte est homo disputans.

10   Aliter potest probabiliter dici concedendo istam:

> Iste Sortes et nihil aliud ab isto Sorte est homo disputans,

dicendo quod ibidem ly .nihil. est negatio infinitans cuius virtus terminatur ad istum terminum 'aliud ab isto Sorte' et non transit in compositionem totam. Et tunc negatur ista consequentia ex qua infertur quod tantum
15 Sortes est homo disputans. Nec ibi arguitur ab exponentibus ad expositam, quia antecedens est una propositio de copulato extremo. Sed si sic argueretur, antecedens deberet esse una copulativa talis:

> Iste Sortes est homo disputans, et nihil aliud ab isto Sorte est homo
> disputans.

20 Et sic conceditur consequentia et negatur antecedens pro minori.

Eodem modo respondetur ad aliud, negando consequentiam, quia ly .nihil. in consequente tenetur mere negative in antecedente vero infinite. Et ulterius cum allegatur regula, dico quod non recte arguitur per regulam. Deberet enim sic argui:

25   Iste Sortes et nihil aliud ab isto Sorte est homo disputans; igitur ens
>   nihil aliud ab isto Sorte est homo disputans.

Et isto modo conceditur consequentia et consequens.

Sed contra istam responsionem arguitur sic. Ex ipsa sequitur quod ista sophismata sunt vera:

30   Sortes et nullus alius mihi respondet, et tamen plures sophistae mihi
>   respondent;

---

4 iste *om. M*   ens *om. E*   aliud a Sorte *M*   8 est ille homo *M*   14 ex *om. E*
16–17 Sed si sic argueretur, *om. M*   17 antecedens enim deberet *M*   20 negetur *M*   23 non *om. M*   28 sic *om. E*   30 respondit *E*

consequent as purely negative.[p] One would, therefore, have to argue in the following way.

> This is a man engaging in disputation, and this is this Socrates and nothing other than this Socrates; therefore this Socrates and a being that is nothing other than this Socrates is a man engaging in disputation.

And in that case I grant both the inference and the consequent. Similarly, from the proposition

> A man engaging in disputation is this Socrates and nothing other than this Socrates

it follows only that this Socrates and a being that is nothing other than this Socrates is a man engaging in disputation.

> Alternatively, one can reply acceptably by granting the proposition

> This Socrates and nothing other than this Socrates is a man engaging in disputation,

maintaining that the 'nothing' is an infinitating negation the force of which terminates with the term 'other than this Socrates' and does not extend into the whole composition.[q] In that case one rejects the inference from which it is inferred that only Socrates is a man engaging in disputation. Nor is it an argument from the exponents to what is expounded,[r] since the antecedent is a proposition with a conjoined extreme. If one were to argue in that way the antecedent would have to be a conjunctive proposition such as

> This Socrates is a man engaging in disputation, and nothing other than this Socrates is a man engaging in disputation.

And in that case the inference is granted but the antecedent is denied in respect of the minor premiss.

One replies in the same way to the other argument, by rejecting the inference, for in the consequent 'nothing' is taken as merely negative but in the antecedent as infinitating. As for the rule that is appealed to, I maintain that it is not correctly argued under that rule. One would have to argue in the following way.

> This Socrates and nothing other than this Socrates is a man engaging in disputation; therefore a being that is nothing other than this Socrates is a man engaging in disputation.

And in that case both the inference and its consequent are granted.

⟨Sophismata directed against Reply 2.62R⟩

> It follows from this that these sophismata are true:
> Socrates and no one else replies to me, and yet several logicians reply to me;

A propositio et nulla alia ab *A* propositione est propositio, et tamen *B* est contradictorium *A*;

Animal et homo currit, et tamen animal et nihil quod est homo currit;

Sortes est aliud quam Plato et nihil aliud quam Plato, et tamen Sortes
5   non est Plato;

Tu es aliud quam asinus et nihil aliud quam asinus, et tamen tu non es asinus.

Huic dicitur breviter concedendo omnes istas conclusiones.

⟨1⟩ Arguitur tamen contra istam ultimam, nam si Sortes est aliud quam
10 Plato et nihil aliud quam Plato, igitur Sortes est aliud quam Plato et non aliud quam Plato. Tenet consequentia ab uno convertibili ad reliquum. Et consequens illius includit contradictionem eo quod nullus terminus copulatus ex duobus contradictoriis incomplexis praedicatur affirmative de isto termino 'Sortes'.

15 ⟨2⟩ Item sequitur:

Sortes est aliud quam Plato et non aliud quam Plato; igitur Sortes est aliud et non aliud quam Plato.

Consequens patet esse falsum, et consequentia probatur, eo quod cum quocumque vere (12ʳᵇ E) praedicatur terminus inferior cum eodem vere
20 praedicatur terminus superior, dummodo terminus cui fit copulatio non aliter supponit nec aliud significat cum uno quam cum alio, qualiter est in proposito.

⟨3⟩ Item si aliud quam Plato et nihil aliud quam Plato est Sortes, ergo Sortes est Plato. Probo consequentiam, quia si non, signo certum sup-
25 positum pro quo verificatur, et sit *B*. Tunc sic: ly .nihil. includit in se negationem et distributionem. Et ratione (15ᵛᵇ M) distributionis distribuit istum terminum 'aliquid quam Plato' pro omni alio a Platone et per consequens pro *B*. Et ratione negationis negat praedicatum ab omni illo pro quo fit distributio. Igitur, cum pro *B* fit distributio, sequitur quod a *B*
30 negatur praedicatum. Et si sic, sequitur illud antecedens asserere *B* esse Sortem et *B* non esse Sortem, et per idem Sortem esse Platonem et Sortem non esse Platonem.

⟨4⟩ Item ista propositio in mente

Nihil aliud quam Plato est Sortes

1 Et quod *A* propositio *M et E* tamen conclusiones ⟨?⟩ *B M* 2 contradictionum *E*
3 Similiter sequitur quod animal *M et E* 4 Similiter sequitur quod Sortes *M et E*
et (2) *om. E* 8 concedo *E* 9 Sed arguitur contra *M* 10–11 et nihil
aliud *E* 13 praedicatur pure affirmative *M* quam (2) *om. M* 16–17 est
aliquid et *M* 18 Consequens est falsum *M* 19 quocumque copulatur
aliquis terminus *M* 19–20 praedicatur vere *E* 20 cui fuit copulatio *M*
24 signo certo certum *M* 29 pro *om. M* 33 in mente *om. M*

Proposition *A* and no other than proposition *A* is a proposition, and yet *B* is the contradictory of *A*;

An animal and a man is running, and yet an animal and nothing that is a man is running;

Socrates is other than Plato and nothing other than Plato, and yet Socrates is not Plato;

You are other than a donkey and nothing other than a donkey, and yet you are not a donkey.

⟨*The Sophismata Granted*⟩

One replies to this briefly by granting all those conclusions.

⟨*Arguments against the Granting of the Sophismata*⟩

⟨1⟩ There are arguments against this last ⟨reply⟩, however, for if Socrates is other than Plato and nothing other than Plato, then Socrates is other than Plato and not other than Plato. The inference holds good: from one interchangeable term to the other. And its consequent includes a contradiction, because no term that is a conjunction of two non-complex contradictories is affirmatively predicated ⟨truly⟩ of the term 'Socrates'.

⟨2⟩ This follows:

Socrates is other than Plato and not other than Plato; therefore Socrates is other and not other than Plato.

The consequent is obviously false, but the inference is proved, for a superior term is predicated truly along with whatever an inferior term is predicated truly along with, provided that the term with which it is conjoined does not supposit otherwise or signify another thing with the one than it does with the other. And that is the way it is in the example in question.

⟨3⟩ If other than Plato and nothing other than Plato is Socrates, then Socrates is Plato. Proof of the inference: If that is not the case, then I choose a certain suppositum for which it comes true—let it be *B*. Then: 'Nothing' involves both negation and distribution. By reason of the distribution it distributes the term 'other than Plato' over everything other than Plato and consequently over *B*. By reason of the negation it denies the predicate of everything over which it produces the distribution. Therefore, since it produces the distribution over *B*, it follows that it denies the predicate of *B*. And if that is the case, it follows that the antecedent asserts that *B* is Socrates and *B* is not Socrates, and by the same token that Socrates is Plato and Socrates is not Plato.

⟨4⟩ Again, the mental proposition

Nothing other than Plato is Socrates

est negativa. Igitur manente isto termino 'aliud quam Plato' subiecto eiusdem, manebit propositio negativa.

⟨1R⟩ Ad primum dico concedendo consequentiam et consequens, non obstante quod terminus copulatus ex contradictoriis incomplexis prae-
5 dicatur affirmative de isto termino 'Sortes'. Et causa est quia prima pars istius copulati includit in se negationem cuius virtus transit ad hoc totum 'Plato et non aliud quam Plato'. Unde si terminaretur ad primum terminum, ipsa esset impossibilis. Et ideo sicut in ista

Sortes est aliud quam tantum Plato

10 virtus negationis inclusae in ly .aliud. transit in hoc totum 'tantum Plato', et sic in proposito.

⟨2R⟩ Ad secundum negatur consequentiam. Et ad probationem

Cum quocumque vere praedicatur terminus inferior, etc.,

dico quod hoc saepe fallit, videlicet quando terminus inferior includit in
15 se negationem transeuntem in subsequens, vel quando terminus inferior est terminus officiabilis, vel quando terminus inferior significat aliquid in obliquo denominans significatum ipsius termini in recto denominatione extrinseca. Ut non sequitur:

Hoc esse est scitum hic; igitur hoc esse est aliquid hic,

20 nam ly .scitum. significat scientiam in obliquo denominantem hoc esse scitum denominatione extrinseca. Nec tenet cum verbalibus nominibus. Unde non sequitur:

Tu es amator vini; igitur tu es aliquid vini.

⟨3R⟩ Ad aliud nego consequentiam. Et pro toto argumento dico, sicut
25 prius, quod ly .nihil. ibidem non tenetur mere negative sed infinite, cuius virtus terminatur ad istum terminum 'aliud quam Plato' et non transit in compositionem totam. Si enim sic transiret, bene sequeretur inconveniens deductum.

⟨4R⟩ Et tunc ad argumentum quando arguitur quod ista propositio in
30 mente Sortis est negativa, concedo. Dico tamen quod illud aggregatum ex ipsa et isto addito non est propositio negativa, sicut nec ista est negativa:

Aliquid non asinus currit,

---

1 Igitur adveniente isto *M*   Plato *om. M*   6 negationem ratione cuius *M* totum *om. M*   9 tantum *om. E*   11 sic est in *M*   13 etc., *om. M*   14 quod *om. M*   fallit, unde nec quando *M*   15 subsequens, nec quando *M*   16 significat aliud in *M*

is negative. Therefore as long as the term 'other than Plato' remains the subject of that proposition it will remain a negative proposition.

⟨*Replies to the Arguments against the Granting of the Sophismata*⟩

⟨1R⟩ I grant both the inference and its consequent, despite the fact that a term that is a conjunction of non-complex contradictories is affirmatively predicated of the term 'Socrates'. This is because the first part of the conjoined term includes a negation the force of which extends to the whole 'Plato and not other than Plato'. If it were to terminate with the first term, the proposition would be impossible. Therefore just as in the proposition

Socrates is other than only Plato

the force of the negation involved in 'other' extends to the whole 'only Plato', so also in the example in question.

⟨2R⟩ I reject the inference. As for the proof

⟨A superior term is predicated truly of⟩ whatever an inferior term is predicated truly of, etc.,

I maintain that this often fails to hold good—e.g. when the inferior term involves a negation that extends into what follows it, or when the inferior term is a functionalizable term,*s* or when the inferior term in an oblique case*t* signifies something denominating the significatum of that same term in the nominative case by an extrinsic denomination.*u* For example, this does not follow:

This being so (*hoc esse*) is known here; therefore this being so (*hoc esse*) is something here.

'Known' (*scitum*) signifies knowledge in an oblique case which denominates this known being by an extrinsic denomination. Nor does it hold good in the case of verbal nouns.*v* Thus this does not follow:

You are a lover of wine; therefore you are something belonging to wine.

⟨3R⟩ I reject the inference. And with reference to the whole argument I say, as before, that the 'nothing' in it is taken not as merely negative but as infinitating, and its force terminates with the term 'other than Plato' and does not extend into the whole composition. If it did extend in that way, the deduced absurdity would follow.

⟨4R⟩ As for the argument in which it is argued that that proposition in Socrates' mind is negative, I grant it. But I maintain that the combination of it with that addition does not constitute a negative proposition, just as this is not negative:

Something not a donkey is running,

et tamen haec est simpliciter negativa:

> Non asinus currit.

In una enim negatio tenetur negative et in alia negatio infinite.

⟨2.63R⟩ Ad tertium argumentum principale nego istam consequentiam:

5   Tantum homo est Sortes; igitur tantum Sortes est homo.

Et tunc ad probationem, concedo totum quousque infertur quod omne idem homini est Sortes, quam consequentiam nego. Et tunc ad regulam, dico quod intelligitur quando negatio tenetur negative et sequitur immediate post terminum distributum. Modo sic non est in proposito, quia ly .non. ibidem non tenetur negative sed infinite solum. Et etiam non sequitur immediate post terminum distributum immo ponitur inter partes subiecti, ut patet. Si enim iste modus arguendi valeret, per idem et iste valeret:

> Nihil non asinus currit; igitur omne ens asinus currit.

Et tamen non valet, quia stat antecedens esse verum sine consequente, ut satis patet intuenti, et eo quod ex negativa non solet sequi affirmativa.

Et sic patet responsio ad multa alia argumenta consimilia.

⟨2.71⟩ Amplius arguitur ad principale sic. Si ego scio te non stare, Sortes est omnis homo; sed ego scio te non stare; ergo Sortes est omnis homo. Consequentia et minor patent, et maior sic arguitur. Ego non scio te non stare nisi Sortes sit omnis homo; igitur si ego scio te non stare, Sortes est omnis homo. Probatur consequentia per consimile, (16ra M) nam sequitur:

> Ego non scio te esse asinum nisi tu sis capra; igitur si ego scio te esse asinum, tu es capra.

Et antecedens principale probatur sic. Et signetur ista propositio:

25   Tu non stas nisi Sortes sit omnis homo.

Tunc sic: ista propositio est falsa (12va E) primarie significando; igitur tu non scis sicut ista tibi primarie significat. Et ista tibi primarie significat

---

9–10 ly .non idem. non *E*   10 Et tunc non *M*   11 distributum ideo ponitur *M*   14 quia . . . consequente, *om. E*   15 et *om. E*   22 tu scis capra *M*

although this is simply negative:

Not a donkey is running.

For in one the negation is taken as negative and in the other as infinitating negation.[w]

⟨Continuation of Replies to the Sixth Set of Arguments against Opinion 2⟩

⟨2.63R⟩ In reply to the third main argument I reject the inference

Only a man is Socrates; therefore only Socrates is a man.

As for the proof, I grant all of it up to the point at which it is inferred that everything the same as a man is Socrates, and that inference I reject. As for the rule, I maintain that it is meant to apply when the negation is taken as negative and follows immediately after the distributed term. But that is not the way it is in the example in question, for the 'not' there is taken not as negative but as infinitating only. Besides, it does not follow immediately after the distributed term but is instead put between parts of the subject, as is perfectly clear. If that mode of arguing were acceptable, then by the same token this, too, would be acceptable:

Nothing not a donkey is running; therefore everything being a donkey is running.

But it is not acceptable, for it is consistent that the antecedent be true without the consequent, as is clear enough to anyone who considers it, and also because an affirmative does not, as a rule, follow from a negative.

And thus the reply to many other similar arguments is manifest.

⟨Seventh Set of Arguments against Opinion 2⟩

⟨2.71⟩ If I know that you are not standing, Socrates is every man, but I do know that you are not standing; therefore Socrates is every man. The inference and the minor premiss are obvious, and the major premiss is supported by the following argument. I do not know that you are not standing unless Socrates is every man; therefore if I do know that you are not standing, Socrates is every man. This inference is proved by means of one equiform to it, for this follows:

I do not know that you are a donkey unless you are a nanny-goat; therefore if I do know that you are a donkey, you are a nanny-goat.

The principal antecedent is proved in the following way. Take the proposition

You are not standing unless Socrates is a man.

Then: That proposition is false in its primary signification; therefore you do not know the case to be as that proposition primarily signifies to you.

quod tu non stas nisi Sortes sit omnis homo; igitur tu non scis te non stare nisi Sortes sit omnis homo. Et per idem sequitur quod ego non scio te non stare nisi Sortes sit omnis homo, quod erat probandum.

⟨2.72⟩ Secundo sic. Sortes est quando impossibile est aliam rem esse
5 quam Sortem esse; igitur Sortes est omnis homo. Patet consequentia, cuius antecedens sic probatur. Sortes est et impossibile est aliam rem esse quam Sortem esse; igitur, etc. Consequentia patet ex hoc quod temporalis et copulativa in eisdem terminis convertuntur cum verbo principaliter significante. Et antecedens probatur. Et signetur propositio impossibilis,
10 quae sit alia res quam Sortes. Isto posito, patet prima pars antecedentis. Et minor sic probatur. Hoc est aliam rem esse quam Sortem esse, et hoc est impossibile; igitur, etc. Antecedens arguitur sic. Hoc est istam rem esse (demonstrando seipsam), et ipsam esse est aliam rem esse quam Sortem esse; igitur, etc.

15 ⟨2.73⟩ Tertio arguitur sic. Quod Sortes est omnis homo Sortes scit, et nihil scitur nisi verum; igitur Sortes est omnis homo. Antecedens sic arguitur. Quod Sortes est ab omni homine Sorte scitur, et quicquid scitur ab omni homine Sorte omnis homo Sortes scit; igitur quod Sortes est omnis homo Sortes scit. Tenet consequentia, et antecedens praesupponitur
20 in casu.

⟨2.71R⟩ Ad ista tria argumenta respondetur. Ad primum nego istam:

Si ego scio te non stare, Sortes est omnis homo.

Et tunc ad probationem:

Ego non scio te non stare nisi Sortes sit omnis homo; igitur, etc.,
25 dicitur dubitando consequentiam eo quod illud verbum 'scio' in antecedente potest determinare totum sequens vel solum primam partem, videlicet, 'te non stare'.

Si autem determinat totum sequens, concedo antecedens et nego consequentiam, eo quod in consequente non potest esse consimilis determina-
30 tio cum antecedens sit categorica de conditionato extremo et consequens

---

7 hoc quia temporalis *M*   8–9 cum . . . significante *om. E*   11 probatur iterum. *M*   13 ipsum *E*

And it primarily signifies to you that you are not standing unless Socrates is every man; therefore you do not know that you are not standing unless Socrates is every man. By the same token it follows that I do not know that you are not standing unless Socrates is every man, which is what was to be proved.

⟨2.72⟩ Socrates is at a time when it is impossible that there is another thing that Socrates is ⟨or: that another thing is than Socrates is⟩; therefore Socrates is every man. The inference is obvious, and its antecedent is proved in the following way. Socrates is and it is impossible that there is another thing that Socrates is ⟨or: that another thing is than Socrates is⟩; therefore, etc. This inference is obvious because a temporal and a conjunctive proposition with the same terms are interchangeable when the verb has its principal signification. The antecedent is proved in the following way. Take an impossible proposition, which is another thing than Socrates. On that hypothesis the first part of the antecedent is obvious. The minor premiss is proved in the following way. This is that there is another thing that Socrates is ⟨or: that another thing is than Socrates is⟩, and this is impossible; therefore, etc. The antecedent is argued in the following way. This (indicating itself) is this thing existing, and this thing existing is that there is another thing that Socrates is ⟨or: this thing existing is that another thing than Socrates is⟩; therefore, etc.

⟨2.73⟩ That Socrates is every man Socrates knows, and nothing is known unless it is true; therefore Socrates is every man. The antecedent is supported by the following argument. That Socrates is is known by every man Socrates, and whatever is known by every man Socrates every man Socrates knows; therefore that Socrates is every man Socrates knows. The inference holds good, and the antecedent is presupposed in the hypothesis.

⟨*Replies to the Seventh Set of Arguments against Opinion 2*⟩

⟨2.71R⟩ I deny the proposition

If I know that you are not standing, Socrates is every man.

And as for the proof

I do not know that you are not standing unless Socrates is every man; therefore, etc.,

I reply by expressing doubt about the inference. For the verb 'know' in the antecedent can govern either the whole of what follows it or only the first part—viz. 'that you are not standing'.

If, on the one hand, it governs the whole of what follows it, I grant the antecedent and reject the inference, for there cannot be a determination of that sort in the consequent because the antecedent is a categorical with

conditionalis pura. Et tunc ad similitudinem, dico quod non est ad propositum cum in antecedente ibidem non possit fieri talis determinatio.

Si autem ly .scio. determinat solum primam partem, concedo consequentiam et nego antecedens.

5 Et tunc ad probationem, dico quod ista consequentia non valet nisi illud verbum 'scio' in consequente determinat totum sequens. Unde si non determinaret, argumentum non fieret ad propositum.

⟨2.72R⟩ Ad secundum cum proponitur

Sortes est quando impossibile est, etc.,

10 dico quod ly .impossibile. potest teneri nominaliter (resolutorie) vel modaliter (officiabiliter). Si nominaliter, concedo antecedens et nego consequentiam. Si vero modaliter, concedo consequentiam et nego antecedens. Et tunc ad probationem illius:

Impossibile est aliam rem esse quam Sortem esse; ergo, etc.,

15 nego consequentiam, quia tunc talis propositio non debet resolvi sed officiari, videlicet,

Haec propositio est impossibilis: 'alia res est quam Sortes est', quae sic primarie significat; igitur, etc.

Et sic arguendo, concedo consequentiam et nego antecedens pro maiori.

20 ⟨2.73R⟩ Ad tertium dicitur quod ista propositio

Quod Sortes est omnis homo Sortes scit

potest esse universalis aut indefinita. Si universalis, concedo eam, ut argumentum probavit. Si indefinita, nego eam. Et tunc ad argumentum:

Quod Sortes est ab omni homine Sorte scitur; igitur, etc., nego

25 consequentiam. Nec arguitur ab activa ad suam passivam, ut clare patet.

Vel potest dici quod ly .omnis homo. potest regi ab isto verbo 'est' aut (16rb M) ab isto verbo 'scio'. Primo modo haec est falsa:

Quod Sortes est omnis homo Sortes scit.

30 Sed secundo modo est vera.

Plura alia argumenta possent fieri in hac materia quae pro nunc gratia brevitatis dimittuntur.

---

7 non foret ad *E*   10 dubito quod *M*   (resolutorie) *om. E*   11 (officiabiliter) *om. E*   14 ergo, etc., *om. M*   15–16 officiabiliter *M*   17 est (2) *om. E*   23 probat *M*   eam *om. E*   27 Vel *om. E*   27–8 'est' et ab *E*   31 pro *om. M* dimittuntur, etc. *M*

a conditional extreme and the consequent is a pure conditional. As for the analogous argument, I say that it is not like the example in question because such a determination could not occur in its antecedent.

If, on the other hand, the 'know' governs only the first part, then I grant the inference but deny the antecedent.

As for the proof, I maintain that that inference is acceptable only if the verb 'know' in the consequent governs the whole of what follows it. If it does not govern that, the argument is irrelevant to the example in question.

⟨2.72R⟩ In reply to the proposition

> Socrates is at a time when it is impossible, etc.,

I maintain that 'impossible' can be taken either as a name (in connection with resolution)[x] or as a modal (in connection with functionalization).[y] If it is taken as a name,[z] I grant the antecedent but reject the inference. But if it is taken as a modal, I grant the inference and reject its antecedent. As for the proof of the antecedent

> It is impossible that there is another thing that Socrates is ⟨or: that another thing is than Socrates is⟩; therefore, etc.,

I reject the inference. In that case such a proposition must not be resolved but functionalized—viz.

> This proposition is impossible: 'another thing is than that Socrates is' ⟨or: 'another thing is than Socrates is'⟩, which primarily signifies that; therefore, etc.

And if one argues in that way I grant the inference but deny the antecedent because of the major premiss.

⟨2.73R⟩ The proposition

> That Socrates is every man Socrates knows

can be either universal or indefinite. If it is universal, I grant it, as the argument has proved. If it is indefinite, I deny it. As for the argument

> That Socrates is is known by every man Socrates; therefore, etc.,

I reject the inference. Nor is this an argument from an active verb to its passive, as is perfectly clear.

Alternatively, one can say that 'every man' can be governed either by the verb 'is' or by the verb 'know'. In the first case this is false:

> That Socrates is every man Socrates knows.

But in the second case it is true.

Several other arguments could be produced on this topic, but they are omitted now for the sake of brevity.

⟨*Quarta Divisio Terminorum*   *Capitulum Quartum*⟩

Quia variatio propositionis ex terminis propositionis habet ortum, ideo notanda est iuxta doctrinas universales logicorum praecedentium particularis distinctio terminorum. Sunt enim quantum ad propositum pertinet 5 quidam termini immediati et quidam termini mediati.

Termini immediati dicuntur termini simplices vel pronomina demonstrativa in singulari numero, ut 'ego', 'tu', 'ille', 'ipse', 'iste', 'hic', et 'is', et adverbia demonstrandi, ut 'nunc', 'tunc', 'hic', 'ibi', et hoc verbum 'est' praesentis temporis et numeri singularis.

10 Et causa est quia quorundam aliorum nominum et verborum pro aliquibus supponentur, cum possunt intrare probationem respectu eorundem terminorum, et non (12vb E) econtra, sicut notius. Et non dico 'sicut superius' vel 'inferius', quia ly .hoc. intrat probationem illius termini 'iste homo' et tamen non est inferius nec superius ad ly .iste homo. 15 Sed bene est notius. Sequitur enim:

Hoc currit, et hoc est iste homo; igitur iste homo currit.

Ideo talis propositio est immediata:

Hoc est,

quia non potest probari per aliquod notius per sensum vel intellectum.

20 Sed est differentia inter istos terminos immediatos, eo quod nomina, pronomina, et adverbia sic sunt immediata quod nullum terminum inferiorem habent se secundum praedicationem per quem possint probari. Sed illud verbum 'sum', 'es', 'est' praesentis temporis et numeri singularis sic est immediatum quod nullum habet supra se terminum sed sub eo 25 omnia alia verba continentur.

In hoc vero conveniunt, quod sicut non est aliquid in quo possit resolvi hoc pronomen 'hoc', ita non est aliud verbum in quo possit resolvi hoc verbum 'sum', 'es', 'est'.

Contra ista dicta arguitur, et primo probando quod pronomina demon- 30 strativa sunt termini mediati, et hoc sic.

⟨D.11⟩ Ly .hoc. est terminus communis pluribus univoce competens; igitur ly .hoc. est terminus mediatus. Patet consequentia, et antecedens probatur. Et assigno intentionem correspondentem huic pronomini 'hoc' quae competit Sorti, quae sit *A*. Et sit *B* una alia intentio demonstrativa,

---

2 propositionis (2) *om. M*   10 quia quorumlibet aliorum *M*   11 supponere *M*; supponentur, unde possunt *E*   respectu *om. M*   19 notius nisi per *M*   21 et *om. M*   22 se habent secundum praedicamentum per *M* quod possint *E*   23 'est' est praesentis *E*   25 alia *om. M*.   26 conveniunt, quia sicut *M*   est aliud in *E*

⟨Chapter Four: The Fourth Division of Terms—Immediate and Mediate⟩

⟨The Distinction between Immediate and Mediate Terms⟩

Variety in propositions has its source in the terms of the proposition. Consequently we must take note of a particular distinction among terms which is in accordance with the universal teachings of earlier logicians.[a] In so far as the distinction pertains to our discussion it maintains that some terms are immediate and other terms are mediate.

Immediate terms are simple terms or demonstrative pronouns in the singular number, such as 'I', 'you', 'that', 'itself', 'this', 'he', and indexical adverbs, such as 'now', 'then', 'here', 'there', and the verb 'is' in the present tense and the singular number.

⟨They are called immediate⟩ because they are put in place of certain other nouns and verbs, for they, as the better known, can enter into a proof in respect of those other terms, but not vice versa. I do not say 'as the superior' or 'as the inferior', for the word 'this' enters into a proof in respect of the term 'this man' and yet is neither inferior nor superior to 'this man'. But it is indeed better known. For this follows:

This is running, and this is this man; therefore this man is running.

Thus a proposition such as

This is

is an immediate proposition, for it cannot be proved by anything better known to the senses or the understanding.

But there is a difference among immediate terms. On the one hand, the nouns, pronouns, and adverbs are immediate in the sense that they are not related by predication to any inferior term by means of which they can be proved. On the other hand, the verb 'am', 'are', 'is' in the present tense and the singular number is immediate in the sense that it has no term over it but all other verbs are contained under it.

Immediate terms are alike, however, in that just as there is nothing in respect of which the pronoun 'this' can be resolved, so there is no other verb in respect of which the verb 'am', 'are', 'is' can be resolved.

⟨First Set of Arguments against the Distinction⟩

One argues against these claims first by proving in the following way that demonstrative pronouns are mediate terms.

⟨D.11⟩ 'This' is a common term, being univocally suited to more than one thing; therefore 'this' is a mediate term. The inference is obvious, and the antecedent is proved in the following way. Take the intention corresponding to the pronoun 'this' which is suited to Socrates and let it be A.

quae sit intentio Platonis. Et sint Sortes et Plato simillimi. Tunc sic: quarumcumque intentionum duarum omnino similium quicquid significatur per unam illarum significatur per reliquam, sed A et B sunt intentiones omnino similes; igitur quicquid significatur per A significatur per B et econverso. Sed Sortes significatur per A; igitur Sortes significatur per B. Et similiter Plato significatur per idem B; igitur B intentio demonstrativa est communis pluribus. (Et consimiliter arguitur de A, quod est terminus mediatus.) Iste discursus est bonus, et maior probatur. Quicquid intentio significat significat propter convenientiam intentionis cum re, etc., quia est similitudo sive imago rei. Sed quaecumque intentiones omnino consimiles aequaliter conveniunt cum omni re cum qua altera earundem convenit. Igitur quarumcumque intentionum ⟨duarum omnino⟩ similium quicquid significatur per unam significatur per reliquam, et econverso.

⟨D.12⟩ Secundo arguitur sic. Et pono quod pro quolibet instanti futuro obiciatur tibi unus homo omnino similis Sorti, ita quod pro nullis duobus instantibus tibi obiciatur idem, et sint sic similes quod distinctio non appareat, et maneat continue A intentio demonstrativa, quae est intellectio Sortis, in (16va M) anima tua. Quaero tunc utrum continue manebit A intentio Sortis in anima tua absque alia de novo causata continue vel erit alia de novo causata secundum novitatem apparentium.

Si primum, respectu cuiuslibet istorum habebis intentionem significantem Sortem, et solum habebis A intentionem; igitur A intentio est communis. Consequentia tenet cum antecedente.

Nec potest dici quod respectu cuiuslibet istorum ⟨habebis⟩ distinctam intentionem, quia si sic, sit A intentio Sortis et B intentio Platonis. Tunc sic: A et B apprehendis, vel igitur ut distinctas vel ut similes. Si ut distinctas, igitur distinctionem inter A et B apprehendis. Consequens falsum. Cum non apprehendas distinctionem rerum, igitur nec intentionum. Nec ut similes, quia tunc similitudinem apprehendis. Sed similitudo apprehensa praesupponit sua extrema apprehendi ut distincta. Igitur prius apprehendis illas intentiones ut distinctas.

Ad haec omnia potest unica responsione responderi eodem modo, quod pronomen demonstrativum plura significat, non tamen est terminus

2 quarumque M   quidquid M   4 quidquid M   9–10 re ex qua est M
19–20 vel continue M et E   21 primum, et respectu M   23 cum maiori. E
24–5 istorum istam intentionem M   26–7 Si ut similes, M   28 apprehendis M
intentionem M

Let B be another demonstrative intention, which is an intention of Plato. And let Socrates and Plato be as much alike as possible. Then: Whatever is signified by one of any two altogether similar intentions is signified by the other, but A and B are altogether similar intentions; therefore whatever is signified by A is signified by B and vice versa. But Socrates is signified by A; therefore Socrates is signified by B. And Plato likewise is signified by that same B; therefore the demonstrative intention B is common to more than one thing. (There is a precisely similar argument to prove that A is a mediate term.) This reasoning is good, and the major premiss is proved in the following way. Whatever an intention signifies it signifies because of an association of the intention with the thing, etc., because it is a likeness or image of the thing. But altogether similar intentions are associated equally with every thing with which any one of them is associated. Therefore whatever is signified by one of any two altogether similar intentions is signified by the other, and vice versa.

⟨D.12⟩ Suppose that at each future instant a man altogether similar to Socrates is perceived by you in such a way that for no two instants is one and the same man perceived by you, and that they are so similar that there is no apparent difference among them, and that the demonstrative intention A, which is a concept of Socrates, remains in your mind all the while. In that case I ask whether (1) the intention A, of Socrates, will remain in your mind all the while apart from another, newly caused intention or (2) there will be another intention, newly caused in accordance with the newness of the appearances.

If (1), then in respect of each of them you will have the intention signifying Socrates, and you will have only that intention A; therefore intention A is common. The inference holds good, along with the antecedent.

Nor can it be said that (2) you will have a distinct intention in respect of each of them. For suppose in that case that A is the intention of Socrates and B the intention of Plato. Then: You apprehend A and B; therefore you apprehend them either as distinct or as alike. If as distinct, then you apprehend a distinction between them. This consequent is false. Since you do not apprehend a distinction between the things, neither do you apprehend one between the intentions. Nor, on the other hand, do you apprehend A and B as alike, for in that case you apprehend the likeness. But an apprehended likeness presupposes that its extremes have been apprehended as distinct. Therefore you previously apprehend those intentions as distinct.

⟨*Replies to the First Set of Arguments against the Distinction*⟩

One can make a single reply to all of these, replying in one and the same way by saying that although a demonstrative pronoun signifies more than

communis quia non pro quolibet quod significat potest supponere sed
solummodo pro uno. Sicut iste terminus 'hoc album' est terminus singularis et tamen significat plura, videlicet, hoc album et albedinem, ab illo
realiter distinctam. Sed pro albedine non potest supponere. Sic ly .istius.
5 plura significat, quia aliud in ista:

> Tu es frater istius

et aliud in ista:

> Tu es aliquid istius.

Et tamen non est terminus communis, quia non potest pro illis supponere,
10 sed praecise pro uno quocumque demonstrato.

Et ita in proposito dicitur quod tam *A* quam *B* significat plura. Non
tamen pro illis potest supponere, (13ʳᵃ E) sed *A* pro Sorte solummodo,
B vero pro Platone.

Aliter respondetur dicendo quod *A* significat Sortem solummodo et *B*
15 praecise Platonem.

⟨D.11R⟩ Et tunc ad argumentum primum, nego maiorem. Et ad probationem, concedo consequentiam cum prima parte antecedentis et nego
secundam, videlicet, quod quaecumque intentiones omnino consimiles
aequaliter conveniunt cum omni re cum qua altera illarum convenit.
20 Quoniam *A* convenit cum Sorte ut similitudo illius, *B* vero cum Platone
ut similitudo eius. Unde sicut non est possibile quod *A* fiat a Platone in
potentia intellectiva sed a Sorte solummodo, ita non est possibile quod sit
Platonis imago aut similitudo foret. Enim impossibile, ut docet experien-
tia, Sortem et Platonem, qualitercumque similes, eandem imaginem in
25 speculo causare, licet consimiles. Et ita foret impossibile unius imaginem
aliud repraesentare, sed eiusdem solummodo principium effectivum.

Verumtamen concedo quod per notitiam Sortis possum devenire in
notitiam Platonis. Sed Platonis notitia necessario altera est a Sortis
similitudine vel notitia.

30 ⟨D.12R⟩ Ad secundum argumentum dicitur ut prius, admisso casu,
quod respectu cuiuslibet istorum habebis distinctam intentionem. Et
tunc ad argumentum:

> *A* et *B* apprehendis; igitur ut distinctas aut similes,

dicitur ad antecedens quod non est necesse ipsum concedere in casu isto.
35 Quoniam sicut possibile est quod aliquid videam non videndo visionem
istius, ita est possibile quod aliquid intelligam non intelligendo intentionem aut intellectionem illius. Quare patet quod non oportet si intelligo
vel apprehendo Sortem et Platonem quod *A* et *B* apprehendam.

---

3 plura, quia hoc *M et E*   37 oportet quod si *M*

one thing, it is not a common term because it cannot supposit for every thing it signifies but for one only. In the same way the term 'this white thing' is a singular term that nevertheless signifies more than one thing— viz. this white thing and the whiteness, which is really distinct from it. But it cannot supposit for the whiteness. Thus 'of his' signifies more than one thing, for it signifies one thing in

> You are a brother of his

and another in

> You are something of his.

Still, it is not a common term. It cannot supposit for both of them but only for just whichever one is indicated.

Thus in the example in question it is said that A as well as B signifies more than one thing. It cannot supposit for them, however; A can supposit only for Socrates and B for Plato.

Alternatively one replies by saying that A signifies Socrates only and B signifies just Plato.

⟨D.11R⟩ In reply to the first argument, then, I deny the major premiss. As for the proof, I grant the inference along with the first part of the antecedent and I deny the second part of it—viz. that any altogether similar intentions are associated equally with every thing with which any one of them is associated. For A is associated with Socrates as his likeness, but B with Plato as *his* likeness. Thus just as it is not possible that A should be produced in the intellective power by Plato but only by Socrates, so it is not possible that it should be the image or likeness of Plato. As experience teaches, it is impossible that Socrates and Plato, however much alike, should cause one and the same image in a mirror even though ⟨they may cause images⟩ just alike. In the same way it is impossible that the image of the one should represent the other. It represents its effective source only.

I do grant, however, that I can arrive at a cognition of Plato by means of a cognition of Socrates. But the cognition of Plato is necessarily other than the likeness or cognition of Socrates.

⟨D.12R⟩ Having accepted the hypothesis, I say as before that you will have a distinct intention in respect of each of them. As for the argument

> You apprehend A and B; therefore you apprehend them either as
> distinct or as alike,

I reply that it is not necessary to grant the antecedent *ex hypothesi*. For just as it is possible that I see something without seeing the seeing of it, so is it possible that I conceive of something without conceiving of the intention or the concept of it. For that reason it is obvious that if I conceive of or apprehend Socrates and Plato I need not apprehend A and B.

Concessa tamen antecedente, nego consequentiam quoniam si ap-
prehenderem ista ut similia vel (16vb M) ut distincta ego apprehen-
derem ista esse plura. Consequens est contra casum. Et ita concedo quod
ista duo apprehendo; sed non apprehendo ista duo quia apprehendo ista
5 esse duo.

Secundo arguitur ad principale probando quod hoc verbum 'est' est
terminus mediatus.

⟨D.21⟩ Quoniam omnis terminus resolubilis est terminus mediatus,
sed ly .est. est terminus resolubilis; ergo est terminus mediatus. Patet
10 discursus cum maiori. Et minorem probo per Aristotelem secundo *Peri
Hermeneias*, dicentem quod non refert dicere hominem ambulare et
hominem ambulantem esse.

⟨D.22⟩ Secundo sicut se habet ly .ambulans. ad ⟨ly⟩ .ambulare., ita
se habet ly .ens. ad ⟨ly⟩ .esse. Igitur qua ratione ly .ambulans. includitur
15 in ly .ambulare., eadem ratione ly .ens. in ly .esse.

⟨D.23⟩ Tertio

Sortes est in domo

convertitur in istam:

Ens in domo est Sortes.

20 Sed non videtur ratio quare ly .ens. additur in convertente nisi quia
includitur in ly .est. Igitur, etc.

⟨D.24⟩ Quarto nisi ly .ens. includatur in ly .est., sequitur quod staret
propositionem aliquam categoricam esse sine praedicato. Consequens
falsum, ex quo propositio categorica est illa quae habet subiectum, prae-
25 dicatum, et copulam principales partes sui.

Respondetur quod illud verbum 'est' est terminus immediatus. Et
cum dicitur quod est terminus resolubilis, nego, loquendo de resolutione
propria, quando illud quod resolvitur non capitur in eius resolutione nec
probatione. Dicere namque

30   Sortes est, id est, Sortes est ens,

haec non est resolutio propria. Sed haec est propria:

Sortes currit, id est, Sortes est currens,

quia ly .currit. non sumitur in eius probatione nec resolutione.

⟨D.21R⟩ Et tunc ad primum argumentum. Concedo quod sicut non
35 refert dicere hominem ambulare et hominem ambulantem esse, et ita nec

---

1 tamen maiori, nego *E*   2 ut demonstrata ego *M*   3 concedendo *M*
6 Secundo *om. M*   8 terminus (2) *om. M*   9 est (2) *om. M*   12 esse
om. E   14 se habet *om. E*   15 ly (3) *om. M*   31 Sed haec est propria: *om. M*

But even granting the antecedent, I reject the inference that if I were to apprehend them either as alike or as distinct I would apprehend that they are more than one. The consequent is contrary to the hypothesis. Thus I grant that I do apprehend those two; but I do not apprehend those two because I apprehend that they are two.

⟨Second Set of Arguments against the Distinction⟩

One argues against the main thesis in the second place by proving that the verb 'is' is a mediate term.[b]

⟨D.21⟩ Every resoluble term is a mediate term, but 'is' is a resoluble term; therefore it is a mediate term. The reasoning is obvious, along with the major premiss. I prove the minor premiss by reference to Aristotle in *De interpretatione* ⟨Chapter 12, 21^{b}10⟩, where he says that it makes no difference whether one says that a man walks or that a man is walking.

⟨D.22⟩ Just as 'walking' is related to 'to walk', so is 'being' related to 'to be'. Therefore for the same reason as 'walking' is included in 'to walk', 'being' is included in 'to be'.

⟨D.23⟩ The proposition

Socrates is in the house

converts into the proposition

⟨A⟩ being in the house is Socrates.

But evidently the only reason why 'being' is added in the process of converting is that it is included in 'is'. Therefore, etc.

⟨D.24⟩ Unless 'being' is included in 'is', it follows that it is consistent that there should be a categorical proposition without a predicate. This consequent is false, for a categorical proposition is that which has a subject, a predicate, and a copula as its principal parts.

⟨Replies to the Second Set of Arguments against the Distinction⟩

The verb 'is' is an immediate term. I deny the claim that it is a resoluble term, speaking of proper resolution, in which what is resolved is not included in its own resolution or proof. For to say

Socrates is, i.e. Socrates is being

is not proper resolution. But this is proper:

Socrates runs, i.e. Socrates is running,

since 'runs' is not used in its proof or resolution.

⟨D.21R⟩ In reply to the first argument I grant that just as it makes no difference whether one says that a man runs or a man is running, neither does it make any difference whether one says that a man is or that

hominem esse et hominem esse ens. Ex hoc tamen non sequitur quod si illud verbum 'ambulat' sit resolubile, ita illud verbum 'est'.

⟨D.22R⟩ Ad secundum argumentum dicitur concedendo quod ly .ens. includitur in ly .esse. Non tamen sequitur quod illud verbum 'est' sit 5 resolubile.

⟨D.23R⟩ Ad tertium concedo quod ista propositio

Sortes est in domo

sic convertitur:

Ens in domo est Sortes,

10 et quod ⟨ly⟩ .esse. includit ⟨ly⟩ .ens. Non tamen sequitur quod ⟨illud verbum 'est'⟩ sit resolubile.

⟨D.24R⟩ Ad quartum concedo conclusionem adductam immo et fortiorem quod aliqua est propositio categorica quae non habet subiectum, praedicatum, nec copulam. Et tunc ad regulam allegatam, dicitur quod 15 intelligitur propositionem categoricam habere implicite vel explicite illas partes, secundum quod declarabitur in secunda parte. Quare, etc.

Terminorum mediatorum quidam sunt resolubiles, ut nomina, verba, adverbia, (13rb E) et participia habentia inferiora secundum praedicationem, ut 'homo', 'movetur', 'alicubi', quibus inferiora sunt ista: 'hoc', 'currit', 20 'ibi'.

Alii autem termini sunt exponibiles, ut signa universalia affirmativa, dictiones exclusivae et exceptivae, 'incipit' et 'desinit', omnes comparativi et superlativi gradus, termini modales, et breviter omnes termini ratione quorum sunt propositiones in quibus ponuntur expositionem assignandae, 25 ut sunt 'talis', 'differt', 'aliud', 'inquantum', 'per se', 'necessario', et 'contingenter'.

Alii vero sunt termini officiabiles, ut termini limitantes ad sensum compositum et sensum divisum et ad diversas compositiones secundum diversas ordinationes in propositionibus, ut sunt termini significantes 30 actus animae, sicut est 'scire', 'intelligere', 'velle', 'imaginari', 'percipere', 'credere', 'dubitare', et similia.

Iuxta hoc tamen est notandum quod ista trimembris divisio secundum viam communem non est ex opposito assignata, cum contingat eundem terminum esse resolubilem, exponibilem, et officiabilem, (17ra M) ut 35 patet de isto termino 'necessarium' in ista propositione:

Necessarium est Deum esse

vel

Necessarium est aliquid non esse,

quae potest tripliciter probari. Primo resolutorie sic:

40 Hoc est Deum esse, et hoc est necessarium; ergo necessarium est Deum esse.

---

2 'ambulo' M et E   4 ly om. E   10 quod (1) om. E   12 et om. M
17 nomina et verba M   17–18 verba et adverbia E   18 adverbia, signa, et M
19 'movetur', 'alicui', quibus M   21 termini om. E   24 sunt om. E   ponuntur
sunt exponibiliter assignandae E   assignare M   25 et om. E   28 divisum aliqui
ad E   32–3 secundum viam communem om. E   38 non om. E   39 resolubiliter E   40 et hoc est necessum E

a man is being. But it does not follow from this that if the verb 'walks' is resoluble the verb 'is' is resoluble as well.

⟨D.22R⟩ I grant that 'being' is included in 'to be'. But it does not follow that the verb 'is' is resoluble.

⟨D.23R⟩ I grant that the proposition

Socrates is in the house

converts to

⟨A⟩ being in the house is Socrates,

and that 'to be' includes 'being'. But it does not follow that the verb 'is' is resoluble.

⟨D.24R⟩ I grant the derived conclusion and even the stronger one that there is a categorical proposition that does not have a subject, a predicate, or a copula. As for the rule appealed to, I say that it means that a categorical proposition has these parts either implicitly or explicitly, as will be explained in Part Two.ᶜ Therefore, etc.

⟨Resolution, Exposition, and Functionalization of Mediate Terms⟩

Of mediate terms some are resoluble, such as nouns, verbs, adverbs, and participles that have inferiors in predication. For example, 'man', 'moves', 'somewhere', with respect to which these are inferior: 'this', 'runs', 'there'.

Other mediate terms are exponible, such as universal affirmative signs, exclusive and exceptive words, 'begins' and 'ceases', all comparative and superlative degrees, modal terms, and, in short, all terms because of which the propositions in which they occur can be assigned an exposition. For example, 'such', 'differs', 'other', 'in so far as', 'as such', 'necessarily', and 'contingently'.

Still others are functionalizable terms, such as terms that limit ⟨a proposition⟩ to the compounded sense or the divided sense and to various compositions according to various arrangements in propositions. For example, terms signifying mental acts, such as 'know', 'understand', 'wish', 'imagine', 'perceive', 'believe', 'doubt', and the like.

It must be noted, however, that this tripartite division in accordance with the common way is not exclusive, for it can happen that one and the same term is resoluble, exponible, and functionalizable. This is clear in the case of the term 'necessary' in the proposition

It is necessary that God is

or

It is necessary that something is not,

which can be proved in three different ways. (1) By means of resolution:

This is that God is, and this is necessary; therefore it is necessary that God is.

Secundo expositorie sic:

> Deus est, et non potest esse quin Deus est; igitur necessarium est Deum esse.

Tertio officiabiliter sic:

5   Talis propositio est necessaria: 'Deus est', quae praecise primarie significat Deum esse; igitur necessarium est Deum esse.

Consimili modo potest dici de isto termino 'contingens', qui potest etiam resolubiliter, exponibiliter, et officabiliter teneri, ut

> Contingens est te esse.

10 Probatur primo resolutorie sic:

> Hoc est te esse, et hoc est contingens; igitur contingens est te esse.

Secundo expositorie sic:

> Tu es, et potest esse quod tu non es; igitur contingens est te esse.

Tertio officiabiliter sic:

15   Talis propositio est contingens: 'tu es', quae praecise primarie significat te esse; igitur contingens est te esse.

Ex istis elicitur talis regula, quod universalis propositio exposita convertitur cum suis exponentibus sumptis simul, sed propositio resolutorie vel officiabiliter probata cum suo antecedente resolutorie vel officiabiliter

20 ipsum inferente non convertitur nisi gratia terminorum. Verbi gratia, sequitur:

> Deus est, et non potest esse quin Deus est; ergo necessarium est Deum esse,

et econtra:

25   Necessarium est Deum esse; igitur Deus est, et non potest esse quin Deus est.

Et sequitur:

> Haec propositio est necessaria: 'Deus est', quae primarie significat Deum esse; igitur necessarium est Deum esse,

30 sed non sequitur econtra, quia licet nulla propositio esset adhuc necessarium esset Deum esse. Similiter sequitur resolutorie:

> Hoc currit, et hoc est homo; igitur homo currit,

sed non sequitur econtra, ut patet intuenti.

1 exponitur E   4 officiatur E   5 necessaria est E   praecise om. M
7–8 potest exponi, resolvi, et officiari, ut M   13 igitur . . . esse om. E
18 exponentibus sufficienter sumptis, sed M   18–19 resolutorie et officiabiliter M
19 resolubiliter M   29 igitur necesse est E   30 esset ad hoc M   31 resolubiliter M

(2) By means of exposition:

God is, and it cannot be but that God is; therefore it is necessary that God is.

(3) By means of functionalization:

This proposition is necessary: 'God is', and it primarily signifies just that God is; therefore it is necessary that God is.

The same sort of thing can be said about the term 'contingent', which can also be taken as resoluble, as exponible, or as functionalizable, as in

It is contingent that you are.

This is proved in the following ways: (1) by means of resolution:

This is that you are, and this is contingent; therefore it is contingent that you are.

(2) By means of exposition:

You are, and it can be that you are not; therefore it is contingent that you are.

(3) By means of functionalization:

This proposition is contingent: 'you are', and it primarily signifies just that you are; therefore it is contingent that you are.

From these considerations the following rule is derived. An expounded universal proposition is interchangeable with its exponents taken together, but a proposition that is proved by means of resolution or functionalization is not interchangeable with the antecedent that implies it in the resolution or functionalization unless as a consequence of the terms themselves. For example, this follows:

God is, and it cannot be but that God is; therefore it is necessary that God is,

and vice versa:

It is necessary that God is; therefore God is, and it cannot be but that God is.

This follows also:

This proposition is necessary: 'God is', and it primarily signifies that God is; therefore it is necessary that God is,

but it does not follow the other way round, for even if there were no proposition it would still be necessary that God is. Similarly, this follows by means of resolution:

This is running, and this is a man; therefore a man is running,

but it does not follow the other way round, as is obvious to anyone who considers it.

Et notanter dicebatur 'nisi gratia terminorum', quia bene sequitur:

Hoc est, et hoc est Deus; igitur Deus est,

et econtra. Similiter sequitur:

Hoc lucet, et hoc est sol; igitur sol lucet,

5 et econtra. Et universaliter est hoc verum quando talium indefinitarum resolventes sunt necessariae. Item officiabiliter sequitur:

Tu scis talem propositionem 'aliquid est', quae primarie significat aliquid esse; igitur tu scis aliquid esse,

et econtra. Sequitur enim:

10 Tu scis aliquid esse; igitur tu scis talem propositionem 'aliquid est', quae primarie significat aliquid esse.

Redeundo, igitur, ad probationem terminorum resolubilium, est sciendum quod omnis terminus communis pro aliquo supponens et omne verbum (praeter verbum substantivum praesentis temporis et numeri sin-15 gularis) est resolubilis. Omnis enim propositio in qua subicitur communis terminus habet probari per duo demonstrativa sibi correspondentia. Et hoc universaliter est verum in indefinita affirmativa in quocumque numero vel casu fuerit, et cum quocumque verbo de praesenti, praeterito, et futuro, ut

20 Homo est animal

sic resolvitur:

Hoc est animal, et hoc est homo; igitur homo est animal.

Aliquid fuit homo

sic resolvitur:

25 Hoc fuit homo, et hoc est vel fuit aliquid; igitur aliquid fuit homo.

Aliquis homo curret:
Hoc curret, et hoc est vel erit aliquis homo; igitur . . .

Album incipit esse:
Hoc incipit esse, et hoc est vel incipit esse album; igitur . . .

30 Aliquod animal desinit esse:
Hoc desinit esse, et hoc est vel desinit esse aliquod animal; igitur . . .

11 Igitur tu scis aliquid esse. *add. E*   13 suppositivus *E*   15–16 subicitur huiusmodi terminus *E*   16 duo pronomina demonstrativa *E*   25 est aliquid vel *E*
igitur, etc. *E*   aliquid...homo *om. E*   26 currit *M*   27 currit *M*   29 est
album vel *E*   30 Aliquid *E*

The phrase 'unless as a consequence of the terms themselves' is important ⟨to the rule⟩, for this follows rightly:

This is, and this is God; therefore God is,

and the other way round as well. Similarly, this follows:

This is shining, and this is the sun; therefore the sun is shining,

and the other way round as well. This is universally true whenever the
resolvends of such indefinite propositions are necessary propositions.
Again, this follows by means of resolution:

You know the proposition 'something is', and it primarily signifies
that something is; therefore you know that something is,

and the other way round as well. For this follows:

You know that something is; therefore you know the proposition 'something is', which primarily signifies that something is.

⟨*Mediate Terms in Indefinite or Particular Affirmative Propositions*⟩

Returning, then, to the proof of resoluble terms, it must be known that
every common term suppositing for something and every verb (except the
substantive verb in the present tense and the singular number) is resoluble.
For every proposition in which a common term is the subject has to be
proved by means of two demonstrative ⟨propositions⟩ corresponding to it.
This is universally true as regards an indefinite affirmative proposition
in any number or case and with any verb in the present, past, or future
tense. For example,

A man is an animal

is resolved as follows:

This is an animal, and this is a man; therefore a man is an animal.

Something was a man

is resolved as follows:

This was a man, and this is or was something; therefore something was
a man.

Some man will be running:

This will be running, and this is or will be some man; therefore . . .

A white thing begins to be:

This begins to be, and this is or begins to be white; therefore . . .

Some animal ceases to be:

This ceases to be, and this is or ceases to be some animal; therefore . . .

Episcopus potest praedicare:

Hoc potest praedicare, et hoc est vel potest esse episcopus; igitur . . .

Episcopus potuit praedicare:

Hoc potuit praedicare, et hoc est vel potuit esse episcopus; igitur

5   episcopus potuit praedicare.

Episcopus poterit praedicare:

Hoc poterit praedicare, et hoc est vel poterit esse episcopus; igitur . . .

Homo (13ra E) videtur ab omni homine:

Hoc videtur ab omni homine, (17rb M) et hoc est homo; igitur . . .

10   Ab aliquo homine differt homo:

Ab hoc differt homo, et hoc est homo; igitur . . .

Contradictoriorum eadem est disciplina:

Horum eadem est disciplina, et haec sunt contradictoria; igitur . . .

Hominibus albis homines nigri fuerunt similes:

15   Istis homines nigri fuerunt similes, et isti sunt homines albi vel
          fuerunt homines albi; igitur . . .

Aliquos homines videbunt aliqui homines:

Istos videbunt aliqui homines, et isti sunt aliqui homines vel erunt
          aliqui homines; igitur . . .

20 Exempla de adverbiis resolutoriis, ut

          Aliqualiter est

resolvitur isto modo:

          Sic est, et sic est aliqualiter; igitur . . .

          Aliquando eris:

25   Tunc eris, et tunc est vel erit aliquando; igitur . . .

          Post A tempus erit Sortes episcopus:

          Tunc erit Sortes episcopus, et tunc est vel erit post A tempus;
          igitur . . .

          Ante crastinam diem dormies:

30   Tunc dormies, et tunc est vel erit ante crastinam diem; igitur . . .

          Alicubi est sol:

          Ibi est sol, et ibi est alicubi; igitur . . .

Per hoc igitur patet quod non est aliqua particularis vel indefinita affirmativa quae non habeat vel habere possit duo demonstrativa sibi correspon-
35 dentia.

2 igitur . . . *om.* E   3–9 -tuit . . . Hoc *om.* E   18 fuerunt *M et* E   19 igitur,
etc. *add.* E   22 resolvitur *om.* M   26 Sortes erit *M*   27 est post *A* tempus vel E

A bishop can preach:
This can preach, and this is or can be a bishop; therefore . . .

A bishop was able to preach:
This was able to preach, and this is or was able to be a bishop; therefore . . .

A bishop will be able to preach:
This will be able to preach, and this is or will be able to be a bishop; therefore . . .

A man is seen by every man:
This is seen by every man, and this is a man; therefore . . .

From some man a man differs:
From this a man differs, and this is a man; therefore . . .

Of contradictories the science is one and the same:
Of these the science is one and the same, and these are contradictories; therefore . . .

To white men black men were similar:
To these things black men were similar, and these things are or were white men; therefore . . .

Some men other men will see:
These things other men will see, and these things are or will be some men; therefore . . .

Examples of resoluble adverbs.

Somehow it is:
Thus it is, and thus is somehow; therefore . . .

Sometime you will be:
Then you will be, and then is or will be sometime; therefore . . .

After time t Socrates will be a bishop:
Then Socrates will be a bishop, and then is or will be after time t; therefore . . .

Before tomorrow you will sleep:
Then you will sleep, and then is or will be before tomorrow; therefore . . .

Somewhere is the sun:
There is the sun, and there is somewhere; therefore . . .

As a result of this it is clear that there is not any particular or indefinite affirmative proposition that does not have or could not have two demonstratives corresponding to it.

Indefinita vel particularis negativa potest tripliciter probari. Uno modo per duo demonstrativa, quemadmodum est indefinita affirmativa, ut

Homo non currit:

Hoc non currit, et hoc est homo; igitur homo non currit.

5 Secundo modo potest probari recurrendo ad eorum contradictoria, ipsa probando vel improbando, quo facto statim patebit veritas indefinitae vel particularis negativae. Tertio modo potest probari per universalem negativam sibi subalternantem, ut

Aliquid non currit

10 probatur sic:

Nihil currit; igitur aliquid non currit.

⟨Animal non currit:⟩

Nullum animal currit; igitur animal non currit.

Et per istum modum probandi patet veritas talium indefinitarum vel

15 particularium, ut

Aliquis homo qui est asinus non est asinus,

Differens ab ente non est,

Aliqua res nolita a chimaera non est nolita a chimaera,

Chimaera non est,

20   Aliquis homo quem asinus genuit non est filius eius,

et ita de infinitis, quae omnes probari possunt per earum subalternas universales negativas.

Et sicut dictum est de infinita vel particulari affirmativa vel negativa, eodem modo est dicendum de singulari affirmativa vel negativa de subiecto

25 demonstrativo praeter 'hoc', quod non potest probari in singulari negativa per suam subalternam, cum talem non habeat. Ideo ista propositio

Iste homo albus currit

debet sic probari:

Hoc currit, et hoc est iste homo albus; igitur . . .

30   Iste homo vel asinus est asinus:

Hoc est asinus, et hoc est iste homo vel asinus; igitur . . .

2 quemadmodum et indefinita *M*   8 ut illa: *M*   19 chimaera . . . est *om. E*
24 de non subiecto *M et E*   25 in *om. M*

⟨Mediate Terms in Indefinite or Particular Negative Propositions⟩

An indefinite or particular negative proposition can be proved in three different ways. (1) By two demonstratives, as in the case of an indefinite affirmative. For example,

A man is not running:
This is not running, and this is a man; therefore a man is not running.

(2) By having recourse to the contradictories of ⟨the two demonstratives⟩ and proving them or disproving them. Once that has been done the truth of the indefinite or particular negative proposition will be immediately apparent. (3) By the universal negative which is its subaltern.[d] For example,

Something is not running

is proved as follows:

Nothing is running; therefore something is not running.

An animal is not running:
No animal is running; therefore an animal is not running.

And in this way, obviously, one can prove the truth of such indefinite or particular propositions as these:

Some man who is a donkey is not a donkey,
What is different from being is not,
Some thing willed against by a chimera is not willed against by a chi-
    mera,
A chimera does not exist,
Some man whom a donkey has begotten is not his son,

and so on as regards infinitely many, all of which can be proved by their subaltern universal negatives.

⟨Mediate Terms in Singular Affirmative or Negative Propositions⟩

The sort of thing that has been said about an indefinite or particular affirmative or negative proposition must also be said about a singular affirmative or negative proposition with a demonstrative subject other than 'this', which cannot be proved in the singular negative by means of its subaltern ⟨universal negative⟩ because it has none. Thus the proposition

This white man is running

must be proved as follows:

This is running, and this is this white man; therefore, etc.

This man or a donkey is a donkey:
This is a donkey, and this is this man or a donkey; therefore . . .

Ex hoc sequitur quod iste syllogismus non est expositorius:

> Iste homo vel asinus est asinus, iste homo vel asinus est homo; igitur
> homo est asinus,

quia medius terminus deberet esse pronomen demonstrativum simplex,
5 qualiter non est in proposito.

Et ex alio sequitur quod ad particularem affirmativam aut sibi aequi-
valentem resolutorie inferendam oportet maiorem esse singularem propositionis inferendae, et minorem esse singularem de subiecto synonymo
cum priori et verbo et praedicato proportionato verbo et praedicato
10 propositionis principaliter inferendae. Sed sic non est in proposito, quia
singularis illius

> Homo est asinus

non est aliqua talis

> Iste homo vel asinus est asinus,

15 ut patet.

⟨1⟩ Sed forte contra quaedam superius dicta arguitur probando quod
non omnis indefinita affirmativa vera habet duo demonstrativa vera. Et
assigno istam propositionem:

> Chimaera intelligitur.

20 (17ᵛᵃ M) Tunc certum est quod ipsa est vera, et tamen non habet aliquam
talem demonstrativam veram:

> Hoc est chimaera,

cum ipsa sit impossibilis.

> Hoc idem patet de ista:

25 > Antichristum significat ly .Antichristus.,

quae vera est et tamen non habet aliquam talem veram

> Hoc est Antichristus.

Huic potest multipliciter responderi.

⟨1R1⟩ Primo modo quod in talibus indefinitis in quibus verba prin-
30 cipalia sunt verba importantia officium vel consignificantia actum mentis
non requiritur nisi solum una demonstrativa. Ideo pro veritate illius

> Chimaera intelligitur

sufficit veritas illius:

> Hoc intelligitur,

5 quare non E   6 alio etiam quia ad M   8 singularem om. E   9 priori
verbo ac praedicato M   9-10 et subiecto propositionis M et E   29 modo om. M
31 solum om. M

It follows from this that this is not an expository syllogism:[e]

This man or a donkey is a donkey, this man or a donkey is a man; therefore a man is a donkey,

for the middle term would have to be a simple demonstrative pronoun, which it is not in the example.

And from the other it follows that in order to infer a particular affirmative or its equivalent by means of resolution the major premiss must be the singular proposition corresponding to the inferred proposition, and the minor premiss must be a singular proposition having its subject synonymous with the earlier subject and having its verb and predicate proportionate to the verb and predicate of the principally inferred proposition. But that is not the way it is in the example in question, since the singular proposition corresponding to

A man is a donkey

is obviously not anything like

This man or a donkey is a donkey.

⟨*Argument against a Claim regarding Indefinite Affirmative Propositions*⟩

⟨1⟩ One may, however, argue against some of what was said above[f] by proving that not every true indefinite affirmative proposition has two true demonstratives. Take the proposition

A chimera is thought of.

It is certainly true, but it has no such true demonstrative as

This is a chimera,

for that is an impossible proposition.

The same thing is clear in the case of

An Antichrist is signified by 'Antichrist',[g]

which is true and yet has no such true proposition as

This is an Antichrist.

⟨*Replies to this Argument*⟩

This argument can be replied to in many ways.

⟨1R1⟩ In indefinite propositions in which the principal verbs are verbs implying a function or consignifying a mental act only one demonstrative is required. Thus for the truth of the proposition

A chimera is thought of

the truth of this suffices:

This is thought of,

demonstrando chimaeram. Similiter, pro veritate istius

    Antichristum significat ly .Antichristus.

sufficit veritas solum huius

    Hoc significat ly .Antichristus.,

5 demonstrando Antichristum.

    ⟨1R2⟩ Secundo modo potest responderi quod ista non est sua secunda demonstrativa

    Hoc est chimaera,

sicut nec istius

10   Homo incipit (13ᵛᵇ E) esse

est secunda demonstrativa haec, scilicet,

    Hoc est homo,

sed haec

    Hoc est homo vel incipit esse homo.

15 Eodem modo est dicendum quod secunda demonstrativa istius

    Chimaera intelligitur

erit ista, scilicet,

    Hoc est vel intelligitur esse chimaera,

quae est vera. Similiter, secunda demonstrativa istius

20   Antichristum significat ly .Antichristum.

erit haec

    Hoc est Antichristus vel significatur esse Antichristus,

quod verum est.

    ⟨1R3⟩ Tertio modo potest dici quod talis demonstrativa debet dari per

25 unam conditionalem, ut

    Chimaera intelligitur:

    Hoc intelligitur et hoc esset chimaera si esset; igitur . . .

Eodem modo dicitur ad aliam de Antichristo.

    ⟨1R4⟩ Quarto modo respondetur, et melius, dicendo quod talia verba

30 'intelligitur', 'opinatur', 'significat', 'supponit', etc., ampliant eorum subiecta et praedicata pro praesenti, praeterito, et futuro, possibili vel imaginabili. Ideo ista propositio

    Chimaera intelligitur

debet sic resolvi:

35   Hoc intelligitur, et hoc est chimaera vel est imaginabile esse chimaera;

        igitur . . .

Similiter, ista

    Antichristum significat ly .Antichristus.

---

1 istius *om.* E   2–3 Antichristum . . . solum *om.* E   6 sua *om.* M   11 est *om.* M
15 est *om.* M   17 scilicet *om.* M   19 vera est M   demonstrativa *om.* E
istius *om.* M   21 est E   24 potest intelligi quod M   30 opinamur E
31 possibili *om.* E   35 chimaera (1) *om.* E

indicating a chimera. Similarly, for the truth of the proposition

An Antichrist is signified by 'Antichrist'

the truth of this alone suffices:

This is signified by 'Antichrist',

indicating an Antichrist.

⟨1R2⟩ One can reply that

This is a chimera

is not its second demonstrative, just as the second demonstrative of

A man begins to be

is not

This is a man

but rather

This is or begins to be a man.

In the same way it must be said that the second demonstrative of

A chimera is thought of

will be

This is or is thought to be a chimera,

which is true. Similarly, the second demonstrative of

An Antichrist is signified by 'Antichrist'

will be

This is or is signified to be an Antichrist,

which is true.

⟨1R3⟩ One can say that a demonstrative of that sort must be expressed by means of a conditional. For example,

A chimera is thought of:

This is thought of, and this would be a chimera if it existed; therefore . . .

One replies in the same way to the example regarding Antichrist.

⟨1R4⟩ A better reply than the others is to say that such verbs as 'is thought of', 'believes', 'signifies', 'supposes', etc., ampliate[h] their subjects and predicates over what is present, past, and future, possible or imaginable. Thus the proposition

A chimera is thought of

must be resolved as follows:

This is thought of, and this is a chimera or is imaginable to be a
chimera; therefore . . .

Similarly, the proposition

An Antichrist is signified by 'Antichrist'

debet sic resolvi:

> Hoc significat ly .Antichristus., et hoc est Antichristus vel erit Anti-
> christus; igitur . . . ,

ita quod semper in secunda parte disiunctivae ponatur pars pro qua
5 potest verificari.

⟨1⟩ Secundo arguitur contra unum aliud implicite concessum, videlicet,
quod omne verbum activum est resolubile in suum participium et verbum
substantivum. Nam dato hoc, sequitur quod Antichristus est, posito tamen
quod nullus Antichristus sit. Probatur sic arguendo.

10   Antichristus disputabit; igitur Antichristus est disputaturus.

Tenet consequentia per concessum, et ex consequente sequitur quod Antichristus est, a tertio adiacente ad secundum adiacens valet consequentia.

⟨2⟩ Item arguitur haec

> Sortes leget

15 non potest resolvi in illam

> Sortes erit legens;

igitur a pari nec in illam

> Sortes est lecturus.

Consequentia tenet, et antecedens probatur. Et pono quod non sit aliquis
20 Sortes sed erit et leget. Tunc sic: Sortes leget; ergo Sortes erit legens.
Et ex consequente sequitur quod Sortes est. Igitur, a primo, Sortes leget;
ergo Sortes est, quod est falsum.

> Et quod sequitur

> Sortes erit legens; igitur Sortes est

25 probatur, nam ista propositio

> Sortes est lecturus

infert istam

> Sortes erit

ratione praedicati futuritive consignificantis. Igitur a pari ista:

30   Sortes erit legens

must be resolved as follows:

> This is signified by 'Antichrist', and this is or will be an Antichrist; therefore . . .

in such a way that the part for which it can come out true is always put in the second part of the disjunctive.

⟨*Arguments against Claims regarding the Resolution of Verbs*⟩

⟨1⟩ In the second place one argues against something else that was taken for granted[i]—viz. that every active verb is resoluble into its participle and the substantive verb. For in that case it follows that Antichrist is even if one has supposed that there is no Antichrist. This is proved by arguing in the following way.

> Antichrist will engage in disputation; therefore Antichrist is a future disputant.

Because of what was taken for granted the inference holds good, and as a consequence it follows that Antichrist is, since an inference from the third component to the second component is acceptable.[j]

⟨2⟩ The proposition

> Socrates will lecture

cannot be resolved into

> Socrates will be lecturing;

therefore by parity of reasoning not into

> Socrates is a future lecturer.

The inference holds good, and the antecedent is proved in the following way. Suppose there is not any Socrates but there will be and he will lecture. Then: Socrates will lecture; therefore Socrates will be lecturing. It follows from this consequent that Socrates is. Therefore, from the first premiss we have: Socrates will lecture; therefore Socrates is, which is false.

Proof that the inference

> Socrates will lecture; therefore Socrates is

does follow: The proposition

> Socrates is a future lecturer

implies the proposition

> Socrates will be

because of the predicate, which consignifies with reference to the future.[k] Therefore by parity of reasoning the proposition

> Socrates will be lecturing

infert istam

    Sortes est

ratione praedicati mere praesentialiter consignificantis. Probatur consequentia: non sequitur

5   Sortes (17vb M) est iustus; igitur Sortes erit,

nec sequitur

    Sortes est futurus; igitur Sortes erit.

Igitur tota causa quare ista

    Sortes est lecturus

10 vel aliqua consimilis, scilicet

    Sortes est futurus,

    Sortes est praedicaturus,

    Sortes est iturus,

infert istam de futuro

15   Sortes erit

est quia praedicatum istius consignificat per modum futuri. Ergo pari
ratione ista

    Sortes erit legens,

sumendo ly .legens. participialiter, infert istam

20   Sortes est

ex quo ipsius praedicatum praesentialiter consignificat.

    ⟨1R⟩ Ad hoc respondetur ad primum negando istam consequentiam

    Antichristus est disputaturus; igitur Antichristus est.

Et tunc ad rationem, dico quod a tertio adiacente ad secundum adiacens
25 non valet argumentum cum termino distrahente, qualis est iste terminus
'disputaturus', ut inferius ostendetur.

    ⟨2R⟩ Ad secundum concedo istam consequentiam

    Sortes leget; igitur Sortes erit legens,

Sed nego illam

30   Sortes erit legens; igitur Sortes est.

Et cum dicitur bene sequitur

    Sortes est lecturus; igitur Sortes erit,

ita a pari sequitur

    Sortes erit legens; igitur Sortes est,

    7 igitur Sortes fuit *M*   13 Sortes ... iturus, *om. E*   19 ly *om. E*

implies the proposition

Socrates is

because of the predicate, which consignifies with reference to nothing but the present.[l] Proof of the inference: This does not follow:

Socrates is just; therefore Socrates will be,

nor does this follow:

Socrates is future; therefore Socrates will be.

Therefore the whole reason why the proposition

Socrates is a future lecturer

or any like it, such as

Socrates is future,
Socrates is a future preacher,
Socrates is a future walker,

implies the future-tense proposition

Socrates will be

is that its predicate consignifies by way of the future. Therefore by parity of reasoning the proposition

Socrates will be lecturing,

taking 'lecturing' participially, implies the proposition

Socrates is

because of the fact that its predicate consignifies with reference to the present.[m]

⟨*Replies to these Arguments*⟩

⟨1R⟩ I reject the inference

Antichrist is a future disputant; therefore Antichrist is.

As for the reason given, I say that an argument from the third component to the second component is unacceptable when there is a distracting term,[n] such as 'a future disputant', as will be shown below.[o]

⟨2R⟩ I grant the inference

Socrates will lecture; therefore Socrates will be lecturing.

But I reject this one:

Socrates will be lecturing; therefore Socrates is.

And in response to the claim that this follows rightly:

Socrates is a future lecturer; therefore Socrates will be,

and that thus by parity of reasoning this follows:

Socrates will be lecturing; therefore Socrates is,

nego consequentiam. Et ad probationem, dico quod prima consequentia valet non praecise ex hoc quia praedicatum est consignificans futuritive (quoniam tunc ista consequentia valeret:

Adam fuit futurus; igitur Adam erit),

5 sed ideo quia praedicatum est futuri temporis et non limitatur per aliquid aliud. Sed potius distrahit et limitat verbum praesentis temporis. Ideo deberet sic argui:

Prima consequentia est bona quia praedicatum est futuri temporis non limitatum, sed secundae consequentiae antecedentis praedica-
10 tum est praesentis temporis et non limitatum; igitur et secunda consequentia est bona.

Concedo argumentum, sed nego minorem quoniam ly .legens. limitatur per verbum praecedens ad standum praecise pro illo de quo erit verum dicere

15 Hoc est legens.

Pro quo notandum quod participium praesentis temporis, puta 'legens' aut aliquod tale, non significat solummodo ea quae nunc principaliter sunt, immo et omnia de quibus est, fuit, aut erit verum dicere quod illa sunt simpliciter vel talia aut talia. Et ita ly .futurus. non solum (14ra E)
20 significat ea quae erunt sed omnia de quibus est, fuit, aut erit verum ⟨dicere⟩ quod illa erunt. Et ita de participio praeteriti temporis est dicendum suo modo.

Huiusmodi igitur termini habentes istam significationem possunt per verba praecedentia limitari, ut

25 Antichristus erit legens vel praeteritus

non infert Antichristum esse vel fuisse, quoniam ly .legens. et .praeteritus. limitantur per verbum praecedentium ad standum pro illo quod erit solummodo. Et ita cum dicitur

Adam fuit futurus

30 non supponit ly .futurus. pro illo quod iam est futurum, sed pro illo de quo aliquando erat verum dicere quod est futurum, et hoc propter limitationem verbi praeteriti temporis, ut dictum est.

Adhuc arguitur contra illam propositionem concessam

Aliquis homo qui est asinus non est asinus.

I reject the inference. As for the proof, I maintain that the first inference is acceptable not precisely because the predicate is consignificant with reference to the present (since in that case this inference would be acceptable:

Adam was future; therefore Adam will be),

but because the predicate is of the future tense and is not limited by anything else.[b] Rather, it distracts and limits the present-tense verb. Thus one would have to argue as follows:

The first inference is good because the predicate is of the future tense and is not limited, but the predicate of the antecedent of the second inference is of the present tense and is not limited; therefore the second inference is also good.

I grant this argument, but I deny its minor premiss. 'Lecturing' is limited by the preceding verb to standing precisely for that of which it will be true to say

This is lecturing.

In this connection it must be noted that a present-tense participle—e.g. 'lecturing' or any of that sort—signifies not only those things that now principally are, but also those things of which it is or will be true to say that they are—either that they are simply or that they are such and such. And so 'future' signifies not only the things that will be but also all the things of which it is or was or will be true to say that they will be. The same sort of thing must be said about the past-tense participle, *mutatis mutandis*.

Terms of this sort, having that sort of signification, therefore, can be limited by the preceding verb. Thus

Antichrist will be lecturing or past

does not imply that Antichrist is or was, since 'lecturing' and 'past' are limited by the preceding verb to standing only for that which will be. And so when one says

Adam was future

the 'future' does not supposit for that which now is future but for that of which it was at some time true to say that it is future. As has been said, that is a consequence of the limitation belonging to the past-tense verb.

⟨*Arguments against the Granting of a Certain Proposition*⟩

In addition one argues against the proposition I granted

Some man who is a donkey is not a donkey.[q]

⟨1⟩ It follows from this that some man is a donkey, but that is false; therefore . . . Proof of the inference: In the proposition

Some man who is a donkey is not a donkey

⟨1⟩ Nam ex ipsa sequitur quod aliquis homo est asinus, et hoc est falsum; igitur . . . Consequentia probatur sic. In ista propositione

Aliquis homo qui est asinus non est asinus

sunt duae compositiones quarum prima ponit et asserit hominem esse asi-
5 num. Sed negatio subsequens non negat compositionem praecedentem. Igitur adhuc post adventum istius negationis manebit prima compositio non negata. Et per consequens consequentia est bona.

⟨2⟩ Item per idem (18ra M) debet concedi ista:

Sortes qui est asinus non differt ab asino.

10 Et si concedatur, arguitur sic:

Sortes qui est asinus non differt ab asino, et Sortes est, et asinus est; igitur Sortes est asinus.

Consequens falsum; igitur et antecedens. Consequentia probatur a simili, sequitur enim:

15 Tu non differs a Platone, et tu es, et Plato est; igitur tu es Plato.
Ita in proposito.

⟨1R⟩ Respondetur ad primum negando consequentiam primam et ultimam, quia ante adventum negationis ista propositio est tota affirmativa, asserens hominem esse asinum. Sed post adventum negationis est pro-
20 positio negativa, et sic non debet asserere.

Vel aliter dicitur negando assumptum ad probandum consequentiam primam, quia nihil nisi propositio asserit vel ponit aliquid esse. Cum igitur ista prima compositio non sit propositio, igitur non sic asserit.

⟨2R⟩ Ad secundum concedo quod Sortes qui est asinus non differt ab
25 asino. Et cum concluditur quod Sortes est asinus, nego consequentiam. Et tunc ad similitudinem, dico quod non est similitudo, quia ista propositio

Tu differs a Platone

bene sic exponitur:

Tu es, et Plato est, et tu non es Plato.

30 Sed ista propositio

Sortes qui est asinus differt ab asino

non sic exponitur:

Sortes est, et asinus est, et Sortes non est asinus,

sed sic:

35 Sortes qui est asinus est, et asinus est, et Sortes qui est asinus non est asinus.

5 neget *E*   13 igitur *om. M*   23 non scit propositio *E*   24 Et ad *M*

there are two compositions, the first of which posits and asserts that a man is a donkey.[r] But a subsequent negation does not negate a preceding composition. Therefore even after the arrival of that negation the first composition will remain unnegated. Consequently the inference is good.

⟨2⟩ By the same token the proposition

Socrates who is a donkey does not differ from a donkey

must be granted. And if that is granted, one argues in the following way.

Socrates who is a donkey does not differ from a donkey, and Socrates is, and a donkey is; therefore Socrates is a donkey.

The consequent is false; therefore so is the antecedent. The inference is proved by analogy, for this follows:

You do not differ from Plato, and you are, and Plato is; therefore you are Plato.

And that is the way it is in the example in question.

⟨*Replies to these Arguments*⟩

⟨1R⟩ I reject the first and the last inference. Before the arrival of the negation the proposition is wholly affirmative, asserting that a man is a donkey. But after the arrival of the negation it is a negative proposition and must not assert that.

Alternatively, one may reply by denying what is assumed in order to prove the first inference, for nothing but a proposition asserts or posits that something is the case. Therefore since the first composition is not a proposition, it does not assert that.

⟨2R⟩ I grant that Socrates who is a donkey does not differ from a donkey. And I reject the inference in which it is concluded that Socrates is a donkey. As for the analogy, I say there is no analogy. The proposition

You differ from Plato

is expounded as follows:

You are, and Plato is, and you are not Plato.

But the proposition

Socrates who is a donkey differs from a donkey

is not expounded as follows:

Socrates is, and a donkey is, and Socrates is not a donkey,

but rather in this way:

Socrates who is a donkey is, and a donkey is, and Socrates who is a donkey is not a donkey.

Ideo in consequentia priori deberet sic argui:

> Sortes qui est asinus non differt ab asino, et Sortes qui est asinus est, et asinus est; igitur, etc.

Et sic conceditur consequentia et negatur prima pars antecedentis.

5 Universalis negativa probanda est per assumptionem sui contradictorii, quo proposito, apparebit veritas ipsius universalis negativae. Multae enim sunt negativae verae quae apparent falsae propter in considerationem suorum contradictoriorum. Ideo conceduntur tales conclusiones quod

> Nihil et chimaera sunt fratres, geniti de eodem patre, et tamen nihil et
10 chimaera sunt homo et asinus.
> Nihil et Antichristus sunt omnia quae sunt, et tamen nihil et Antichristus differunt ab omnibus quae sunt.
> Nihil et chimaera sunt plura infinita, et tamen nihil et chimaera sunt tantum duo.

15 Sed hoc caveas de negatione, quia non sequitur

> Nihil et chimaera differunt ab homine; igitur nihil et chimaera sunt homo,

quia ex consequente sequitur quod omne ens et chimaera differunt ab homine, quod est falsum. Et consequentia patet per istam regulam: negatio
20 postposita, etc.

Et si dicitur quod ibi arguitur ab exposita ad unam suarum exponentium, respondetur negando. Et causa est quia nulla universalis negativa debet exponi sed solum probari per suum contradictorium, ut dictum est.

Sequitur de universali affirmativa specialiter pertractandum, et maxime
25 quomodo expositione probari debeat.

Et patet, iuxta regulas communes, quod propositio universalis affirmativa debet exponi per suam subalternam et universalem (14rb E) negativam sibi convenientem.

Et notanter dico 'sibi convenientem', quia multipliciter contingit expo-
30 nentes universalis affirmativae variari: vel ⟨1⟩ ratione signi, vel ⟨3⟩ ratione subiecti simplicis vel compositi, vel ⟨4⟩ ratione verbi, vel ⟨2⟩ ratione praedicati.

---

1 in *om. M*   sic deberet *M*   3 et asinus est *om. M*   etc. *om. M*   4 negatur secunda pars *M*   9 de eadem matre, et *E*   12–17 omnibus ... homo *om. M*   12–18 differunt ab homine. Et si arguitur sic: nihil et chimaera differunt ab homine; igitur nihil et chimaera non sunt homo, negatur consequentia, quia *M*   23 De expositione universalis affirmativae. *add. E*   26 quod primo universalis *E*

Thus in the earlier inference one would have to argue in the following way.

> Socrates who is a donkey does not differ from a donkey, and Socrates who is a donkey is, and a donkey is; therefore, etc.

And in that case the inference is granted and the first part of its antecedent is denied.

⟨Mediate Terms in Universal Negative Propositions⟩

A universal negative proposition must be proved by means of the assumption of its contradictory. Once that has been propounded, the truth of the universal negative itself will be apparent. For there are many true negatives that appear false except in respect of a consideration of their contradictories. Thus such conclusions as these are granted:

> Nothing and the chimera are brothers, begotten of the same father, and yet nothing and the chimera are a man and a donkey.
>
> Nothing and Antichrist are all the things there are, and yet nothing and Antichrist differ from all the things there are.
>
> Nothing and the chimera are infinitely many, and yet nothing and the chimera are only two.

But be careful as regards negation, for this does not follow:

> Nothing and the chimera differ from man; therefore nothing and the chimera are man,

because it follows from that consequent that every being and the chimera differ from man, which is false. This inference is obvious under the rule that a negation placed after, etc.[s]

And if anyone claims that that is an argument from what is expounded to one of its exponents, I deny it. A universal negative proposition must not be expounded, but only proved by means of its contradictory.

⟨Mediate Terms in Universal Affirmative Propositions⟩

Next, the universal affirmative proposition must be thoroughly discussed as a type, particularly as regards the way in which it must be proved by means of exposition.

It is clear, in accordance with common rules, that a universal affirmative propostition must be expounded by means of its subaltern and the universal negative corresponding to it.

I quite deliberately say 'corresponding to it', because it can happen that the exponents of a universal affirmative proposition vary in several different ways: either ⟨1⟩ by reason of the sign, or ⟨3⟩ by reason of the simple or compound subject, or ⟨4⟩ by reason of the verb, or ⟨2⟩ by reason of the predicate.

⟨1⟩ Exemplum primi: nam aliquod est signum restrictivum ad masculos, ut 'quilibet', 'unus', 'quisque', 'uterque', etc., et aliquod est signum communis generis, ut ly .omnis. Ideo aliter debet ista propositio probari et exponi:

5   Quilibet homo currit,

et aliter ista:

Omnis homo currit.

Prima enim sic exponitur:

Aliquis homo currit, et nullus est homo quin ille currat,

10 vel sic:

Homo masculus currit, et nihil est homo masculus quin illud currat.

Secunda sic exponitur:

Homo currit, et nihil est homo quin illud currat; igitur . . .

Ex quo patet quod ista non sunt (18rb M) contraria:

15   Omnis homo currit

et

Nullus homo currit.

Nec ista sunt contradictoria:

Omnis homo currit

20 et

Aliquis homo non currit.

Nec ista sunt subalterna:

Omnis homo currit

et

25   Aliquis homo currit.

Et causa est quia haec copulativa est possibilis:

Omnis homo currit et nullus homo currit,

supposito quod nullus esset homo nisi una mulier, praegnans cum fetu masculo, quae curreret.

30   Similiter cum isto signo 'uterque' oportet proportionari ambas exponentes suae significationi, ut

Uterque istorum currit

---

2 'utrique' *E*   20 et *om. M*   28 quod nihil esset *E*   29 curret *E*
30 'utrumque' *E*   32 Utrumque *E*

⟨1 *How the Sign Affects Exposition*⟩

One sort of sign is restrictive to things of the masculine gender—e.g. '*quilibet*' (each or any), '*unus*' (one), '*quisque*' (each), '*uterque*' (both)—and another sort is a sign of common gender, such as '*omnis*' (every). Thus the proposition

(1) Each man (*homo*) is running

must be proved and expounded in one way, and the proposition

(2) Every human being (*homo*) is running

in another. For proposition (1) is expounded as follows:

Some man is running, and no one is a man but that he is running,

or as follows:

A male human being is running, and nothing is a male human being but that it is running.

Proposition (2) is expounded as follows:

A human being is running, and nothing is a human being but that it is running; therefore . . .

From this it is clear that these propositions are not contraries:

Every human being is running

and

No man is running.

Nor are these propositions contradictories:

Every human being is running

and

Some man is not running.

Nor are these subalterns:

Every human being is running

and

Some man is running.

And the reason is that this conjunctive proposition is possible:

Every human being is running and no man is running,

supposing that there were no man but a woman, pregnant with a male foetus, who was running.

In the case of the sign 'both' it is similarly necessary that each of the two exponents be proportioned to its signification. For example,

Both of them are running

sic exponitur:

Alter istorum currit, et neuter istorum est quin ille currit; igitur . . .

vel sic:

Alter istorum currit, et non est alter istorum quin ille currit; igitur . . .

5   Similiter cum istis signis 'quantuslibet', 'qualislibet', 'quomodolibet' oportet aliter proportionari exponentes, ut

Quantuslibet homo currit

debet sic exponi:

Aliquantus homo currit, et non est aliquantus homo quin ille currit;

10   igitur . . .

Item,

Quantalibet homo currit

exponitur sic:

Aliquanta homo currit, et non est aliquanta homo quin illa currit;

15   ⟨igitur . . .⟩

Item,

Quantumlibet animal currit

exponitur sic:

Aliquantum animal currit, et non est aliquantum animal quin illud

20   currat; igitur . . .

Item cum isto signo 'qualislibet', ut

Qualislibet homo currit

exponitur sic:

Aliqualis homo currit, et nihil est aliqualis homo quin illud currat;

25   igitur . . .

Qualelibet ⟨animal⟩ currit:

Aliquale ⟨animal⟩ currit, et non est aliquale ⟨animal⟩ quin illud currit;

igitur . . .

Similiter cum isto signo 'quomodolibet', ut

30   Quomodolibet homo currit

exponitur sic:

Aliquo modo homo currit, et non est aliquis modus quin isto modo

homo currit; igitur . . .

Item,

35   Quotienscumque homo currit homo movetur

5 'qualiscumque' M   17 animal om. M   19 animal om. M   20 currit E
23 exponitur sic: om. M   24 est aliquale quin M   currit E   26–8 Qualelibet . .
igitur . . . om. E

is expounded as follows:

> One or the other of them is running, and neither of them is but that he is running; therefore . . . ,

or as follows:

> One or the other of them is running, and there is not one or the other of them but that he is running; therefore . . .

In the case of the signs 'of every size', 'of every sort', and 'in every way' the exponents must likewise be proportioned in different ways. For example

> A man of every size is running

must be expounded as follows:

> A man of some size is running, and there is no man of any size but that he is running; therefore . . .

Again,

> A female human being of every size is running

is expounded as follows:

> A female human being of some size is running, and there is no female human being of any size but that she is running; therefore . . .

Again,

> An animal of every size is running

is expounded as follows:

> An animal of some size is running, and there is no animal of any size but that it is running; therefore . . .

Likewise with the sign 'of every sort'. For example,

> A human being of every sort is running

is expounded as follows:

> A human being of some sort is running, and nothing is a human being of any sort but that it is running; therefore . . .
> An animal of every sort is running:
> An animal of some sort is running, and there is no animal of any sort but that it is running; therefore . . .

Likewise with the sign 'in every way'. For example,

> A man is running in every way

s expounded as follows:

> A man is running in some way, and there is not any way but that a man is running in that way; therefore . . .

Likewise ⟨with the sign 'however often'. For example,⟩

> However often a man is running a man is moving

exponitur sic:

> Aliquotiens homo currit quotiens ipse movetur, et non est aliquotiens
> homo currens quin totiens ipse movetur; ergo quotienscumque, etc.

⟨2⟩ Secundo variantur exponentes ratione praedicatorum adiectivorum,
5 quorum unum est adiectivum masculini generis vel feminini generis et
alterum neutri generis. Ideo diversimode exponuntur tales propositiones:

> Omnis homo est album

et

> Omnis homo est albus.

10 (Cuius oppositum solet poni, dicendo quod ambae aequaliter exponuntur.)
Prima enim sic exponitur:

> Homo est album, et nihil est homo quin illud est album.

Secunda sic exponitur:

> Homo est albus, et nihil est homo quin illud est homo albus; igitur . . .

15 Et sic patet quod prima est vera et secunda falsa, istae enim propositiones
convertuntur:

> Omnis homo est albus

et

> Omnis homo est homo albus,

20 sicut et istae:

> Omnis homo est unus solus

et

> Omnis homo est unus solus homo.

Ideo tales propositiones uniformiter exponi debent.

25   Eodem modo est dicendum de illis propositionibus

> Omnis homo est futurum

et

> Omnis homo est futurus,

quarum prima est vera et secunda falsa. Prima enim aequivalet huic:

30   Omnis homo erit,

et secunda aequivalet isti

> Omnis homo erit homo masculus,

---

1 sic exponitur: *M*   2 est *om. M*   3 quotiescumque, etc. *om. M*   5 erat *M*
generis (1&2) *om. E*   6 generis *om. E*   23 homo et unus *E*   24 debent
uniformiter exponi *M*   29 secunda est falsa *M*   31 et *om. E*

is expounded as follows:

> At some time at which a man is running at that time he is moving, and there is not any time at which a man is running at which he is not moving; therefore however often, etc.

⟨*How the Predicate Affects Exposition*⟩

In the second place the exponents vary by reason of predicate adjectives, of which one sort is of the masculine or feminine gender and the other of the neuter gender. Thus such propositions as

(1) Every human being is ⟨a⟩ white ⟨thing⟩

and

(2) Every human being is ⟨a⟩ white ⟨man⟩

are expounded differently. (Usually the opposite view is maintained—viz. that both are expounded alike.) For proposition (1) is expounded as follows:

> A human being is ⟨a⟩ white ⟨thing⟩, and nothing is a human being but that it is white.

Proposition (2) is expounded as follows:

> A human being is ⟨a⟩ white ⟨man⟩, and nothing is a human being but that it is a white man; therefore . . .

Thus it is clear that (1) is true and (2) false, for the propositions

> Every man is white

and

> Every man is a white man

are interchangeable, as are these:

> Every man is only one

and

> Every man is only one man.

Therefore such propositions must be expounded in one and the same way.

The same sort of thing must be said of the propositions

(1) Every human being is ⟨a⟩ future ⟨thing⟩

and

(2) Every human being is ⟨a⟩ future ⟨man⟩.

(1) is true and (2) is false. For (1) is equivalent to

> Every human being will be

and (2) is equivalent to

> Every human being will be a male human being,

quae falsa est et impossibilis. Ideo illa

>Omnis homo est futurum

habet sic exponi:

>Homo est futurum, et nihil est homo vel erit homo quin illud est
>5   futurum,

quod verum est. Secunda sic exponitur, videlicet,

>Omnis homo est futurus:

>Homo est futurus, et nihil est homo vel erit homo quin illud erit
>homo masculus vel aliquis homo.

10 Modo hoc est falsum quia multae mulieres erunt quarum nulla est nec
erit aliquis homo. Verumtamen conceditur quod quilibet homo est futurus,
quia aliquis homo est futurus, et nullus est homo vel erit homo quin ille
est futurus.

>Ex his patet istam consequentiam non valere:

>15   Omnis homo fuit vel erit; igitur omnis homo est praeteritus vel
>futurus.

Sed bene sequitur quod omnis homo est praeteritum vel futurum. (18va M)
Sicut nec sequitur

>(14va E) Iste populus currit; igitur iste populus est currens,
>20 vel

>Iste binarius est; igitur iste binarius est ens

(tenendo ly .ens. nominaliter). Sed bene sequitur

>Iste populus currit; igitur iste populus est currens vel currentia.

Similiter:

>25   Iste binarius est; igitur iste binarius est ens vel entia,

et sic de infinitis.

>⟨3⟩ Tertio ratione subiecti contingit exponentes multipliciter variari.
Quandoque enim est subiectum simplex, quandoque compositum.

>Si simplex, vel in recto vel in obliquo. Si in recto, exponatur modo
30 superius dicto. Si in obliquo, est alius modus tenendus, videlicet, quod
terminus relativus erit in eodem casu et in eodem numero in quo casu et in
quo numero fuerit terminus recipiens distributionem.

>Ut

>Cuiuslibet hominis est asinus currens

35 exponitur sic:

>Hominis est asinus currens, et nihil est homo quin illius asinus currit.

6 sic *om. E*   26 et *om. M*   29 exponantur *E*   36 et non est *E*

which is false and impossible. Thus (1) has to be expounded as follows:

> A human being is ⟨a⟩ future ⟨thing⟩, and nothing is or will be a human being but that it is future,

which is true. Propsition (2) is expounded as follows:

> A human being is ⟨a⟩ future ⟨man⟩, and nothing is or will be a human being but that it will be a male human being or some man.

But that is false because there will be many women, none of whom is or will be some man. Nevertheless it is granted that each man is future, for some man is future, and no one is or will be a man but that he is future.

From these considerations it is clear that this is not an acceptable inference:

> Every human being was or will be; therefore every human being is ⟨a⟩ past or ⟨a⟩ future ⟨man⟩.

But it does follow rightly that every human being is ⟨a⟩ past or ⟨a⟩ future ⟨thing⟩. In the same way, this does not follow:

> The crowd runs; therefore the crowd is ⟨a⟩ running ⟨thing⟩.

Nor does this follow:

> This pair is; therefore this pair is ⟨a⟩ being

(taking 'being' as a name).[t] But this does follow rightly:

> The crowd runs; therefore the crowd is ⟨a⟩ running ⟨thing⟩ or running ⟨things⟩.

Similarly:

> This pair is; therefore this pair is ⟨a⟩ being or beings,

and so on in infinitely many cases.

⟨3 How the Subject Affects Exposition⟩

In the third place it can happen that the exponents vary in many different ways by reason of the subject. Sometimes the subject is simple, and sometimes it is compound.

If the subject is simple, it is so either in the nominative or in an oblique case. If in the nominative, the proposition may be expounded in the way described above. If in an oblique case, there is another way that must be kept in mind—viz. that the relative term will be in the same case and number as was the term receiving the distribution.

⟨In the genitive case,⟩ for example,

> Belonging to each man is a running donkey

is expounded as follows:

> Belonging to a man is a running donkey, and nothing is a man but that its donkey is running.

Cuiuslibet hominis est oculus dexter:

Alicuius hominis est oculus dexter, et nihil est homo quin illius est oculus dexter; igitur . . .

Exemplum in dativo casu, ut

5   Cuilibet respondenti concluditur

sic exponitur:

Alicui respondenti concluditur, et nihil est respondens quin illi concludatur.

Exemplum in accusativo casu, ut

10   Omnem hominem omnis homo videt

sic exponitur:

Hominem omnis homo videt, et nihil est homo quin illud omnis homo videt; igitur, etc.

Exemplum in ablativo casu, ut

15   Ab omni homine Sortes differt

exponitur sic:

Ab homine Sortes differt, et nihil est homo quin ab illo Sortes differt.

Universalis affirmativa in plurali numero sic exponitur, ut

Omnes homines currunt:

20   Homines currunt, et nulla sunt homines quin illa currunt.

Omnium contradictoriorum alterum est verum

sic exponitur:

Aliquorum contradictoriorum alterum est verum, et nulla sunt contradictoria quin istorum alterum est verum,

25 et sic ulterius discurrendo per omnes casus pluralis numeri.

Circa haec est tamen advertendum, iuxta sententiam aliquorum, quod proposita tali propositione

Cuiuslibet hominis asinus currit

vel

30   Cuiuslibet hominis oculus est dexter

est simpliciter dubitanda, eo quod rectus sequens obliquum potest se teneri a parte praedicati vel a parte subiecti. Si tenet se a parte praedicati, tunc talis propositio est universalis, cuius obliquus stat confuse et

---

2–3 oculus est *E*   13 etc. *om. M*   16 sic *om. E*   20 nulli *M*   illi *M*
26 tamen *om. M*   31 est *om. M*

Belonging to each man is a right eye:

Belonging to some man is a right eye, and nothing is a man but that belonging to it is a right eye; therefore . . .

Example in the dative case:

To each respondent it is demonstrated

is expounded as follows:

To some respondent it is demonstrated, and nothing is a respondent but that to it it is demonstrated.

Example in the accusative case:

Every man every man sees

is expounded as follows:

A man every man sees, and nothing is a man but that it every man sees; therefore, etc.

Example in the ablative case:

From every man Socrates differs

is expounded as follows:

From a man Socrates differs, and nothing is a man but that from it Socrates differs.

A universal affirmative in the plural number is expounded as follows:

All human beings are running:

Human beings are running, and no things are human beings but that they are running.

The proposition

Of all contradictories one or the other is true

is expounded as follows:

Of some contradictories one or the other is true, and no things are contradictories but that one or the other of them is true,

and so on, going through all the cases in the plural number.

In this connection it must be noted, however, that in the opinion of some men when a proposition such as

Belonging to each man a donkey is running

or

Belonging to each man an eye is right

is at issue, this proposition taken *simpliciter* must be neither affirmed nor denied. For a nominative following something in an oblique case can belong either to the predicate or to the subject. If it belongs to the predicate, then such a proposition is universal, and the oblique part of it has distributive confused *suppositio* while the nominative has merely confused

distributive, et rectus confuse tantum. Si autem rectus est pars subiecti, obliquus stat confuse et distributive et rectus determinate. Et tunc talis propositio non est exponibilis, cum non sit universalis, sed resolubilis, sicut et quaelibet alia indefinita. Ut

5   Cuiuslibet hominis asinus currit

sic resolvitur:

Hoc currit, et hoc est cuiuslibet hominis asinus; igitur . . .

Et sic patet quod illae convertuntur:

Cuiuslibet hominis asinus currit

10 et

Asinus cuiuslibet hominis currit.

Et sicut una est indefinita, ita est alia, praesupposito semper quod rectus utrobique sit pars subiecti.

Ex isto patet hanc consequentiam non valere vel saltim dubitandam:

15   Cuiuslibet hominis est asinus currens; igitur cuiuslibet hominis asi-
        nus currit.

Similiter:

Cuiuslibet hominis est dexter oculus; igitur cuiuslibet hominis oculus
est dexter.

20 Et si dicitur quod quaelibet singularis illius est vera, videlicet,

Istius hominis oculus est dexter, et istius hominis oculus est dexter;
        igitur . . . ,

hinc dicitur quod illae singulares non sunt singulares istius:

Cuiuslibet hominis oculus est dexter

25 si ly .oculus. tenet se a parte subiecti, sed bene si teneret se a parte praedicati, vel saltem illius:

Cuiuslibet hominis est oculus dexter.

Ex his sequitur quod istae duae:

Cuiuslibet hominis asinus currit

30 et

Cuiuslibet hominis asinus non currit

non (18ᵛᵇ M) sunt contraria sed subcontraria, quarum unius contradictorium est hoc:

Quilibet asinus cuiuslibet hominis currit

35 et alterius est hoc:

Nullus asinus cuiuslibet hominis currit.

3 exponibilis probabilis, cum *M*   resolubiliter *M*   8 Et *om. M*   patet *om. M*
20-1 videlicet . . . dexter *om. E*   25-6 sed . . . praedicati *om. M*   31 hominis
om. M

suppositio. But if the nominative is part of the subject, then the oblique element has distributive confused *suppositio* and the nominative has determinate *suppositio*. In the latter case such a proposition is not exponible, since it is not a universal proposition, but rather resoluble, just like any other indefinite proposition. For example,

Belonging to each man a donkey is running

is resolved as follows:

This is running, and this is belonging to each man a donkey; therefore...

Thus it is clear that the propositions

Belonging to each man a donkey is running

and

A donkey belonging to each man is running

are interchangeable. And just as the one is indefinite, so is the other, always assuming that the nominative in both is part of the subject.

From this it is clear that the following inference is not acceptable, or ought at least to be doubted:

Belonging to each man is a running donkey; therefore belonging to each man a donkey is running.

Likewise:

Belonging to each man is a right eye; therefore belonging to each man an eye is right.

If someone says that each of this proposition's singulars is true—viz.

Belonging to this man an eye is right, and belonging to this man an eye is right, ⟨etc.⟩; therefore . . . ,

the reply is that those singulars are not the singulars of

Belonging to each man an eye is right

if 'eye' belongs to the subject, but are so if it belongs to the predicate—or are at any rate the singulars of

Belonging to each man is a right eye.

From these considerations it follows that the two propositions

Belonging to each man a donkey is running

and

Belonging to each man a donkey is not running

are not contraries but subcontraries, the contradictory of the one being

Each donkey belonging to each man is running

and of the other being

No donkey belonging to each man is running.

Similiter ista non sunt contradictoria:

> Cuiuslibet hominis asinus currit

et

> Alicuius hominis asinus non currit.

5 Immo sunt simpliciter impertinentes, nec simul stant in figura.

Haec autem omnia conceduntur et similia, dato quod rectus teneat se a parte subiecti et non a parte praedicati. Si autem teneret se a parte praedicati, haec omnia negarentur.

Est etiam diversitas exponendi propositionem universalem de subiecto 10 composito, scilicet copulato vel disiuncto. Unde proposita tali

> Omnis homo vel asinus est asinus

aut

> Omnis propositio vel eius contradictoria est vera

est immediate dubitanda et distinguenda, quaerendo an signum univer- 15 sale distribuat totum disiunctum aut partem primam solummodo.

Si distribuit totum disiunctum, tunc quaelibet talis est (14vb E) neganda et per istum modum exponenda, ut

> Homo vel asinus est asinus, et nihil est homo vel asinus quin illud est
> asinus,

20 quod est falsum, quia quilibet homo est homo vel asinus et tamen non est asinus. Similiter,

> Omnis propositio vel eius contradictoria est vera

sic exponitur:

> Aliqua propositio vel eius contradictoria est vera, et nulla est pro-
> 25   positio vel eius contradictoria quin ipsa est vera.

Modo hoc est falsum, quia haec

> Homo est asinus

est propositio vel eius contradictoria et tamen non est vera.

Exemplum in obliquo, ut

> 30   Ab omni homine vel ab asino differs

exponitur sic:

> Ab homine vel ab asino differs, et nihil est homo vel asinus quin ab
> isto differs.

Exemplum in plurali numero, ut

> 35   Omnes homines vel asini currunt

4 currit, vel nullus asinus currit. M   5 Ideo sunt M   13 vel cuius
contradictoria E   17 exponendi M

Similarly, the propositions

>Belonging to each man a donkey is running

and

>Belonging to some man a donkey is not running

are not contradictories. They are, rather, simply independent of each other, since they do not stand together in a square of opposition.

All these things and others like them are granted provided that the nominative belongs to the subject and not to the predicate. But if it belongs to the predicate, all these things are denied.

If, on the other hand, the subject of a universal proposition is compound —i.e. conjoined or disjoined—there is also more than one way to expound the proposition. Thus when a proposition such as

>Every man or ⟨a⟩ donkey is a donkey

or

>Every proposition or its contradictory is true

is at issue, one must immediately express a doubt and draw a distinction by asking whether the universal sign distributes the whole of the disjoined term or the first part only.

If it distributes the whole of the disjoined term, then each such proposition is to be denied and to be expounded in the following way.

>A man or ⟨a⟩ donkey is a donkey, and nothing is a man or ⟨a⟩ donkey but that it is a donkey,

which is false, since each man is a man or ⟨a⟩ donkey and yet is not a donkey. Similarly,

>Every proposition or its contradictory is true

is expounded as follows:

>Some proposition or its contradictory is true, and there is no proposition or its contradictory but that it is true.

But that is false, since

>A man is a donkey

is a proposition or its contradictory and yet is not true.

Example in an oblique case:

>From every man or from a donkey you differ

is expounded as follows:

>From a man or from a donkey you differ, and nothing is a man or donkey but that from it you differ.

Example in the plural number:

>All men or donkeys are running

exponitur sic:

> Homines vel asini currunt, et nulla sunt homines vel asini quin illa
> currunt.

Exemplum in obliquo et in plurali numero, ut

5　　Omnium verorum vel falsorum alterum est verum

exponitur sic:

> Verorum vel falsorum alterum est verum, et nulla sunt vera vel falsa
> quin illorum alterum est verum.

Eodem modo est dicendum de propositione universali de copulato ex-
10 tremo ipsam taliter exponendo, dato quod signum distribuat totum copulatum, ut

> Omnis homo et asinus currunt

debet sic exponi:

> Homo et asinus currunt, et nulla sunt homo et asinus quin illa
15　　currunt,

et sic de aliis.

Ex his sequitur quod tales universales sunt falsae secundum istum
modum loquendi:

> Omnia duo et tria sunt quinque.
20　　Omnes duo homines et duo animalia sunt plura quam duo quia
> omnia quattuor sunt duo et tria, et nulla quattuor sunt quinque;
> igitur non omnia duo et tria sunt quinque.

Igitur ista exponens est falsa, videlicet,

> Nulla sunt duo et tria quin ista sunt quinque,

25 eo quod omnia quattuor sunt duo et tria communicantia. Sed hoc est
verum, quod omnia duo sunt aliqua quae et tria sunt quinque vel duo
et tria communicantia. Secunda etiam est falsa, quia omnes duo homines
sunt duo homines et duo animalia, sed non sunt duo et duo, et nulli duo
homines sunt plura duobus. Ideo non omnes duo homines et duo animalia
30 sunt plura quam duo, quamvis forte omnes duo homines sint aliqua quae
et duo animalia sunt quattuor. Similiter nego illam:

> Omnis homo et duo homines sunt tres homines,

sed concedo quod omnis homo est aliquid quod et duo homines sunt tres.
Si autem signum distribuit solum primam partem disiuncti vel copulati,
35 tunc (19ᵃ M) quaeritur an totum disiunctum sit subiectum vel solum
prima pars et residuum tenet se a parte praedicati. Si detur primum, dicatur tunc quod talis propositio non est universalis sed indefinita resolutorie

---

6 exponitur sic: *om.* E　　14 nulla homo et asinus sunt M　　22 et tertia sunt E
24 Non sunt M　　26 sunt aliquod quae M *et* E　　27 Secunda autem est E
28 animalia, et non E　　32 homines (2) *om.* E　　34–5 copulati, iterum quaeritur E
35 solum *om.* M　　36 Si dicitur primum, M

is expounded as follows:

> Men or donkeys are running, and no things are men or donkeys but that they are running.

Example in an oblique case in the plural number:

> Of all things true or false one or the other is true

is expounded as follows:

> Of things true or false one or the other is true, and no things are true or false but that of them one or the other is true.

The same sort of thing must be said regarding a universal proposition with a conjoined extreme, provided that the sign distributes the whole conjoined term. For example,

> Every man and donkey are running

must be expounded as follows:

> A man and donkey are running, and no things are a man and donkey but that they are running,

and so on as regards other cases.

From these considerations it follows that such universal propositions as

> Any two and three are five

are false according to this way of speaking.

> Any two men and two animals are more than two because any four are two and three, and no four are five; therefore not any two and three are five.

Therefore that exponent is false—viz.

> No things are two and three but that they are five,

for any four are two and three overlapping. But this is true, viz. that any two are things which together with three are five, or ⟨else are⟩ two and three overlapping. The second proposition also is false, for any two men are two men and two animals, but they are not two and two, and no two men are more than two. Thus not any two men and two animals are more than two, although as it happens any two men are things which together with two animals are four. Similarly, I deny the proposition

> Every man and two men are three men,

but I grant that every man is something which together with two men is three.

If, on the other hand, the sign distributes only the first part of the disjoined or conjoined term, then one asks whether (1) the whole disjoined term is the subject or (2) the first part only is the subject while the rest belongs in the predicate. If (1), then it may be said that such a proposition is not a universal proposition but rather an indefinite proposition that must be proved by means of resolution. But if (2), then it may be granted that the

probanda. Si vero datur secunda pars, concedatur talem esse universalem
et aliter quam prius exponendam, ut

> Omnis homo vel asinus est asinus

sic exponitur, dato isto:

5   Homo vel asinus est asinus, et nihil est homo quin illud vel asinus
        est asinus; igitur . . .

Similiter,

> Omnis propositio vel eius contradictoria est vera

sic exponitur:

10   Propositio vel eius contradictoria est vera, et nulla est propositio
        quin illa vel eius contradictoria est vera.

Et sic exponendae sunt tales propositiones verae:

> Omnis homo vel asinus est asinus,
> Omnis propositio vel eius contradictoria est vera,

15   Omnia duo et tria sunt quinque,
> Omnis homo et duo homines sunt tres,

et similia.

    ⟨1.1⟩ Contra ista dicta arguitur, probando primo quod haec propositio

> Omnis homo vel asinus est asinus

20 est vera et simpliciter concedenda. Nam quaelibet eius singularis est vera,
et cuilibet supposito subiecti correspondet una singularis; igitur . . .
Consequentia tenet cum minori, et maior arguitur, nam haec est vera:

> Iste homo vel asinus est asinus,

et haec similiter:

25   Iste homo vel asinus est asinus,
homine vel asino demonstrato; igitur, etc.

    ⟨1.2⟩ Secundo sic. Quaelibet exponentium est vera; igitur exposita est
vera. Consequentia patet, et antecedens probatur, quia homo vel asinus est
asinus, et nihil est homo quin illud vel asinus est asinus; igitur omnis homo
30 vel asinus est asinus.

    ⟨1.3⟩ Tertio sic. Omnis asinus est asinus; igitur omnis homo vel asinus
est asinus. Consequentia patet: a parte disiuncti ad totum disiunctum.

    ⟨1.4⟩ Quarto sic. Nisi teneatur ibi secundus rectus a parte praedicati
sequitur quod illae non sunt singulares:

35   Iste homo vel asinus est asinus, et iste . . . , etc.,

---

1 conceditur *E*   14 vel cuius contradictoria *E*   22 tenet *om. E*   minori
patet, et *E*   26 igitur, etc. *om. M*

proposition is a universal proposition that must be expounded otherwise than at first. For example,

Every man or ⟨a⟩ donkey is a donkey

is, on that hypothesis, expounded as follows:

A man or ⟨a⟩ donkey is a donkey, and nothing is a man but that it or a donkey is a donkey; therefore . . .

Similarly,

Every proposition or its contradictory is true

is expounded as follows:

A proposition or its contradictory is true, and there is no proposition but that it or its contradictory is true.

Expounded in that way such propositions as these are true:

Every man or ⟨a⟩ donkey is a donkey,
Every proposition or its contradictory is true,
Any two and three are five,
Every man and two men are three.

⟨*Arguments in Favour of Simply Granting Such Propositions*⟩

⟨1.1⟩ One argues against these remarks first by proving that the proposition

Every man or ⟨a⟩ donkey is a donkey

is true and, taken *simpliciter*, is to be granted. Each of its singulars is true, and one singular corresponds to each thing supposited by its subject; therefore . . . The inference holds good, along with the minor premiss. The following argument supports the major premiss. The proposition

This man or ⟨a⟩ donkey is a donkey

is true, and so is this one:

This man or ⟨a⟩ donkey is a donkey,

indicating a man or ⟨a⟩ donkey; therefore, etc.

⟨1.2⟩ Each of the exponents is true; therefore what is expounded is true. The inference is obvious, and the antecedent is proved in the following way. A man or ⟨a⟩ donkey is a donkey, and nothing is a man but that it or a donkey is a donkey; therefore every man or ⟨a⟩ donkey is a donkey.

⟨1.3⟩ Every donkey is a donkey; therefore every man or ⟨a⟩ donkey is a donkey. The inference is obvious: from a part of the disjoined term to the whole disjoined term.

⟨1.4⟩ Unless the second nominative in the proposition belongs to the predicate, it follows that these are not singular propositions:

This man or ⟨a⟩ donkey is a donkey and this . . . , etc.,

quia cuiuslibet istarum subiectum supponit pro pluribus et pro eisdem (15ʳᵃ E) divisim est praedicabilis.

⟨2.1⟩ Iam arguitur quod talis universalis est falsa et simpliciter neganda, nam eius contradictoria est vera, videlicet,

5   Aliquid quod est homo vel asinus non est asinus,

quia aliquid quod est homo non est asinus; igitur aliquid quod est homo vel asinus non est asinus. Consequentia tenet: a parte disiuncti ad totum disiunctum. Similiter: Hoc non est asinus (demonstrando Sortem), et hoc est aliquid quod est homo vel asinus; igitur, etc. Et sic patet falsitas istius
10 universalis.

⟨2.2⟩ Secundo sua contraria est vera; igitur ipsa universalis est falsa. Consequentia tenet, et antecedens probatur per sua singularia. Nam quocumque homine demonstrato vel asino, patet quod iste homo vel asinus non est asinus, et iste homo vel asinus non est asinus, et per con-
15 sequens nihil quod est homo vel asinus est asinus, quod est contrarium universalis datae.

⟨2.3⟩ Tertio exclusiva sua, secum convertibilis de terminis transpositis, est falsa; igitur ipsa universalis falsa. Consequentia tenet, et antecedens probatur, nam haec est falsa:

20   Tantum asinus est homo vel asinus,

et haec est sua exclusiva; igitur . . . Et quod ista sit falsa patet, quia aliud ab homine est homo vel asinus, puta Brunellus.

⟨2.4⟩ Quarto ista est universalis affirmativa cuius multa supposita capiuntur sub subiecto, quorum nullum capitur sub praedicato; igitur ista non
25 est vera. Consequentia tenet, quia si ipsa esset vera esset ibi dici de omni; igitur nihil contingeret capi sub subiecto de quo non dicatur (19ʳᵇ M) praedicatum. Quod patet per Aristotelem primo *Priorum*, ubi describit dici de omni et dici de nullo. Quod autem multa supposita inveniantur sub subiecto de quo non dicatur praedicatum probatur, nam nec de Sorte
30 nec de Platone dicitur praedicatum, cum neuter eorum sit asinus. Et de quolibet illorum dicitur subiectum, quia quilibet illorum est homo vel asinus. Igitur, etc.

⟨2.5⟩ Quinto arguitur sic. Omnis homo vel asinus est asinus, omnis homo vel asinus est homo; igitur homo est asinus. Consequens falsum;
35 igitur aliqua praemissarum. Et consequentia patet, quia syllogismus in *Darapti*.

2 est divisim M   10 universalis, etc. M   11 est (2) *om.* M   21 haec *om.* M
26 contingit M   capere M et E   dicantur E   27 Quod *om.* E   28 Quod
aut multa E   30 Tunc de M   32 etc. *om.* E   35 praemixarum M; praemitivorum
E   35–6 syllogismus enim *Darapti.* E

because the subject of each of them supposits for more than one thing and is separately predicable for them.

⟨*Arguments in Favour of Simply Denying Such Propositions*⟩

⟨2.1⟩ One argues next that such a universal proposition is false and simply to be denied. Its contradictory is true—viz.

Something that is a man or ⟨a⟩ donkey is not a donkey,

for something that is a man is not a donkey; therefore something that is a man or ⟨a⟩ donkey is not a donkey. The inference holds good: from a part of the disjoined term to the whole disjoined term. Similarly: This is not a donkey (indicating Socrates), and this is something that is a man or ⟨a⟩ donkey; therefore, etc. And so the falsity of the universal is apparent.

⟨2.2⟩ Its contrary is true; therefore the universal itself is false. The inference holds good, and the antecedent is proved by means of its singulars. For when any man or ⟨a⟩ donkey is indicated, it is clear that this man or ⟨a⟩ donkey is not a donkey, and this man or ⟨a⟩ donkey is not a donkey, ⟨etc.⟩, and consequently nothing that is a man or ⟨a⟩ donkey is a donkey, which is the contrary of the given universal proposition.

⟨2.3⟩ Its exclusive, which is interchangeable with it with the terms transposed, is false; therefore the universal proposition itself is false. The inference holds good, and the antecedent is proved in the following way. The proposition

Only a donkey is a man or ⟨a⟩ donkey

is false, and it is the exclusive of the universal proposition; therefore . . . And clearly this is false, for something other than a man is a man or ⟨a⟩ donkey—e.g. Brownie.

⟨2.4⟩ The proposition in question is a universal affirmative whose many supposita are contained under the subject, none of which is contained under the predicate; therefore it is not true. The inference holds good, for if it were true it would be a case of *dici de omni*, and so nothing could be contained under the subject of which the predicate was not said. This is clear from what Aristotle has to say in *Prior Analytics* ⟨Book I, Chapter 1, 24ᵇ26⟩, where he describes the *dici de omni* and *dici de nullo*.ᵘ That many supposita are found under the subject of which the predicate is not said is proved in the following way. The predicate is said neither of Socrates nor of Plato, since neither of them is a donkey. And the subject is said of each of them, since each of them is a man or ⟨a⟩ donkey. Therefore, etc.

⟨2.5⟩ Every man or ⟨a⟩ donkey is a donkey, every man or ⟨a⟩ donkey is a man; therefore a man is a donkey. This consequent is false; therefore so is one of the premisses. And the inference is obvious, since it is a syllogism in *Darapti*.

Similiter: omnis homo vel asinus est asinus, omnis homo est homo vel asinus; igitur omnis homo est asinus. Consequens falsum; igitur aliqua praemissarum. Non minor; ergo maior, quod erat probandum.

Ad ista argumenta respondetur sustinendo continue responsionem
5 priorem, videlicet, quod quandoque tales propositiones proponuntur sine limitatione dubitandae sunt, quia intellectus liber est, et libere potest utrumque rectum distribuere vel solum unum, sicut sibi placet. Ideo nescitur an talis universalis sit vera vel falsa cum primo proponitur.

⟨1.1R⟩ Et tunc ad argumenta tum probantia illam

10   Omnis homo vel asinus est asinus

esse veram et simpliciter concedendam, nego. Immo praesupposita limitatione quod uterque rectus distribuatur nego istam. Et tunc ad probationem, dico dubitando numquid tales singulares sint singulares istius universalis, eo quod nota disiunctionis continue potest teneri divisive vel collective.
15 Si divisive, dico quod tales non sunt eius singulares, sed istius:

Omnis homo est aliquid quod vel asinus est asinus.

Si autem teneatur nota disiunctionis collective, dico tunc quod istae bene sunt singulares istius universalis, sed multae sunt falsae, nam demonstrando Sortem est ista falsa:

20   Iste homo vel asinus est asinus,

quia tunc sic debet resolvi:

Hoc est asinus, et hoc est iste homo vel asinus; igitur . . .

Unde hic est notandum quod in proposito ly .vel. tenetur collective quando cadit super totum disiunctum pronomen demonstrativum. Et si
25 dicitur quod ly .iste. non potest cadere super totum disiunctum, dicatur quod non est magis inconveniens quam quod ly .omnis. cadat super eodem. Et si opponens non esset contentus de illis singularibus, assigna istas, scilicet,

Hoc quod est homo vel asinus est asinus, et hoc quod est homo vel
30   asinus est asinus, et sic ultra,

quarum multae sunt falsae.

---

3 praemixarum *M*; praemitivorum *E*   5 quod *om. E*   7 rectum distinguere vel *M*
8 talis *om. E*   universalis *om. M*   9 tum *om. M*   11–12 Ideo semper supposita
limitatione *M*   13 talis *M*   14 divise *E*   17 teneantur *E*   22 igitur
om. M   23 Unde *om. E*   27 assignata *E*   28 scilicet, *om. M*   29–30 et hoc
quod est homo vel asinus est asinus, *rep. E*

Similarly: Every man or ⟨a⟩ donkey is a donkey, every man is a man or ⟨a⟩ donkey; therefore every man is a donkey. This consequent is false; therefore so is one of the premisses. Not the minor premiss; therefore the major, which is what was to be proved.

⟨*General Reply to These Arguments*⟩

I reply to these arguments by maintaining throughout a reply I made earlier[v]—viz. that whenever such propositions are put forward without limitation they are subject to doubt since the understanding is free and can choose to distribute both nominatives or only one, just as it pleases. Thus one does not know whether such a universal proposition is true or false when it is first put forward.

⟨*Replies to the First Set of Arguments*⟩

⟨1.1R⟩ I reject the claim that the proposition

Every man or ⟨a⟩ donkey is a donkey

is true and simply to be granted. I reject it having assumed the limitation that both nominatives are distributed. As for the proof, I reply by doubting whether such singulars are the singulars belonging to that universal, because the mark of disjunction can be taken dividedly or collectively throughout. If it is taken dividedly, I say that they are not the singulars of the proposition in question but of

Every man is something such that it or a donkey is a donkey.

But if the mark of disjunction is taken collectively, then I say that they are indeed the singulars belonging to that universal proposition, although many of them are false. For the proposition

This man or ⟨a⟩ donkey is a donkey

is false, indicating Socrates, since in that case it must be resolved in the following way:

This is a donkey, and this is this man or ⟨a⟩ donkey; therefore . . .

Thus it must be noted here that in the example in question the 'or' is taken collectively when the demonstrative pronoun covers the whole disjoined term. And if it is said that 'this' cannot cover the whole disjoined term, it may be pointed out that that is no more absurd than that 'every' should cover it. And if the opponent is not satisfied with those singulars, take these:

This which is a man or ⟨a⟩ donkey is a donkey, and this which is a man or ⟨a⟩ donkey is a donkey, and so on,

many of which are false.

Non enim mihi verum videtur quod aliqui dicunt, quod singulares istius universalis sunt istae:

Iste homo est asinus, et iste asinus est asinus, et sic de aliis.

Oportet enim in singularibus debitis assignatis esse consimilis praeiacens
5 universalis et singularium, cuius oppositum est hic, ut patet intuenti.
Immo si eius singulares converterentur, non propter hoc essent singulares
(15rb E) eiusdem universalis, sicut sunt illae:

Iste homo est

et

10 Hoc risibile est.

Prima enim est singularis istius:

Omnis homo est

et non secunda. Similiter secunda est singularis istius:

Omne risibile est

15 et non prima. Et hoc est solum ratione praeiacentium. Quare, etc.

⟨1.2R⟩ Ad secundum dico quod istae non sunt exponentes istius universalis

Omnis homo vel asinus est asinus,

sed istae sunt eius exponentes:

20 Homo vel asinus est asinus, et nihil est homo vel asinus quin illud est
asinus.

Modo certum est quod ista secunda exponens est falsa.

⟨1.3R⟩ Ad tertium nego consequentiam. Et ad probationem a parte disiuncti, etc., dico quod regula intelligit quando disiunctum non praecedit
25 signum aliquod (19va M) habens vim confundendi, Qualiter non est in proposito, eo quod illud signum universale 'omnis' habet vim confundendi et distribuendi, et etiam praecedit disiunctum.

⟨1.4R⟩ Ad ultimum dicendum quod non est inconveniens in omnibus propositionibus in quibus subiectum est terminus compositus ex diver-
30 sis terminis communibus quorum quilibet requirit distinctas singulares. Ideo non mirum est si subiecta istarum singularium supponunt pro pluribus et pro eisdem divisim sunt praedicabilia.

Ad alia argumenta probantia illam

Omnis homo vel asinus est asinus

3 Iste om. M   de singulis. M   4 debite E   5 sit M   6 Ideo M
eius om. M   convertuntur E   hoc dicuntur singulares E   7 illae om. E
15 Quare om. E   16–17 universalis om. M   18 Omnis om. M   24 etc. om. M
quod ibi intelligit E   26–7 vim concedendi et E   28 dicitur M   32 etc. add. E

Some men claim that the singulars belonging to that universal proposition are these:

This man is a donkey, and this donkey is a donkey, and so on.

This does not strike me as true, for as regards the singulars that ought to be assigned it is necessary that the prejacent of the universal and of the singulars be just alike.[w] But the opposite is the case here, as is obvious to anyone who considers it. Indeed, if the singulars were interchangeable, they would not for that reason be the singulars of one and the same universal proposition. Take for example

(1) That man is

and

(2) This risible thing is.

Proposition (1) but not proposition (2) is a singular belonging to

Every man is.

Similarly, (2) but not (1) is a singular belonging to

Every risible thing is.

And in both cases it is solely because of the prejacents. Therefore, etc.

⟨1.2R⟩ I maintain that those are not the exponents of the universal proposition

Every man or ⟨a⟩ donkey is a donkey.

Instead its exponents are these:

A man or ⟨a⟩ donkey is a donkey, and nothing is a man or ⟨a⟩ donkey but that it is a donkey.

But the second exponent is certainly false.

⟨1.3R⟩ I reject the inference. As for the proof from a part of the disjoined term, etc., I maintain that the rule means ⟨that such an inference holds good⟩ when the disjoined term is not preceded by some sign with the power of producing confused *suppositio*. But that is not the way it is in the example in question, for the universal sign 'every' has the power of producing distributive confused *suppositio*, and it precedes the disjoined term.

⟨1.4R⟩ It is not the case that there is an absurdity in all propositions in which the subject is a term compounded out of different common terms each of which requires distinct singulars. And so it is not remarkable if the subjects of those singulars supposit for many things and are separately predicable for them.

⟨*Replies to the Second Set of Arguments*⟩

As for the other arguments, those proving that the proposition

Every man or ⟨a⟩ donkey is a donkey

esse falsam et simpliciter negandam, dicitur negando assumptum quod solum primus rectus distribuatur et secundus teneat se a parte praedicati.

⟨2.1R⟩ Et tunc ad primum argumentum nego quod contradictorium istius sit verum. Et ad probationem dico quod illud non est suum con-
5 tradictorium:

    Homo vel asinus non est asinus,

sed illud:

    Non homo vel asinus est asinus.

Ideo nec illae aequipollent:

10   Non aliquid quod est homo vel asinus non est asinus

et

    Omnis homo vel asinus est asinus,

quia in una ly .asinus. stat determinate vel confuse tantum et in alia confuse et distributive ratione praecedentis negationis.

15   Et si allegatur ista regula: ⟨negatio⟩ prae contradictorium, ⟨etc.,⟩ dicitur concedendo regulam. Sed ex ista non sequitur quod dictae propositiones aequipollent sicut istae:

    Non quilibet homo currit

et

20   Aliquis homo non currit.

Et est ratio diversitatis quia in una termini stant opposito modo et non in alia. Cum ibidem praedicatum, quod est terminus compositus, non distribuatur.

⟨2.2R⟩ Propter consimilem causam concedendo illam:

25   Omnis homo vel asinus non est asinus,

et dico quod non contrariatur illi:

    Omnis homo vel asinus est asinus

nec illi aequipollet:

    Nihil quod est homo vel asinus est asinus.

30 Nec sequitur:

    Iste homo vel asinus non est asinus, et iste . . . , etc.; igitur nullus
        homo vel asinus est asinus.

Sed bene sequitur quod quilibet homo vel asinus non est asinus, quae conceditur, sicut et alia.

35   Ad inferendum igitur illa:

    Nullus homo vel asinus est asinus

oportet praeponere negationem in antecedente isto modo:

    Nec iste homo vel asinus est asinus, nec iste . . . etc.; igitur nullus
        homo vel asinus est asinus.

---

1 negando ad se quod *M*   2 secundo *M*   8 Homo non *M et E*   vel *om.*
E   9 Immo nec ista *E*   10 Non aliud quod *E*   14 ratione dictionis
praecedentis includentis negationem. *E*   15 allegetur *E*   15 prae contra
dicitur *E*; prae contra dic dicitur *M*   21 uno *E*   22–3 compositus, nullibi
distribuatur. *E*   35 illa *om. E*

is false and simply to be denied, I deny the assumption that only the first nominative is distributed while the second belongs to the predicate.

⟨2.1R⟩ I deny that the contradictory of the universal proposition is true. As regards the proof, I maintain that its contradictory is not

> A man or ⟨a⟩ donkey is not a donkey

but

> Not a man or ⟨a⟩ donkey is a donkey.

Thus the propositions

> Not something that is a man or ⟨a⟩ donkey is not a donkey

and

> Every man or ⟨a⟩ donkey is a donkey

are not equipollent. In the one 'donkey' has determinate or merely confused *suppositio* and in the other distributive confused *suppositio* because of the preceding negation.

If someone appeals to the rule that a negation before the contradictory, etc.,[*] I grant the rule. But it does not follow from that rule that the above-mentioned propositions are equipollent as are these:

> Not each man is running
> Some man is not running.

The root of the difference is that in one but not the other the terms stand in an opposed way. For in that case the predicate, which is a compound term, is not distributed.

⟨2.2R⟩ For much the same reason I grant the proposition

> Every man or ⟨a⟩ donkey is not a donkey,

but I say that it is neither contrary to

> Every man or ⟨a⟩ donkey is a donkey

nor equipollent to

> Nothing that is a man or ⟨a⟩ donkey is a donkey.

Nor does this follow:

> This man or ⟨a⟩ donkey is not a donkey, and this . . . , etc.; therefore no man or ⟨a⟩ donkey is a donkey

But it does follow rightly that each man or ⟨a⟩ donkey is not a donkey, and that proposition, along with the other, is granted.

Therefore in order to infer the proposition

> No man or ⟨a⟩ donkey is a donkey

one must put the negation ahead in the antecedent in this way:

> Neither this man or ⟨a⟩ donkey is a donkey, nor this . . . , etc.; therefore no man or ⟨a⟩ donkey is a donkey.

Conceditur consequentia et negatur antecedens. Unde istae non convertuntur:

> Iste homo vel asinus non est asinus

et

5   Non iste homo vel asinus est asinus

propter diversam suppositionem a parte subiecti, ut patet intuenti. Et per hoc patet responsio ad secundum argumentum.

⟨2.3R⟩ Ad tertium dico quod ista exclusiva data non est exclusiva convertibilis cum ista universali, nec directe ⟨nec⟩ de terminis transpositis.
10 Nam tunc quod praedicaretur in universali foret subiectum exclusivae. Sed sic non est in proposito, quia in exclusiva solum subicitur ly .asinus. et in universali praedicatur totum hoc: 'aliquid quod vel asinus est asinus'. Ideo exclusiva istius est ista:

> Tantum aliquid quod vel asinus est asinus est homo,

15 et hoc conceditur.

⟨2.4R⟩ Ad quartum dico quod non est inconveniens aliquam esse universalem affirmativam veram et aliquid sumi sub subiecto de quo non dicatur praedicatum explicite sumptum, sed quod de ipso non dicatur praedicatum implicite sumptum falsum est et inconveniens. Et haec est
20 intentio Philosophi in loco praeallegato. Unde praedicatum implicitum istius universalis est 'aliquid quod vel asinus est asinus', et hoc dicitur de quolibet contento sub subiecto universalis.

⟨2.5R⟩ Per hoc ergo patet responsio ad quintum argumentum, negando discursum istum. Nec est in *Darapti*, quia maior extremitas non praedicatur
25 de minori extremitate. Ideo deberet talis conclusio inferri, videlicet,

> Aliquid (15va E) quod vel asinus est homo est aliquid quod vel asinus est asinus,

et hoc conceditur.

Eodem modo est respondendum si fieret talis syllogismus:

30   Omnis propositio vel eius contradictoria est vera, omnis propositio vel eius contradictoria est falsa; igitur falsum est verum.

Negatur consequentia. Sed debet concludi talis propositio, videlicet,

> Propositio quae vel eius (19vb M) contradictoria est falsa est propositio quae vel eius contradictoria est vera.

35 Et sic arguendo, concedo consequentiam et consequens.

Ad confirmationem, nego consequentiam quia plus praedicatur in

---

5 Non *om. M*   13 erit *M*   14 Tantum aliud quod *E*   16–22 Ad . . . universalis *om. M*   23 quartum *M et E*   25 minori in extremitate *M*   debet *E*

The inference is granted but its antecedent is denied. Thus the propositions

This man or ⟨a⟩ donkey is not a donkey

and

Not this man or ⟨a⟩ donkey is a donkey

are not interchangeable, because of the different *suppositio* belonging to the subject, as is clear to anyone who considers it. As a consequence, the reply to the second argument is obvious.

⟨2.3R⟩ I maintain that the given exclusive proposition is not an exclusive interchangeable with that universal proposition, whether directly or with the terms transposed. For in that case what would be predicated in the universal proposition would be the subject of the exclusive proposition. But that is not the way it is in the example in question, for in the exclusive proposition 'a donkey' alone is the subject, and in the universal proposition the whole phrase 'something such that it or a donkey is a donkey' is predicated. Thus the exclusive beonging to that universal is this proposition:

Only something such that it or a donkey is a donkey is a man,

and that is granted.

⟨2.4R⟩ I say that it is not absurd that there should be a true universal affirmative and that something is taken under the subject of which the predicate taken explicitly is not said, but that it is false and absurd that the predicate taken implicitly is not said of it. And that is what the Philosopher means in the passage cited. Thus the implicit predicate of that same universal proposition is 'something such that it or a donkey is a donkey', and that is said of each thing contained under the subject of the universal.

⟨2.5R⟩ As a consequence of this it is clear that the reply to the fifth argument is to reject that reasoning. It is not an instance of *Darapti*, since the major term is not predicated of the minor term. Therefore the conclusion one ought to infer is

Something such that it or a donkey is a man is something such that it or a donkey is a donkey,

which is granted.

One must reply in the same way if a syllogism such as this is produced:

Every proposition or its contradictory is true, every proposition or its contradictory is false; therefore what is false is what is true.

This inference is rejected. The conclusion one ought to infer instead is

A proposition such that it or its contradictory is false is a proposition such that it or its contradictory is true.

And if one does argue in that way, I grant the inference and its consequent.

As for the confirmation,[y] I reject the inference. There is more in the predicate of the minor premiss than there was in the subject of the major

minori quam fuerat subiectum maioris, praecise enim subiciebatur ly .homo. in maiori, et in minori totum illud: 'homo vel asinus'.

Propter consimilem causam negantur omnes tales consequentiae:

Omnia duo et tria sunt quinque, quattuor sunt duo et tria; igitur
5   quattuor sunt quinque.

Similiter:

Omnes duo homines et duo animalia sunt quattuor, sed Sortes et
    Plato sunt duo animalia; igitur Sortes et Plato sunt quattuor.

Utrobique enim plus praedicatur in minori quam subiciebatur in maiori.

10   Non obstante quod haec de obliquo et termino composito probabiliter dicta sunt, tamen mihi videtur aliter posse dici absque distinctione aliqua praetermittendo.

Primo, quod in ista

Omnis homo vel asinus est asinus

15 ly .homo vel asinus. est subiectum. Nullus enim grammaticus diceret quod altera pars disiuncti teneret se a parte appositi.

Secundo, praemitto iuxta sententiam antiquorum logicorum quod signum universale affirmativum non distribuit terminum mediate sequentem nisi de per se accidens ratione determinationis aut regiminis aut restricti-
20 onis.

Dico 'determinationis' propter tales:

Omnis homo albus currit,
Omnis homo niger disputat,

ubi adiectiva stant distributive.

25   Dico secundo 'regiminis' propter istas propositiones:

Omnis asinus hominis currit,
Omnis oculus dexter equi est dexter,

ubi genitivus casus supponit distributive.

Dico tertio 'restrictionis' propter huiusmodi propositiones:

30   Omne quod est homo est risibile,

ubi ly .homo. et ly .quod. stant confuse et distributive.

Ex praedictis suppositionibus sequitur quod in ista propositione

Omnis homo vel asinus est asinus

subiectum est ly .homo vel asinus. Et tamen non totum distribuitur, sed

---

1 maioris, cum subiciebatur M   subiciebam E   15 Nullus ei grammaticus E
16 disiuncta E   17 praemittendo M   19 aut (1) om. M   27 dexter (1) om.
M   31 ly .quot. stant M

premiss, for just 'man' was the subject of the major premiss, and in the minor premiss the whole phrase 'a man or donkey' ⟨is the predicate⟩.

For much the same reason all such inferences as these are rejected:

> Any two and three are five, four are two and three; therefore four are five.
>
> Any two men and two animals are four, but Socrates and Plato are two men and two animals; therefore Socrates and Plato are four.

In both instances there is more in the predicate of the minor premiss than there was in the subject of the major premiss.

⟨*Alternative Treatment of Oblique and Compound Terms*⟩

Although the things that have already been said about the oblique and the compound term were acceptable, it seems to me that it can be presented otherwise without omitting any distinction.

⟨1⟩ In the proposition

> Every man or ⟨a⟩ donkey is a donkey

the subject is 'man or ⟨a⟩ donkey'. No grammarian would say that one or the other part of the disjoined term belongs to the neighbouring term.

⟨2⟩ In keeping with the older logicians' view I take it for granted that a universal affirmative sign does not distribute a term that follows it mediately unless it does so *per accidens*, in virtue of a determination belonging either to a governing position or to a restriction.

'Of a determination' because of such propositions as

> Every white man is running,
> Every black man is engaged in disputation,

in which the adjectives have distributive confused *suppositio*.

'Belonging to a governing position' because of the propositions

> Every donkey belonging to a man is running,
> Every right eye belonging to a horse is right,

in which ⟨the term in⟩ the genitive case has distributive confused *suppositio*.

'Belonging to a restriction' because of propositions of this sort:

> Everything which is a man is risible,

in which 'man' and 'which' have distributive confused *suppositio*.

From the foregoing hypotheses it follows that in the proposition

> Every man or ⟨a⟩ donkey is a donkey

the subject is 'man or ⟨a⟩ donkey'. And yet it is not the whole of it that is distributed but nothing more nor less than 'man'. The term 'donkey' has

praecise ly .homo. Et ly .asinus. stat confuse tantum tam a parte subiecti quam a parte praedicati. Unde in ista propositione

> Omnis homo asinus non est

ly .asinus. stat confuse tantum, ut patet. Sed cuiuslibet virtus magis debet
5 se extendere in propinquum quam in remotum. Igitur a fortiori in ista:

> Omnis homo vel asinus est asinus

ly .asinus. in subiecto non stat confuse distributive.

Si ergo mihi proponitur ista:

> Omnis homo vel asinus est asinus,

10 concedo eam. Et si quaeritur de eius exponentibus, dico quod sunt tales:

> Homo vel asinus est asinus, et nihil est homo quin illud vel asinus est
> asinus,

ita quod semper totum quod stat confuse tantum sequatur ly .quin. et quod distribuitur praecedat. Contradictorium istius est

15 > Non homo vel asinus est asinus,

et est contradictorium per negationem praepositam, vel sic:

> Homo non vel asinus est asinus,

cuius veritas vel falsitas requiratur in suo contradictorio. Singulares vero sunt istae:

20 > Iste homo vel asinus est asinus, et iste homo vel asinus . . . , et sic de
> aliis.

Et non est inconveniens in propositionibus singularibus subiecta pro pluribus supponere dummodo compositionem gerant.

Item sequitur quod in argumento syllogistico non oportet subiectum
25 maioris (nec sibi proportionabile) praedicari in minori implicite vel explicite, sed solum quod distribuatur. Unde ista consequentia non valet:

> Omnis homo vel asinus est asinus, tu es homo vel asinus; igitur tu es
> asinus.

Sed debet sumi pro minori quod tu es homo, et concludi quod tu vel
30 asinus es asinus. Et (20ra M) si aliquando aliqua dixi vel dicam quae non videantur suffragari hinc, intelligo ea quando subiectum distribuitur.

Item sequitur quod aliqua est propositio universalis cuius subiectum non distribuitur, sed solum pars. Nec hoc est contra aliquam regulam,

1 stat *om.* M   10 concedendo E   13 itaque semper E   sequitur M
16 est *om.* M   18 falsitas recipiatur in M   20 et ista homo M   26 distribuitur M

merely confused *suppositio* in the subject as it has in the predicate. Thus in the proposition

Every man ⟨a⟩ donkey is not

'donkey' obviously has merely confused *suppositio*. But a thing's power must be extended more in the near vicinity than far away. Therefore *a fortiori* in the proposition

Every man or ⟨a⟩ donkey is a donkey

the term 'donkey' in the subject does not have distributive confused *suppositio*.

If, therefore, I am confronted with the proposition

Every man or ⟨a⟩ donkey is a donkey,

I grant it. And if I am asked about its exponents, I say that they are these:

A man or ⟨a⟩ donkey is a donkey, and nothing is a man but that it or a donkey is a donkey,

with the result that the element that has merely confused *suppositio* always follows the 'but that' and the distributed element precedes it. The contradictory is

Not a man or ⟨a⟩ donkey is a donkey,

a contradictory by prefixed negation, or

A man not or ⟨a⟩ donkey is a donkey,[z]

the truth or falsity of which is required in its contradictory. But its singulars are these:

This man or ⟨a⟩ donkey is a donkey, and this man or ⟨a⟩ donkey . . . , and so on.

Moreover, it is not absurd that the subjects in the singular propositions supposit for more than one thing, as long as they give rise to the composition ⟨of the universal proposition⟩.

Again, it follows that in syllogistic argument it is not required that the subject of the major premiss (and not one proportionable to it) be predicated implicitly or explicitly in the minor premiss, but only that it be distributed. Thus the following inference is not acceptable:

Every man or ⟨a⟩ donkey is a donkey, you are a man or ⟨a⟩ donkey; therefore you are a donkey.

Instead what must be taken as the minor premiss is that you are a man, and what must be concluded is that you or a donkey are a donkey. And if at any time I have said or shall say things that seem not to support this, I mean them to apply in cases in which the subject is distributed.

Again, it follows that there is a universal proposition the subject of which is not distributed, but only a part thereof. Nor is that contrary to any rule,

quia licet oporteat subiectum in universali affirmativa implicite vel explicite
determinari per signum universale, non tamen oportet distribui. Quia
forte signum (15vb E) non ad tantum se potest extendere determinando,
cum se extendit non solum ad distributionem sed etiam ad confusionem,
5　quae oritur a signo in distante sicut in propinquo.

Consimiliter dicatur de obliquis casibus. Unde licet in ista

Omnis asinus hominis currit

rectus et obliquus distribuantur, hoc non est uniformiter et univoce, nam
rectus de per se distribuitur, obliquus autem de per accidens ratione recti
10　merentis suam distributionem in ipsum propter regimen. Tam in ista

Cuiuslibet hominis asinus currit

distribuitur ly .hominis. et non ly .asinus., sed supponit confuse tantum,
non obstante quod sit pars subiecti. Cum non se habeat ad obliquum
aliquo dictorum modorum ratione quorum de per accidens possit dis-
15　tribui.

Si ergo quaeritur de suis exponentibus, dico quod sunt istae:

Hominis asinus currit, et non est homo quin istius asinus currit.

Contradictorium etiam et contrarium dantur per oppositas suppositiones.
Et ita syllogistice arguendo debet sic argui:

20　　Cuiuslibet hominis asinus currit, Sortes est homo; igitur Sortis asinus
　　currit,

ita quod illud quod distribuitur in maiori ponatur in minori, et non plus.

Ex praedictis sequitur quod istae non convertuntur:

Cuiuslibet hominis asinus currit

25　et

Quilibet asinus hominis currit.

Et non sequitur istae negativae convertuntur, scilicet,

Nullius hominis asinus currit

et

30　　Nullus asinus hominis currit.

---

3 non additum se *M*　determinatio *M*　　　　4 distributum *M*　　　5 in proposito. *M*　　　9-10 recti tendentis suam *E*　　16 expositionibus *E*　　　30 currit
om. E

for although the subject in a universal affirmative proposition must be implicitly or explicitly determined by a universal sign, it need not be distributed. Perhaps a sign can extend itself by governing not only so far and no farther, since it extends itself not only to distribution but also to confusion,[a] which results from a sign some distance away just as from one in the near vicinity.

The same sort of thing is to be said as regards the oblique cases. Thus although both the nominative and the oblique terms are distributed in

> Every donkey belonging to a man is running,

they are not uniformly and univocally distributed, for the nominative is distributed *per se* but the oblique *per accidens* because the nominative term acquires its distribution in itself as a result of its governing position. In the same way in the proposition

> Each man's donkey is running

'man's' is distributed and not 'donkey', which has merely confused *suppositio* instead, despite the fact that it is part of the subject. For it is not related to the oblique term in any of the ways described as a consequence of which it could be distributed *per accidens*.

If, therefore, I am asked about the exponents of that proposition, I say that they are these:

> A man's donkey is running, and there is not a man but that his donkey is running.

Its contradictory and its contrary are given by the opposite hypotheses. Thus in arguing syllogistically one must argue in the following way:

> Each man's donkey is running, Socrates is a man; therefore Socrates' donkey is running,

with the result that what is distributed in the major premiss is predicated in the minor premiss, and no more.

From the foregoing considerations it follows that these propositions are not interchangeable:

> Each man's donkey is running

and

> Each donkey belonging to a man is running.

And it does not follow that these negative propositions are interchangeable:

> No man's donkey is running

and

> No donkey belonging to a man is running.

Sed istae contrariantur illis affirmativis. Igitur et illae affirmativae convertuntur. Sicut non sequitur istae duae convertuntur:

> Alicuius hominis asinus currit

et

5   Asinus alicuius hominis currit.

Sed istae sunt subcontrariae istarum, videlicet,

> Alicuius hominis non asinus currit

et

> Asinus alicuius hominis non currit.

10 Igitur et istae convertuntur. Data enim quod omnis asinus hominis curreret
et quod Sortes esset homo qui nullum haberet asinum, haec esset vera:

> Omnis asinus hominis currit,

et haec falsa:

> Cuiuslibet hominis asinus currit.

15 Et haec similiter esset vera:

> Alicuius hominis nullus asinus currit,

et haec esset falsa:

> Asinus alicuius hominis non currit.

Et sic patet quod non semper convertuntur illi termini 'hominis asinus'
20 et 'asinus hominis', cuius tamen oppositum solet supponi.

〈4〉 Quarto contingit expositionem universalis affirmativae variari
ratione verbi. Quia aliter debet exponens negativa capi cum verbo ampliativo, et aliter cum verbo non ampliativo; et aliter cum verbo de praesenti,
et aliter cum verbo de praeterito vel de futuro. Unde potest pro regula
25 sustineri quod sicut omnis universalis affirmativae cuius principale verbum
non est ampliativum principale verbum secundae exponentis erit verbum
substantivum de praesenti, sic omnis talis universalis cuius principale
verbum est ampliativum verbum secundae exponentis erit verbum distinctum ex verbo substantivo et ampliativo synonymo cum verbo propo-
30 sitionis principaliter exponendae.

> Verbi gratia, ut exponendo illam

> Omne animal currit

---

2 duae *om.* M   5 alicuius *om.* M   7 hominis nullus asinus E   9 alicuius *om.* M
non *om.* M   10 et *om.* M   Dico enim M   currit M   11 Sortes erit homo E
15 Et *om.* M   22 aliter *om.* E   24 potest sub regula M   26 exponentis
est M   verbum (2) *om.* M

But they are the contraries of those affirmatives. Therefore those affirmatives too are interchangeable. In the same way it does not follow that these two propositions are interchangeable:

Some man's donkey is running

and

A donkey belonging to some man is running.

But their subcontraries are these propositions:

Of some man not a donkey is running

and

A donkey belonging to some man is not running.

Therefore those too are interchangeable. For given that every donkey belonging to a man is running and that Socrates is a man who has no donkey, this proposition would be true:

Every donkey belonging to a man is running,

and this one false:

Each man's donkey is running.

Similarly, the proposition

Of some man no donkey is running

would be true, and this one false:

A donkey belonging to some man is not running.

Thus it is clear that the terms 'a man's donkey' and 'a donkey belonging to a man' are not always interchangeable. The opposite is, however, usually assumed.

⟨4 *How the Verb Affects Exposition*⟩

The exposition of a universal affirmative proposition can vary by reason of the verb. For the negative exponent must be taken in one way with an ampliating verb and in another with a non-ampliating verb,[b] and in one way with a present-tense verb and in another with a verb of the past or future tense. Thus it can be upheld as a rule that just as in the case of every universal affirmative proposition the principal verb of which is non-ampliating the principal verb of the second exponent will be the substantive verb in the present tense, so in the case of every universal affirmative the principal verb of which is ampliating the verb of the second exponent will be a verb distinct from the substantive verb and the ampliating verb synonymous with the verb of the proposition that is principally to be expounded.

For example, it is clear from the foregoing remarks that in expounding

Every animal is running

patet ex praedictis quod secunda exponens est talis:

> Nihil est animal quod non currit.

Et sic de omni universali de praesenti (20rb M) affirmativa, sive verbum substantivum sive adiectivum non ampliativum praedicetur.

5   Exempla secundae partis multa sunt. Et primo de praeterito, ut

> Omnis homo fuit

exponitur sic:

> Homo fuit, et nihil est homo vel fuit homo quin illud fuit.

Exemplum de futuro, ut

10   Omne animal erit

exponitur sic:

> Aliquid animal erit, et nihil est animal vel erit animal quin illud erit.

Exemplum de verbo ampliativo:

> Omne album potest esse nigrum

15 exponitur sic:

> Aliquod album potest esse nigrum, et non est aliquod album vel potest esse aliquod album quin illud potest esse nigrum.

Exemplum de praeterito cum verbo ampliativo, ut

> Omnis homo potuit currere

20 exponitur sic:

> Homo potuit currere, et nihil est homo vel potuit esse homo quin illud potuit currere.
>
> Omne currens poterit esse sedens

sic exponitur:

25   Aliquod currens poterit esse sedens, et nihil est currens vel poterit esse currens quin illud poterit esse sedens.

Exempla cum isto verbo 'incipit', ut

> Omne *A* incipit esse verum

exponimus sic:

30   *A* incipit esse verum, et nihil est *A* vel incipit esse *A* quin illud incipit esse verum.

> Omne *A* incepit esse falsum

---

4 non ampliativum *om.* M   12 igitur . . . *add.* E   13–17 Exemplum . . . nigrum. *om.* E   25 Aliquid E   27 illa verba M   28 verum *om.* E   29 exponitur M 30 illud *om.* E   32 incipit M

the second exponent is the proposition

Nothing is an animal that is not running.

And the same holds good regarding every universal affirmative proposition of the present tense, whether the substantive verb or a non-ampliating adjective is predicated.

There are many examples of the second part. First, an example involving the past tense,

Every man was,

is expounded as follows:

A man was, and nothing is or was a man but that it was.

An example involving the future tense,

Every animal will be,

is expounded as follows:

Some animal will be, and nothing is or will be an animal but that it will be.

An example involving an ampliating verb,

Everything white can be black,

is expounded as follows:

Something white can be black, and there neither is nor can be anything white but that it can be black.

An example involving the past tense together with an ampliating verb,

Every man was able to run,

is expounded as follows:

A man was able to run, and nothing is or was able to be a man but that it was able to run.

The proposition

Everything running will be able to be sitting

is expounded as follows:

Something running will be able to be sitting, and nothing is or will be able to be running but that it will be able to be sitting.

Examples involving the verb 'begins'. The proposition

Every A begins to be true

we expound as follows:

A begins to be true, and nothing is or begins to be A but that it begins to be true.

The proposition

Every A began to be false

sic exponitur:

> A incepit esse falsum, et nihil est vel incepit esse A quin illud incepit
> esse falsum.

Omne A incipiet esse dubium

5 exponitur sic:

> A incipiet esse dubium, et nihil est A vel incipiet esse A quin illud
> incipiet esse dubium.

Exemplum cum verbis distractivis vel concernentibus actum mentis, ut

> Omnis res intelligitur (apprehenditur, significatur, est (16ra E) volita
> 10 ⟨vel⟩ imaginata, et sic de aliis verbis quibuscumque passivis dis-
> trahentibus).

Nam secunda exponens primae erit talis:

> Nulla est vel intelligitur res quin ista intelligitur,

et sic de aliis.

15 Sed hic forte dubitatur qualiter debent illae exponi:

> Omnis homo praeteritus est,
> Omnis homo futurus est animal in hoc instanti.

Dicitur quod quaelibet istarum est dubitanda eo quod ly .praeteritus. et
ly .futurus. possunt teneri nominaliter vel participialiter.

20 Si nominaliter, quaelibet istarum potest satis bene concedi. Prima enim
sic exponitur:

> Homo praeteritus est, et nihil est homo praeteritus quin illud est,

et hoc est verum. Secunda sic exponitur:

> Homo futurus est animal in hoc instanti, et nihil est homo futurus
> 25 quin illud est animal in hoc instanti,

et hoc similiter est verum.

> Si autem ly .futurus. et ly .praeteritus. tenentur participialiter, tunc
quaelibet illarum est neganda. Et prima sic exponitur:

> Homo praeteritus est, et nihil est vel fuit homo quin illud fuit homo
> 30 masculus,

et hoc est falsum. Secunda sic exponitur:

> Homo futurus est animal in hoc instanti, et nihil est vel erit homo
> quin illud sit futurum animal in hoc instanti,

iterum hoc est falsum.

---

2 incipit (1) (2) (3) M   illud *om.* E   4 incipit E   6 A incipit   esse E
vel incipit esse M   7 incipit M; incepit E   8 Igitur exemplum E   distractivis
vel *om.* M   10 de ceteris verbis M   15 hoc E   deberet M   20 satis bene
om. M   22 et nullus est E   23 est *om.* M   28 illarum *om.* E   32 futurus
erit animal E   32–3 et . . . instanti, *om.* M

is expounded as follows:

A began to be false, and nothing is or began to be A but that it began to be false.

The proposition

Every A will begin to be doubtful

is expounded as follows:

A will begin to be doubtful, and nothing is or will begin to be A but that it will begin to be doubtful.

An example involving verbs that are distractive[c] or that concern a mental act:

Every thing is understood (or is apprehended, is signified, is willed, or is imagined, and so on as regards other verbs with distractive passives).

For the second exponent of the first of these propositions will be

None is or is understood to be a thing but that it is understood,

and so on as regards the others.

But there may be some doubt as to how the propositions

(1) Every past human being is

and

(2) Every future human being is an animal at this instant

are to be expounded. It is said that each of them must be doubted because the words 'past' and 'future' can be taken either as names or as participles.[d]

If they are taken as names, each of the propositions can be readily granted. For (1) is expounded as follows:

A past human being is, and nothing is a past human being but that it is,

and that is true. Proposition (2) is expounded as follows:

A future human being is an animal at this instant, and nothing is a future human being but that it is an animal at this instant,

and that, likewise, is true.

If, on the other hand, 'future' and 'past' are taken as participles, then each of the propositions is to be denied. Proposition (1) is expounded as follows:

A past human being is, and nothing is or was a human being but that it was a male human being,

and that is false. Proposition (2) is expounded as follows:

A future human being is an animal at this instant, and nothing is or will be a human being but that it is a future animal at this instant,

and this, too, is false.

Vel potest aliter dici concedendo secundam propositionem, eo quod ly .futurus. necessario tenet se a parte subiecti. Si autem teneret se a parte praedicati esset incongrua locutio, cum ibidem esset discordantia adiectivi cum suo substantivo. Ly .futurus. enim est masculini generis, et ly .animal. 5 est neutri generis. Igitur, etc.

1 concedo *M*   3 erit incongrua *E*   erit discordantia *E*   4 enim *om. M*   esset *M* 5 est *om. M*   Ideo, etc. *E*   Nota bene istam sententiam, eo quod multa poteris solveris argumenta. *add. E*

Alternatively, one can grant proposition (2) because 'future' necessarily belongs to the subject. But if it were taken to be part of the subject it would be an ungrammatical locution, since there would be a disagreement between the adjective and its substantive. For 'future' is of the masculine gender and 'animal' is of the neuter gender. Therefore, etc.

NOTES TO *PART I, FASCICULE 1*

Chapter *1*

p. 3 n. a What is equiform to a sign-occurrence is another occurrence of the same sign, another token of the same type.

p. 3 n. b See p. 5 below, para. ⟨4⟩.

p. 5 n. c I know of no other instance of this claim that verbs in general are not categorematic terms, but the reason given for ruling them out suggests that it is primarily the substantive verb 'to be' in its role as copula that is under consideration, and the substantive verb in that role was frequently taken to be syncategorematic.

p. 5 n. d i.e. producing confused *suppositio* in some categorematic term.

p. 5 n. e On p. 3 above, para. ⟨3⟩.

p. 9 n. f On p. 5 above, where a syncategorematic term is defined, in part, as one that '. . . is significant *per se* of nothing other than itself and what is equiform to it'.

p. 9 n. g Earlier on p. 9.

p. 9 n. h i.e. such syncategorematic words as 'every' or 'no', which ordinarily give rise to 'merely confused' or 'distributive confused' *suppositio* in terms on which they exercise their functions.

p. 9 n. i Broadly speaking, the extremes of a proposition are its subject and predicate terms; strictly speaking, the extremes are the major and minor terms of a syllogism, connected through the middle.

p. 9 n. j i.e. taken as having 'personal' *suppositio*.

p. 9 n. k On p. 5, para. ⟨5⟩, where it is indirectly denied that 'every' and 'no' ever signify personally—i.e. signify something 'distinct from such terms and things equiform to them'. Cf. p. 5 at foot, para. ⟨4⟩. Such words can be the subject terms of propositions only if they are taken as signifying materially, as in ' "Every" is a distributive syncategorematic word'. See p. 7 above: 'any such ⟨syncategorematic⟩ term materially signifies itself.'

p. 11 n. l On taking modal words as names or as modalities see p. 195 below, especially n. e.

p. 11 n. m On terms taken as functionalizable and as resoluble see pp. 225–9 below.

p. 11 n. n Apparently a reference to the definition of a syncategorematic term on p. 5 above: '. . . a sign that carries out a function . . .'.

p. 11 n. o In the proposition '*Possibile est contingens*' ('What is possible is contingent') '*possibile*' is taken as resoluble and '*contingens*' as functionalizable.

p. 13 n. p A transcendental term is a simple term, such as 'being', that can be the predicate term in a true affirmative proposition about absolutely anything there is. See p. 97 below. Each transcendental term can therefore be the predicate term in a true affirmative proposition in which any other transcendental term is the subject term.

p. 13 n. q Term 'A' is inferior to term 'B' if and only if 'Every ⟨or all⟩ A is B' is true and 'Every ⟨or all⟩ B is A' is false.

p. 13 n. r In a proposition such as 'Every man is a being', which might seem to fill the bill, it is 'man' and not 'every man' that is the subject term. See Paul's solution to this difficulty in his reply, p. 23 below.

p. 13 n. s i.e. putting together the elements of the judgement. See p. 25 below: 'to compound is nothing other than to affirm one intention ⟨or concept⟩ of another.'

p. 15 n. t The inverted Latin word-order ('*Homo animal non est*') conveys the sense 'A man is not a certain animal' rather than 'A man is not an animal' ('*Homo non est animal*'). The inverted word-order is retained here in the English because of special features of this objection. See the reply ⟨1.6R⟩, p. 27 below; see also pp. 33–5 below.

p. 17 n. u i.e. the rule of obversion: 'Every A is non-B; therefore no A is B'; 'Some A is non-B; therefore some A is not B'.

p. 17 n. v 'Every A is B; therefore no non-B is non-A'; 'Some A is B; therefore some non-B is not non-A'.

p. 17 n. w Cf. *In librum de interpretatione editio prima*, Migne *PL* 64. 387C–D; *editio secunda*, 64. 577B; 628B.

p. 21 n. x Collectively as distinct from distributively, for one cannot validly infer 'therefore these men are all men', or 'therefore these three of God's apostles are all of God's apostles'. See the discussion of this distinction in Norman Kretzmann, *William of Sherwood's Treatise on Syncategorematic Words* (Minneapolis: University of Minnesota Press, 1968), pp. 39–40.

p. 23 n. y Because it is not a simple term. See p. 13 above, n. p.

p. 23 n. z Reduction in this context is the classification of a composite in accordance with some part of it. For example, substantial change considered as a whole would ordinarily be classified as change, but it might be *reduced* to the category of substance.

p. 23 n. a Thereby generating the true proposition that there is at least one entity such that it is every man (the sum total of all human beings extant at any given time or at all times) and it is a being, just as a herd of sheep is a being.

p. 25 n. b The exclusive proposition corresponding to the universal affirmative proposition 'Every A is B' is 'Only B is A'. The inference from the universal affirmative to the corresponding exclusive is therefore a kind of conversion.

p. 25 n. c The word '*homo*', like the word 'man', is ambiguous as between 'human being' and 'adult male human being'. It is, therefore, ordinarily correctly translated as 'man'. This group of examples and the group immediately following turn on the ambiguity. The '*homo*' in '*quilibet homo*', '*unus homo*', '*aliquis homo*', and '*nullus homo*' is read as 'man' in the narrow sense, while '*homo*' without a modifier in the masculine gender is read as 'man' in the broad sense—'human being'. Cf. pp. 167 and 249 below.

p. 25 n. d i.e. at least one woman but no man is running.

p. 29 n. e On p. 21.

p. 33 n. f Ampliation is the expansion of the natural or normal *suppositio* of a common term by means of certain verbs or modifiers. If the natural *suppositio* of 'man' is taken to be every extant individual human being, then the verb 'can' produces ampliation in the proposition 'A man can travel outside the solar system', as does the adverb 'necessarily' in 'A man is necessarily an animal'.

p. 33 n. g The assumption is that because no chimera exists there is no term that

can serve as the predicate term in a true, affirmative, non-ampliative proposition beginning 'A chimera is . . .', where 'is' is taken not as a tenseless copula but as a present-tense verb form.

p. 33 n. h The sense of the first proposition is 'It is not the case that every man is a certain animal'; see p. 15 above. The sense of the second is 'It is not the case that every man is an animal'. The first proposition is not merely true but necessary; see p. 35 below.

p. 35 n. i i.e. at least one woman but no man is running. See p. 25 above, n. c.

p. 41 n. j On mediate terms see Chapter Four, especially p. 217 below.

Chapter 2

p. 41 n. a i.e. a mental image associated necessarily with one and only one original.

p. 45 n. b In this passage term-tokens and not term-types are being discussed.

p. 45 n. c This passage evidently covers both lost term-types (e.g. obsolete words) and lost term-tokens (e.g. the marks on the pages of a destroyed book).

p. 47 n. d i.e. the mental image.

p. 49 n. e A first intention is one that is naturally significant (of itself and) of some entity other than an intention. The mental term *man* may be considered a first intention. An intention that is naturally significant (of itself and) of another intention only is a second intention. The mental term *genus* may be considered to be a second intention.

p. 51 n. f The second point concerns intention in the ordinary sense of the English word 'intention', a sense usually irrelevant to this discussion.

p. 51 n. g The individual I perceive may in fact be Socrates, but unless I perceive him as Socrates I do not perceive Socrates. See John Buridan (d. 1356) on the different interpretation of terms occurring before (*a parte ante*) and after (*a parte post*) a verb of cognition (such as '*cognosco*') in Theodore Kermit Scott, *John Buridan: Sophisms on Meaning and Truth* (New York: Appleton–Century–Crofts, 1966), pp. 126–8.

p. 53 n. h In argument ⟨1⟩ on pp. 47–9.

p. 53 n. i The notions of the compounded and divided senses are flexible, but even so it is difficult to see how 'It appears that Plato is Plato' can be considered to be the compounded sense of 'Plato is Plato'. For more detailed examples of Paul's application of these notions see, for example, pp. 167, 183–5, 193–5, and 203 below. And see especially *Logica magna*, Part I, Treatise 21, '*De sensu composito et diviso*'.

p. 53 n. j This passage seems confused, but the sense is clear enough. If it is a man that I perceive, then the appearance produced in my mind must be the appearance of a man. But in some circumstances this appearance will be so obscure that I will associate it with a memory image of something other than a man—e.g. a donkey—and thus believe that I perceive something other than a man. What I perceive is a man, but because I do not perceive him as a man I do not perceive a man. Similarly, it is the man himself that his appearance represents, but because it does not represent him as a man it does not represent a man. See p. 51 above, n. g. Buridan considers this sort of case as well: 'we apply names for the purpose of signifying ⟨things⟩ based on the ways in which we understand the things. Thus the verb "I signify" produces appellations in the same way as do "I understand", "I perceive", and even "it appears" ' (cf. Scott, op. cit., p. 127, where this passage is differently translated). On Buridan's use of '*appellatio*', a use which Paul seems

to have adopted here, see Scott, op. cit., pp. 42–9, esp. p. 42 n. 76. Paul discusses cases similar to this one on pp. 217–23 below.

p. 53 n. k On pp. 41–3 above.

p. 53 n. l On pp. 45–7 above.

p. 53 n. m On pp. 41 and 47 above.

p. 55 n. n *In librum de interpretatione editio secunda*, Migne *PL* 64. 394A; 420A–C; 423B–C.

p. 55 n. o I have chosen this example rather than translating the Latin example because the occurrence of an article in the possible translations—'A chimera is' or 'The chimera is'—would destroy the possibility of generating the *reductio ad absurdum* intended in this argument. Pegasus, of course, is not a chimera; but for present purposes the differences between a winged horse and a chimera are nugatory.

p. 57 n. p This interpretation is less bizarre when, as in the Latin example, the predicate term does not include an article.

p. 59 n. q See Part II, Treatise 10: '*De veritate et falsitate propositionum*'.

p. 61 n. r See, for example, the discussion of primary and secondary signification on pp. 109–21 below.

p. 63 n. s See p. 25 above, n. c.

p. 69 n. t The medieval Latin particle '*ly*' (or '*li*'), a close relative of the definite article in the Romance languages, was used in much the same way as inverted commas (single quotation marks) are used by contemporary philosophers to indicate that the word or expression within them is being mentioned rather than used. The medieval practice was even closer to our own when (as in this edition of the Latin text) dots were placed before and after the word or expression with which the '*ly*' was associated.

p. 71 n. u The point evidently is that this or that term-token signifies even though not it but one equiform with it has been imposed for the purpose of signifying.

p. 71 n. v I have found no passage in the *Sophistical Refutations* which looks exactly right, but all the following seem more or less closely relevant: 165^a6, 168^a28, ch. 10 (170^b11 ff.), 173^b12, 175^b28, ch. 19 (177^a9 ff.), 178^a24. *Topics*, Book I, ch. 18, 108^a18, looks more nearly right than do any of those in *Sophistical Refutations*.

p. 73 n. w Personal verbs are those that take subject terms of the ordinary kinds in the ordinary way, as distinct from impersonal verbs, such as '*videtur*' ('it seems'), '*oportet*' ('it is necessary'), '*pluit*' ('it is raining').

p. 79 n. x The *ars obligatoria* lays down the conditions under which formal disputation takes place, the obligations assumed by each party to the disputation. See *Logica magna*, Part II, Treatise 14, '*De obligationibus*'.

p. 81 n. y i.e. in connection with propositions as well as with terms. The type of sophisma referred to is described at the end of ⟨1⟩ above: an argument from an inferior to its superior in which the operative verb is 'signify'.

p. 81 n. z See p. 51 above, n. g.

p. 85 n. a On mediate terms see Chapter Four, especially p. 217 below.

p. 87 n. b On exposition and exponents see pp. 225–9 below.

p. 89 n. c See p. 51 above, n. g, and p. 53 above, n. j.

p. 89 n. d This resolution, from '*significatur*' to '*significatum est*', does not appear

in this grammatical form in the translation, where the transition is from 'is signified' to 'what is signified . . . is'.

p. 89 n. e *Isagoge*, ed. Busse, p. 13, l. 10.

p. 91 n. f I have not found such a passage in Avicenna. Richard Feribrigge and Johannes Venator Anglicus, two late fourteenth-century logicians on whose works Paul drew, also cite this passage, locating it in Book V of Avicenna's *Metaphysics*. The passage is not there.

p. 91 n. g The grammatically correct and usually appropriate translation of '*Sortes est homo*' is 'Socrates is a man'. Because the example in this case is intended to emphasize the occurrence of simple terms in it, I have bracketed the indefinite article.

p. 97 n. h See p. 13 above, n. p. Ordinarily only six transcendental terms were recognized: '*ens*', '*aliquid*', '*unum*', '*verum*', '*bonum*', and '*res*'.

p. 97 n. i On immediate terms see p. 217 below.

p. 97 n. j A compound noun consisting of modifier+simple noun is related to the component simple noun in the mode of apposition. See p. 107 below.

p. 99 n. k On primary and secondary signification see pp. 109–21 below.

p. 99 n. l On p. 97.

p. 99 n. m According to William of Sherwood (d. 1266/71), 'the matter of statements is of three kinds, viz. natural, contingent, and separate. The matter is natural in case the subject receives the predicate by its very nature, as in "a man is an animal". It is contingent in case the subject receives the predicate contingently, as in "a man is running". It is separate in case the predicate is naturally separated from the subject, as in "a man is an ass".' Norman Kretzmann, *William of Sherwood's Introduction to Logic* (Minneapolis: University of Minnesota Press, 1966), p. 33 (hereafter *WSIL*).

p. 103 n. n i.e. the verb 'to be'.

p. 107 n. o i.e. inferentially inferior. See pp. 103–5.

p. 107 n. p For the standard medieval Porphyrian Tree see *WSIL*, p. 54. 'Animate body' and 'rational animal' are the only two complex terms occurring in the figure.

p. 109 n. q On pp. 97–9.

p. 109 n. r i.e. secondarily.

p. 111 n. s This conclusion is contrary not to any reply in particular but to the explanation on pp. 97–9 (and p. 109) above, which later on p. 111 is called 'the exposition'. It seems, therefore, that '*responsionem*' here is a mistake for '*expositionem*' and '*responsione*' in the next line a mistake for '*expositione*'.

p. 111 n. t i.e. the explanation on pp. 97–9 above, the gist of which is repeated on p. 109.

p. 111 n. u In the kind of analysis known as exposition the expounded is the analysed proposition and the exponents are the results of the analysis. Cf. analysis in respect of one or another term on p. 177 below.

p. 113 n. v The ablative '*B modo*' is an ablative of manner modifying '*significat*' and thereby, according to Paul, constituting an impediment to the inference from inferior to superior.

p. 117 n. w See p. 111 above, n. u.

p. 119 n. x See Part II, Treatise 10: '*De veritate et falsitate propositionum*'.

p. 119 n. y It seems likely that *'responsione'* here is a mistake for *'expositione'*. See p. 111 above, n. s.

p. 119 n. z In 'Every man is running' 'man' has mobile distributive confused *suppositio*. One can therefore argue to any of the corresponding singular propositions ('Socrates is running', 'Plato is running', and so on) or from all the corresponding singular propositions to the original universal proposition. In 'Only every man is running' the distributive confused *suppositio* of 'man' has been immobilized by 'only'. Thus one cannot argue to any of the corresponding singular propositions ('Only Socrates is running', 'Only Plato is running', and so on) or, except trivially, from all the corresponding singular propositions to the original universal proposition. These are standard instances of the difference between mobile and immobile *suppositio*. As instances more closely approximating the one under discussion here consider (1) 'Jane is meeting a man', (2) 'Jane would like to meet a man'. In (1) 'a man' does not have distributive confused *suppositio*, much less mobile. In (2) the situation is not so clear. One might suppose that from (2) and 'Tom is a man' one could infer 'Jane would like to meet Tom', although such an inference would be strictly invalid. But all doubts about the mobility of 'a man' are removed in (3) 'Jane would primarily like to meet a man'. No one would suppose that from (3) and 'Tom is a man' one could infer 'Jane would primarily like to meet Tom'. 'Primarily' does not, speaking strictly, immobilize 'a man', but it does make its immobility obvious. The same situation seems to obtain in the instance under discussion here.

p. 121 n. a On terms taken as exponible and as functionalizable see pp. 225–9 below.

p. 121 n. b Apparently a reference to ⟨5R⟩ on pp. 117–19 above.

Chapter 3

p. 127 n. a The reference is to the first discussion of equivocation in *Sophistical Refutations*. At 166ᵃ15 Aristotle uses 'dog' as an example of a name that properly signifies more than one thing and so can give rise to equivocation. He does not however, introduce this particular inference, which is a medieval example of equivocation. See, for example, *WSIL*, p. 135.

p. 129 n. b On ampliation see p. 33 above, n. f.

p. 131 n. c i.e. terms in cases other than the nominative.

p. 133 n. d On p. 131.

p. 135 n. e e.g. *De interpretatione*, ch. 10, 20ᵃ23 ff., where 'Socrates' is used as the subject term in a proposition illustrating the case in which 'the subject is individual'.

p. 135 n. f *Categories*, ch. 5, 2ᵃ11 ff.

p. 135 n. g *Categories*, ch. 5, 2ᵃ17 ff.

p. 135 n. h This seems to be a mistake. Aristotle regularly uses the Greek words ὥστε and οὖν where we would use 'therefore', and either of these words has the sense of 'therefore' even apart from (and before) Aristotle. William of Moerbeke translated the οὖν at *De interpretatione* 17ᵃ17 as *'igitur'*, Boethius as 'ergo'. William and Boethius both translated the ὥστε at *De interpretatione* 18ᵇ10 as *'quare'*.

p. 135 n. i The passage cited in angles comes closer than any other I have found in *Prior Analytics* to making this point, but it says nothing about effecting agreement among the interlocutors. Similar passages occur at *Posterior Analytics* 76ᵇ39 and *Metaphysics* 1078ᵃ18.

p. 139 n. j Ordinarily *per se* predications are all analytic propositions; they are exemplified here by an identity proposition.

p. 145 n. k See p. 53 above, n. j. Paul's use of *'appellatio'* there seems to agree with Buridan's. His use of it here seems in keeping with the use made of it by older logicians. William of Sherwood, for example, describes it as the property a term has just in case there is at least one extant individual to which the term applies at the time at which it is used. See *WSIL*, pp. 106 and 122–3.

p. 147 n. l The modal term here is *'scio'* ('I know').

p. 147 n. m e.g. on pp. 137 and 145 above.

p. 147 n. n See p. 79 above, n. x.

p. 149 n. o On p. 145.

p. 151 n. p i.e. pronouns the antecedents of which are proper names. Personal pronouns often occur as proper pronouns.

p. 153 n. q i.e. he is in doubt about each case taken separately though not about the disjunction of all the cases taken together.

p. 153 n. r i.e. when it occurs without the special, artificial support of the hypothesis. See p. 151 above.

p. 155 n. s See Part II, Treatise 14: *'De obligationibus'*.

p. 155 n. t i.e. a common name.

p. 157 n. u Paul's own account of an accidental term is clarified on pp. 157–9 below, and he defines the connotative term on p. 159 below.

p. 157 n. v This is Porphyry's definition of accident (*Isagoge*, ed. Busse, p. 12 ll. 24–5), which concludes 'apart from the corruption of the subject'. See later on p. 157.

p. 157 n. w See p. 23 n. z above.

p. 157 n. x William Ockham (d. 1347/9) often explains accident along this line. See Léon Baudry, *Lexique philosophique de Guillaume d'Ockham* (Paris: Lethielleux, 1958) art. *'Accidens'*.

p. 157 n. y Both Aristotle and Porphyry treat it from an ontological point of view. See Aristotle's *Topics*, Book I, ch. 5 ($102^{b}4$–26) and Porphyry's *Isagoge*, ed. Busse, p. 12, ll. 24–5.

p. 159 n. z The term 'God' was said to belong to no category whatever. See p. 107 above.

p. 159 n. a On analogical terms see pp. 55 and 57–9 above.

p. 159 n. b I have not found this reference.

p. 161 n. c This is said by Porphyry (*Isagoge*, ed. Busse, p. 4, ll. 15–20) but not by Aristotle, as far as I know.

p. 161 n. d *Categories*, ch. 5, $2^{b}7$–22.

p. 163 n. e I have not found this reference.

p. 165 n. f i.e. the minor premiss 'Plato is a man or will be a man'.

p. 167 n. g In the divided sense a division is made between the second occurrence of 'this man' and what follows it, so that the whole proposition is copulative. In the compounded sense the second occurrence of 'this man' is compounded with what follows it so that the whole proposition is a proposition with a copulated extreme.

p. 167 n. h See p. 25 above, n. c.

p. 171 n. i On exposition and resolution see pp. 225–9 below.

p. 171 n. j Indicating a specific time, as shown in ⟨2.24R⟩ on page 169 above.

p. 171 n. k See p. 111 above, n. u.

p. 173 n. l See p. 33 above, n. f.

p. 173 n. m A distractive term is one (such as 'past' or 'future', 'understood' or 'imagined') which when used as a predicate term distracts the 'is' of the copula from being interpreted as a present-tense existential 'is' in an inference 'from the third component to the second component'. See p. 239 below, n. j.

p. 173 n. n See p. 111 above, n. u.

p. 175 n. o On the primary and secondary signification of propositions see pp. 97–9 and 109–21 above.

p. 177 n. p See p. 111 above, n. u.

p. 177 n. q On resolution see pp. 225–9 below.

p. 179 n. r See p. 111 above, n. u.

p. 181 n. s See p. 111 above, n. u.

p. 183 n. t i.e., in this case, the word '*vel*' ('or').

p. 185 n. u See *Logica magna*, Part I, Treatise 21: 'De sensu composito et diviso'.

p. 189 n. v Restriction is the converse of ampliation. The effect of a modifier or a verb is much more frequently restriction than it is ampliation of a term's natural or normal *suppositio*. See p. 33 above, n. f.

p. 191 n. w The full rule is that a negation placed after a universal negative sign produces a combination equipollent to a universal affirmative sign. Cf. *WSIL*, p. 36.

p. 193 n. x i.e. a predicate term falling under an infinitating negation—'*non*' read as 'non-' rather than as 'not'. See p. 195 below, n. g.

p. 193 n. y i.e. the minor premiss 'That proposition is'.

p. 193 n. z The antecedent of this argument is true *ex hypothesi* if and only if it is given the natural interpretation 'Socrates is the same as (somebody drawing a conclusion with reference to (Socrates and every man))'. But it can be made to yield the conclusion if and only if it is given the unnatural, unsupported interpretation 'Socrates is the same as ((somebody drawing a conclusion with reference to Socrates) and (every man))'. I am grateful to Professor Geach for suggesting this analysis.

p. 193 n. a It is very difficult—perhaps impossible—to translate this paragraph so as to display the pattern of the reasoning in a readable English text. Professor Geach has suggested the following translation, which aims especially at showing how the argument is supposed to go. 'Similarly, if in regard to Socrates, the one who draws a conclusion, and in regard to every man—that is what Socrates identically is: then, in regard to some man and in regard to every man, that is what Socrates identically is. The inference is obvious: it goes from an inferior to a superior term, ⟨both⟩ taken affirmatively. The main antecedent is proved as follows: this is what Socrates identically is, and this is, in regard to Socrates, the one who draws a conclusion, and in regard to every man; ergo: in regard to Socrates, the one who draws a conclusion, and in regard to every man—that is what Socrates identically is.' The string of words 'in regard to Socrates, the one who draws a conclusion, and in regard to every man' is intended to be syntactically ambiguous as between (1) a construction in which 'the one who draws a conclusion' is in apposition to 'Socrates'—'In regard to (Socrates, the one who draws a con-

clusion), and in regard to every man: that is what Socrates identically is'—and (2) a construction in which the 'in regard to' phrases are governed by 'draws a conclusion'—'In regard to Socrates, and in regard to every man, Socrates identically is one who draws a conclusion ⟨about them⟩'. From (1), but not from (2), this follows: 'In regard to some man, and in regard to every man: that is what Socrates identically is'. I am grateful to Professor Geach for this translation and analysis.

p. 195 n. b It is the role of the word 'true' in the proposition that makes it modal. Medieval logicians regularly recognized six modes—true, false, necessary, impossible, possible, contingent—based on Aristotle, *De interpretatione*, ch. 12, 22^{a}11.

p. 195 n. c See Part II, Treatise 12: '*De possibilitate, impossibilitate, et contingentia propositionum*'.

p. 195 n. d On resolution see pp. 225–9 below.

p. 195 n. e To take '*verum*' as a name is to take it as a substantive ('what is true') or adjective ('true') the occurrence of which in a proposition does not affect the assertoric status of the proposition; e.g. 'What is true is an expression of what is real', 'A true proposition results from the denial of a false proposition'. See also ⟨2.72R⟩ on p. 215 below.

p. 195 n. f An expository syllogism is a syllogism of the third figure with two singular premisses supporting a particular, singular, or indefinite conclusion; e.g. 'Socrates is running, Socrates is white; therefore something white is running'. In this case the syllogism is 'The proposition "God is" is not Socrates differing from every man, the proposition "God is" is something true; therefore something true is not Socrates differing from every man'.

p. 195 n. g An infinitating occurrence of '*non*' produces an infinite term; a purely negative occurrence produces the negation of a proposition. '*Non homo currit*' read in the first way is 'A non-man is running'; in the second, 'It is not the case that a man is running'.

p. 197 n. h The first of these inferences is unacceptable because the word 'not', a sign with the power of producing confused *suppositio* in a term, precedes the copulated term 'a man and a donkey'. The unacceptability of the second inference depends on the occurrence in it not of a sign but of the correlative terms 'whole' and 'half'. (The emendation which completes the second inference was suggested by Professor Geach.) The text used for the translation here is that of the 1499 printed edition. The manuscript presents a significant variant up to 'As for the confirmation . . .' later on p. 197. The translation of the variant reads as follows: '. . . I maintain that it does not always hold good because the same governance is not signified in the antecedent and in the consequent, provided that the "in relation to every man" is governed by the participial phrase ⟨"drawing the conclusion"⟩ in the antecedent and by the same in the consequent.'

p. 199 n. i See p. 195 above, n. f.

p. 199 n. j On resolution see pp. 225–9 below.

p. 199 n. k Professor Geach has suggested the following translation of this paragraph with the same aim as in his translation in n. a to p. 193 above. 'In reply to the confirmatory argument: When it was said—If in regard to Socrates, the one who draws a conclusion, etc.; then, in regard to some man, and in regard to every man, that is what Socrates identically is—what I say is to deny that it follows. First, this is not an argument from an inferior to a superior term, because "Socrates, the one who draws a conclusion" is not ⟨in the context of the antecedent⟩ a term inferior to the term "man". Even if it were an inferior term, even so the inference would be invalid, because the argument relates not to the whole subject term but only to part of it. Now such a form is invalid; e.g. this does not follow—

You are what appears a donkey; therefore you are a donkey of some sort—and yet "of some sort" is a term superior to "what appears". Similarly this does not follow—You are Plato's owner; therefore you are some one of Plato's things—and yet "owner" is a term inferior to "thing". If, however, in the previous argument the conclusion were this—In regard to some man, that is what Socrates identically is—I allow the inference, and the conclusion is true. But if in the main antecedent the phrase "in regard to every man" is governed by "identically is", I allow the inference but deny the antecedent. In reply to the proof of this antecedent—This is what Socrates identically is, and this is in regard to Socrates, the one who draws a conclusion, and in regard to every man; *ergo*, etc.—I deny the inference. First, in the antecedent the phrase "in regard to every man" is governed by "the one who draws a conclusion", but in the consequent it is governed by "identically is". Alternatively, we may deny that this is an expository syllogism. First, because in the proposition to be resolved only "Socrates, the one who draws a conclusion" has the role of subject: "in regard to every man" falls on the side of the predicate. The argument ought to be:

> In regard to this, and in regard to every man: that is what Socrates identically is;
> And this is Socrates, the one who is drawing a conclusion;
> *Ergo*: In regard to Socrates, the one who is drawing a conclusion, and in regard to every man: that is what Socrates identically is.

In that case I allow the inference and deny the antecedent.'

p. 201 n. l See p. 195 above, n. f.

p. 201 n. m On resolution see pp. 225–9 below.

p. 203 n. n See p. 111 above, n. u.

p. 203 n. o See p. 191 above, n. w.

p. 205 n. p On this distinction, ordinarily associated with uses of '*non*', see p. 195 above, n. g.

p. 205 n. q i.e. into the whole predication.

p. 205 n. r See p. 111 above, n. u.

p. 209 n. s On functionalizable terms see pp. 225–9 below.

p. 209 n. t i.e. in any case other than the nominative.

p. 209 n. u On extrinsic denomination see, for example, St. Thomas Aquinas, *Summa theologiae* Ia, q. 6, a. 4: 'In cases involving relation there is nothing to prevent something's being denominated by what is extrinsic to it, as when something is denominated "located" from location, or "measured" from measure.' On denomination, or paronymy, generally see D. P. Henry, *The De Grammatico of St. Anselm* (Notre Dame, Ind.: Notre Dame University Press, 1964).

p. 209 n. v A verbal noun is a noun formed on the present stem of a verb or, more broadly, any noun or adjective obviously derived from a verb. E.g. '*dominus*' ('lord') from '*dominor*' (as Paul evidently believes; see p. 197 above) and '*amator*' ('lover') from '*amo*'.

p. 211 n. w See p. 195 above, n. g.

p. 215 n. x On resolution see pp. 225–9 below.

p. 215 n. y On functionalization see pp. 225–9 below.

p. 215 n. z On taking a modal word as a name see p. 195 above, n. e.

Chapter 4

p. 217 n. a Johannes Venator Anglicus (d. *c.* 1427?), whose work was used by Paul, devotes much of the first chapter of the first treatise of his *Logica* (MS. Cod. Vat. Lat. 2130), fols. 49ra–51ra, to a discussion of this distinction. A closely related distinction was often drawn between immediate and mediate propositions.

See, for example, William Ockham, *Summa logicae* III, ii, c. 14; *Ordinatio*, Prol., q. 4c. See also Paul of Pergula, a student of Paul of Venice, *Logica*, ed. Brown, p. 45.

p. 223 n. b Venator, loc. cit., offers these four arguments against the view of Richard Billingham that '*est*' is an immediate term.

p. 225 n. c See *Logica magna*, Part II, Treatise 2, '*De propositione categorica*'.

p. 233 n. d 'Subaltern' is a generic term designating the subalternants (the universal propositions) and the subalternates (the particular propositions) in the traditional square of opposition.

p. 235 n. e On expository syllogisms see p. 195 above, n. f.

p. 235 n. f. Particularly on p. 231 above.

p. 235 n. g Because Latin lacks an indefinite article, this proposition is theoretically interpretable either as a singular or as an indefinite proposition. The latter interpretation, although bizarre, seems to be required by the context.

p. 237 n. h On ampliation see p. 33 above, n. f.

p. 239 n. i Apparently on pp. 223–5 above.

p. 239 n. j A proposition of the form '*A* is' is one in which 'is' is the second component; one of the form '*A* is *B*' is one in which 'is' is the third component. The claim here is that an inference of the form '*A* is *B*; therefore *A* is' is acceptable. Venator, loc. cit., offers this argument against Billingham's view that every active verb is resoluble into its participle and the verb 'is'.

p. 239 n. k The predicate term in this case is taken to be '*erit*' ('will be').

p. 241 n. l The predicate term in this case is taken to be the present participle '*legens*' ('lecturing').

p. 241 n. m Venator, loc. cit., offers a similar argument against Billingham's analysis of '*Sortes leget*'.

p. 241 n. n See p. 173 above, n. m.

p. 241 n. o See, e.g., pp. 287–9 below.

p. 243 n. p i.e. it is not affected by other elements in the sentence in such a way as to supposit for anything other than future lecturers. Paul seems to be using '*limitatio*' here as a synonym for '*restrictio*'. See p. 189 above, n. v.

p. 243 n. q See p. 233 above.

p. 245 n. r The first composition is 'man who is a donkey'; the second is the entire proposition.

p. 247 n. s The negation here is the negation of 'are' implicit in 'differ from', and the full rule is that a negation placed after a universal affirmative sign produces a combination equipollent to a universal negative sign.

p. 255 n. t i.e. rather than as a participle.

p. 267 n. u The *dici* (or *dictum*) *de omni* (*et nullo*) was the most widely accepted formula for the essence of syllogistic reasoning. Aristotle introduces it in these words in the passage cited: 'That one term should be included in another as in a whole is the same as for the other to be predicated of all of the first. And we say that one term is predicated of all of another whenever no instance of the subject can be found of which the other term cannot be asserted: "to be predicated of none" must be understood in the same way.'

p. 269 n. v On p. 261 above.

p. 271 n. w The prejacent of the universal and of the singulars is the proposition

without the universal sign or the demonstrative pronoun—e.g. 'Man is running' is the prejacent of 'Every man is running' and of 'This man is running'.

p. 273 n. x The full rule is that a negation before the contradictory produces a proposition equipollent to the original proposition.

p. 275 n. y i.e. the second inference under ⟨2.5⟩, on p. 269 above.

p. 279 n. z In order to see how he arrives at such bizarre forms as these one must be prepared to recognize '. . . or a donkey is a donkey' as a predicate term and to accept the occurrence of predication in the absence of an ordinary copula. Then if 'a man' is taken as the subject term, we have 'Every man or a donkey is a donkey' as the universal affirmative and 'A man or a donkey is a donkey' as the corresponding indefinite proposition. The negation of the indefinite may then be effected in either of two ways, as in 'Not (i.e. it is not the case that) a man is a stone' and 'A man is not a stone'.

p. 281 n. a i.e. confused *suppositio*.

p. 283 n. b On ampliation see p. 33 above, n. f.

p. 287 n. c See p. 173 above, n. m.

p. 287 n. d '*Praeteritus*' ('past') is not only a name (substantival or adjectival) but also a participle of '*praeterire*' ('to pass by'); and '*futurus*' is a participle of '*esse*' ('to be').

GENERAL INDEX

(Paul of Venice, *Logica magna*, Fascicule 1)

[This index contains no entries for the Introduction (pp. xv–xx)]